Taxation, Human Rights, and Sustainable Development

This book investigates the relationship between human rights and taxation, exploring how human rights have been impeded or enhanced through tax laws and policies, and what this means for sustainable development in the Global South.

Drawing on cases from across the Global South, the book demonstrates the benefits of embedding human rights into tax policies and legislation. The authors not only highlight the role of legislative measures and other human rights regulations in the realisation of international treaty rights but also argue that it creates an environment whereby individuals feel duty-bound to pay taxes, when necessary, thereby securing a sustainable revenue source for the state to meet their socio-economic responsibilities. The book investigates key topics such as compliance, redistribution, e-commerce, tax havens, and the role of key stakeholders.

This book will be useful for researchers from across the fields of law, human rights, taxation, and sustainable development.

Eghosa O. Ekhator is Associate Professor of International Environmental Law at the University of Derby, United Kingdom. His main research areas include International Environmental Law, African International Legal History, and Natural Resources Governance. Dr Ekhator has published extensively on his research areas and his academic papers have been cited by a plethora of public and international agencies including the U.K. Parliament's International Trade Committee and the United Nations Refugee Council. Dr Ekhator is also the Chair Committee on the Teaching of International Law and the SDGs, International Law Association (Nigerian Branch), and Senior Fellow of Environmental Law and Sustainable Development – Institute for Oil, Gas, Energy, Environment and Sustainable Development (OGEES Institute), Afe Babalola University, Nigeria.

Newman U. Richards is a Senior Lecturer in Law at the University of Nigeria, Enugu Campus, Enugu, Nigeria. His research interest includes Tax Laws and Policies, Sustainable Development Goals and Cybercrimes. Most of his works examine how tax policies can catalyse domestic resource mobilisation. Some of his works also looked at how taxation could bridge the funding gap in the actualisation of the SDGs in developing countries. He has presented papers at several international and local seminars, workshops, and law conferences in his areas of interest.

Chisa Onyejekwe is an academic and Associate Director at Bristol Law School, University of the West of England (UWE). She is an accomplished scholar with research expertise in Human Rights and economic development in Africa. Her work critically engages with key issues shaping the African continent, including regional integration, the role of the African Union, taxation systems, and the advancement of Human Rights. In the field of taxation, Dr Onyejekwe investigates how fiscal policies and legal structures impact economic justice and development. Her work often intersects with human rights, emphasising the need for equitable systems that uplift marginalised populations while fostering national and regional growth. Beyond her research, Dr Onyejekwe is dedicated to teaching and mentoring the next generation of legal professionals and scholars. Her role as Associate Director at UWE reflects her leadership and commitment to advancing academic excellence and fostering a culture of innovation and critical thinking within the legal field.

Taxation, Human Rights, and Sustainable Development

This book investigates the relationship between human rights and taxation, exploring how human rights have been impeded or enhanced through tax laws and policies, and what this means for sustainable development in the Global South.

Drawing on cases from across the Global South, the book demonstrates the benefits of embedding human rights into tax policies and legislation. The authors not only highlight the role of legislative measures and other human rights regulations in the realisation of international treaty rights but also argue that it creates an environment whereby individuals feel duty-bound to pay taxes, when necessary, thereby securing a sustainable revenue source for the state to meet their socio-economic responsibilities. The book investigates key topics such as compliance, redistribution, e-commerce, tax havens, and the role of key stakeholders.

This book will be useful for researchers from across the fields of law, human rights, taxation, and sustainable development.

Eghosa O. Ekhator is Associate Professor of International Environmental Law at the University of Derby, United Kingdom. His main research areas include International Environmental Law, African International Legal History, and Natural Resources Governance. Dr Ekhator has published extensively on his research areas and his academic papers have been cited by a plethora of public and international agencies including the U.K. Parliament's International Trade Committee and the United Nations Refugee Council. Dr Ekhator is also the Chair Committee on the Teaching of International Law and the SDGs, International Law Association (Nigerian Branch), and Senior Fellow of Environmental Law and Sustainable Development – Institute for Oil, Gas, Energy, Environment and Sustainable Development (OGEES Institute), Afe Babalola University, Nigeria.

Newman U. Richards is a Senior Lecturer in Law at the University of Nigeria, Enugu Campus, Enugu, Nigeria. His research interest includes Tax Laws and Policies, Sustainable Development Goals and Cybercrimes. Most of his works examine how tax policies can catalyse domestic resource mobilisation. Some of his works also looked at how taxation could bridge the funding gap in the actualisation of the SDGs in developing countries. He has presented papers at several international and local seminars, workshops, and law conferences in his areas of interest.

Chisa Onyejekwe is an academic and Associate Director at Bristol Law School, University of the West of England (UWE). She is an accomplished scholar with research expertise in Human Rights and economic development in Africa. Her work critically engages with key issues shaping the African continent, including regional integration, the role of the African Union, taxation systems, and the advancement of Human Rights. In the field of taxation, Dr Onyejekwe investigates how fiscal policies and legal structures impact economic justice and development. Her work often intersects with human rights, emphasising the need for equitable systems that uplift marginalised populations while fostering national and regional growth. Beyond her research, Dr Onyejekwe is dedicated to teaching and mentoring the next generation of legal professionals and scholars. Her role as Associate Director at UWE reflects her leadership and commitment to advancing academic excellence and fostering a culture of innovation and critical thinking within the legal field.

Routledge Explorations in Development Studies

This Development Studies series features innovative and original research at the regional and global scale. It promotes interdisciplinary scholarly works drawing on a wide spectrum of subject areas, in particular politics, health, economics, rural and urban studies, sociology, environment, anthropology, and conflict studies.

Topics of particular interest are globalization; emerging powers; children and youth; cities; education; media and communication; technology development; and climate change.

In terms of theory and method, rather than basing itself on any orthodoxy, the series draws broadly on the tool kit of the social sciences in general, emphasizing comparison, the analysis of the structure and processes, and the application of qualitative and quantitative methods.

Arts-based Research in Global Development
Performing Knowledge
Edited by Vicki-Ann Ware, Kirsten Sadeghi-Yekta, Tim Prentki, and Wasim al Kurdi

Youth Voice and Participatory Arts in Global Development
The May Group

Human Rights and the United Nations
Paradox and Promise
Edited by Abigail B. Bakan and Yasmeen Abu-Laban

Civil Society and Local Ownership in the Global South
Responses to Conflict and Militarism
Edited by Ibrahim Natil

Taxation, Human Rights, and Sustainable Development
Global South Perspectives
Edited by Eghosa O. Ekhator, Newman U. Richards, and Chisa Onyejekwe

For more information about this series, please visit: www.routledge.com/Routledge-Explorations-in-Development-Studies/book-series/REDS

Taxation, Human Rights, and Sustainable Development

Global South Perspectives

Edited by Eghosa O. Ekhator, Newman U. Richards, and Chisa Onyejekwe

Routledge
Taylor & Francis Group
LONDON AND NEW YORK

First published 2025
by Routledge
4 Park Square, Milton Park, Abingdon, Oxon OX14 4RN

and by Routledge
605 Third Avenue, New York, NY 10158

Routledge is an imprint of the Taylor & Francis Group, an informa business

British Library Cataloguing-in-Publication Data
A catalogue record for this book is available from the British Library

ISBN: 978-1-032-55913-1 (hbk)
ISBN: 978-1-032-55916-2 (pbk)
ISBN: 978-1-003-43289-0 (ebk)

DOI: 10.4324/9781003432890

Typeset in Times New Roman
by SPi Technologies India Pvt Ltd (Straive)

Contents

Contributors

Dr Adebolarin Adekanle is an Associate Professor of Law at Ambrose Alli University, Nigeria. He specialises in Human Rights Law and is currently in active law practice in Nigeria.

Ohene Yaw Ampofo-Anti has an LLB from the University of Cape Town and an LLM from the University of California, Los Angeles (UCLA) with specialisations in Critical Race Studies as well as Public Interest Law and Policy. He was a Program Associate at the Center for Economic and Social Rights (CESR).

Marie-Louise F. Aren is an international lawyer and is currently a concluding doctoral candidate (International Tax Law) at the University of Pretoria, South Africa.

Dr Augustine Edobor Arimoro is a Senior Lecturer in Law at the School of Law, University of West London. Also, he is a Research Partner at the Centre for Comparative Law in Africa, University of Cape Town, South Africa.

Professor Emeka Duruigbo is the Roberson King Professor of Law at Thurgood Marshall School of Law, Texas Southern University, U.S.A., where he teaches courses in Property, Business Organisations, Oil and Gas and Energy Law. Prior to law teaching, he was a resource development associate at Law Finance Group, Inc., a senior legal counsel at Natural Heritage Institute, both in San Francisco, and a research fellow at the Program on Energy and Sustainable Development, Center for Environmental Science and Policy, Stanford University, U.S.A.

Dr Eghosa O. Ekhator is Associate Professor of International Environmental Law at the University of Derby, United Kingdom. His main research areas include International Environmental Law, African International Legal History, and Natural Resources Governance. Dr Ekhator has published extensively on his research areas and his academic papers have been cited by a plethora of public and international agencies including the U.K. Parliament's International Trade Committee and the United Nations Refugee Council. Dr Ekhator is also the Chair Committee on the Teaching of International

Law and the SDGs, International Law Association (Nigerian Branch) and Senior Fellow of Environmental Law and Sustainable Development – Institute for Oil, Gas, Energy, Environment and Sustainable Development (OGEES Institute), Afe Babalola University, Nigeria.

Dr Olaniyi Evans is an Economic Researcher and University Lecturer at Pan Atlantic University in Lagos, where he specialises in teaching, research and mentoring. He held previous roles as an Adjunct Lecturer at the University of Lagos (DLI), Research Assistant at Lagos Business School, and Assistant Consultant at Acadapages Ltd.

Dr Antonius R. Hippolyte is the current Dean (Interim) of the Faculty of Law at the University of the West Indies, Cave Hill Campus. He has research interest in International Economic Law and Governance. However, most of his work so far has examined developing countries' participation in foreign investment law, specifically investor-State arbitration. He examines how international investment law may be at odds with the sovereign interest of developing countries.

Dr Carika Keulder holds the degrees LLB, LLM, and LLD from the University of Pretoria and is an admitted attorney and notary public. She is a professor at the Law School of the University of Witwatersrand, South Africa and lectures on undergraduate and postgraduate level. She frequently presents research papers, locally and abroad, and has published several articles in peer-reviewed accredited journals. Her research focus is tax administration and taxpayers' rights, and she holds a C2-rating from the National Research Foundation in South Africa.

Dr María Emilia Mamberti is Research and Policy Lead Manager at the Center for Economic and Social Rights (CESR). She holds doctoral (J.S.D) and master's (LL.M) degrees from Columbia University in New York, and a law degree from the University of La Plata in Argentina.

Dr Magalie Masamba serves as an Extraordinary Lecturer at the Centre for Human Rights, University of Pretoria; Senior Associate at Zenizeni Sustainable Finance, Senior Fellow at the African Debt Justice Network (AfSDJN), and a Non-Executive Director on the board of the Cubango-Okavango River Basin (CORB) Fund. Dr. Magalie Masamba is an international legal scholar and policy advisor specialising in global economic governance, sovereign debt, climate finance, and international economic law.

Olivia Minatta holds a law degree from Universidad Nacional de La Plata, Argentina, and an LLM from Columbia Law School, U.S.A.

Professor Habiba Musa is the Deputy Dean of Postgraduate Studies and a Law Professor at the Nasarawa State University, Keffi-Nigeria. She holds an LLB (Hons) degree from the University of Maiduguri, and a PhD degree in Law from the Nasarawa State, University Keffi and an MSc in Cyber Security from the University of Law, United Kingdom.

Dr Philip Oamen is a Lecturer in Law and LLM Associate Course Director at the Birmingham City University (BCU), United Kingdom. Philip obtained his PhD in Law from the University of Birmingham, and he is a Fellow of the Higher Education Academy (Advance HE). He is licensed to practise as a Barrister and Solicitor of the Supreme Court of Nigeria. Before joining the academia, Philip practised with reputable law firms in Nigeria where he had extensive experience as a litigator. Philip's research interests are generally in the field of International Human Rights Law, with special interests on socioeconomic rights of vulnerable people.

Dr Chisa Onyejekwe is an academic and Associate Director at Bristol Law School, University of the West of England (UWE). She is an accomplished scholar with research expertise in Human Rights and economic development in Africa. Her work critically engages with key issues shaping the African continent, including regional integration, the role of the African Union, taxation systems, and the advancement of Human Rights. In the field of taxation, Dr Onyejekwe investigates how fiscal policies and legal structures impact economic justice and development. Her work often intersects with human rights, emphasising the need for equitable systems that uplift marginalised populations while fostering national and regional growth. Beyond her research, Dr Onyejekwe is dedicated to teaching and mentoring the next generation of legal professionals and scholars. Her role as Associate Director at UWE reflects her leadership and commitment to advancing academic excellence and fostering a culture of innovation and critical thinking within the legal field.

Luiza Leite de Queiroz is Marie Skłodowska-Curie Fellow with the ADAPTED programme and a Joint PhD candidate at the Faculty of Law of Vrije Universiteit Amsterdam and at the Institute of Development Research and Development Policy of Ruhr-Universität Bochum. A qualified lawyer admitted to the Brazilian Bar, she holds a Bachelor of Laws (LLB) from the Federal University of Rio de Janeiro with an exchange semester at the University of Coimbra, a Master of Laws in International and Comparative Law (LLM) from Trinity College Dublin and a Master of International Affairs (MA) from the Hertie School. Her work on transnational tax justice has been published in EJIL: Talk!, Emory International Law Review, and Transnational Legal Theory.

Dr Newman U. Richards is a Senior Lecturer in Law at the University of Nigeria, Enugu Campus, Enugu, Nigeria. His research interest includes Tax Laws and Policies, Sustainable Development Goals, and Cybercrimes. Most of his works examine how tax policies can catalyse domestic resource mobilisation. Some of his works also looked at how taxation could bridge the funding gap in the actualisation of the SDGs in developing countries. He has presented papers at several international and local seminars, workshops, and Law Conferences in his areas of interest.

Dr Olusegun Vincent is an Associate Professor in the School of Management & Social Sciences of Pan-Atlantic University, Lagos, Nigeria, where he teaches (undergraduate & postgraduate) courses in taxation, financial management, research methodology, and advanced quantitative techniques. Before now, Segun had a stint as a lecturer at the University of Lagos, Director of Economic Intelligence Unit at Lagos State Ministry of Economic Planning & Budget, senior roles in the banking industry, and advisory services manager at Ernst & Young.

Foreword

Damilola S. Olawuyi

It is my great pleasure to write a foreword to this monumental book titled *Taxation, Human Rights, and Sustainable Development in the Global South*. The connection between taxation, human rights, and sustainable development is one of profound significance, especially in the context of the Global South. This book is a significant effort aimed at unpacking the intricacies of these links, offering an exploration of how fiscal policies and tax systems impact social economic development and environmental sustainability. By anchoring its focus on the Global South, particularly Africa, this book provides a timely and necessary contribution to global debates on equity, governance, and development.

Taxation, in addition to its role as a critical tool for resource mobilisation, is a cornerstone of governance and an essential mechanism for redistributing resources to promote equality and inclusivity. In the Global South, however, tax systems often contend with structural challenges such as weak institutions, illicit financial flows, and informality. These challenges compound the issue of low revenue generation, which aggravate issues of inequality and inhibit the capacity of governments to provide social services such as healthcare, education, and infrastructure which are imperatives of sustainable development. This book challenges the conventional perception of taxation and sustainable development by framing it as a human rights issue. It highlights how unfair or poorly designed tax systems can promote poverty and social injustice.

There is a significant relationship between human rights and taxation, which is often overlooked in contemporary scholarship on taxation in the Global South. Tax policies directly affect the attainment of sustainable development and the enjoyment of human rights (including economic and social rights). However, the realisation of social and economic rights such as the rights to education, health, and an adequate standard of living are largely determined by the availability of public funds. An unfair tax system disproportionately puts more burden on marginalised communities, undermining their rights and entrenching their cycle of poverty. The attainment of sustainable development (including the SDGs), as anticipated in the 2030 Agenda for Sustainable Development, demands innovation in the ways resources are mobilised and allocated. This book underscores how an equitable tax system can catalyse sustainable development and the actualisation of sustainable development goals. An effective and equitable tax system can mobilise significant domestic resources, reduce over-dependence on foreign grants and aid, and ensure the equitable development of any given society. The editors of this book, leading scholars in the fields of environment, energy and international economic law, must therefore be commended for their exemplary dedication to filling the gap in the literature on the intricate intersections of tax, human rights and sustainable development.

I recommend this book to all and sundry for their reading and application. The book is an essential resource for policymakers, academics, practitioners, and advocates who seek to understand the critical role of taxation in fostering sustainable development anchored on justice. Through rigorous analysis and case studies, it highlights both the challenges and prospects in reconsidering taxation as a tool for promoting human rights and sustainable development. As you engage with the insights and arguments presented in this book, I encourage you to reflect on the profound implications of taxation in shaping developed and equitable societies. The future of the Global South will be largely determined by how it navigates the complexities of taxation, human rights, and sustainable development.

Professor Damilola S. Olawuyi, SAN
Independent Expert, United Nations Working Group on Business and Human Rights
Professor and UNESCO Chair on Environmental Law and Sustainable Development
Hamad Bin Khalifa University, Doha, Qatar

1 Introduction

The Nexus between Taxation, Human Rights and Sustainable Development in the Global South

Eghosa O. Ekhator, Newman U. Richards, and Chisa Onyejekwe

Human Rights play an integral role in State revenue sourcing and taxation.[1] The relevance of these ideas is twofold: first, to reinforce a state's obligation to enact legislative measures and other regulations for the realisation of treaty rights. The second is to recommend a foundation or premise whereby individuals are duty-bound to pay taxes when necessary. Additionally, states are obligated to protect human rights under Customary International Law and international human rights treaties. These treaties and customs ensure that states enact legislation (and policies) that guarantee the enjoyment of the rights and freedoms of citizens.[2]

This book examines whether human rights can be invoked in the debate on creating a successful tax regime thereby enhancing the quest to actualise sustainable development in the Global South. There exists a plethora of linkages between taxation and human rights. For example, scholars including Alston and Reisch have categorised the linkages via different headings including accountability and resource mobilisation.[3] This book takes a taxpayer-centred approach to the linkage between taxation and human rights. Recent literature and reports agree that tax and development go hand in hand to achieve the best possible human rights objectives.[4] This takes on more prominence in several countries in the Global South. Hence, the tax policy of a country is in part, among the steering instruments of governments. Arguably, at the crux of every tax policy is the political and economic interests of a plethora of business groups, stakeholders and individuals who seek to enjoy tax reliefs, exemptions and compensation.[5]

There are controversies and divergent academic (including stakeholder) perspectives regarding the meaning or definition of the 'Global South'; hence, this book adopts a broad conceptualisation of the Global South. It is widely agreed that African countries majorly are in the Global South. Thus, according to Kavuri and Ramanathan, the Global South comprises countries in Africa, Latin and Central America and most parts of Asia and the Global South comprises of majority of the countries in the world.[6] However, the conceptualisation of the Global South in this book does not include 'Global South' sites or locations in the Global North.[7] Thus, this book focuses on countries in the

DOI: 10.4324/9781003432890-1

Global South including case studies from several countries in Africa. Notwithstanding the criticisms of the utility of the term 'Global South', it is valid and widely accepted in political, governance and academic circles.[8]

Arguably, there are divergent academic and stakeholder perspectives on the definition of taxpayer rights.[9] The conceptualisation/definition of taxpayer rights in this book also encompasses civil and political rights and socio-economic rights amongst others. Furthermore, issues on taxpayer rights in the tax system including due process, procedural fairness, rule of law and the right of judicial review will also be in focus. For example, this is reflected in chapter 7 by Carika Keulder. Thus, tax justice and human rights analysis form the critical human rights perspective underpinning various chapters of the book.

As many countries in the Global South intensify efforts to increase their tax revenue and sustain an effective tax system, concerns about tax justice are often implicated in the process. These issues revolve around how tax systems deal with issues of inequality, financing public services, redistribution of wealth, equitable development and maintaining a fair and sustainable tax regime. Tax justice highlights the need for a fair tax system that is collaborative and demands proportional contributions based on the capacity or ability of the taxpayers to pay.[10] It recognises systemic and structural inequalities in Global South countries that often accentuate issues of tax evasion and tax avoidance. The tax structure of several countries in the Global South is largely influenced by their colonial heritage.[11] Taxation during the colonial era was primarily intended to raise revenue to support the activities of the government. Hence, it was extractive in nature and prioritised revenue mobilisation above other objectives of taxation which often leads to structural inequalities. Unfortunately, many of the countries in the Global South have weak economies and large informal sectors which is difficult to tax.[12] The resultant effect is a low tax-to-GDP ratio, which inhibits the efforts of the state to fund social services.

In many countries in the Global South, there are challenges to tax justice. Some of these challenges include weak governance structure and lack of public trust which discourages voluntary tax compliance as revenue is often mismanaged or inequitably distributed.[13] Furthermore, ineffective tax administration systems and weak enforcement mechanisms which often allow corruption to undermine the collection and payment of taxes fairly and efficiently are commonplace in several countries.[14] This is further exacerbated by regressive tax structures that promote inequality and increase the tax burden of low-income earners. Likewise, it is further compounded by the lack of comprehensive legal frameworks to deal with illicit financial flows, money laundering and tax evasion. In addition, some countries as a strategy to attract foreign investment often offer too generous tax concessions which leads to huge revenue losses and unfair tax competition and gives foreign companies an unfair advantage over their local competitors.[15] These challenges often make taxpayers unwilling to pay taxes and undermines the capacity of the government to address the developmental challenges in developing countries. This calls for tax reforms in the Global South to enhance efficiency, equity and accountability in tax administration. Tax justice therefore demands for a fairer tax system that reduces inequality and promotes sustainable development, economic growth and strengthens the domestic tax systems to address structural and systemic inequalities.[16]

The attainment of tax justice through international human rights law and the actualisation of sustainable development (including the Sustainable Development Goals – SDGs) in the Global South is the crux of the book. For example, chapter 4 by Oamen and Adekanle relies on the Third World Approaches to International Law (TWAIL) to underpin their analysis of socio-economic rights and taxation in the Global South. Furthermore, Leite de Queiroz's chapter is also premised on critical legal theory.

Rationale

Human rights play an integral role in State revenue sourcing and taxation in different parts of the world. For countries in the Global South, it should be an obligation to consider human rights in their tax policies and legislation as they need a sustainable revenue source to meet their socio-economic responsibilities (the welfare state) of which tax revenue is one. This goes to the foundations of a good tax system. Drawing lessons from the Global South, this book examines whether human rights can be invoked in the debate on creating effective tax regimes across the various jurisdictions. Recent literature and reports agree that tax and development are integral in achieving human rights objectives and sustainable development.

Arguably, there is a small number of research on the disconnect between human rights, taxation laws and sustainable development policies in the Global South (including several African and Latin American countries).[17] This book attempts to mitigate the gap by providing contemporary perspectives on these issues. It analyses the extent to which human rights have been hindered or enhanced through tax laws and policies with overarching implications for the quest to attain sustainable development in the Global South.

Scope

This book argues for the integration of human rights and sustainable development considerations in policies and taxation laws in the Global South. Contributions to the book contain conceptual analyses and country studies on taxation, human rights and sustainable development in several countries in the Global South. The goal is to present comparative and contemporary accounts that will enable cross-exchange of solutions and practices for taxation and human rights and improving its effectiveness in the Global South. Thus, countries in the Global South can draw lessons from selected jurisdictions in this book. Centralising lessons from countries in focus, this book can be useful to other countries whether in the Global South or Global North. This book is divided into three parts that contains 11 chapters written by authors from several countries in the Global South. This chapter, which is the introduction, is jointly authored by the editors of the book – Eghosa O. Ekhator, Newman U. Richards and Chisa Onyejekwe. This chapter provides an overview of the book and discusses some introductory issues regarding human rights and taxation and their implications in the quest to actualise sustainable development in the Global South.

The second chapter of the book is by Luiza Leite de Queiroz. The chapter is titled 'What Normativity for International Tax? Towards Alignment with Human Rights and the Sustainable Development Goals'. This chapter discusses the practical steps towards ensuring international taxation's alignment with human rights normativity. The third chapter titled 'Human Rights as a Normative Tool to Promote Fiscal Justice in Africa' is jointly written by Olivia Minatta, Ohene Yaw Ampofo-Anti and María Emilia Mamberti. Hence, this chapter demonstrates how human rights and the rights-based economy can act as a powerful and transformative normative framework for radically rethinking fiscal policy in Africa. The fourth chapter is by Philip Oamen and Adebolarin Adekanle and titled 'Taxation and the Realisation of Socioeconomic Rights in Africa: What Is the Role of International Cooperation?' This chapter draws on existing human rights instruments and literature to develop an international cooperation model, as a useful vehicle for realisation of socio-economic rights in Africa through the lens of TWAIL.

The fifth chapter titled 'Supporting Infrastructure Development Initiatives Using Tax Frameworks in Emerging Economies' is co-authored by Augustine Edobor Arimoro and Habiba Musa. This chapter explores the potential opportunities presented by leveraging the tax system to facilitate private sector investment in infrastructure procurement in emerging markets (which are predominantly found in the Global South). The sixth chapter is titled 'Unpacking the Mobile Money Tax Conundrum: Insights from Case Studies of Kenya, Uganda and Tanzania' and jointly authored by Marie-Louise F. Aren and Magalie Masamba. Chapter 6 examines how the growth of mobile money services has contributed to development and human rights and within the context of domestic resource mobilisation (DRM). The seventh chapter is titled 'The South African Revenue Service's role in Providing Access to Justice to Taxpayers' written by Carika Keulder. The chapter argues that the South African Revenue Services (SARS) role in facilitating access to justice for taxpayers depends on its adherence to the rule of law and relevant legislation to ensure that SARS respect taxpayers' rights while efficiently and effectively collecting taxes. The eighth chapter is titled 'Refuting its "Tax Haven" Characterisation: The BVI's Offshore Financial Services Industry and its Right to Economic Self-Determination' and written by Antonius R. Hippolyte. This chapter focuses on the categorisation of British Virgin Island (BVI) as a 'tax haven' by demonstrating the BVI's commitment to cooperation, good governance and transparency through the BVI's numerous regulatory initiatives and the enactment of numerous pieces of legislations all aimed at continuously enhancing regulation of its financial services industry in the BVI. The ninth chapter is by Emeka Duruigbo and it is titled 'IMF, World Bank and Fossil Fuel Subsidies'. The chapter by Emeka Duruigbo advances the notion that while subsidy reforms are necessary for economic and environmental reasons, they must be carefully planned and implemented to avoid negative social impacts.

The tenth chapter is by Olusegun Vincent and Olaniyi Evans and it is titled 'Digital Taxation: Sustainable Use of Digitalization and Tax Justice in Africa'. This chapter discusses how tax authorities invest in digital technologies to improve tax collection and reduce fraud and evasion, while businesses leverage these advancements to streamline operations and increase competitiveness. The 11th chapter is written by Newman U. Richards and it is titled 'Tax Implications of Fiscal Social Contract on Sustainable Development in Nigeria'. Chapter 11 argues that sustainable development is a consequence of good governance and collaborative citizenship participation in governance.

Notes

1 According to the UN Special Rapporteur on Extreme Poverty and Human Rights (UN Special Rapporteur on poverty), Report: Taxation and Human Rights, 22 May 2014, UN Doc. A/HRC/26/28, 1 'Taxation is a key tool when tackling inequality and for generating the resources necessary for poverty reduction and the realisation of human rights, and can also be used to foster stronger governance, accountability and participation in public affairs'. Also cited in Amnesty International, 'What's tax got to do with it: A resource guide on tax and human rights' (2024) 8 https://www.amnesty.org/en/documents/pol30/8134/2024/en/#:~:text=Governments%20use%20tax%20to%20ensure,implement%20its%20policies%20and%20programmes accessed 15 November 2024.

2 For a critical analysis of the failings of international law from the Third World Approaches to International Law (TWAIL) perspective, see Bhupinder S. Chimni, 'Crisis and international law: A third world approaches to international law perspective' in Makane M. Mbengue and Jean D'Aspremont (eds.) *Crisis Narratives in International Law* (Brill Nijhoff, 2021) 40–53.

3 Nikki Reisch, 'Taxation and human rights: Mapping the landscape' in Philip G. Alston and Nikki Reisch (eds.) *Tax, Inequality, and Human Rights* (Oxford University Press, 2019) 33–58. Also, see Kenny Ng, 'Sustainable sides of taxation: An international law approach' (2024) 26 (1) *Environmental Law Review* 33–52; Benjamín Sevilla-Bernabéu and Estrella Del-Valle-Calzada, 'Tax policies with a human rights perspective: Towards greater tax justice' (2024) 38 (3) *South African Journal of Accounting Research* 264–277; Reuven S. Avi-Yonah and Gianluca Mazzoni, 'Taxation and human rights: A delicate balance' in Philip G. Alston and Nikki R. Reisch (eds.) *Tax, Inequality, and Human Rights* (Oxford, 2019) 259–277.

4 Generally, see United Nations Economic Commission for Africa (UNECA), 'Technical report: Promoting effective tax cooperation at the United Nations' (October 2023) https://repository.uneca.org/handle/10855/49954 accessed 15 November 2024; Daniel Olika, 'Taxation and human rights: Towards a sustainable realisation of minimum core obligations in Nigeria' (2024) 24 (1) *African Human Rights Law Journal* 31–57.

5 Eghosa Ekhator, Chisa Onyejekwe and Newman Richards, 'Human rights and taxation in developing countries: A case for tax justice and accountability in Africa' in Damilola Olawuyi and Oyeniyi Abe (eds.) *Business and Human Rights Law in Africa* (Edward Elgar, 2022) 127–150.

6 Sudha Kavuri and Anjana Ramanathan, 'Climate change litigation: Chronicles from the Global South. A comparative study' (2022) 28 *Comparative Law Review* 169–199. On the other hand, according to Louisa Brooke-Holland, 'What is the Global South' (House of Commons Library, 11 July 2024) https://commonslibrary.parliament.uk/what-is-the-global-south/#:~:text=The%20%27Global%20South%27%20has%20become,such%20as%20China%20and%20India accessed 15 November 2024, 'There is no definitive definition of the Global South, which means there is no definitive list of countries'.

7 B. D. S. Santos, 'Epistemologies of the South and the future' (2016) 1 *From the European South: A Transdisciplinary Journal of Postcolonial Humanities* 17–29, 18–19. Hence, according to Santos, the Global South is not a geographical description but rather a metaphor for the human suffering caused by capitalism and colonialism on the global level… and speaks of a South that also exists in the geographic North (Europe and North America), in the form of excluded, silenced and marginalised populations….

Also, see Prakash Kashwan, 'Climate justice in the Global North: An introduction' (2021) 5 (1) *Case Studies in the Environment* 1–13.

8 Also, see Aude Darnal, 'The 'Global South' is real. Deal with it' (World Politics Review, 28 September 2023) https://www.worldpoliticsreview.com/global-south-countries-term-brics/ accessed 15 November 2024; Brooke-Holland (n 6).

9 Generally, see Jeffrey Owens and Jonathan L. Pemberton, *Cooperative Compliance: A Multi-stakeholder and Sustainable Approach to Taxation* (Kluwer Law International BV, 2021); Reisch (n 3).

10 Generally, see Amnesty International (n 1).

11 Abel Gwaindepi, 'Taxation in since colonial times' African Economic History Network https://www.aehnetwork.org/textbook/taxation-in-africa-since-colonial-times/ accessed 15 November 2024.

12 Newman U. Richards and Benedicta Ikwuegbu, 'Examination of the challenges and prospects of taxing the informal sector in Nigeria' (2024) 20 (1) *UNIZIK Law Journal* 118.

13 Sonnur Aktas Guzel, Gokhan Ozer and Murat Ozcan, 'The effect of the variables of tax justice perception and trust in government on tax compliance: The case of Turkey' (2019) 78 *Journal of Behavioral and Experimental Economics* 80.

14 Transparency International, 'Exploring the relationships between corruption and tax revenue: U4 expert answer' 1 (January 2010) https://www.u4.no/publications/exploring-the-relationships-between-corruption-and-tax-revenue.pdf accessed 15 November 2024.

15 Martin Hearson, 'The challenges for developing countries in international tax justice' (2018) 53 (10) *The Journal of Development Studies* 1932.

16 Also, see Okanga Okanga and Lyla Latif, 'Effective taxation in Africa: Confronting systemic vulnerability through inclusive global tax governance' (2021) 2 *African Journal of International Economic Law* 100.

17 However, see Serges D. Kamga, 'Taxation, tax injustice, and the right to development in Africa' in Emmanuel E. K. Kamga, et al. (eds.) *Right to Development and Illicit Financial Flows from Africa: Dynamics, Perspectives, and Prospects* (Lexington Books, 2024) 273–286; Irma M. Valderrama, 'How can regional cooperation help the enhancement of regional economic development and strengthen the voices of developing countries in global tax negotiations?' (2024) 25 (2) *The Journal of World Investment & Trade* 201–236.

Bibliography

Reuven S. Avi-Yonah and Gianluca Mazzoni, 'Taxation and human rights: A delicate balance' in Philip G. Alston and Nikki R. Reisch (eds.) *Tax, Inequality, and Human Rights* (House of Commons Library, 2019) 259–277.

Louisa Brooke-Holland, 'What is the Global South' (House of Commons Library, 11 July 2024) https://commonslibrary.parliament.uk/what-is-the-global-south/#:~:text=The%20%27Global%20South%27%20has%20become,such%20as%20China%20and%20India accessed 15 November 2024.

Bhupinder S. Chimni, 'Crisis and international law: A third world approaches to international law perspective' in Makane M. Mbengue and Jean D'Aspremont (eds.) *Crisis Narratives in International Law* (Brill Nijhoff, 2021) 40–53.

Aude Darnal, 'The 'Global South' is real. Deal with it' (World Politics Review, 28 September 2023) https://www.worldpoliticsreview.com/global-south-countries-term-brics/ accessed 15 November 2024.

Eghosa Ekhator, Chisa Onyejekwe and Newman Richards, 'Human rights and taxation in developing countries: A case for tax justice and accountability in Africa' in Damilola Olawuyi and Oyeniyi Abe (eds.) *Business and Human Rights Law in Africa* (Edward Elgar, 2022) 127–150.

Sonnur Aktas Guzel, Gokhan Ozer and Murat Ozcan, 'The effect of the variables of tax justice perception and trust in government on tax compliance: The case of Turkey' (2019) 78 *Journal of Behavioral and Experimental Economics* 80.

Abel Gwaindepi, 'Taxation in since colonial times' African economic History Network https://www.aehnetwork.org/textbook/taxation-in-africa-since-colonial-times/ accessed 15 November 2024.

Martin Hearson, 'The challenges for developing countries in international tax justice' (2018) 53 (10) *The Journal of Development Studies* 1932.

Serges D. Kamga, 'Taxation, tax injustice, and the right to development in Africa' in Emmanuel E. K. Kamga, et al. (eds.) *Right to Development and Illicit Financial Flows from Africa: Dynamics, Perspectives, and Prospects* (Lexington Books, 2024) 273–286.

Prakash Kashwan, 'Climate justice in the Global North: An introduction' (2021) 5 (1) *Case Studies in the Environment* 1–13.

Sudha Kavuri and Anjana Ramanathan, 'Climate change litigation: Chronicles from the Global South. A comparative study' (2022) 28 *Comparative Law Review* 169–199.

Kenny Ng, 'Sustainable sides of taxation: An international law approach' (2024) 26 (1) *Environmental Law Review* 33–52.

Okanga Okanga and Lyla Latif, 'Effective taxation in Africa: Confronting systemic vulnerability through inclusive global tax governance' (2021) 2 *African Journal of International Economic Law*100.

Daniel Olika, 'Taxation and human rights: Towards a sustainable realisation of minimum core obligations in Nigeria' (2024) 24 (1) *African Human Rights Law Journal* 31–57.

Jeffrey Owens and Jonathan L. Pemberton, *Cooperative Compliance: A Multi-stakeholder and Sustainable Approach to Taxation* (Kluwer Law International BV, 2021).

Nikki Reisch, 'Taxation and human rights: Mapping the landscape' in Philip G. Alston and Nikki Reisch (eds.) *Tax, Inequality, and Human Rights* (Oxford University Press, 2019) 33–58.

Newman U. Richards and Benedicta Ikwuegbu, 'Examination of the challenges and prospects of taxing the informal sector in Nigeria' (2024) 20 (1) *UNIZIK Law Journal* 118.

B. D. S. Santos, 'Epistemologies of the South and the future' (2016) 1 *From the European South: A Transdisciplinary Journal of Postcolonial Humanities* 17–29.

Benjamín Sevilla-Bernabéu and Estrella Del-Valle-Calzada, 'Tax policies with a human rights perspective: Towards greater tax justice' (2024) 38 (3) *South African Journal of Accounting Research* 264–277.

Transparency International, 'Exploring the relationships between corruption and tax revenue: U4 expert answer' 1 (January 2010) https://www.u4.no/publications/exploring-the-relationships-between-corruption-and-tax-revenue.pdf accessed 15 November 2024.

UN Special Rapporteur on Extreme Poverty and Human Rights (UN Special Rapporteur on Poverty), Report: Taxation and Human Rights, 22 May 2014, UN Doc. A/HRC/26/28. https://digitallibrary.un.org/record/773515?ln=en&v=pdf

United Nations Economic Commission for Africa (UNECA), 'Technical report: Promoting effective tax cooperation at the United Nations' (October 2023) https://repository.uneca.org/handle/10855/49954 accessed 15 November 2024.

Irma M. Valderrama, 'How can regional cooperation help the enhancement of regional economic development and strengthen the voices of developing countries in global tax negotiations?' (2024) 25 (2) *The Journal of World Investment & Trade* 201–236.

Part A

Conceptualisation and Evolution

Role of Human Rights in Taxation

2 What normativity for international tax?

Towards alignment with human rights and the Sustainable Development Goals

*Luiza Leite de Queiroz**

2.1 Introduction

Since its inception a hundred years ago, the international tax architecture has remained largely unchanged. Incrementalism[1] and the monopoly of international tax law-making by a handful of developed countries[2] allowed for calculated tweaks over the years that were rather successful in preventing fundamental revisions or a complete overhaul of the system in place. Yet, as happens with many structures that withstand the test of time, the regime's foundation was plagued by small cracks that progressively grew to become unsustainable rifts. The 2008 financial crisis added pressure to these fractures[3] as much as it exposed them to the wider public. Unable to overlook anachronic concepts any longer and to sweep embedded inequalities under the rug, the architects of the international tax regime eventually headed the call for change. The Base Erosion Profit Shifting (BEPS) Project launched by the Organisation for Economic Cooperation and Development (OECD) in 2012 and initiatives that followed are the first tangible effort made to reform parts of the international tax design.

The establishment of the OECD/G20 Inclusive Framework on BEPS in 2016 marked the onset of a period of fast-paced change. From its adoption in October 2021, the so-called Two-Pillar Solution took centre stage in discussions, discourse and analyses of international tax law. Only two years later, a parallel move towards establishing a United Nations (UN) framework convention on international tax cooperation was successfully spearheaded by a group of developing, mostly African, countries.[4] As we witness a tipping point in history, many questions remain unanswered, including whether some of the currently discussed solutions have any real transformative capacity[5] or if they represent only a modest take on what true change could be.[6] But preceding these assessments comes the initial interrogation: Why is it that the system needs repairing in the first place? Although more than one answer applies, this

* Luiza Leite de Queiroz, Marie Skłodowska-Curie Fellow (ADAPTED) | Joint PhD candidate at the Faculty of Law of Vrije Universiteit Amsterdam and at the Institute of Development Research and Development Policy of Ruhr-Universität Bochum (Germany). This work was supported by the European Union's Horizon 2020 Research and Innovation Programme under Marie Skłodowska-Curie Grant Agreement No. 956909 (ADAPTED)

DOI: 10.4324/9781003432890-3

chapter's focus is on one fundamental reason behind calls for reform which was explicitly removed from the scope of BEPS[7] and corollary initiatives[8]: the unequal allocation of taxing rights between countries.

From its early days, the international tax regime was moored to the main objective of preventing double taxation of corporate income in cross-border trade. Aside from giving rise to a framework inherently characterised by a rivalry between sovereigns,[9] this original framing was conspicuously conceived from the vantage point of private corporate actors (rather than that of individuals). Hand-in-hand with such commercial orientation is the pursuit of efficiency, a goal that came to be seen as the non-normative reflection of strictly technical economic thinking. Opposing such notion, this chapter argues that, not only is that *not* the case, but the observed lack of an identifiable normative compass in international taxation results in a constraint of developing countries' ability to fulfil human rights' obligations within their borders. To that end, the analysis proceeds gradually and in relation to two axial claims. First, we centrally contend that, due to its historical trajectory, the regime is underlined by an arbitrary pragmatism that merely aims for economic efficiency in its distribution of taxing rights (as opposed to relying on human rights principles as guideposts). Its alleged normative neutrality, we submit, comes at the expense of the pursuit of justice between nations, which has negative consequences for individuals (often the most vulnerable) in developing countries. In light of that, a pivoting exercise in the way that international tax law is intellectually envisaged, anchored in Critical Legal Studies (CLS) and Third World Approaches to International Law (TWAIL), is briefly sketched out.

In advancing the chapter's second central claim, we indicate that human rights – and, most notably, socio-economic rights – need financial resources (among others) to be realised. A skewed allocation of taxing rights effectively impacts how much tax revenue different countries – developed and developing – get to collect from transnational corporate activity. This, we argue, interferes with states' ability to discharge their territorial and, relevantly, extraterritorial human rights obligations. As will be advanced, while the territorial state ought to procure all available resources to fulfil human rights within its borders, the non-territorial state must refrain from interfering with such obligation. Finally, recognising that the realisation of these topical ties in practice requires mutual understanding between those working in international tax and human rights, it is noted that, so far, international tax circles have remained aloof to human rights vernacular. On the other hand, they have become increasingly aware of the omnipresent concept of sustainable development which, we observe, is staked in human rights normativity, especially as framed in the Sustainable Development Goals (SDGs). It is therefore posited that the SDGs may be leveraged in international tax circles as the *lingua franca* that allows a push for alignment of the rules on the allocation of taxing rights with human rights normativity.

2.2 International tax structure and the inequalities it produces

2.2.1 Past to present

The current international tax structure was conceived under the auspices of the League of Nations in the 1920s to 'remove the evil consequences of double taxation'.[10] Crucially, the historical context in which discussions on the topic arose was one of post-war financial recovery.[11] Resurfacing from World War I, Europe was still reeling from huge economic losses and reckoning with growing external debt contracted to meet war demands. Looking into ways out of the financial crisis thus became an imperative, which led the League to convene an International Finance Conference early on in its works in February 1920. Representing the business community which saw in states increased fiscal appetite a real threat to profits, the International Chamber of Commerce significantly lobbied proceedings.[12] As a result, the Conference's outcome document recognised the issue of double taxation as an obstacle to investments abroad.

In October 1920, a Financial Committee was established to follow up on the recommendations made. One year later, it commissioned a report on double taxation from four academics, often referred to as the Four Economists. Seeking to answer five theoretical questions about double taxation, they drafted a report in 1923 whose contents are widely regarded as the starting point of our current international tax regime.[13] Importantly, the 1923 report 'outlined economic principles, not legal language to implement them'.[14] It was then the task of a group of tax officials, the Technical Experts to the Financial Committee of the League of Nations, to give legal expression to the *doctrine of economic allegiance* articulated by the Four Economists. The Technical Experts produced a new report in 1925 and drafted the first model treaties on double taxation – considered the cornerstone of current Model Tax Conventions[15] – in 1928.

Upon the League's demise,[16] the OECD, initially through its precursor, the Organisation for European Economic Cooperation (OEEC), took over the role and connected responsibilities of 'world leader in international coordination on tax'.[17] This, in effect, meant that the OECD, 'a club of advanced industrialized countries',[18] automatically inherited the power to delineate the contours of international taxation rules applicable worldwide without inclusive or further deliberations. The implications of such a set up are manifold.[19] But, on a more fundamental level, briefly looking on the historical path that led to the adoption of the international tax framework in its standing format is vital in understanding that particular interests in a very specific historical context[20] informed the normative preferences that still govern international tax matters today.

2.2.2 What purpose does it serve?

Unlike most branches of international law,[21] international tax law is, as we stand, made up of a patchwork of over 3,000 bilateral agreements that dictate which country gets to tax what – or, in other words, allocate taxing rights (or entitlements) between countries. This is no coincidence as the Technical

Experts already discarded a multilateral solution to double taxation as practically unfeasible when proposing the first Model Conventions.[22] While talks of replacing the bilateral system for a multilateral convention resurfaced in the 1960s when work on the Conventions resumed, they were short lived. Most bilateral agreements – Double Taxation Agreements (DTAs) – signed to date follow the OECD Model Tax Convention,[23] a document firstly drafted in 1963 (following the outlines of the League of Nations Model Conventions, as seen) and periodically revised ever since. Broadly speaking, DTAs that do not adopt the OECD template reproduce the content of the UN Model Double Taxation Convention. Although the UN Model largely drew its structure and wording from the OECD's, the two models significantly differ in how they allocate taxing rights between countries.

Since the adoption of the regime via DTAs in the 1960s, scholars have befittingly raised concerns about the suitability of the framework to achieve the primary goal of eradicating double taxation[24] and even dispelled its necessity to attain said goal altogether.[25] Fulfilling some expectations, a network of DTAs allowed some common ground for coordination, legal harmony and a great deal of certainty for investors. But, on a deeper level, it marshalled a certain point of view – that of capital exporting (developed) countries, as will be discussed below – and made it so that normative prescriptions of the past became so interwoven with technical concepts that disentangling them became virtually impossible in practice. To discuss the imbalances between countries that the international tax regime produces became synonymous with discussing the regime itself.[26] As its 100-year stability has shown, making the two indissociable proved to be an effective way of keeping critics at bay.

2.2.3 *A story of rough approximation to justice*

Tracing back its history, it emerges that the propelling motive to erect an international taxation framework was to ensure that a specific barrier to cross-border trade (double taxation) was eliminated so that a welcoming environment for foreign investment could be fostered.[27] As sedimented by the regime, states' power to tax – an aspect typically linked to sovereignty itself[28] – became, in a way, *subordinate* to the policy goal of avoidance of double taxation. DTAs, it must be said, embody, first and foremost, compromise and (rules of) mutual concession on whose domestic legislation applies when. Accepting that *some* concessions may be required in a globalised market economy, however, does not equate to accepting that *any* concession is, or should be, valid. The continuum between the two is precisely the space in which considerations of distribution are debated.

Appealing to a discourse of tax is technical or tax is the realm of the expert,[29] the OECD has so far successfully prevented an ample debate on the rules that define the allocation of taxing entitlements from occurring. A virtue of portraying a topic as technical is its almost immediate depoliticisation[30] and consequent removal from political scrutiny.[31] Taken in tandem with the notable absence of a court-like structure[32] that allows for contestation of allocation rules on technical grounds, such discourse effectively insulated the current system from dissident voices. While specific aspects of taxation may well claim the neutrality that technicality lends (e.g., defining optimal tax rates for different goods), some others run, by definition, into value-laden deliberations. As discussed below, at the heart of the *quid pro quo* lies the dichotomy *source* (or debtor or host) vs. *residence* (or creditor or home) countries.

In broad terms, the nomenclature refers, respectively, to countries where an economic activity gives rise to transnational wealth (profit/income), as opposed to countries where the investor is domiciled or resident. Incidentally, this division largely overlaps with the known divide between developing and developed nations because the former are predominantly capital-importing nations (and thus the source of economic activity, generally speaking) and the latter are typically capital-exporting nations (and therefore the home or residence of investors).[33] The issue – already flagged by scholars for some five decades[34] – is that, as endorsed by the Four Economists, the Technical Experts and subsequently enshrined in the OECD Model Conventions (hence, in most DTAs), the current allocation of taxing rights between source and residence countries significantly privileges the latter over the former. Indeed, the current international tax regime reflects the endorsement of what this chapter shall call a *normative triad* which made contextual sense in 1920s post-war Europe and that continued to make sense, later on, to the OECD's membership. That triad is composed of one economic doctrine, one economic assumption and one arbitrary choice.

First, the doctrine of economic allegiance articulated by the Four Economists initially ascribed taxing rights according to varying degrees of proximity between different categories of *active* or *passive* income and four factors. As previously alluded to, these factors were eventually condensed into only two, deemed of ultimate relevance by the 1923 report: source (of income) and residence (of investor). Central to the doctrine, as crystalised in DTAs, are two elements: a) *a priori* restriction of source taxation of (most) passive income[35]; and b) the concept of permanent establishment (PE) with respect to source taxation of active income. Draped in apparent (normative) neutrality, both elements effectively allow for more taxing rights to be granted to residence rather than source which has far from negligible consequences for poorer developing countries.[36]

As it may be seen as less obviously problematic than an *a priori* restriction on taxation of an entire income category, it is important to note that the PE concept is equally prejudicial to source countries' tax bases. As conceived, it requires the physical presence of a non-resident corporate taxpayer in a source jurisdiction as a trigger for tax liability of active income. Not only does the OECD Model Convention define what is considered physical presence for tax purposes but it further limits source taxation to 'the income "attributable" to that permanent establishment'.[37] Within the BEPS scaffolding and subsequent proposals, the PE concept was partially revisited under Action 7[38] and Pillar

One (Amount A) of the Two-Pillar Solution.[39] Nevertheless, neither of these initiatives completely abandons the concept as the main parameter for source taxation of corporate (active) income.

Second, the economic assumption upon which the regime was built – considered a mitigating factor of the restrictions imposed on source taxation – was that signatory countries to bilateral taxation agreements shared similar flows of investment.[40] This should mean, in short, that signatory countries display(ed) comparable volumes of outward investment. The follow-up premise to this assumption is that, where reciprocity or symmetry exists, tax revenue foregone as source on the one hand will be offset by tax revenue collected as residence on the other. After all, source and residence are non-static concepts that are concretely determined depending on the specific economic situation observed in each bilateral relationship. Notably, though, where asymmetry is observed and outward flows of investment are markedly unequal, the follow-up premise ceases to apply. Asymmetric bilateral agreements have thus the actual effect of reducing 'tax revenues available for the developing country'.[41]

Third, owing to the Four Economists' original framing of international taxation (rules) as 'a zero-sum game [in which] one country's gain in revenue is another's loss',[42] choosing between competing interests became a necessity. As seen, the choice made was to adopt an economic model in which 'the country of origin [source] should exempt all non-residents from taxation imposed on income drawn from sources within its borders, [because it] recognises the theoretical fact that the country wanting the money cannot successfully 'tax the foreigner'.[43] Quite evidently, the model was (and still is) premised on the source country's renunciation of its primary right to tax (all) wealth produced within its borders as it deems fit. In justifying their partial preference for the model, the Four Economists emphasised that its 'rough approximation to justice'[44] was the 'most desirable practical method for avoiding the evils of double taxation'[45] for countries 'in which conditions are fairly equal'.[46] Rather tellingly, they did acknowledge that it could be reasonably argued that the chosen model did 'violence to what are at present their [debtor countries] instinctive ideas as to their rights to origin taxation'.[47]

Particularly striking about this fundamentally arbitrary[48] choice is the admitted absence of economic reasoning to support it aside from the proposition that a country wanting investments cannot introduce barriers to their flows.[49] In the end, the main justifications offered by the Four Economists to vouch for a residence-based taxation model were *convenience* – in conforming to selected states' practice at that time – and *pragmatism* – in avoiding the lack of theoretical basis for an exact quantification of proportions of income that should be taxed in each jurisdiction (as per economic allegiance). Both existing treaty practice and pragmatism continued to be central considerations in the subsequent work carried out by the Technical Experts. As the international tax regime slowly stretched itself to envelop a more frequent reality of asymmetric bilateral relationships, the choice was continuously renewed, and the normative triad gradually became synonymous with the system.

Against this background, it is truly worrying that the arbitrary pragmatism which underlies the triad eventually came to be seen as the non-normative reflection of sound economic thinking.[50] As will be argued in the following section, brushing aside the regime's roots, and portraying exclusionary decisions of the past as the pristine standard against which to measure progress is tantamount to what has been termed in the literature *coloniality of being*.[51] It has been noted, it is true, that the economic power of developed countries alone cannot fully explain the international tax regime's formation.[52] But it is equally important not to lose sight of the fact that, as the regime evolved, power relations 'secured consent without the presence of struggles'[53] as well as 'shield[ed] the policy agenda from certain discussions and [brought] others to the fore of the debate'.[54] As empirical research has shown, for developing countries, 'the decision to negotiate and the eventual negotiated content [of a DTA] are a function of power and knowledge-based variables'.[55]

2.3 From mainstream economics to critical legal theory and TWAIL

2.3.1 The pursuit of efficiency

It is commonly said that the training we receive widely shapes the way we rationalise problems and propose solutions. The original framing of international taxation as a zero-sum game and its consequent unequal allocation of taxing rights certainly illustrates that point well. Tax scholarship has long been populated by a great assortment of academics[56] whose background disciplines fall somewhere within the broad spectrum of the social sciences.[57] While philosophers and political scientists have extensively scrutinised the foundations and normative underpinnings of international tax law,[58] practically speaking, it has been tax lawyers, accountants and (mainstream) economists who have taken the lead in shaping it. This *quasi* monopoly of law-making and interpreting by scholars, technocrats and professionals with an accentuated proclivity for mainstream economic reasoning has largely led to the establishment of the normative triad's *status quo* described above.

In the absence of an *overtly* normative framework that orients action, international tax rules were ultimately fashioned to achieve the goal of economic efficiency,[59] generally perceived as normatively neutral in economic circles. Relevantly, we argue, this pursuit comes at the expense of other relevant policy goals, such as justice between nations,[60] and a more *earnest engagement* with normative deliberations that necessarily surround distribution processes. Going beyond the pertinent question as to whether considerations of efficiency in taxation can really be neutral,[61] it is crucial to note that economic appeals to efficiency have not and, in fact, *cannot* solve the problem of injustice in the allocation of taxing rights.[62] Discipline-related epistemological boundaries constrain what queries economics alone (particularly mainstream) can or cannot answer.[63] Normative reflections imbued in distributive matters are, by their own concession, usually out of economists' reach.[64] Efficiency and justice are, indeed, not synonymous and, if anything, the two are frequently antagonistic.[65]

Conventional economic wisdom indicates that, domestically, 'it is typically welfare-enhancing to adopt the efficient rule and then redistribute it through taxes'.[66] The rationale behind the proposition is that 'efficiency maximizes the size of the economic pie that taxes and transfers can then redistribute to address concerns about distribution'.[67] Moreover, 'across a large number of efficient policies, distributional consequences will even out'.[68] Irrespective of the arguments that can be wielded in favour or against these claims, it is reasonable to conceive that the inherent difficulties of speaking of aggregate welfare *within* national borders can only be magnified at the international level. Can we practically speak of *aggregate global* welfare vis-à-vis our Westphalian paradigm of sovereignty in which the territorial state is the primary duty-bearer and guarantor of rights? If so, to whom must we direct appeals for redistribution[69] of transnational wealth? Could the notion of aggregate global welfare perhaps imply the existence of a global community?

The fact that tax policies came to be seen as the instrument through which redistribution may happen at the national level only emphasises the intrinsically different locations within the paragon of economic efficiency that domestic and international tax law occupy. While domestic taxation should in theory represent the second step that legitimises a purely efficient outcome, international taxation is confined to the bounds of the first step as it only goes as far as distributing taxing entitlements with no recourse to a subsequent redistribution mechanism. If international tax law were to follow the logic of its domestic counterpart, the distributional offset assumption could hold true if a supranational authority was entrusted with the task of redistributing national gains and losses across borders. Alternatively, a mechanism of redistribution could be directly embedded into the legal framework concerned. But fundamentally, both would still have to be informed by *a* normative compass in conceiving the redistribution[70] which is precisely what economics alone[71] cannot provide.

2.3.2 If not (law &) economics, which legal lens and why?

The main argument sketched out thus far – i.e., that the current biased regime is partly a product of its contingent historical path, partly of mainstream economic thinking which extols efficiency and normative neutrality – largely echoes assertions postulated in more abstract terms by scholars affiliated with the CLS[72] movement. In view of the OECD's automatic inheritance of the post of world tax authority – which effectively enabled the normative triad to become synonymous with the regime – the argument advanced also harmonises rather well with voices within the TWAIL[73] movement. Particularly, this chapter aligns itself with CLS and TWAIL in three interrelated, and sometimes overlapping, ways.

First, in deploying a historical analysis and illuminating the normative partiality disguised as technical neutrality embraced by the regime, we largely adhere to the critique levied by CLS proponents on liberal legalism.[74] Second, in fleshing out the triad and discussing how it consistently privileges developed countries – many of which were colonial powers in the 1920s – the argument advanced is similar to Anthony Anghie's main thesis that 'the colonial encounter has ineluctably shaped the fundamental doctrines of international law'.[75] Third, in drawing attention to the fact that the parlance of justice has not been prioritised within international tax experts' lexicon, we subscribe to James Thuo Gatti's writings on the Regime Bias approach to international economic governance.[76] Specifically, it is maintained that the scarcity of discussions on justice in the international tax regime obscures the very fact that *a* facet of justice was chosen and adopted – that which prioritises corporate private actors' interests – over others.

To decry international tax law as biased necessarily implies the qualification: towards/against whom? For that reason, the arguments espoused here have attempted to shed light on the symbiotic relationship between developed countries' legal praxis and mainstream economic reasoning as they breathed life into the international tax law project. Legal inventiveness arguably provided *a posteriori* justification for the doctrine of economic allegiance in the 1920s and bestowed credibility upon the normative triad. Throughout the decades such credibility sedimented the notion that the concepts adopted by the international tax regime were *universal*[77] and, indeed, universally desirable – something dangerously close to neo-colonialist reasoning.[78] Taken together, variations of these observations and connected claims have been submitted more broadly by scholars examining inherent biases in international economic law.[79] But international tax rules deserve special attention for at least one pivotal reason: their impact on states' ability to comply with their human rights obligations.

The *lex mercatoria* lens so far employed in the allocation exercise does not go beyond the goal of economic efficiency as it conveniently sustains the normative triad. But such a lens is as insufficient as it is inadequate. It does not provide an answer to the question of which guiding (justice) principles (should) apply in international taxation and, worse yet, ignores the human rights consequences of the current skewed distribution of taxing entitlements. As will be further explored in the next section, the allocation rules here discussed hinder human rights' realisation in two complementary ways. First, by constraining the ability of developing countries to mobilise the financial resources required for the realisation of human (particularly socio-economic) rights within their borders and second, by enabling developed countries to evade their own extraterritorial human rights obligations. Owing to its overt and intrinsic normativity, we argue that international human rights law provides a more suitable conceptual lens through which to critically appraise international taxation.

2.4 Towards a necessary alignment between human rights normativity and the international tax regime

2.4.1 Why is international taxation relevant to socio-economic rights' realisation?

In a state-centric international order where sovereigns are rights-holders, duty-bearers, makers and sometimes enforcers of international law, speaking of equity between nations[80] does not require much creative effort. If one takes to heart the basic proposition that sovereigns are equals,[81] any imbalances that were not freely agreed upon are, by definition, chipping away at the world equilibrium that the law of nations purports to curate. Ultimately, though, it is not a fondness for the legal fiction of statehood that justifies arguments for a just distribution of taxing rights. It is rather the recognition that inequalities produced by the international tax regime on the world stage *trickle down* to the individual level on the domestic plane and effectively hinder the realisation of human rights recognised in numerous international treaties ratified by most countries.[82]

Constant reference in the international tax literature to the all-encompassing term *taxpayer* dangerously obscures the different spaces that corporations and individuals occupy within the international tax regime. As seen, individuals' interests and needs were not really considered when the regime's theoretical underpinnings were being conceived. In addition to being disenfranchised[83] individuals everywhere, but especially the poorer ones[84] in developing countries, stand to lose the most from any lesser availability, or scarcity, of (transnational) corporate tax revenue. Socio-economic rights enshrined in the International Covenant on Economic, Social and Cultural Rights (ICESCR), such as the rights to health, an adequate standard of living, and education, patently depend on financial resources to be realised. Adequate infrastructure needs to be built, healthcare systems need to be maintained, schools need to be staffed, etc. Although funds can be raised from several different sources, there is great consensus among fiscal policy specialists that the bulk of it should ideally come from (progressive) tax collection.[85]

In the last decade, several UN Special Rapporteurs have spoken of the repercussions that different sources and modes of revenue collection can have on human rights.[86] UN Committees have also made explicit the link between domestic tax practices of (individually considered) developed countries and the respective consequences to the attainment of human rights in developing countries.[87] In the meantime, human rights scholarship has turned its gaze to historically unorthodox themes such as the effects of regressive taxation on human rights. The commonality broadly shared by those researching (transnational) tax justice in the human rights field is the general understanding that there should be a call for alignment of the international tax regime with human rights normativity.[88] Significantly, however, the relationship between allocation rules' biased nature and states' ability to comply with human rights obligations, both within and beyond their borders,[89] remains deficiently addressed in the literature.

2.4.2 *Maximum available resources & international cooperation and assistance*

The economic facet of the realisation of socio-economic rights gained shape in the ICESCR under the expression *maximum available resources*[90] contained in Article 2 (1). Albeit relatively underdeveloped as a legal concept, the term has been gradually clarified by the UN Committee on Economic, Social and Cultural Rights (the Committee) in successive General Comments. In General Comment No. 3 the UN body inaugurally noted that the phrase 'was intended (...) to refer to both the resources existing within a State and those available from the international community through international cooperation and assistance'.[91] Sorely lacking in this interpretation were any further explanations of what constituted a *resource*, which types of resources could be available internationally for (developing) countries, and what the expression *international cooperation and assistance* entailed. While the Committee's approach to filling these gaps has been piecemeal, its understanding has considerably evolved over the last 20 years.

For example, it has repeatedly been observed that unwillingness and resource constraints do not constitute an objective and reasonable justification to excuse a domestic state's non-compliance with its human rights obligations.[92] Only by demonstrating that *every* effort[93] has been made to use *all* available resources at its disposal can the state be deemed not to be in violation of its duties. The Committee has also noted that 'insufficient expenditure (...) which results in the non-enjoyment of the right to health by individuals or groups, particularly the vulnerable or marginalized'[94] may constitute a violation of a domestic state's obligation to fulfil human rights. Human rights scholars have often provided complementary analyses of the parameters found in Article 2 (1). Regarding the term *international cooperation and assistance*, it is generally understood that developing states have an obligation to seek and developed states have the corresponding duty to offer it. Although the precise contents of the duty to *render international cooperation and assistance* are yet to be settled, it is incontrovertible that the duty itself sits alongside other duties within the *protect, respect and fulfil framework*[95] which will be touched upon below.

2.4.3 *Extraterritorial obligations within the protect, respect and fulfil framework*

Adopted by international human rights law in the 1980s, the protect, respect and fulfil framework has since provided a conceptual typology against which to gauge whether states are compliant with their human rights obligations or not. Within this taxonomy, the domestic (territorial) state may be the principal but is not the sole duty-bearer when it comes to human rights attainment. The gradient nature of the different duties ensures that all states have some shared responsibility towards the realisation of human rights everywhere. While *protecting* and *fulfilling* human rights generally involve positive duties whereby states are effectively required to act, *respecting* human rights is widely regarded as entailing 'a negative obligation of abstention from interference, which by and large corresponds to the 'global minimum standard' of 'do no harm'.[96]

In this scenario, extraterritorial human rights obligations are understood as duties attributable to states beyond their domestic borders.[97] At a minimum, a state party to the ICESCR has the 'duty to abstain from activities or measures that will have a negative impact on the enjoyment of economic, social and cultural rights outside its own territory'.[98] Interpreting the Covenant's provisions, the Committee has noted that the negative duty to respect acquires particular relevance in the negotiation and conclusion of trade agreements and tax treaties.[99] It has further spoken on the obligation that states have 'to ensure that the policies and decisions of the international financial institutions of which they are members are in conformity with the obligations imposed by the Covenant'.[100] In the realm of international taxation, we see that, while the OECD itself may, strictly speaking, not be bound by human rights duties almost all its member states are.[101]

Irrespective of whether developed states can be said to have a legal duty to provide assistance, developing countries have an obligation to procure all available resources, domestically and internationally, to fulfil human rights within their borders. Correspondingly, *non-interference* with such obligation is an *integral* part of (non-territorial) countries' extraterritorial duty to respect. Moreover, to the extent that *cooperation* and *assistance* can be understood separately, while *providing assistance* may be viewed in connection with the duty to *fulfil, cooperating* should in principle be framed within the duty to respect.[102] In that sense, the Committee has also explicitly indicated that 'international cooperation requires States parties to refrain from actions that interfere, directly or indirectly, with the enjoyment of the right to water in other countries'.[103] This interpretation was adopted in successive Comments[104] and the same formula was later repeated with respect to the right to social security.[105]

It is important, then, to note that discussions about a just allocation of taxing rights have conspicuously revolved around moral or charitable duties of distributive justice rather than around legal human rights obligations. As a charitable action falls entirely within the discretion and goodwill of a donor, it effectively cannot be seen as a legal obligation. Development aid and efficiency thus seem to go hand-in-hand as, from the perspective of developed countries, additional revenue collected as a result of an (allegedly) efficient international tax regime can, in principle, be rightfully redistributed through aid.[106] This paternalistic view not only neglects states' general obligation to respect socio-economic rights abroad, but also overlooks the fact that redistributing additional tax revenue gains through aid cannot possibly be conceived as charity. If at all connected to the idea of offsetting previous distortions,[107] the redistribution logic leans closer to the legal notion of compensation or reparation.

2.4.4 But is it human rights or (sustainable) development?

It is important to say that any real furtherance and clarification of the ties between international taxation and human rights here articulated would require a solid common ground from which to start discussions. Truthfully, the almost complete absence of human rights language in the field of international taxation certainly gives the impression that the two worlds are far too removed for anyone to be conceiving bridges between them. That suspicion, whilst valid, is fortunately not true as, – we argue – one paramount concept already provides the middle ground that should spark mutual understanding between the two spheres. Development, in its usual dimensions of economic growth and (expected) social progress, has been a long acquaintance of the international tax expert. Its evolved, qualified form of *sustainable* development, so ubiquitous in policies, domestic and international, of the last 20 years is, in fact, *soaked* in human rights normativity.

A product of two distinct moments of the 20th century, these two fields evolved separately for decades: human rights with its language of treaties, obligations and legal parameters[108] and development as a technical endeavour allegedly devoid of political affiliations and normative inclinations. After decades of modest to no improvement in the socio-economic outlook of developing countries in spite of development projects, the question of whether development could be achieved purely following prescriptions of macroeconomics, without corresponding aspects of what came to be known as *good governance*,[109] eventually rose to the surface of the literature. The adoption of good governance as a benchmark for project planning provided an entry point for normative considerations to pierce through the sturdy wall of technocratic development.

The Millennium Development Goals (MDGs) adopted in the year 2000 were arguably the first step in the direction of alignment between the two, although Philip Alston aptly observed that '[U]nfortunately the great majority of analyses undertaken on the MDGs do not approach them as being situated within a human rights framework'.[110] Relevantly, his analysis of the sophisticated links between development and human rights emphasised that extreme poverty simultaneously thwarts the former – poverty is both a known obstacle to, and *the* issue that scripts of economic growth attempt to address – and results in a denial or violation of the latter. In other words, at the highest level of abstraction[111] *poverty* binds human rights and development together. Intersecting development, poverty and human rights lies taxation, a government tool that can hinder or foster the first, deepen or alleviate the second, and promote or breach the third. Such powerful instrument should be steered in a way that, rather than leaving these links at the fringes, fully acknowledges and strives to contemplate all of them in public finance planning and management.

Sufficiency of tax revenue as a share of a country's Gross Domestic Product has been hailed in tax scholarship as a key element of fiscal self-determination[112] and operationalised in public finance terms as part of the concept of *domestic revenue mobilisation* (DRM). The OECD, the World Bank, the International Monetary Fund (IMF) and the UN all have singled out DRM as a core priority of (development) projects worldwide, emphasising the desired sustainability of a country's capacity to domestically mobilise resources to finance public goods and services within its borders. DRM is generally prescribed as the antidote to developing countries' usual reliance on foreign debt and development aid[113] in ensuring the proper functioning of government activities. In that sense, the OECD's incoherent stance in advocating for DRM while leaving the allocation of taxing rights essentially untouched by the reforms proposed following BEPS seems rather puzzling. But, quite interestingly, the concept of DRM itself is aligned with the premise that the domestic (territorial) state is the primary, but not the sole, duty-bearer when it comes to the realisation of human rights within its borders.

2.4.5 *The missing link or lingua franca: Sustainable Development Goals*

Calls for a holistic rights-based approach to development picked up pace in the last 20 years just as the concept of sustainability resurged in the global agenda. Human rights and the SDGs contained in Agenda 2030 have often been described as two sides of the same coin given that the realisation of the former invariably leads to the fulfilment of the latter. Presented in a packaging of aspirational goals and measurable targets that more readily resonate with the rationale of economics generally embraced by tax experts, the SDGs overwhelmingly reflect already codified human rights.[114] Their substance finds not only moral justification in human rights, but an actual echo in the contents of numerous treaties. Besides formalising the concept of global partnership for sustainable development under Goal 17, the SDGs span several topics of common interest to those working in international taxation,[115] development and human rights, beginning with the overarching pledge to end poverty in all its forms everywhere contained in Goal 1.

The relevance of embracing the SDGs as the *lingua franca* that sparks discussions in traditionally non-intersecting circles cannot be overstated. The normativity they convey has remarkably seeped through tax policy documents that persistently remain aloof to human rights language. Not only were the SDGs formally endorsed by the OECD Council[116] but the institution has actively sought, in the last few years, to produce and publish informative materials on how different areas of its work could be aligned with Agenda 2030's framework. It is then interesting to note that the OECD Secretariat's continued resistance to human rights language noticeably fizzles out before the SDGs which suggests that perhaps it is not human rights normativity that is not compelling enough but rather the way it is presented. We submit, therefore, that the SDGs framework should be *openly* leveraged to allow international tax experts, human rights scholars and development practitioners to speak a similar language and to ultimately find potential synergies and opportunities for collaborative work on a suitable normative compass for international taxation.

2.5 Conclusion

This chapter probed for a fresh normative angle to the problem of unequal allocation of inter-state taxing entitlements. Dispelling the harmful notion that the normative preferences which were imbued in the international tax regime over a century ago are the product of *neutral* economic thinking is truly a matter of urgency if socio-economic rights are to be progressively realised in developing countries. Notwithstanding the domestic state's primary responsibility in mobilising all available resources to realise human rights within its own borders, non-territorial states, particularly OECD member states, have the equally relevant legal obligation of non-interference with the former's ability to discharge its duties. In the same vein, a genuine commitment to attaining the goals contained in Agenda 2030 necessarily requires a stern appraisal of the international tax rules in place, and a thorough understanding of the deep interconnectedness of human rights, sustainable development and taxation. While alignment of the international tax regime with human rights normativity is no panacea for the ailments posed by extreme poverty, it fundamentally represents a step in the right direction.

Notes

1 Ruth Mason, 'The Transformation of International Tax' (2020) 114 *American Journal of International Law* 353.
2 Thomas Rixen, *The Political Economy of International Tax Governance* (Transformations of the State, Palgrave Macmillan, Hampshire 2008) 87–99.
3 Rasmus Corlin Christensen and Martin Hearson, 'The New Politics of Global Tax Governance: Taking Stock a Decade after the Financial Crisis' (2019) 26 *Review of International Political Economy* 1068, 1083.
4 Rasmus Colin Christensen, 'Between Revolution and Rhetoric: The UN Vote and the Future of International Tax Cooperation' (2024) 19 *British Tax Review*.
5 Aitor Navarro, 'The Allocation of Taxing Rights under Pillar One of the OECD Proposal' in Florian Haase and Georg Kofler (eds), *The Oxford Handbook of International Tax Law* (Oxford University Press 2023); Suranjali Tandon, 'Assessing the Impact of Pillar Two on Developing Countries' (2022) 50 *INTERTAX* 923.
6 Annet Wanyana Oguttu and Monica Iyer, 'Tax Abuse and Implications for Human Rights in Africa' in Philip G. Alston and Nikki R. Reisch (eds), *Tax, Inequality, and Human Rights* (Oxford University Press 2019) 194/95.
7 OECD, 'Action Plan on Base Erosion and Profit Shifting' (2013), 11.
8 Although a new nexus rule on the allocation of *some* taxing rights is foreseen under Amount A of Pillar One, currently discussed proposals merely redistribute a *portion* of *in-scope* companies' profits in *selected* activities. Additionally, Pillar One's viability has recently been questioned should the United States of America (USA) decide not to implement it.
9 Mason, 'The Transformation of International Tax' 387.
10 Bruins and others, 'Report on Double Taxation Submitted to the Financial Committee' (1923) E.F.S.73. F.19.
11 Sunita Jogarajan, 'The 100th Anniversary of International Institutions and International Taxation' (2020) 48 *INTERTAX* 929.
12 Rixen, *The Political Economy of International Tax Governance* (n 2).
13 Sunita Jogarajan, *Double Taxation and the League of Nations* (Cambridge Tax Law Series, Cambridge University Press, Cambridge 2018) 31–32.
14 Elliott Ash and Omri Marian, 'The Making of International Tax Law: Empirical Evidence from Natural Language Processing' Legal Studies Research Paper Series, 9.
15 Jogarajan, *Double Taxation and the League of Nations*.

16 The intellectual work produced by former members of the disbanded Committee during the inter-war period is thoroughly analysed in: Nikki J. Teo, *The United Nations in Global Tax Coordination Hidden History and Politics* (Cambridge Tax Law Series, Cambridge University Press 2023).
17 Allison Christians and Laurens van Apeldoorn, *Tax Cooperation in an Unjust World* (Oxford University Press, Oxford 2021) 3.
18 Irma Mosquera Valderrama, Dries Lesage and Wouter Lips, 'Tax and Development: The Link between International Taxation, The Base Erosion Profit Shifting Project and The 2030 Sustainable Development Agenda' (2018) W-2018/4, 31 Although, in recent years the OECD has expanded its membership to include member states that are classified by the World Bank as developing countries. See: Reuven S. Avi-Yonah, 'Globalization, Tax Competition, and the Fiscal Crisis of the Welfare State' (2020) 113 *Harvard Law Review* 1573 1664.
19 Ivan Ozai, 'Two Accounts of International Tax Justice' (2020) 33 *Canadian Journal of Law & Jurisprudence* 317.
20 Diane M. Ring, 'International Tax Relations: Theory and Implications' (2007) 60 *Tax Law Review* 83–126.
21 Reuven S. Avi-Yonah, 'International Tax as International Law' (2004) 57 *Tax Law Review* 483 (on whether international tax law can be seen as part of the international law *corpus juris*).
22 The amount of reservations allowed to the provisions of the *Multilateral Convention to Implement Tax Treaty Related Measures to Prevent BEPS* (MLI), which came into force in 2018, illustrates the difficulties of reaching consensually agreed multilateral solutions with respect to international taxation.
23 Christians and Apeldoorn, *Tax Cooperation in an Unjust World.*
24 Kim Brooks and Richard Krever, 'The Troubling Role of Tax Treaties' in Geerten M M Michielse and Victor Thuronyi (eds), *Tax Design Issues Worldwide*, vol 51 (Series on International Taxation, Kluwer Law International 2015).
25 Tsilly Dagan, 'The Tax Treaties Myth' (2000) 32 *New York University Journal of International Law and Politics*.
26 Ring, 'International Tax Relations: Theory and Implications' 151.
27 Peter Dietsch and Thomas Rixen, 'Global Tax Governance: What It Is and Why It Matters' in Peter Dietsch and Thomas Rixen (eds), *Global Tax Governance – What's Wrong, and How to Fix It* (ECPR Press, Colchester 2016) 5.
28 Laurens van Apeldoorn, 'International Taxation and the Erosion of Sovereignty' in Peter Dietsch and Thomas Rixen (eds), *Global Tax Governance: What is Wrong with It and How to Fix It* (ECPR Press, Colchester 2016).
29 Attiya Waris, 'Kenya's Fiscal Accountability Revisited: A Review of the Historical Erosion of the Country's Fiscal Constitution from 1962 to 2010' in Morris Kiwinda Mbondenyi and others (eds), *Human Rights and Democratic Governance in Kenya: A Post-2007 Appraisal* (Pretoria University Law Press 2015) 304.
30 Cassandra Vet, Danny Cassimon and Anne Van de Vijver, 'Getting the Short End of the Stick: Power Relations and Their Distributive Outcomes for Lower-Income Countries in Transfer Pricing Governance' in Irma Johanna Mosquera Valderrama, Dries Lesage and Wouter Lips (eds), *Taxation, International Cooperation and the 2030 Sustainable Development Agenda* (United Nations University Series on Regionalism, Springer 2021) 5.
31 Mason, 'The Transformation of International Tax' 393.
32 Tarcisio Diniz Magalhães, 'What Is Really Wrong with Global Tax Governance and How to Properly Fix It' (2018) 10 *World Tax Journal.*
33 Arthur J. Cockfield, 'Shaping International Tax Law and Policy in Challenging Times' (2018) 54 *Stanford Journal of International Law* 227.
34 Charles R. Irish, 'International double taxation agreements and income taxation at source' (1974) 23 *International and Comparative Law Quarterly* 292 496.

35 OECD, 'Model Tax Convention on Income and on Capital: Condensed Version' (2017) 16–17.
36 In 2020, the OECD estimated that, on average, 19.3% of *total* tax revenue in African countries was raised through *corporate taxes* (as opposed to OECD countries' average of 9%). In notably poorer countries, corporate income tax represented between 25% and 40% of total tax revenue. This is illustrative of developing countries' higher reliance on corporate taxes as a key source of revenue. See: OECD, 'Corporate Tax Statistics' (2023).
37 Mason, 'The Transformation of International Tax' 356.
38 The more stringent guidelines proposed within Action 7 do not alter the dynamic of making source taxation of active income conditional on the physical presence of a permanent establishment. Furthermore, anti-fragmentation rules were made optional under the MLI.
39 See note 8.
40 Jalia Kangave, 'The Dominant Voices in Double Taxation Agreements: A Critical Analysis of the "Dividend" Article in the Agreement between Uganda and the Netherlands' (2009) 11 *International Community Law Review* 387 400.
41 Dagan, 'The Tax Treaties Myth' 989.
42 Reuven S. Avi-Yonah, 'Structure of International Taxation: A Proposal for Simplification' (1996) 74 *Texas Law Review* 1301–1303.
43 Bruins and others, 'Report on Double Taxation Submitted to the Financial Committee' 42.
44 Bruins and others, 'Report on Double Taxation Submitted to the Financial Committee' 48.
45 Bruins and others, 'Report on Double Taxation Submitted to the Financial Committee' 51.
46 Bruins and others, 'Report on Double Taxation Submitted to the Financial Committee' 48.
47 Bruins and others, 'Report on Double Taxation Submitted to the Financial Committee' 49.
48 Ivan Ozai, 'Internation Equity Revisited' (2020) 12 *Columbia Journal of Tax Law* 75.
49 Economic literature on the relationship between DTAs and foreign direct investment (FDI) is flagrantly divided and sometimes conflicting.
50 Mason, 'The Transformation of International Tax' 393.
51 Peer Zumbansen, 'Transnational Law as Socio-Legal Theory and Critique: Prospects for "Law and Society" in a Divided World' (2019) 67 *Buffalo Law Review* 950–951 (paraphrasing Nelson-Maldonado Torres for whom coloniality of being refers to long-standing patterns of power that surfaced from colonialism).
52 Ring, 'International Tax Relations: Theory and Implications' 145–148.
53 Vet, Cassimon and Vijver, 'Getting the Short End of the Stick: Power Relations and Their Distributive Outcomes for Lower-Income Countries in Transfer Pricing Governance'.
54 Vet, Cassimon and Vijver, 'Getting the Short End of the Stick: Power Relations and Their Distributive Outcomes for Lower-Income Countries in Transfer Pricing Governance'.
55 Martin Hearson, 'When Do Developing Countries Negotiate Away Their Corporate Tax Base?' (2018) 30 *Journal of International Development* 233–251.
56 Traditional tax scholarship, however, has been made up of a specific intellectual structure. See: Alex Raskolnikov, 'Accepting the Limits of Tax Law and Economics' (2013) 98 *Cornell Law Review* 523.
57 Diane M. Ring, 'The Promise of International Tax Scholarship and its Implications for Research Design, Theory and Methodology' (2010) 55 *Saint Louis University Law Journal* 307 13–14.
58 Peter Hongler, *Justice in International Tax Law: A Normative Review of the International Tax Regime* (IBFD 2019).

59 David Elkins, 'A Critical Reassessment of the Role of Neutrality in International Taxation' (2019) 40 *Northwestern Journal of International Law & Business* 36.
60 Tsilly Dagan, 'International Tax and Global Justice' (2017) 18 *Theoretical Inquiries in Law* 5.
61 Nancy J. Knauer, 'Critical Tax Policy: a Pathway to Reform?' (2014) 9 *Northwestern Journal of Law & Social Policy* 222.
62 Allison Christians, 'Taxing According to Value Creation' (2018) 90 *Tax Notes International* 1379 3.
63 Robert C. Hockett, 'Human Persons, Human Rights, and the Distributive Structure of Global Justice' (2009) 40 *Columbia Human Rights Law Review* 343–404.
64 Eric Posner, 'The Boundaries of Normative Law and Economics' (2021) 38 *Yale Journal on Regulation* 657–662.
65 Margot E. Salomon and Colin Arnott, 'Better Development Decision-making: Applying International Human Rights Law to Neoclassical Economics' (2014) 32 *Nordic Journal of Human Rights* 65–66.
66 Zachary Liscow, 'Is Efficiency Biased?' (2018) 85 *The University of Chicago Law Review* 1649–1663.
67 Zachary Liscow, 'Is Efficiency Biased?' (2018) 85 *The University of Chicago Law Review* 1661.
68 Zachary Liscow, 'Is Efficiency Biased?' (2018) 85 *The University of Chicago Law Review* 1661.
69 Nancy Fraser, 'Who Counts? Dilemmas of Justice in a Postwestphalian World' (2009) 41 *Antipode* 281.
70 For example, one commonly proposed solution to corporate tax avoidance is that of *formulary apportionment*. While the formula for apportionment may be 'purely mathematical', the decision about *what relative weight to assign* to each factor is not.
71 Posner, 'The Boundaries of Normative Law and Economics' 676.
72 Roberto Mangabeira Unger, *The Critical Legal Studies Movement: Another Time, A Greater Task* (3rd edn, Verso 2015); Duncan Kennedy, 'Form and Substance in Private Law Adjudication' (1976) 89 *Harvard Law Review* 1686.
73 Makau Mutua and Antony Anghie, 'What is TWAIL?'(Proceedings of the Annual Meeting (American Society of International Law), 5–8 April 2000).
74 Unger, *The Critical Legal Studies Movement: Another Time, A Greater Task.*
75 Anthony Anghie, *Imperialism, Sovereignty and the Making of International Law* (Cambridge University Press 2005) 243–244.
76 James Thuo Gathii, 'Third World Approaches to International Economic Governance' in Richard Falk, Balakrishnan Rajagopal and Jacqueline Stevens (eds), *International Law and the Third World: Reshaping Justice* (Routledge-Cavendish 2008) 261–265.
77 James Thuo Gathii, 'The Promise of International Law: A Third World View' (2021) 36 *American University International Law Review* 379.
78 Anghie, *Imperialism, Sovereignty and the Making of International Law.*
79 B.S. Chimni, 'Critical theory and international economic law: a third world approach to international law (TWAIL) perspective' in John Linarelli (ed), *Research Handbook on Global Justice and International Economic Law* (Edward Elgar 2013).
80 The idea that taxing entitlements should be distributed fairly between countries is encapsulated by the concept of *inter-nation equity*. See: Richard A. Musgrave and Peggy B. Musgrave, 'Inter-nation Equity' in Richard M. Bird and John G. Head (eds), *Modern Fiscal Issues: Essays in Honor of Carl S Shoup* (University of Toronto Press, Toronto 1972).
81 Something vehemently disputed by TWAIL scholars.
82 Magdalena Sepúlveda Carmona, 'Report of the Special Rapporteur on extreme poverty and human rights' (2014) A/HRC/26/28, 11.

83 Nancy Fraser's *all-subjected principle* states that 'all those who are jointly subject to a given governance structure have a moral standing as subjects of justice in relation to it.', in: Fraser, 'Who Counts? Dilemmas of Justice in a Postwestphalian World' 292–293.

84 Olivier De Schutter, 'Taxing for the Realization of Economic Social and Cultural Rights' in Nikki R. Reisch Philip G. Alston (ed), *Tax, Inequality, and Human Rights* (Oxford University Press 2019) 71.

85 In OECD countries the so-called tax-to-GDP ratio – an important measure of a country's fiscal fitness – was, on average, 34% in 2022. By contrast, in 33 African countries surveyed in a 2023 joint report, the average ratio was 15.6% in 2021. See: OECD, 'Revenue Statistics 2023: Tax Revenue Buoyancy in OECD Countries 1965–2022' (2023); African Tax Administration Forum (ATAF), African Union Commission (AUC) and Organisation for Economic Co-operation and Development (OECD), 'Revenue Statistics in Africa 2023' (2023).

86 See, for example, Juan Pablo Bohoslavsky,

Guiding principles on human rights impact assessments of economic reforms: Report of the Independent Expert on the effects of foreign debt and other related international financial obligations of States on the full enjoyment of human rights, particularly economic, social and cultural rights (2018) A/HRC/40/57.

87 See, for example, UN Committee on the Rights of the Child, 'Concluding observations on the combined fifth and sixth periodic reports of the Kingdom of the Netherlands' (2022) CRC/C/NLD/CO/5-6; UN Committee on the Elimination of Discrimination against Women, 'Concluding observations on the combined fourth and fifth periodic reports of Switzerland' (2016) CEDAW/C/CHE/CO/4-5.

88 Nikki Reisch, 'Taxation and Human Rights: Mapping the Landscape' in Philip G. Alston and Nikki R. Reisch (eds), *Tax, Inequality, and Human Rights* (Oxford University Press 2019).

89 Olivier De Schutter, Nicholas J. Lusiani and Sergio Chaparro, 'Re-righting the International Tax Rules: Operationalising Human Rights in the Struggle to Tax Multinational Companies' (2020) 24 *The International Journal of Human Rights* 1370, 1377.

90 Anja Rudiger, 'A Framework for Fiscal Justice: How Human Rights Can Change Public Finance' in Gillian MacNaughton, Diane Frey and Catherine Porter (eds), *Human Rights and Economic Inequalities* (Cambridge University Press 2021) 149.

91 UN Committee on Economic Social and Cultural Rights, 'General Comment No. 3: The nature of States parties' obligations' (1990) E/1991/23, para. 13.

92 UN Committee on Economic Social and Cultural Rights, 'General cComment No. 20: Non-discrimination in economic, social and cultural rights' (2009) E/C.12/GC/20, para. 13.

93 Including by adopting a plan of action or national strategy delineating the steps the state intends to take to progressively realise socio-economic rights and *identifying* the resources available to do so.

94 UN Committee on Economic Social and Cultural Rights, 'General Comment No. 14: The Right to the Highest Attainable Standard of Health' (2000) E/C.12/2000/4, para. 52.

95 Wouter Vandenhole and Wolfgang Benedek, 'Extraterritorial Human Rights Obligations and the North-South Divide' in Malcolm Langford and others (eds), *Global Justice, State Duties: The Extraterritorial Scope of Economic, Social and Cultural Rights in International Law* (Cambridge University Press 2012) 333.

96 Vandenhole and Benedek, 'Extraterritorial Human Rights Obligations and the North-South Divide'.

97 Mark Gibney and others (eds), *The Routledge Handbook on Extraterritorial Human Rights Obligations* (Routledge 2021).
98 Magdalena Sepúlveda, 'Obligations of International Assistance and Cooperation in an Optional Protocol to the International Covenant on Economic, Social and Cultural Rights' (2006) 24 *Netherlands Quarterly of Human Rights* 271–280.
99 UN Committee on Economic Social and Cultural Rights, 'General Comment No. 24: State obligations under the International Covenant on Economic, Social and Cultural Rights in the context of business activities' (2017) E/C.12/GC/24, para. 29.
100 Sepúlveda, 'Obligations of International Assistance and Cooperation in an Optional Protocol to the International Covenant on Economic, Social and Cultural Rights' 284.
101 Except for the USA.
102 UN Committee on Economic Social and Cultural Rights, 'General Comment No. 15: The Right to Water' (2002) E/C.12/2002/11, 1086.
103 UN Committee on Economic Social and Cultural Rights, 'General Comment No. 15: The Right to Water' (2002) E/C.12/2002/11, 1086 para. 31.
104 UN Committee on Economic Social and Cultural Rights, 'General Comment No. 21: Right of Everyone to Take Part in Cultural Life' (2009) E/C.12/GC/21, para. 58.
105 UN Committee on Economic Social and Cultural Rights, 'General Comment No. 19: The Right to Social Security' (2008) E/C.12/GC/19, para. 53.
106 Johanna Stark, 'Tax Justice Beyond National Borders: International or Interpersonal?' (2022) 42 *Oxford Journal of Legal Studies* 133 23.
107 Julia Braun and Martin Zagler, 'The True Art of the Tax Deal: Evidence on Aid Flows and Bilateral Double Tax Agreements' (2018) 41 *The World Economy*.
108 Tahmina Karimova, *Human Rights and Development in International Law* (Routledge 2016).
109 Anghie, *Imperialism, Sovereignty and the Making of International Law*.
110 Philip Alston, 'Ships Passing in the Night: The Current State of the Human Rights and Development Debate Seen through the Lens of the Millennium Development Goals' (2005) 27 *Human Rights Quarterly* 755–780.
111 Stephen P. Marks, 'Poverty and Human Rights' in Daniel Moeckli and others (eds), *Textbook on International Human Rights Law* (3rd edn, Oxford University Press 2017).
112 Laurens van Apeldoorn, 'BEPS, Tax Sovereignty and Global Justice' (2018) 21 *Critical Review of International Social and Political Philosophy* 478–491.
113 Okanga Okanga and Lyla Latif, 'Effective Taxation in Africa: Confronting Systemic Vulnerability through Inclusive Global Tax Governance' (2021) 2 *African Journal* 100–101.
114 International Institute for Sustainable Development, 'DIHR Presents Tools Outlining SDGs and Human Rights Links' (2019) https://sdg.iisd.org/news/dihr-presents-tools-outlining-sdgs-and-human-rights-links/ accessed 5 April 2024.
115 Most notably, target 17.1.
116 OECD, 'Better Policies for 2030: An OECD Action Plan on the Sustainable Development Goals' (2016).

Bibliography

Alston P, 'Ships Passing in the Night: The Current State of the Human Rights and Development Debate Seen through the Lens of the Millennium Development Goals' (2005) 27 *Human Rights Quarterly*. 755–829.

Anghie A, *Imperialism, Sovereignty and the Making of International Law* (Cambridge University Press 2005).

Apeldoorn L v, 'International Taxation and the Erosion of Sovereignty' in Dietsch P and Rixen T (eds), *Global Tax Governance: What Is Wrong with It and How to Fix It* (ECPR Press 2016).
Apeldoorn L v, 'BEPS, Tax Sovereignty and Global Justice' (2018) 21 *Critical Review of International Social and Political Philosophy*. 478–499.
Ash E and Marian O, 'The Making of International Tax Law: Empirical Evidence from Natural Language Processing' Legal Studies Research Paper Series (ATAF) A T A F, (AUC) A U C and (OECD) O f E C-o a D, *Revenue Statistics in Africa 2023*, 2023. https://www.oecd.org/en/publications/2023/10/revenue-statistics-in-africa-2023_3d0cafc8.html
Avi-Yonah R S, 'Structure of International Taxation: A Proposal for Simplification' (1996) 74 *Texas Law Review*. 1301–1360.
Avi-Yonah R S, 'International Tax as International Law' (2004) 57 *Tax Law Review*. 483–501.
Avi-Yonah R S, 'Globalization, Tax Competition, and the Fiscal Crisis of the Welfare State' (2020) 113 *Harvard Law Review*. 1573–1676.
Bohoslavsky J P, *Guiding Principles on Human Rights Impact Assessments of Economic Reforms: Report of the Independent Expert on the Effects of Foreign Debt and Other Related International Financial Obligations of States on the Full Enjoyment of Human Rights, Particularly Economic, Social and Cultural Rights* (2018). https://www.ohchr.org/en/documents/thematic-reports/ahrc4057-guiding-principles-human-rights-impact-assessments-economic.
Braun J and Zagler M, 'The True Art of the Tax Deal: Evidence on Aid Flows and Bilateral Double Tax Agreements' (2018) 41 *The World Economy*. 1478–1507.
Brooks K and Krever R, 'The Troubling Role of Tax Treaties' in Michielse G M M and Thuronyi V (eds), *Tax Design Issues Worldwide*, vol 51 (Series on International Taxation, Kluwer Law International 2015).
Bruins G W J and et al., *Report on Double Taxation Submitted to the Financial Committee* (1923) League of Nations.
Carmona M S, *Report of the Special Rapporteur on Extreme Poverty and Human Rights* (2014). https://digitallibrary.un.org/record/773516?v=pdf
Child U C o t R o t, *Concluding Observations on the Combined Fifth and Sixth Periodic Reports of the Kingdom of the Netherlands* (2022). https://digitallibrary.un.org/record/3963980?ln=en&v=pdf
Chimni B S, 'Critical Theory and International Economic Law: A Third World Approach to International Law (TWAIL) Perspective' in Linarelli J (ed), *Research Handbook on Global Justice and International Economic Law* (Edward Elgar 2013). 2–12.
Christensen R C, 'Between Revolution and Rhetoric: The UN Vote and the Future of International Tax Cooperation' (2024) 1 *British Tax Review*. 2–12.
Christensen R C and Hearson M, 'The New Politics of Global Tax Governance: Taking Stock a Decade after the Financial Crisis' (2019) 26 (5) *Review of International Political Economy*. 1068–1088.
Christians A, 'Taxing According to Value Creation' (2018) 90 *Tax Notes International*. 1379–1383.
Christians A and Apeldoorn L V, *Tax Cooperation in an Unjust World* (Oxford University Press 2021).
Cockfield A J, 'Shaping International Tax Law and Policy in Challenging Times' (2018) 54 *Stanford Journal of International Law*. 223–240.
Dagan T, 'The Tax Treaties Myth' (2000) 32 *New York University Journal of International Law and Politics*. 939–996.
Dagan T, 'International Tax and Global Justice' (2017) 18 *Theoretical Inquiries in Law*. 1–35.

Development I I f S, 'DIHR Presents Tools Outlining SDGs and Human Rights Links' (2019)https://sdg.iisd.org/news/dihr-presents-tools-outlining-sdgs-and-human-rights-links/ accessed 5 April 2024.

Dietsch P and Rixen T, 'Global Tax Governance: What It is and Why It Matters' in Dietsch P and Rixen T (eds), *Global Tax Governance – What's Wrong, and How to Fix It* (ECPR Press 2016).

Elkins D, 'A Critical Reassessment of the Role of Neutrality in International Taxation' (2019) 40 *Northwestern Journal of International Law & Business*. 1–46.

Fraser N, 'Who Counts? Dilemmas of Justice in a Postwestphalian World' (2009) 41 *Antipode*. 265–278.

Gathii J T, 'Third World Approaches to International Economic Governance' in Falk R, Rajagopal B and Stevens J (eds), *International Law and the Third World: Reshaping Justice* (Routledge-Cavendish 2008).

Gathii J T, 'The Promise of International Law: A Third World View' (2021) 36 *American University International Law Review*. 377–478.

Gibney M and et al. (eds), *The Routledge Handbook on Extraterritorial Human Rights Obligations* (Routledge 2021).

Hearson M, 'When Do Developing Countries Negotiate Away Their Corporate Tax Base?' (2018) 30 *Journal of International Development*. 233–255.

Hockett R C, 'Human Persons, Human Rights, and the Distributive Structure of Global Justice' (2009) 40 *Columbia Human Rights Law Review*. 343–424.

Hongler P, *Justice in International Tax Law: A Normative Review of the International Tax Regime* (IBFD 2019).

Irish C R, 'International Double Taxation Agreements and Income Taxation at Source' (1974) 23 *International and Comparative Law Quarterly*. 292–316.

Jogarajan S, *Double Taxation and the League of Nations* (Cambridge Tax Law Series, Cambridge University Press 2018).

Jogarajan S, 'The 100th Anniversary of International Institutions and International Taxation' (2020) 48 *INTERTAX*. 929–933.

Kangave J, 'The Dominant Voices in Double Taxation Agreements: A Critical Analysis of the "Dividend" Article in the Agreement between Uganda and the Netherlands' (2009) 11 *International Community Law Review*. 387–407.

Karimova T, *Human Rights and Development in International Law* (Routledge 2016).

Kennedy D, 'Form and Substance in Private Law Adjudication' (1976) 89 *Harvard Law Review*. 1685–1778.

Knauer N J, 'Critical Tax Policy: A Pathway to Reform?' (2014) 9 *Northwestern Journal of Law & Social Policy*. 206–263.

Liscow Z, 'Is Efficiency Biased?' (2018) 85 *The University of Chicago Law Review*. 1649–1718.

Magalhães T D, 'What Is Really Wrong with Global Tax Governance and How to Properly Fix It' (2018) 10 *World Tax Journal*. 499–536.

Marks S P, 'Poverty and Human Rights' in Moeckli D and others (eds), *Textbook on International Human Rights Law* (3rd edn, Oxford University Press 2017).

Mason R, 'The Transformation of International Tax' (2020) 114 *American Journal of International Law*. 353–402.

Musgrave R A and Musgrave P B, 'Inter-nation Equity' in Bird R M and Head J G (eds), *Modern Fiscal Issues: Essays in Honor of Carl S Shoup* (University of Toronto Press 1972).

Mutua M and Anghie A, 'What is TWAIL?'(*Proceedings of the Annual Meeting* (American Society of International Law), 5–8 April 2000).

Navarro A, 'The Allocation of Taxing Rights under Pillar One of the OECD Proposal' in Haase F and Kofler G (eds), *The Oxford Handbook of International Tax Law* (Oxford University Press 2023).

OECD, *Action Plan on Base Erosion and Profit Shifting* (2013). OECD. https://www.oecd.org/en/publications/2013/07/action-plan-on-base-erosion-and-profit-shifting_g1g30e67.html

OECD, *Better Policies for 2030: An OECD Action Plan on the Sustainable Development Goals* (2016).

OECD, *Model Tax Convention on Income and on Capital: Condensed Version* (2017).

OECD, *Corporate Tax Statistics* (2023a).

OECD, *Revenue Statistics 2023: Tax Revenue Buoyancy in OECD Countries 1965–2022* (2023b).

Oguttu A W and Iyer M, 'Tax Abuse and Implications for Human Rights in Africa' in Alston P G and Reisch N R (eds), *Tax, Inequality, and Human Rights* (Oxford University Press 2019).

Okanga O and Latif L, 'Effective Taxation in Africa: Confronting Systemic Vulnerability through Inclusive Global Tax Governance' (2021) 2 *African Journal of International Economic Law*. 100–121.

Ozai I, 'Inter-nation Equity Revisited' (2020a) 12 *Columbia Journal of Tax Law*. 58–88.

Ozai I, 'Two Accounts of International Tax Justice' (2020b) 33 *Canadian Journal of Law & Jurisprudence*. 317–339.

Posner E, 'The Boundaries of Normative Law and Economics' (2021) 38 *Yale Journal on Regulation*. 657–677.

Raskolnikov A, 'Accepting the Limits of Tax Law and Economics' (2013) 98 *Cornell Law Review*. 523–590.

Reisch N, 'Taxation and Human Rights: Mapping the Landscape' in Alston P G and Reisch N R (eds), *Tax, Inequality, and Human Rights* (Oxford University Press 2019).

Rights U C o E S a C, *General Comment No. 3: The Nature of States Parties' Obligations* (1990).

Rights U C o E S a C, *General Comment No. 14: The Right to the Highest Attainable Standard of Health* (2000). https://www.refworld.org/legal/general/cescr/2000/en/36991

Rights U C o E S a C, *General Comment No. 15: The Right to Water* (2002). https://www.refworld.org/legal/general/cescr/2003/en/39347

Rights U C o E S a C, *General Comment No. 19: The Right to Social Security* (2008). https://www.refworld.org/legal/general/cescr/2008/en/41968

Rights U C o E S a C, *General Comment No. 20: Non-discrimination in Economic, Social and Cultural Rights* (2009a). https://www.refworld.org/legal/general/cescr/2009/en/68520

Rights U C o E S a C, *General Comment No. 21: Right of Everyone to Take Part in Cultural Life* (2009b). https://www.refworld.org/legal/general/cescr/2009/en/83710

Rights U C o E S a C, *General Comment No. 24: State Obligations Under the International Covenant on Economic, Social and Cultural Rights in the Context of Business Activities* (2017). https://www.ohchr.org/en/documents/general-comments-and-recommendations/general-comment-no-24-2017-state-obligations-context

Ring D M, 'International Tax Relations: Theory and Implications' (2007) 60 *Tax Law Review*. 83–154.

Ring D M, 'The Promise of International Tax Scholarship and Its Implications for Research Design, Theory and Methodology' (2010) 55 *Saint Louis University Law Journal*. 307–330

Rixen T, *The Political Economy of International Tax Governance* (Transformations of the State, Palgrave Macmillan 2008).

Rudiger A, 'A Framework for Fiscal Justice: How Human Rights Can Change Public Finance' in MacNaughton G, Frey D and Porter C (eds), *Human Rights and Economic Inequalities* (Cambridge University Press 2021).

Salomon M E and Arnott C, 'Better Development Decision-making: Applying International Human Rights Law to Neoclassical Economics' (2014) 32 *Nordic Journal of Human Rights*.44–74.

Schutter O D, 'Taxing for the Realization of Economic Social and Cultural Rights' in Philip G. Alston (ed), *Tax, Inequality, and Human Rights* (Oxford University Press 2019).

Schutter O D, Lusiani N J and Chaparro S, 'Re-righting the International Tax Rules: Operationalising Human Rights in the Struggle to Tax Multinational Companies' (2020) 24 *The International Journal of Human Rights*. 1370–1399.

Sepúlveda M, 'Obligations of International Assistance and Cooperation in an Optional Protocol to the International Covenant on Economic, Social and Cultural Rights' (2006) 24 *Netherlands Quarterly of Human Rights*. 271–303.

Stark J, 'Tax Justice Beyond National Borders: International or Interpersonal?' (2022) 42 *Oxford Journal of Legal Studies*. 133–160.

Tandon S, 'Assessing the Impact of Pillar Two on Developing Countries' (2022) 50 *INTERTAX*. 923–935.

Teo N J, *The United Nations in Global Tax Coordination Hidden History and Politics* (Cambridge Tax Law Series, Cambridge University Press 2023).

Unger R M, *The Critical Legal Studies Movement: Another Time, A Greater Task* (3rd edn, Verso 2015).

Valderrama I M, Lesage D and Lips W, *Tax and Development: The Link between International Taxation, The Base Erosion Profit Shifting Project and The 2030 Sustainable Development Agenda* (UNI-CRIS Working Paper Series, 2018). United Nations University Institute of Comparative Regional Integration Studies - UNU-CRIS.

Vandenhole W and Benedek W, 'Extraterritorial Human Rights Obligations and the North-South Divide' in Langford M and others (eds), *Global Justice, State Duties: The Extraterritorial Scope of Economic, Social and Cultural Rights in International Law* (Cambridge University Press 2012).

Vet C, Cassimon D and Vijver A V d, 'Getting the Short End of the Stick: Power Relations and Their Distributive Outcomes for Lower-Income Countries in Transfer Pricing Governance' in Valderrama I J M, Lesage D and Lips W (eds), *Taxation, International Cooperation and the 2030 Sustainable Development Agenda* (United Nations University Series on Regionalism, Springer 2021).

Waris A, 'Kenya's Fiscal Accountability Revisited: A Review of the Historical Erosion of the Country's Fiscal Constitution from 1962 to 2010' in Mbondenyi M K and others (eds), *Human Rights and Democratic Governance in Kenya: A Post-2007 Appraisal* (Pretoria University Law Press 2015).

Women U C o t E o D a, *Concluding Observations on the Combined Fourth and Fifth Periodic Reports of Switzerland* (2016). https://www.refworld.org/policy/polrec/cedaw/2016/en/113996

Zumbansen P, 'Transnational Law as Socio-Legal Theory and Critique: Prospects for "Law and Society" in a Divided World' (2019) 67 *Buffalo Law Review*. 909–960.

3 Human rights as a normative tool to promote fiscal justice in Africa

*Olivia Minatta, Ohene Yaw Ampofo-Anti, and María Emilia Mamberti**

3.1 Introduction

At present, many have argued that the world faces multiple intersecting crises: the rising cost-of-living crisis, a sovereign debt crisis for countries in the Global South, rapidly increasing poverty and inequality both within and between countries and the existential threat of climate change.[1] Fiscal policy is arguably at the centre of these crises because, at their essence, these issues are about how societies choose to raise, allocate and distribute resources. In addition, fiscal policies – which we define as the measures which States rely upon to collect and allocate public resources – lie at the heart of the state's economic choices and play a crucial role in confronting these crises. The policies needed to address these intersecting crises, such as the provision of quality public services and universal social protection; mitigation, adaptation and a just transition in response to climate change; and reparations for historic injustices rooted in slavery, colonialism and apartheid all require capable and adequately resourced states that can deliver for people and planet.

Africa has not remained unaffected by these crises. Despite high rates of economic growth in many African countries over the last two decades, progress in reducing poverty and improving the quality of life of citizens has been very limited compared to other regions in the Global South.[2] Poverty rates remain exceedingly high, and due to rapid population growth, the total number of people living in poverty has increased despite economic growth. For instance, in the Sub-Saharan region, extreme poverty exceeds 64%, accounting for two-thirds of the population living in extreme poverty in the globe.[3]

The Southern African Customs Union, consisting of the Sub-Saharan countries of Botswana, Eswatini, Lesotho, Namibia and South Africa, is the world's most unequal region.[4] The top 10% of the population in South Africa, Namibia and Botswana possess 80.6%, 65.5% and 61.2% of financial assets, respectively, while many households in the bottom 10% have almost no assets.[5]

* Olivia Minatta, Ohene Yaw Ampofo-Anti and María Emilia Mamberti, *Center for Economic and Social Rights*.

DOI: 10.4324/9781003432890-4

According to the World Bank, unequal access to education and legacies of apartheid and colonialism including wage inequality and severe inequality in wealth and physical assets are key drivers of income inequality in the region.[6] For example, the historical concentration of agricultural land ownership during the colonial and apartheid eras continues to be a persistent factor contributing to wealth inequality, especially in Namibia and South Africa. These underlying structural factors contribute to the widening wage and skills disparities, as well as restrict employment prospects for specific groups, such as women, black people and rural populations.

The picture painted above poses the question of how governments can generate sufficient revenue and allocate them appropriately to address these challenges whilst being conscious of who will bear the costs resulting from the tricky economic decisions and trade-offs made by states. In this chapter, we will set out how and why we argue that human rights can provide a normative framework which can act as a lodestar for addressing these dilemmas. As we explicate later on, human rights obligations require states to implement equitable fiscal policies which will achieve a more just distribution of income, wealth and resources; eliminate poverty and inequality and enable sufficient fiscal space to resource crucial public services such as education, healthcare, social security as well as provide essential public infrastructure, especially in disadvantaged communities, which will enable people to live a dignified life.

Implementing tax policies which expand the fiscal space of states is necessary to ensure human rights. Additionally, Africa is dealing with the urgent and intractable challenges associated with climate change. Recent examples include Cyclone Idai, Kenneth or Freddy.[7] What these climate disasters demonstrate is that fiscal policies directed at adapting and mitigating the negative effects of climate change are essential, particularly for vulnerable groups such as frontline communities, communities impacted by extractivism, poor people, women and others facing systemic and structural discrimination.

At the Center for Economic and Social Rights (CESR), we seek to demonstrate how the normative principles which undergird human rights might act as a catalyst for a just and equitable economic order (at the local, regional and global levels) which is fit for purpose in tackling the poly-crisis which disproportionately impacts regions such as Sub-Saharan Africa. We seek to demonstrate how human rights principles such as dignity, equality, solidarity, participatory democracy, intersectionality and justice should guide a rights-based economy. We define a rights-based economy as one where every person has the resources to live a dignified life within planetary boundaries.[8] Our most detailed description of what this might entail in relation to fiscal policy is outlined in the Principles on Human Rights in Fiscal Policy, further discussed in this chapter. Whilst the Principles were formulated in the context of Latin America, in this chapter, we will demonstrate how they might serve as a useful framework for articulating rights-aligned fiscal policies in Africa.

This chapter will proceed as follows. First, we will explain why human rights can be utilized as a transformative normative tool to tackle the poly-crisis by emphasizing and outlining the connection between fiscal policies and adequate public services such as healthcare, education and social security. Second, we will highlight how Illicit Financial Flows (IFFs) and international tax abuse in Africa could be addressed effectively if states had regard to the norms and standards advanced by the Principles on Human Rights in Fiscal Policy. Third, in order to place the Principles (which were developed in Latin America) into an African context, we will explore how the human rights principle of substantive racial equality can provide guidance on how a just and equitable fiscal policy framework can be realized in the African context. In doing so, we will explicate how the principle of substantive racial equality can address Africa's distinct challenges namely the historic legacies of slavery, colonialism and apartheid which largely remain unaccounted for today. Furthermore, how substantive racial equality provides an analytical framework to critically examine and interrogate the neocolonial aspects of the global financial architecture which can be regarded as inconsistent with human rights. In conclusion, we will demonstrate how human rights and the rights-based economy can act as a powerful and transformative normative framework for radically rethinking fiscal policy in Africa.

3.2 Why are human rights relevant to fiscal policy?

Traditionally, fiscal policies, have been seen as complex issues handled only by experts in the field of economics. For this reason, the traditional functions assigned to fiscal policy have typically entailed fixing market failures, such as "externalities", rather than pursuing other public goals, such as ensuring the realization of human rights or addressing the unequal distribution of wealth and income in society. Consequently, fiscal policies have often been isolated from broader public debates and perceived as disconnected from the realm of human rights in general, and of international human rights law in particular.[9]

However, fiscal policies and human rights are connected inseparably, in at least two ways. First, fiscal policies are essential for realizing rights. First, every right requires the investment of resources from States to be fully realized. Fiscal policy can also perform other functions (now often referred to as the five "Rs" of fiscal policy) which are closely connected to human rights. Indeed, fiscal policies are not only necessary for "resourcing" rights but also for "redistributing" wealth and income to enable the achievement of equality; for "repricing" goods and services to ensure human rights (for example, by disincentivizing through taxes some behaviours that can harm the right to health); for strengthening democratic "representation"; and to provide "reparations" for historic wrongs such as slavery, colonialism and apartheid.

All these functions have very concrete implications for human rights. For example, to reduce inequality, States may need to ensure that the richest pay their fair share, contributing proportionally more than those in more vulnerable situations. This is of the uttermost relevance for Africa, as 10 of the 19 most unequal countries in the world are from Southern Africa and Central

Africa.[10] Some estimates indicate that in Africa there were 24 billionaires with a combined wealth of $80 billion in 2016 and by 2017, there were 165,000 high-net-worth individuals with combined holdings of $860 billion.[11]

In terms of "re-pricing" or regulating, often taxes and subsidies are employed to incentivize behaviours that are essential for safeguarding human rights, while discouraging actions that are harmful to them, such as imposing higher taxes on sugary drinks which are harmful to the right to health. These fiscal instruments – which include so-called "green taxes" – can be of enormous importance in a world that demands an urgent energy transition and calls on governments for immediate action to tackle climate change and related ecological crises.

Similarly, the application of human rights principles to fiscal policies plays a central role in bolstering democratic institutions. Contrary to what has often been insinuated, fiscal policy decisions are not simply technical formulas dictated by experts. They often require rigorous trade-off analyses and political deliberations, where some may experience losses while others gain advantages. In Latin America and other parts of the world, there are several examples of fiscal policy decisions made without ensuring any transparency or participation of civil society, which ended up delegitimizing governments and prompting widespread protests. Against this backdrop, because of their commitment to transparency, participation and accountability, human rights can serve as an empowering tool for those historically excluded from public decision-making, enabling them to demand equitable outcomes and decisions made through more participatory processes.[12]

The second connection between fiscal policy and human rights lies in the mandatory nature of international human rights' law, which presents some agents as duty-bearers and others as rights' holders. Indeed, because of the normative nature of international human rights law, fiscal policy (as any other field of public intervention) must align with the human rights' obligations undertaken by any given State. This means that fiscal decision-making processes must be guided by human rights principles and obligations and aim to realize human rights. Notably, almost all countries in Africa are parties to the core treaties that set forth human rights' obligations, as will be discussed below.[13]

Overall, under international human rights law, states have an obligation to respect, protect and fulfil human rights (whether civil, political or socio-economic) and resource mobilization and allocation are a key part of those obligations. In other words, the wide range of policies that governments use to generate revenues – for example, issuing public debt or raising taxes – and to allocate their resources – such as investing in social protection – must be guided by normative standards derived from international human rights' law. For example, if governments reduce social spending without first exploring alternatives that are less restrictive of rights – such as scrutinizing tax exemptions – they may be in violation of their human rights obligations.

As a result of these multiple connections, over the last decades, there have been very significant advancements in assessing and explaining in further detail how human rights obligations can impact fiscal policy. Some of the core human rights treaties of the United Nations (UN) system have provided the key basis for such endeavours, speaking to the importance of the normative nature of human rights.

As a starting point, the two core human rights treaties of the UN system, the International Covenant on Economic, Social and Cultural Rights (ICESCR) and the International Covenant on Civil and Political Rights (ICCPR), set forth a series of obligations that States must follow to realize rights and comply with their international commitments which have fiscal policy implications.

For example, Article 2.2 of the ICCPR requires States to adopt all necessary measures to make rights effective, which includes financial measures. Importantly, Article 2.2 of the ICESCR and Art. 2.1 of the ICCPR set forth the principle of equality and non-discrimination. The obligation of non-discrimination has persistently been codified throughout human rights law as a duty for States to guarantee substantive equality and prioritize the protection of historically marginalized groups – such as women, children, persons with disabilities, indigenous peoples and racially marginalized groups amongst others. The principles of substantive equality and non-discrimination have various implications for the ways in which resources are raised and allocated (for example, they may require the allocation of additional resources for some groups in order to ensure the achievement of substantive equality). Notably, even in times of severe resource constraints, State parties must adopt protective measures for people in a position of disadvantage and seek resources through international cooperation.

On top of these overarching standards, the keystone provision from which many human rights' obligations related to fiscal policy have been derived is Article 2.1 of the ICESCR, which states that

> Each State Party to the present Covenant undertakes to take steps, individually and through international assistance and cooperation, especially economic and technical, to the maximum of its available resources, with a view to achieving progressively the full realization of the rights recognized in the present Covenant by all appropriate means…

The Committee on Economic, Social and Cultural Rights – the official entity tasked with interpreting and monitoring the application of the ICESCR by States – as well as other UN human rights mechanisms, have interpreted Article 2.1 of the ICESCR and similar provisions contained in other human rights instruments as requiring States to: (i) guarantee a core content of rights; (ii) advance rights progressively and with no retrogression; (iii) mobilize the maximum available resources in order to discharge their rights' commitments.

The obligation to ensure the core content of rights means that there are non-derogable minimum quantitative and qualitative thresholds that states must guarantee to all people, regardless of circumstances such as the country's level of development or the existence of economic crises, and as a matter of top priority. A state party can only justify its failure to meet these core contents due to a lack of resources after showing that every effort has been made to use all the resources that are at its disposal to satisfy, as a matter of priority, those minimum obligations.

The obligation of progressivity means that states must adopt concrete, deliberate and targeted measures towards the full realization of all the rights contained in the Covenant, which includes "financial measures" to that end, such as allocating sufficient resources. Similarly, non-retrogression prescribes that states must avoid making decisions that represent a step backwards in the enjoyment of rights, such as cutting down budgets.

The duty to mobilize resources has been interpreted to mean that states need to utilize fiscal policy to its fullest potential. Therefore, states must make efficient use of existing resources, as well as expand their fiscal space through a range of tools, such as increasing progressive taxation, combating IFFs or requesting international assistance. At the same time, states must ensure that the mobilization of resources advances the goal of substantive equality. This means that states should not only invest resources to compensate groups who face more barriers in accessing rights but also be cognizant when crafting policies so such groups are not impacted disproportionately when expanding their fiscal space. To achieve this, states should increase their resources by prioritizing alternatives such as taxing those with higher incomes or combating tax evasion and avoidance by multinational corporations.

Furthermore, the human rights obligation to mobilize the maximum available resources encompasses both domestic and international duties. Apart from creating fiscal space internally, States must cooperate internationally to allow resource mobilization in other jurisdictions[14] and promote solutions for international economic problems, such as combating IFFs.[15]

States' extraterritorial obligations (those that States have beyond their borders) to protect and to fulfil prescribe that states must take reasonable measures to prevent human rights violations abroad, as well as take the necessary steps to promote and help create an environment that favours the realization of rights outside their territories. In the context of international economic relations, this means that states must ensure that business actors do not undermine the efforts of the States in which they operate to fully realize the Covenant rights, for instance by resorting to tax evasion or tax avoidance strategies. In order to do so, states must, for instance, refrain from promoting legal frameworks that allow high-net-worth individuals and transnational corporations to evade tax liabilities, such as through the establishment of tax havens.

As these abundant conceptual and normative efforts show, the potential benefits of connecting fiscal policy and human rights are numerous, and key to addressing the problems of rights non-compliance that underlie the current crisis that the world is facing. Indeed, in the last decade, a significant number of activists, movements, civil society organizations and academics have increasingly used the normative standards and conceptual connections just described to advance their fights for fiscal justice and the respect for human rights.

In Latin America, the fruitful synergies between the two fields have led to significant civil society mobilization and engagement with different institutional actors to promote more rights-aligned fiscal debates and policy decisions. Examples of such engagement include advocacy before the Inter-American System of Human Rights, strategic litigation, public campaigning and the production of numerous reports with varied evidence that show how unfair fiscal policies across the region harm states' capacities to deliver on their rights' commitments, and advance policy alternatives to address those gaps.

Building on such efforts, in 2021, the Principles for Human Rights in Fiscal Policy (the Principles),[16] probably the most systematic attempt at the moment to condense existing standards that link human rights and fiscal policy. The Principles were elaborated and launched by the Initiative for Human Rights in Fiscal Policy, a project which brings together eight civil society organizations and a diverse group of experts and for which CESR functions as the Technical Secretariat. The Initiative led a three-year-long participatory process to draft the Principles, which are now increasingly recognized and used by a diverse number of actors in Latin America and elsewhere. Indeed, they have been referenced by different international and regional human rights mechanisms, and incorporated in the work of academic, public entities and civil society organizations.

The Principles systematize the numerous existing human rights standards on fiscal policy derived both from international and inter-American law already discussed and also provide concrete "guidelines" to orient policymakers who seek to align fiscal policies with human rights. Because of this, they can be of use when exploring the connections between human rights and fiscal policy in Africa, in line with efforts that have already been made in the region to pursue that goal.

The following section explores such efforts and the potential uses of the Principles in the African context, noting specific opportunities the region brings and using the issue of IFFs – which is at the heart of the connection between fiscal justice and human rights – as an example to illustrate the powerful connection between rights and fiscal policy.

3.3 A persistent fiscal problem with a human rights' dimension in Africa: Illicit financial flows, and how human rights could help address it

IFFs are a clear example of how the relationship between human rights and fiscal policy plays out in practice. IFFs generally refer to money that countries lose due to diverse practices, some being illegal, such as tax evasion and other criminal activities (corruption, money laundering, etc.) and others not strictly illegal but "contrary to the aims and spirit of the law", such as tax avoidance.

According to the Tax Justice Network, nearly $480 billion worth of tax revenue is lost each year due to international tax abuse and IFFs.[17] As a consequence, IFFs represent a very serious barrier to ensuring human rights, especially for countries in the Global South, impacting their capacity to devote their maximum available resources to this end. Indeed, it is estimated that every year, Africa loses USD 50 to USD 60 billion of revenue to IFFs.[18] According to the Economic Commission for Africa of the United Nations (ECA), between 2001 and 2010 African countries lost up to $407 billion from trade mispricing alone, namely, one of the several strategies used by transnational corporations for tax evasion.[19]

As anticipated, such revenue losses undermine the capacity of African countries to fund public services and ensure human rights, while also reinforcing inequalities and weakening democratic institutions. For instance, a study led by Action Aid uncovered that a brewery company listed in London engaged in various tax avoidance practices with its subsidiaries, resulting in the deprivation of up to £20 million in tax revenue for five African countries – Ghana, Mozambique, Tanzania, South Africa and Zambia. This amount could have been utilized to send a quarter of a million children to school, ensuring their right to education enshrined under ICESCR.

Furthermore, because of these tax planning strategies, Action Aid revealed that, in Ghana, a woman informal trader effectively paid more tax than the subsidiary operating in that country. This not only led to a loss of resources needed to fund public services in Ghana but also highlighted the disproportionate impact of the tax system on informal workers, particularly women. This disparate impact is in tension with the principle of substantive equality that human rights require as discussed in the previous section.[20]

There are many factors operating domestically and internationally that enable IFFs, including legal instruments such as secrecy laws or double-taxation agreements that end up functioning as "none taxation agreements". According to international human rights law, States are responsible when, by failure to address this phenomenon (due to action or inaction), their own capacity or other state's capacity to collect revenue is affected, because they have extraterritorial obligations and a duty "to mobilize the maximum of available resources", as discussed in the previous section. Furthermore, states' duty to protect human rights requires African states to take positive steps against non-state actors, such as multinational corporations, when engaging in abusive tax practices. Equally important, extraterritorial obligations demand states to take proper action when their regulations are partly responsible for human rights violations abroad (such as secrecy laws or legal architecture creating tax havens).

Considering the clear implications that IFFs have for human rights, it is useful to delve into the concrete steps which states could take as duty bearers under the rights' framework to address the problem. Notably, the Principles for Human Rights in Fiscal Policy already systematize many of the actions that States either must or should pursue.

For example, the Principles explain that, because of States' obligation to protect human rights – that is, to safeguard against the actions of third parties who can compromise the realization of rights – they must take a number of fiscal measures in connection to companies and other private actors that engage in fiscally abusive practice.[21] More specifically, States must regulate the role of third parties, establish reporting mechanisms, intervene systematically when they commit infringements, and ultimately sanction them. They must also refrain from granting any form of support or incentive to those who fail to comply with their human rights responsibilities or who commit acts of corruption in connection to IFFs.

The guidelines associated with this Principle – which provide action-oriented suggestions based on best practices, rather than normative duties – further distil what the obligation to protect could mean in the context of tackling IFFs. For example, they recommend States to require companies and other tax-payers to exercise due diligence in identifying, preventing and mitigating the risks of human rights violations arising from their tax practices.[22] They similarly require financial institutions to be held accountable for their role in facilitating tax evasion and avoidance, which would require States' specialized agencies to supervise them rigorously, require a license that can be withdrawn in cases of non-compliance, and subject these institutions to effective monitoring systems. Consequently, States should endow supervisory agencies with appropriate powers, including the authorization to carry out inspections, demand information, and impose sanctions with the goal of fighting IFFs.

However, states duties in relation to IFFs are not limited to supervising and sanctioning the conduct of the private parties who engage in financially abusive practices but also include obligations which they must observe themselves. First, the Principles state that because of the obligation to mobilize the maximum available resources to ensure human rights, states must expand their fiscal space by means of resources that are not currently being mobilized, such as those lost to IFFs.[23]

Also, because of their extraterritorial human rights obligations, states must abstain from any conduct that undermines another state's capacity to fulfil their own obligations, including facilitating tax abuse and other practices related to IFFs.[24] According to the Principles, the first step to ensure that this duty becomes a reality is undertaking assessments of the extraterritorial effects of laws, policies and practices that may unduly restrict the fiscal space of other States.[25] In practical terms, this could mean that states should combat abusive tax practices, especially of transnational companies, for example, by providing high levels of transparency and guaranteeing automatic information exchange on the activities of multinational companies.[26]

Importantly, while the sources on which the Principles built to develop the aforementioned standards apply equally to Africa – as they derive mainly from the international human rights' sources discussed in the previous section, to which virtually all African countries are a party – there are additional standards that can help strengthen the human rights approach to the fight against IFFs in the continent.

Indeed, there have already been important efforts started along these lines. For example, already in 2013, the African Commission on Human and Peoples' Rights issued resolution 236, which among other things, made explicit the connection between IFFs and human rights, and called on states to review their domestic legislation to combat IFFs. Similarly, in its resolution 367 of 2017, the Commission urged States to establish regional mechanisms to fight IFFs in the realm of extractive industries. Unsurprisingly, in 2022, African states successfully acted in coordination to call on the UN General Assembly to establish a new framework that can more inclusively combat IFFs and other related practices.[27]

Interestingly, because of resolution 236 of 2013 of the African Commission, Ms. Asha Ramgobin developed a document undertaking an in-depth study on the impact of illicit capital flight on human rights in Africa which provided an interpretation and systematization effort of human rights' standards that in relevant aspects resembles the Principles for Human Rights in Fiscal Policy. As such, the document is helpful in identifying which regional human rights' standards from Africa, in addition to those used in Latin America, can help in the endeavours of seeking rights-aligned fiscal policies in the African context, and confirms the potential of these efforts.

Importantly, unlike other treaties, the African Charter on Human and Peoples' Rights (the African Charter) recognizes collective rights and rights of the peoples, in addition to individual rights, which can be fruitful tools to further explore the fiscal dimensions of human rights. For example, the Charter recognizes the right of all peoples to "freely dispose of their wealth and natural resources".[28] According to Ramgobin, this right implies an obligation to promote international economic cooperation based on mutual respect, to strengthen African unity and solidarity and to eliminate all forms of foreign economic exploitation. She argues that in the context of IFFs, this would entail, for instance, enacting and enforcing norms that regulate non-state actors and enable the state to undertake investigations specifically the extractive industries supply chain, prosecute and take steps to ensure that lost revenues reach back to the state. Importantly, she also argues that additional revenue is spent in the interests of the people, and not for other non-rights' related purposes.

Similarly, she argues that the collective right to self-determination recognized in the African Charter, which can be asserted against internal and external abuse, would be affected if a state facilitates IFFs and therefore compromises the ability of other states to fulfil their human rights obligations. As a rights holder under the interpretation of this collective right, she proceeds, a State could challenge other State that enables IFFs, for example.

Importantly, by focusing on collective and historical dimensions of rights, these additional sources that African states, movements, academia and civil society organizations could build on in promoting a human-rights approach to fiscal policy make evident a key point: the need to embrace rights from an anti-colonial point of view. The following section delves into this issue.

3.4 Why the principle of substantive racial equality in international human rights law is a powerful normative tool to understand fiscal policy in Africa

In the first three parts of this chapter, we explained how human rights can act as a normative tool to advance fiscal policy and demonstrated why international tax abuse and IFFs can be an impediment to the development and realization of human rights in Africa. We also explained how the Principles for Human Rights in Fiscal Policy explain what rights-aligned measures can be adopted in an African context. Moreover, we explained why fiscal policy is an essential ingredient in tackling the poly-crisis the world, especially Africa, faces today and can make the realization of human rights a reality.

From the perspective of human rights we adopt at CESR, rights are more than political entitlements or claims, or formal tools that remain neutral before political struggles. They also contain important principles or values which should guide both the process by which fiscal policies are created as well as their content. As we stated previously, these principles include dignity, equality, solidarity, participatory democracy and justice.

Africa's developmental and human rights challenges are arguably not an accident but a product of its brutal history of racial subordination and subjugation. Indeed, legal scholars have argued how "the built-in historical headwinds of colonialism ushered in a colonial afterlife in which formal sovereignty, or equality of states, comfortably existed alongside the quasi sovereignty of the Third World".[29]

It was Kwame Nkrumah who first coined the concept of "neo-colonialism" or how political independence did not result in African countries having substantive economic independence from their former colonizers and the various schemes which have been enacted since the nominal end of colonialism to sustain Africa's subordination.[30] For this reason, legal scholars have argued that

> formal inclusion into the international order and the sovereignty recognition it effectuated was not an achievement of substantive equality for Third World nation states. Instead, the very terms of inclusion ensured a persisting global hierarchy with First World nations on top and Third World nations on the bottom that belies the common equation of formal decolonization with the end of colonial relations between the First and the Third World.[31]

In a similar vein, the UN Special Rapporteur on Racism has argued that Africa's "underdevelopment" can be attributed to the neoliberal economic policies imposed upon them by the Bretton Woods Institutions over the last 40 years.[32] Linking human rights to the imperative of decolonization, she explains that "Racial justice, equality and non-discrimination are not compatible with economic structures that continue to privilege and benefit so-called 'developed' countries, their corporations and elites in 'underdeveloped' nations at the expense of 'underdeveloped' nations and the vast majority of their populations".[33]

The International Convention on the Elimination of Racial Discrimination (ICERD), one of the UN human rights' treaties that supplement the conventions already discussed in the previous section, requires substantive racial equality and the elimination of both de jure and de facto discrimination.[34] This means that even laws and policies which are neutral on their face and have no intention to discriminate still fall foul of its provisions if they have a disproportionate impact on racially marginalized groups.[35] The commitment to substantive racial equality contained in ICERD recognises racism as a global system underpinned by white supremacy wherein the structures of historical racism rooted in slavery, colonialism and apartheid must also be eliminated.[36]

The former UN Special Rapporteur on Racism, Tendayi Achiume has argued that the application of the principle of substantive racial equality embodied by ICERD should be understood and applied through four interrelated steps.[37] First, recalling the history of racial subordination as a global project and that ICERD's aim to eradicate all forms of racial discrimination requires paying close attention to how patterns of subordination and exploitation from the colonial era continue to manifest today.

Second, taking what Achiume and other scholars term an "anti-subordination" approach to addressing racial subordination. This entails taking steps to bring about not only formal but substantive racial equality which aims to eliminate structural racial discrimination in all its forms. According to this approach, ICERD not only aims to eliminate intentional and overt forms of racial discrimination but also indirect discrimination. Indirect discrimination refers to laws or policies which are neutral on their face but have a disproportionate impact on racially subordinated groups. Finally, a commitment to substantive racial equality means that where necessary states must take positive measures (including differentiation on the basis of race) if such measures are targeted at empowering previously disadvantaged groups.

Third, Achiume calls for an intersectional approach to racial discrimination. Intersectionality entails an acknowledgement of how intersecting and interlocking systems of oppression result in both distinct and compounded vulnerabilities for groups who face intersecting vulnerabilities based on their race, gender, sexuality, gender identity or expression, disability, nationality or other status. An intersectional approach cautions against regarding those who are subject to racial discrimination as a homogenous group. Instead, it requires one to be alive to how an individual's experience of discrimination may be shaped by all the social identities they hold and the combined impact of multiple oppressions.

Fourth, Achiume borrows from critical race scholars' approach of "looking to the bottom". This approach was coined by legal theorist, Mari Matsuda, who argues that those who have been on the receiving end of racial subordination, know best about what racial emancipation entails. Looking to the bottom requires us to take seriously the lived experiences of those at the frontlines of battles for racial justice and to ensure that their challenges shape the agenda for racial equality as well as shape potential interventions to remedy systemic racial subordination. Looking to the bottom means that those at the frontlines must be recognized as knowledge producers whose lived experiences should define the content of what we understand to be racial justice, racial emancipation and racial equality.

Achiume's robust articulation of racial justice and substantive racial equality has an important bearing on how one conceptualises the relationship between fiscal policy and the advancement of human rights in Africa. First, within countries in Africa, substantive racial equality entails the adoption of fiscal policies which are specifically intended to dismantle the contemporary effects of historic legacies of oppression rooted in slavery, colonialism and apartheid which, as the UN Committee on the Elimination of Racial Discrimination (CERD) has pointed out, remain largely unaccounted for today. Second, taking an intersectional approach means substantive racial equality should come alongside substantive gender equality. The gendered harms of international tax abuse and IFFs as well as unjust fiscal policies are numerous and well documented.

Third, at a global level, the principle of substantive racial equality provides a stronger foundation for critiquing neocolonial arrangements in the international financial architecture which sustains inequality between countries. This is because the legacies of colonialism, slavery and apartheid continue to be largely unaddressed to this day and are embedded in global structures such as the global system concerning international finance, taxation and debt.

In this global racialized system former colonial powers continue to be winners whilst former colonies continue to be the losers. In this regard, a discussion about IFFs, and advancing human rights in fiscal policy in Africa would be incomplete if those human rights norms were not understood through the lens of decolonization. For example, the duties to collaborate or the interpretation of extra-territorial obligations cannot be applied equally and formalistically to all countries, without consideration of how the impacts of colonialism play out in the dynamics of IFFs.

A good illustration of how neocolonialism plays out in the international financial architecture in regard to taxation and fiscal policy is the contestation surrounding the OECD's Two Pillar Solution. Recently a group of eight UN Special Procedures decried the OECD's proposed approach[38] warning that it "could have a discriminatory impact on the grounds of *gender, ethnicity and race*". They warned furthermore that "in reifying patterns of economic extraction with historical origins in systems of colonialism and slavery" the deal has the potential to "prejudice the predominantly non-white nations of the Global South".

Decolonial theorists have argued that colonialism created a relationship of dependency between countries in the Global South and countries in the Global North. According to this argument, colonialism created a centre-periphery relationship whereby colonial powers extracted raw materials and labour from colonial territories and "transformed economies of the Global South into satellites of the Global North".[39] Colonialism made states in the Global South reorient themselves entirely in the economic interests of countries in the Global North which enabled the latter to accumulate capital and wealth at the former's expense.

This created a relationship of dependency whilst deliberately ensuring that countries in the Global South would become underdeveloped. Importantly these theorists have argued that political independence from Global North countries was insufficient to enable economic emancipation and self-determination.

Decolonization and dependency theory are a useful basis upon which to understand how tax havens and IFFs contributes towards Africa's underdevelopment. Essentially, seen in their proper light, they act as neo-colonial constraints on Africa's development and the fiscal capacity of African states to give effect to economic, social, cultural and environmental rights. The more inequality widens between former colonial powers and formerly colonized states, this undermines the achievement of substantive racial equality.

One of the most effective pathways towards decolonization and dismantling structures which sustain subordination is ensuring reparations for racial injustice, a goal that rights-aligned fiscal policies can help secure. The Special Rapporteur has contended that one of the essential ingredients for reparations is the establishment of a just and equitable international order.[40]

In the context of the fight against IFFs and its detrimental impact on Africa's development, human rights shine a light on the extraterritorial obligations and reparations owed by states in the Global North (former colonial powers) to African states (formerly colonized nations). Whilst fiscal policy is first and foremost a concern of each individual government it is also a matter of global concern, and the current global economic framework is rooted in the legacy of slavery and colonialism.

Similarly, the legacies of colonialism are also an important driver of the nationwide inequalities discussed in this chapter, such as wealth and therefore income inequality.[41] The rights-aligned fiscal policies suggested in the previous section can therefore provide promising ways to address this current dimension of the colonial legacy. Overall, human rights through a decolonized lens offer a pathway towards a more just fiscal architecture which may ensure that economic, social, cultural and environmental rights are enjoyed by all.

3.5 Conclusion

Throughout this chapter, we have demonstrated the inseparable relationship between human rights and fiscal policy at the normative, conceptual and historical levels. We have surveyed existing efforts to enhance the materialization of this connection in practice, with a specific focus on the Principles for Human Rights in Fiscal Policy. We hope the Principles can spark an interest in the field in readers and inspire much-needed efforts to use fiscal policy to finally realize the promise of human rights of dignity and equality for all.

In this chapter, we tailored our arguments to the particularities of the African continent, using IFFs as an example of a fiscal problem with a human face. This tailoring exercise showed the urgent need to discuss fiscal problems in a way that puts people and the planet in the centre, to find solutions to dramatic problems such as wealth and income inequality. It also showed the relevant efforts that African countries have made along those lines and the enormous potential that tools available in the continent – such as innovative provisions of the African Charter – can have.

When writing, we are conscious that human rights are not a silver bullet that could resolve all the crises and challenges that the continent faces nowadays. We are also aware that challenges do not happen in a vacuum but are instead the result of historical processes that still today show the dramatic legacies of colonialism. However, we are confident that human rights, understood in a comprehensive manner that acknowledges this legacy, can provide a promising conceptual, political, moral and normative tool to rethink many of the challenges in the realm of fiscal policy that countries are facing.

Notes

1 Ohene Ampofo-Anti and Alina Saba, 'How a rights-based economy can help us overcome the social, economic and environmental challenges of our time' (September 2022) https://www.unrisd.org/en/library/blog-posts/how-a-rights-based-economy-can-help-us-overcome-the-social-economic-and-environmental-challenges-of-?utm_source=pocket_saves accessed 4 June 2023.

2 Habtamu Fuje and Jiaxiong Yao 'Africa's rapid economic growth hasn't closed income gaps', available online: https://www.imf.org/en/Blogs/Articles/2022/09/20/africas-rapid-economic-growth-hasnt-fully-closed-income-gaps#:~:text=Many%20economies%20in%20sub%2DSaharan,over%20the%20past%20two%20decades 21 (September 2022) accessed 4 June 2023.

3 Marta Schoch & Christoph Lakner, 'The number of poor people continues to rise in Sub-Saharan Africa, despite a slow decline in poverty rate' (*World Bank Data Blog*, December 2020) https://blogs.worldbank.org/ accessed 4 June 2023.

4 With an average Gini coefficient of 58.7%. Namibia and South Africa have Gini coefficients of 76%, while Botswana's coefficient is 71%, much higher than for other regions in the world. The World Bank, 'Inequality in Southern Africa: An assessment of the Southern African Customs Union' (2022).

5 The World Bank, 'Inequality in Southern Africa. An assessment of the Southern African Customs Union' (2022) https://documents.worldbank.org/en/publication/documents-reports/documentdetail/099125303072236903/p1649270c02a1f06b0a3ae02e57eadd7a82 3, 12, 41, 43.

6 The World Bank, 'Inequality in Southern Africa. An assessment of the Southern African Customs Union' (2022) https://documents.worldbank.org/en/publication/documents-reports/documentdetail/099125303072236903/p1649270c02a1f06b0a3ae02e57eadd7a82 3, 12, 41, 43.

7 International Monetary Fund, *Regional Economic Outlook, Sub Saharan Africa. The Big Funding Squeeze* (2023) 12.

8 Center for Economic and Social Rights, *Rights-Based Economy: Imagining a System that Supports a Better Life For All* www.cesr.org/rights-based-economy accessed 23 June 2023.

9 Center for Economic and Social Rights, *Dismantling the Dogmas of Austerity and Fiscal Injustice in Latin America* (2019) https://www.cesr.org/dismantling-dogmas-austerity-and-fiscal-injustice-latin-america/ accessed 20 May 2023.

10 Asha Ramgobin, *Illicit Financial Flows and Human Rights in Africa, a Primer* (unpublished manuscript).

11 Global Justice Now, *Honest Accounts 2017: How the World Profits from Africa's Wealth* (2017), available at http://www.globaljustice.org.uk/sites/default/files/files/resources/honest_accounts_2017_web_final_updated.pdf accessed 20 May 2023.
12 María Emilia Mamberti and Olivia Minatta, 'What do human rights have to offer to fiscal policy? Implications of fiscal transparency, participation and accountability' (2022) 46 (2) *Public Sector Economics* http://www.pse-journal.hr/en/archive/what-do-human-rights-have-to-offer-to-fiscal-policy-implications-of-fiscal-transparency-participation-and-accountability_9041/ accessed 20 May 2023.
13 United Nations Human Rights, Office of the High Commissioner, 'Status of ratification', https://indicators.ohchr.org/ accessed 20 May 2023.
14 International Covenant on Economic, Social and Cultural Rights, Art. 2. Universal Declaration of Human Rights, Art. 28.
15 United Nations Charter, Art. 55 and 56. Universal Declaration of Human Rights, Art. 22.
16 Principles for Human Rights in Fiscal Policy (2021) https://derechosypoliticafiscal.org/en/.
The Principles were launched and adopted in May 2021 through a week-long series of events that assembled over 1,000 participants and gathered consistent support for the Principles.
17 Tax Justice Network, The State of Tax Justice 2023 https://taxjustice.net/reports/the-state-of-tax-justice-2023/#:~:text=Key%20findings,tax%20abuse%20by%20wealthy%20individuals accessed 23 June 2023.
18 United Nations. Economic Commission for Africa. *Illicit Financial Flows: Report of the High Level Panel on Illicit Financial Flows from Africa* (2015) https://repository.uneca.org/bitstream/handle/10855/22695/b11524868.pdf?sequence=3&isAllowed=y accessed 23 June 2023.
19 United Nations. Economic Commission for Africa. *Illicit Financial Flows: Report of the High Level Panel on Illicit Financial Flows from Africa* (2015) https://repository.uneca.org/bitstream/handle/10855/22695/b11524868.pdf?sequence=3&isAllowed=y 33, accessed 23 June 2023.
20 UN Convention on the Elimination of all forms of discrimination on women.
21 Principle 2.3 of the Principles for Human Rights in Fiscal Policy (2021), Initiative for the Principles of Human Rights in Fiscal Policy https://derechosypoliticafiscal.org/en/ accessed 23 June 2023.
22 Guideline 4, Principle 2 of the Principles for Human Rights in Fiscal Policy (2021), Initiative for the Principles of Human Rights in Fiscal Policy https://derechosypoliticafiscal.org/en/ accessed 23 June 2023.
23 Principle 10.1. of the Principles for Human Rights in Fiscal Policy (2021), Initiative for the Principles of Human Rights in Fiscal Policy https://derechosypoliticafiscal.org/en/ accessed 23 June 2023.
24 Principle 13.3. of the Principles for Human Rights in Fiscal Policy (2021), Initiative for the Principles of Human Rights in Fiscal Policy https://derechosypoliticafiscal.org/en/ accessed 23 June 2023.
25 Principle 13.3. of the Principles for Human Rights in Fiscal Policy (2021), Initiative for the Principles of Human Rights in Fiscal Policy https://derechosypoliticafiscal.org/en/ accessed 23 June 2023.
26 Guideline 3, Principle 13 of the Principles for Human Rights in Fiscal Policy (2021), Initiative for the Principles of Human Rights in Fiscal Policy. Available at https://derechosypoliticafiscal.org/en/ accessed 23 June 2023.
27 Rui Xu, 'Stopping the haemorrhage: The case for a global framework to stem illicit financial flows from Africa' (United Nations, Office of the Special Adviser on Africa)https://www.un.org/osaa/news/stopping-haemorrhage-case-global-framework-stem-illicit-financial-flows-africa accessed 20 May 2023.

28 Article 21 of the African Charter on Human and People's Rights.
29 E. Tendayi Achiume and Devon W. Carbado, 'Critical race theory meets third world approaches to international law' (2021) 67 *UCLA Law Review* 1462.
30 Kwame Nkrumah, 'Neocolonialism: The last stage of imperialism' (1965, Panaf).
31 Achiume and Carbado (n 29).
32 *2030 Agenda for Sustainable Development, the Sustainable Development Goals and the fight against racial discrimination. Report of the Special Rapporteur on contemporary forms of racism, racial discrimination, xenophobia and related intolerance,* E. Tendayi Achiume, UN General Assembly, Human Rights Council, 50th session, 17 June 2022, https://documents-dds-ny.un.org/doc/UNDOC/GEN/G22/383/75/PDF/G2238375.pdf?OpenElemen.
33 Special Rapporteur on contemporary forms of racism, racial discrimination, xenophobia and related intolerance, E. Tendayi Achiume, *2030 Agenda for Sustainable Development, the Sustainable Development Goals and the fight against racial discrimination* (2022).
34 Committee on the Eradication of Racial Discrimination, General Recommendation on Article 4.
35 Committee on the Eradication of Racial Discrimination, General Recommendation on Article 4.
36 See groundbreaking statement of CERD on vaccine inequity, 'Statement on the lack of equitable and non-discriminatory access to COVID-19 vaccines' (April 2022) https://tbinternet.ohchr.org/_layouts/15/treatybodyexternal/Download.aspx?symbolno=INT%2fCERD%2fSWA%2f9548&Lang=en accessed 23 June 2024.
37 E. Tendayi Achiume, 'Putting racial equality onto the global human rights agenda' (2018) 15 *SUR – International Journal on Human Rights* 141.
38 Tax Justice Network, OECD tax reforms risk violating human rights law, UN experts warn in special intervention (2024) https://taxjustice.net/press/oecd-tax-reforms-risk-violating-human-rights-law-un-experts-warn-in-special-intervention/ accessed 24 June 2023.
39 E. Ndhlovu, 'Decolonisation of development: Samir Amin and the struggle for an alternative development approach in Africa' (2020) 1 (1) *The Saharan Journal* 81–103.
40 Special Rapporteur on contemporary forms of racism, racial discrimination, xenophobia and related intolerance, E. Tendayi Achiume, Reparation, racial justice and equality report (2019), A/74/321.
41 The World Bank, Inequality in Southern Africa (n 5).

Bibliography

E. Tendayi Achiume, 'Putting racial equality onto the global human rights agenda' (2018) 15 *SUR – International Journal on Human Rights* 141.

E. Tendayi Achiume and Devon W. Carbado, 'Critical race theory meets third world approaches to international law' (2021) 67 *UCLA Law Review* 1462.

Ohene Ampofo-Anti and Alina Saba, '*How a rights-based economy can help us overcome the social, economic and environmental challenges of our time*' (September 2022) https://www.unrisd.org/en/library/blog-posts/how-a-rights-based-economy-can-help-us-overcome-the-social-economic-and-environmental-challenges-of-?utm_source=pocket_saves accessed 4 June 2023.

Center for Economic and Social Rights, *Dismantling the Dogmas of Austerity and Fiscal Injustice in Latin America* (2019) https://www.cesr.org/dismantling-dogmas-austerity-and-fiscal-injustice-latin-america/ accessed 4 June 2023.

Center for Economic and Social Rights, *Rights-Based Economy: Imagining a System that Supports a Better Life For All* https://www.cesr.org/rights-based-economy/ accessed 4 June 2023.

Habtamu Fuje and Jiaxiong Yao, '*Africa's rapid economic growth hasn't closed income gaps*' (21 September 2022) https://www.imf.org/en/Blogs/Articles/2022/09/20/africas-rapid-economic-growth-hasnt-fully-closed-income-gaps#:~:text=Many%20economies%20in%20sub%2DSaharan,over%20the%20past%20two%20decades accessed 4 June 2023.

Global Justice Now, *Honest Accounts 2017: How the World Profits from Africa's Wealth* (2017) http://www.globaljustice.org.uk/sites/default/files/files/resources/honest_accounts_2017_web_final_updated.pdf accessed 20 May 2023.

International Monetary Fund, *Regional economic outlook, sub Saharan Africa. The big funding squeeze* (2023). https://www.elibrary.imf.org/display/book/9798400235641/CH001.xml

María Emilia Mamberti and Olivia Minatta, 'What do human rights have to offer to fiscal policy? Implications of fiscal transparency, participation and accountability' (2022) 46 (2) *Public Sector Economics* http://www.pse-journal.hr/en/archive/what-do-human-rights-have-to-offer-to-fiscal-policy-implications-of-fiscal-transparency-participation-and-accountability_9041/ accessed 20 May 2023.

E Ndhlovu, 'Decolonisation of development: Samir Amin and the struggle for an alternative development approach in Africa' (2020) 1 (1) *The Saharan Journal* 81–103.

Kwame Nkrumah, *Neocolonialism: The Last Stage of Imperialism* (Panaf 1965).

Principles for Human Rights in Fiscal Policy, '*Initiative for the principles of human rights in fiscal policy*' (2021) https://derechosypoliticafiscal.org/en/ accessed 4 June 2023.

Asha Ramgobin, *Illicit Financial Flows and Human Rights in Africa, a Primer* (unpublished manuscript n.d.).

Marta Schoch and Christoph Lakner, 'The number of poor people continues to rise in Sub-Saharan Africa, despite a slow decline in poverty rate' (*World Bank Data Blog*, December 2020) https://blogs.worldbank.org/ accessed 4 June 2023.

Tax Justice Network, *The State of Tax Justice* (2023) https://taxjustice.net/reports/the-state-of-tax-justice-2023/#:~:text=Key%20findings,tax%20abuse%20by%20wealthy%20individuals accessed 4 June 2023.

Tax Justice Network, '*OECD tax reforms risk violating human rights law, UN experts warn in special intervention*' (2024) https://taxjustice.net/press/oecd-tax-reforms-risk-violating-human-rights-law-un-experts-warn-in-special-intervention/ accessed 17 November 2024.

The World Bank, '*Inequality in Southern Africa: An assessment of the Southern African Customs Union*' (2022) https://documents.worldbank.org/en/publication/documents-reports/documentdetail/099125303072236903/p1649270c02a1f06b0a3ae02e57eadd7a82 accessed 24 June 2023.

UN Convention on the Elimination of all forms of discrimination on women (1979). https://www.ohchr.org/en/instruments-mechanisms/instruments/convention-elimination-all-forms-discrimination-against-women

United Nations Human Rights, Office of the High Commissioner. '*Status of ratification*' (2015), https://indicators.ohchr.org/ accessed 20 May 2023.

United Nations. Economic Commission for Africa, *Illicit Financial Flows: Report of the High Level Panel on Illicit Financial Flows from Africa* (2015) https://archive.uneca.org/publications/illicit-financial-flows

Rui Xu, 'Stopping the haemorrhage: The case for a global framework to stem illicit financial flows from Africa' (United Nations, Office of the Special Adviser on Africa) https://www.un.org/osaa/news/stopping-haemorrhage-case-global-framework-stem-illicit-financial-flows-africa accessed 20 May 2023.

4 Taxation and the Realisation of Socioeconomic Rights in Africa

What Is the Role of International Cooperation?

Philip Oamen and Adebolarin Adekanle†*

4.1 Introduction

Over the years, taxation has remained an under-explored topic on the human rights agenda.[1] However, there is a current shift as countries have begun to intensify efforts to mobilise sufficient revenue through taxation to finance the much-needed social services including education and health.[2] Taxation unarguably remains a major source of providing the facilities needed to realise Socioeconomic Rights (SR) or meet the Sustainable Development Goals (SDGs). Target 17.1 of the SDGs requires developed states to provide international support to developing countries to strengthen domestic resource mobilisation and improve domestic capacity for tax and other revenue collection. Thus, this chapter examines the relevance of international tax cooperation in realising SR, and it highlights issues around tax injustice and social inequalities, which international cooperation could address.

The importance of realising SR to meet the SDGs cannot be overestimated. SR aim to empower people with the material conditions and facilities necessary to lead a life of dignity. Thus, about 90% of the world's constitutions recognise at least one SR, either in a justiciable or aspirational manner.[3] The International Covenant on Economic, Social and Cultural Rights (ICESCR) recognises SR as including the right to work,[4] the right to just and favourable conditions of work,[5] the right to trade union membership,[6] the right to social security,[7] the right to family life,[8] the right to an adequate standard of living,[9] the right to enjoy the highest attainable standard of physical and mental health[10] and the right to education.[11] This chapter examines the engagement of international tax cooperation as a means of realising SR in Africa which currently suffers an acute dearth of facilities necessary for the realisation of these rights. International cooperation is relevant for the prevention of double taxation and non-taxation of eligible taxpayers.[12]

* Lecturer in Law, Birmingham City University, United Kingdom. Orcid ID: 0000-0002-6684-1270. Email address: philip.oamen@bcu.ac.uk.

† Associate Professor of Law, Ambrose Alli University, Nigeria. Email address: bolaadekanle@aauekpoma.edu.ng.

DOI: 10.4324/9781003432890-5

Over the past 20 years, many African countries have embraced SR by constitutionally recognising them either as justiciable rights[13] or as directive principles of state policy (Directive Principles).[14] Newer constitutions in Africa tilt towards justiciability of SR.[15] This constitutional recognition has fed into an evolving positive judicial approach to SR in Africa. For example, the Supreme Court of Kenya recently observed that the '... question as to when the right to housing accrues, in our view, is not dependent upon its progressive realization. The right accrues to every individual or family, by virtue of being a citizen of this Country'.[16] The Kenyan apex court also stated that

> Where the Government fails to provide accessible and adequate housing to all the people, the very least it must do, is to protect the rights and dignity of those in the informal settlements. The Courts are there to ensure that such protection is realized, otherwise these citizens, must forever, wander the corners of their country, in the grim reality of 'the wretched of the earth'.[17]

Despite this evolving positive approach to SR in Africa, the non-realisation of SR persists. A common argument usually advanced for this non-realisation is that African states cannot fulfil SR owing to resource constraints. The realisation of SR 'depends on the availability of... material resources. Given the fact that our society is incredulously unequal, with the majority ...condemned to grinding poverty', achieving these rights 'remains but a pipe-dream for many'.[18] Successive governments in Africa keep 'erecting the defence of "lack of resources"',[19] in their bid to escape their SR obligations. To navigate this resource concern, some scholars have highlighted the essentialness of an effective state tax assessment and collection system in enhancing the realisation of SR.[20]

However, beyond the state domestic tax system, international treaties and cooperation on taxation are necessary for states' domestic compliance with human rights obligations.[21] This chapter examines the role of international tax cooperation, as a useful vehicle for mobilising resources for SR realisation in Africa. Through the lens of Third World Approaches to International Law (TWAIL), it argues that no matter how much they try and owing to structural and economic imbalances between developed countries and developing countries, African states may not be able to effectively deploy taxation to fully realise SR of their people without the cooperation and assistance from developed states.

To achieve its set out objective, this chapter proceeds in eight sections. While this section introduces the work, Section 4.2 discusses the relationship between taxation and SR realisation. Section 4.3 examines international cooperation in the context of SR realisation and Section 4.4 unpacks TWAIL as an interpretive tool. In Section 4.5, the chapter engages TWAIL to assess the Organisation for Economic Cooperation and Development (OECD) framework on tax cooperation while Section 4.6 examines the UN's current work on tax cooperation. Section 4.7 considers areas where international cooperation will be useful in enhancing SR realisation in Africa and Section 4.8 concludes the chapter.

4.2 Taxation and Realisation of SR

Taxation plays a key role in stimulating economic growth and enhancing sustainable development, leading to the realisation of SR in any given nation. De Schutter notes that taxation is a human rights policy for several reasons.[22] These reasons include the fact that taxation allows states to mobilise resources to realise SR, taxation is a means of wealth redistribution and taxation feeds into democratic participation and accountability.[23] It has been observed that 'healthy collections of tax provide state and local governments the money to improve education, hire police officers and firefighters, build and maintain roads, keep parks clean, and many other public services'.[24] The UN Committee on Economic, Social and Cultural Rights (CESCR) has also observed that a state's obligation to fulfil SR may 'require the mobilization of resources by the State, including by enforcing progressive taxation schemes'.[25] Studies reveal that states which rely on domestic taxes as the main source of realising SR are more likely to be more answerable to their citizens than those who rely on natural resources or international aid.[26]

One of the features of a well-functioning government is the ability to mobilise tax revenue to provide public service or promote social welfare.[27] According to Roach,

> Tax policy has important economic consequences... Taxes can create incentives promoting desirable behavior and disincentives for unwanted behavior. Taxation provides a means to redistribute economic resources towards those with low incomes or special needs. Taxes provide the revenue needed for critical public services such as social security, health care, national defense, and education.[28]

The above assertion finds corroboration in Turk's position that 'progressive...measures of taxation can... lead to gentle and gradual forms of income redistribution within States...thereby creating conditions that enable a larger proportion of society to enjoy economic, social and cultural rights'.[29] Indeed, taxation can provide a foundation for the development of responsive and accountable governance in developing countries.[30] Taxation is central to the Sustainable Development Goals Agenda, because it provides 'a stable flow of revenue to finance development priorities, such as strengthening physical infrastructure, and is interwoven with numerous other policy areas, from good governance and formalizing the economy, to spurring growth'.[31] Thus, in its Concluding Observations on Burundi, the CESCR suggested that the state should design and implement an effective tax collection system that is progressive and laced with social justice, and which takes a cautious approach to tax exemptions scheme which could undermine tax revenue.[32] The CESCR took a similar position on the United Kingdom (the UK) when it cautioned the UK against an increase in regressive indirect taxes and a reduction in corporate income tax rate, which could hamper the domestic mobilisation of resources needed for realising SR.[33]

International cooperation is key to the utilisation of taxes for realising SR. As Chowdhary and Picciotto assert, tax 'is the fundamental means by which States can fund the fulfilment of their domestic and international human rights obligations… International coordination and cooperation at all levels of government and civil society concerned with tax are essential to deliver this'.[34] The importance of the relationship between taxation and the realisation of human rights is evident in relevant instruments.

For example, article 2(1) of ICESCR requires every state to take steps, to the 'maximum of its available resources', to realise SR progressively. This suggests that a state cannot be held accountable for not realising SR if it can show, for example, through its reports to the UN bodies, that it has deployed the maximum of its domestically and internationally sourced available resources towards realising SR. So, without taxes being collected and utilised effectively, a state may not have the maximum available resources needed for SR realisation. Although 'available resources' within the context of article 2(1) of ICESCR go beyond financial resources and include informational, natural, human and technological resources,[35] this chapter essentially focuses on resources from the perspective of finances sourced from taxation.

4.2.1 Tax Duties and SR Realisation in Africa: Nigeria as a Case Study

Article 29(6) of the African Charter on Human and Peoples' Rights (the African Charter) imposes a duty on the individual 'to work to the best of his [read their] abilities and competence, and to pay taxes imposed by law in the interest of the society'. Similarly, the African Commission Principles and Guidelines on the Implementation of Economic, Social and Cultural Rights (the Principles) impose duties on both the individual and the State as it relates to taxation as a means of realising SR. Hence, the Principles recognise that 'States need sufficient resources to progressively realise economic, social and cultural rights' and that there is 'a variety of means through which states may raise these resources, including taxation'.[36] The Principles also state that the

> duty of the individual to pay taxes imposed by the African Charter implies that there is an obligation on the State to institute an effective and fair taxation system and a budgeting process that ensures that economic, social and cultural rights are prioritised in the distribution of resources.[37]

Thus, it is imperative that a state's taxation policy is effective and fair enough to correctly assess and collect taxes which are needed for meeting the SR needs of citizens and residents. Some scholars have argued that poor financial resources should be 'a basis for the enactment of legislation that guarantees revenue-generation for redistribution to the citizens through human rights enforcement'.[38] Indeed, the strength and efficacy of the tax system in a state are factors that feed into whether the state has available resources for human rights realisation.[39] This is because the absence of a strong and effective tax system could trigger leakages that could remove or reduce the resources available for SR realisation.

As regards the duties created under the Principles above, it is unfortunate that some African states often emphasise the individual's duty to pay taxes but they fail to pay equal attention to the corresponding duty of states to use the resources derived from taxes to realise the SR of citizens. For instance, using Nigeria as a case study, the Nigerian Federal Government does not see itself as owing a duty to use taxes for SR realisation. This position is evinced in the Nigerian National Tax Policy (NTP) which defines tax as 'any compulsory payment to government imposed by law without direct benefit or return of value or a service whether it is called a tax or not'.[40] Although the NTP is not a legally binding document,[41] it currently serves as the policy that guides the federal tax system in Nigeria, with its current non-committal position on benefits. This chapter argues that payment of taxes confers a corresponding right on the taxpayer to obtain direct and indirect benefits. As some authors assert, taxation is 'a process in which citizens entrust the government with a share of their income and in return expect efficient delivery of services'.[42] Thus, this chapter argues that if the Nigerian government fails to provide efficient delivery of services in return for payment of taxes, that would be a violation of its SR obligations under ICESCR and domestic laws.

However, the Nigerian national and sub-national governments are always quick to assert that SR are not justiciable because they are provided for as Directive Principles in the Constitution,[43] but the same governments are quick to use the same Directive Principles[44] to argue that individuals owe a duty to pay taxes.[45] An effective and fair tax system should not only generate resources but should also protect the human rights of taxpayers.[46]

The Lagos State Government of Nigeria recently took the issue of taxation to a worrying dimension when it denied some pupils enrolment into the state public schools on the ground that the pupils' parents had no evidence of tax payment.[47] When the matter went to court, the trial court agreed with the government, stating that the right to education, being part of the Directive Principles under the Constitution, is not justiciable.[48] This judgment does not only punish innocent children for the sins of their parents but it also flies in the face of relevant statutes that guarantee children's right to free and compulsory education. For example, sections 14(1) and 39(1) of the Child's Rights Law of Lagos State 2007, sections 13(1) and 14 of the Compulsory Free Universal Basic Education Law of Lagos State, 2005, article 17(1) of the African Charter[49] and article 11(1), (3) (a), (d) and (e) of the African Charter on the Rights and

Welfare of the Child provide for children's right to education. Going by the decision of the Supreme Court of Nigeria in Attorney-General of Ondo State v Attorney-General of the Federation and 35 Others,[50] the enactment of these specific instruments to provide for the otherwise non-justiciable provisions of the Directive Principles is an escape route to navigate the justiciability challenge.[51] As the matter regarding the pupils has proceeded to the Court of Appeal, it is hoped that the appellate court will take a different view on the issue.

Despite the foregoing, it is not all a sorry situation in Nigeria. It is imperative to commend the Federal Government of Nigeria for some steps taken towards utilising taxes to realise the right to education which forms part of SR. For example, through the Tertiary Education Trust Fund (TETFund), the government now collects a 2% education tax from the assessable profits of all registered companies in Nigeria.[52] The proceeds of the tax are then utilised to build infrastructure, train lecturers and carry out other capacity-building activities within the Nigerian Higher and Further Education Sectors.[53] This move has boosted the capacity of Nigerian public universities to compete with their counterparts around the world.[54] This kind of move should be replicated in other sectors to fully realise SR in Nigeria.

That said, this chapter argues that an effective tax assessment and collection system for SR realisation may be unattainable in the absence of international cooperation among States. Research suggests that tax system design often promotes the interests of the elites, in individual and State perspectives, thereby attenuating the social welfare of the poor,[55] hence the need for international cooperation towards tax justice. As Roach argues,

> Political leaders have used tax policy to promote their agendas by initiating various tax reforms: decreasing (or increasing) tax rates…The voluminous tax code is packed with rules that benefit a certain group of taxpayers while inevitably shifting more of the burden to others. Tax policy clearly reflects the expression of power…– those without power or favor are left paying more in taxes while others reap the benefits of lower taxes because of their political influence.[56]

Thus, the formulation of tax policies often comes with the political and economic interests of certain business groups and individuals who seek to take advantage of the policies, thereby attenuating the human rights of vulnerable people.[57] A state's failure to arrest corruption in its tax system amounts to failure to utilise the maximum of its available resources as required under article 2(1) of ICESCR.[58] Also, where a state perceives that national resources are not enough to realise the SR of its citizens, it owes the citizens a duty to request international cooperation and assistance.[59] Richer states to which such a request is made are obligated to provide the needed resources (broadly defined), provided that such provision will not lead to the richer states' failure to meet their own SR obligations to their own citizens domestically.[60]

While a good tax policy 'shapes the environment in which international trade and investment take place',[61] it is also pertinent to note the observation that 'a core challenge for African countries is finding the optimal balance between a tax regime that is business and investment friendly, and one which can leverage enough revenue for public service delivery'.[62] Taxation is one major means of mobilising resources domestically towards meeting social welfare needs.[63] Effective tax policies should support sustainable economic development, reduce inequality and promote growth.[64] Thus, scholars have advanced arguments that African States should be held accountable for how they design tax systems – that enable tax evasion – and how they use tax revenue to eliminate or reduce extreme poverty.[65]

Nonetheless, beyond state tax policy and African states' duty to realise SR domestically, there is an extraterritorial obligation on developed states to help developing states harness taxes to realise SR. It has been suggested that 'economic, social, and cultural rights establish a clear role for the international community to support the realization of rights in low resource countries'.[66] While there are several ways this cooperation can be fostered, the main means will be in terms of providing technical support and cooperation in the fight against tax evasion.

A 2016 report on tax evasion in the United States of America (the US) reveals that, between 2008 and 2010, the gross tax gap due to tax evasion was $458 billion.[67] If such 'capital flight is occurring with [the US] regulatory frameworks commonly perceived as sound, one can imagine how many more opportunities exist for evasive practices in countries with weak regulatory and legal environments'.[68] Despite the challenges associated with the tax systems of developed countries, their systems still work better in terms of tax assessment and collection, and their effective tax collection and utilisation reflect on their better economic and social structures when compared with those of developing countries.[69] The developed countries should, therefore, cooperate with the developing countries to ensure that the latter are able to muster resources from taxation towards SR realisation. In this regard, this chapter echoes the words of developing countries under the auspices of G77 that

> Appropriate emphasis must be placed on an enabling global environment and global partnership for development, balanced against the increased emphasis being placed on domestic resource mobilization.... it is counterproductive to highlight the importance of domestic resource mobilization in developing countries, while at the same time not robustly tackle areas that impede their ability to capture necessary resources.[70]

Thus, the above concern calls for international cooperation and assistance from developed countries in favour of developing countries, especially in Africa, to engender an effective tax legal and institutional regime, both at the domestic and international levels.

4.3 International Cooperation on SR Realisation

The role of international cooperation and assistance in realising SR is recognised in the United Nation's normative framework. Although the nature and contours of this duty to cooperate internationally are still debatable,[71] the duty is, at least, normatively recognised in the ICESCR and the CESCR jurisprudence.[72] For example, article 2(1) of ICESCR provides that

> Each State Party to the present Covenant undertakes to take steps, individually and through international assistance and co-operation, especially economic and technical, to the maximum of its available resources, with a view to achieving progressively the full realization of the rights recognized in the present Covenant by all appropriate means, including particularly the adoption of legislative measures.

It has been observed that the foregoing provisions create a treaty obligation which article 28 of the Universal Declaration of Human Rights (UDHR) inspired but could not achieve on its own.[73] This argument is plausible because, during the drafting of the ICESCR, poorer countries represented by Egypt and India argued that 'the available resources of the smallest [poorest] countries, even if utilised to the maximum, would be insufficient, [and] as a result, those countries would have to fall back on international cooperation'.[74] Thus, Curtis and Darcy assert that

> ...international cooperation can be characterised as a means of addressing the power differential between wealthy influential states and those states unable to realise the rights of their people. The concept of cooperation would then be fundamentally linked to this power differential, and obligations to cooperate would be based on any given State's relative power to affect the realisation of rights in any other given State.[75]

Put in another way, the need for international cooperation is informed by the stark reality on the ground that some states are more powerful and richer than others, thus the need to prevent the use of the international order to suffocate less endowed States.[76] From a TWAIL perspective discussed below, this is particularly important against the backdrop of developed countries' historical expropriation of developing countries through slave trade and colonialism.[77]

Furthermore, several other provisions of ICESCR accentuate the role of international cooperation in realising SR. For example, article 11(1) provides that states shall take steps while 'recognizing ... the essential importance of international cooperation based on free consent', towards the realisation of the right to food. Article 15(4) similarly imposes an obligation on states to, while taking steps to realise the right to cultural life, 'recognize the benefits to be derived from the encouragement and development of international contacts and co-operation…' Also, article 23 requires States to recognise the importance of international action, methods, meetings, assistance and consultation in the realisation of ESR.[78]

In addition, the CESCR has developed a rich jurisprudence to explicate the foregoing provisions of ICESCR. For example, General Comment No. 3 states that

> A final element of article 2 (1), to which attention must be drawn, is that the undertaking given by all States parties is 'to take steps, individually and through international assistance and cooperation, especially economic and technical …'. The Committee notes that the phrase 'to the maximum of its available resources' was intended by the drafters of the Covenant to refer to both the resources existing within a State and those available from the international community through international cooperation and assistance…International cooperation for development and thus for the realization of economic, social and cultural rights is an obligation of all States. It is particularly incumbent upon those States which are in a position to assist others in this regard.[79]

The CESCR also notes that

> in the absence of an active programme of international assistance and cooperation on the part of all those States that are in a position to undertake one, the full realization of economic, social and cultural rights will remain an unfulfilled aspiration in many countries.[80]

This underscores the important role that international cooperation plays in realising SR in developing countries, many of which lack the resources, domestically, to meet the demands of SR. The obligation to cooperate internationally requires states to 'cooperate to mobilize the maximum of available resources for the universal fulfilment of economic, social and cultural rights'.[81]

However, a call for international cooperation does not in any way attenuate states' domestic duty to, as a matter of priority, mobilise resources to realise SR.[82] Coomans' observation that SR obligations are essentially domestic in nature holds true here.[83] Skogly and Gibney also note that a 'person's home state is certainly the first place to look to in terms of the protection of economic rights – and all other human rights as well'.[84] Thus, international cooperation should be complementary rather than substitutive of domestic mobilisation of resources for SR realisation.[85]

There is a debate on whether the duty to cooperate internationally is a binding one. Alston and Quinn argue that it is problematic to uphold 'the argument that the commitment to international cooperation can be accurately characterized as a legally binding obligation upon a particular State to provide any particular form of assistance'.[86] De Schutter, while recognising the challenge of state sovereignty to the duty to cooperate, notes that

> such a duty requires that the State put forward proposals, with a view to strengthening international cooperation, that are both sufficiently concrete and "reasonable", which means in particular that in the distribution of the burdens and benefits, such proposals should take into account the principle of common but differentiated responsibilities and respective capabilities.[87]

Whereas it is true that the imposition of a duty of international cooperation on states seems to negate the principle of sovereignty because it fetters states' ability to pick and choose what actions to undertake, it is argued that in this era of globalisation, there should be a move away from absolute sovereignty to shared sovereignty.[88]

Although shared sovereignty is often conceptualised as the process of sharing governmental powers between the Federation and the federating states within a domestic legal system,[89] Gusy asserts that the concept can be stretched to apply to international or supranational governance levels.[90] So, shared sovereignty would promote transnational identity through 'pragmatic solidarities'[91] among states, which will bring about a continuing rapprochement of the different levels of governance.[92] It 'balances the levers of power and provides a legitimisation forum for the workings of states, international institutions, global actors, individuals and civil society amongst others'.[93]

However, one must note that this international cooperation and its attendant shared sovereignty could result in the 'paradox of the many hands' where

> the larger the number of States involved in a situation that creates obstacles to the ability of any one State to fulfil its human rights obligations, the more difficult it will be to assert a responsibility of any individual State in that situation.[94]

This, however, does not mean that international cooperation should be abandoned. Perhaps, the many hands in the paradox might turn out to be cooperative and effective hands acting for the realisation of SR.

One key area where international cooperation would be helpful in the context of taxation is the creation of legal instruments to prevent double taxation. Double taxation treaties are bilateral and multilateral arrangements that 'serve to harmonize the tax systems of ...countries involved and apply not only to organizations, but also to individuals engaged in cross-border trade and investment'.[95] If no such treaties exist, 'income from cross-border transactions or investments may be subject to double taxation: first, in the country where the income is generated and, second, in the country where the recipient of the income is a resident',[96] and this may reduce the available resources needed for SR realisation in the poorer countries. The OECD's tax treaties and the evolving UN tax cooperation mechanism which seek to address this challenge are assessed below.

4.4 Understanding TWAIL as an Interpretive Tool

This chapter uses TWAIL to problematise the existing attempts at tax cooperation. Particularly, the chapter argues below that the tax cooperation regime that OECD has developed is too Eurocentric and thus largely unbeneficial to developing countries. The chapter thus calls for a more participatory tax cooperation regime that takes the interests of developing countries into account, without mortgaging the equally valid interests of the developed countries.

TWAIL is 'an expansive, heterogeneous and polycentric dispersed network and field of study',[97] which 'offers both theories of, and methodologies for, analysing international law and institutions',[98] especially regarding developing countries. TWAIL '…is both reactive and proactive. It is reactive in the sense that it responds to international law as an imperial project. But it is proactive because it seeks the internal transformation of conditions in the Third World'.[99] Hence, in the realm of SR realisation, a TWAIL perspective reacts to developed countries' non-committal approach to the transformation of the socioeconomic conditions of people in developing countries.[100]

Mainstream international law, the TWAIL perspective argues, does not consider the historical or colonial underpinnings that inform the social and economic inequalities between developed countries and developing countries. Thus, TWAIL seeks to 'unpack the colonial history of …the Third World, foreground colonialism's continual influence on the international system …and focus on achieving some form of justice for peoples of the Third World'.[101] TWAIL challenges the complacency in international law to treat the colonial legacy as a dead letter, overcome by the process of decolonisation.[102] It argues that any reference to the colonial events should not be perceived as 'crying over milk that was split many decades back but about being intuitive in understanding the systemic and structural constraints on the Third World that are heritages of a colonial legacy'.[103]

TWAIL interrogates international law rules, to assess how they 'empower or disempower peoples in the Third World…'[104] TWAIL seeks 'to centre the *rest* rather than merely the *west*, thereby taking the lives and experiences of those who have self-identified as Third World much more seriously than has generally been the case'.[105] It aims 'to transform the international economic system so that it could be an effective mechanism for the development needs of developing countries as much as it was and continues to be of the economic needs of developed countries'.[106] Thus, TWAIL scholars have 'a shared ethical commitment to the intellectual and practical struggle to expose, reform, or even retrench the features of the international system that help create or maintain the generally unequal, unfair, or unjust global order'.[107]

Drawing on TWAIL as an interpretive tool to understand the duty to cooperate, this chapter argues that the historical or colonial impact on SR in developing countries should be given a serious thought.[108] The fact that SR is not being realised in developing countries should not be discussed just in terms of statistics without looking at the historical contexts.[109] Currently, international law helps to legitimise and sustain 'the unequal structures and processes that manifest themselves in the growing North-South divide'.[110] Giving serious thought to this issue should feed into the legal architecture of international tax cooperation.

4.5 OECD Framework on Tax Cooperation: A TWAIL Assessment

The current legal and institutional architecture of tax cooperation is characterised by fragmentation and a multi-layered approach. This section assesses the key players and instruments that currently dominate the international tax system. The essence of this assessment is to highlight how developed countries, through the OECD taxation mechanism, have attenuated the capacity of African states to mobilise resources (derivable from taxation) which are needed for SR realisation. It also seeks to spotlight the importance of incorporating other regional perspectives (in addition to OECD's) in the evolving UN's tax cooperation initiative discussed below.

Institutionally, the OECD is unarguably the frontline body on international tax cooperation. For half a century, 'the most influential international rules and standards for taxing multinational corporations have been formulated by a select group of developed countries, the OECD, with lower-income countries on the outside'.[111] No doubt, the OECD has influenced the development of several international tax law principles that have been codified into a number of bilateral and multilateral instruments.[112] The OECD is made up of 38 countries, 'each with a gross national income per capita that places them in the category of "upper-middle income economy" or "high-income economy", as defined by the World Bank'.[113] Most members of the OECD are from Europe and the Americas, while none is from Africa.[114] As would be seen below, this composition undermines the interests of developing countries not represented in the OECD, because the OECD occupies a predominant position in the framing of international tax cooperation.

The OECD produced the 1963 Model Tax Convention on Income and Capital, which provides residence-country taxation rules most favourable to developed countries and their multinational enterprises (MNEs). The OECD also produced the Convention on Mutual Administrative Assistance in Tax Matters 1988 (amended in 2010 to create a wider participation) and the Global Anti-Base Erosion (GloBE) Model Rules (which provides for the global minimum tax [15%] that jurisdictions can impose on MNEs). It has also produced other salutary tax rules as highlighted below.

From a TWAIL perspective, it is pertinent to observe that, despite the laudable work that OECD has undertaken, it remains an exclusive club for a powerful set of nations which make up the G20, a forum of the world's 20 largest economies. So, there is little or no wonder that some of OECD's policy-making processes do not provide a participatory environment for poorer nations such as African countries. The fact that 'much of international tax governance does not come from the United Nations, the organization whose membership includes all sovereign nations',[115] questions the legitimacy of the OECD legal architecture on tax cooperation. The OECD model tax conventions are premised largely on the concept of reciprocity between the contracting states which are rich and powerful countries.[116] As discussed below, examples of undemocratic practices – which undermine developing countries' participatory rights – abound within the international taxation system of OECD.

In attempts to address this democratic legitimacy concern, the OECD began to carry out some institutional reforms in 2009 by trying to infuse wider participatory tax governance.[117] For example, the Global Forum on Transparency and Exchange of Information for Tax Purposes (the Global Forum) which was established in 2009, the Base Erosion and Profit Shifting (BEPS) and the Inclusive Framework on Base Erosion and Profit Shifting (IF) are some of the leading tax initiatives which the OECD has designed. While the Global Forum, with 170 members, is the leading international body on global transparency aimed at addressing tax evasion,[118] the OECD in collaboration with G20 also launched the BEPS Project (currently with over 140 member-states) in 2013, to tackle the problems of tax avoidance by MNEs.[119] Furthermore, in 2016, the OECD and G20 launched the IF which currently has over 140 members) aimed at ensuring the timely, participatory and effective implementation of the results of the BEPS Project.[120] An essential feature of the IF is that it aims to give all its members 'equal footing' in the design and implementation of international tax cooperation mechanisms.[121] According to the OECD,

> Importantly, developing country members of the Inclusive Framework have played a vital role in shaping the agreement, and have had significant influence on many of the essential components of the reforms. This demonstrates that the new international tax architecture provides not only a seat 'at the table,' but also the potential for developing countries to have a strong voice in ensuring that international tax norms and standards reflect their priorities.[122]

While it is true that the foregoing OECD initiatives have widened the tax governance spaces for developing countries,[123] whether the IF has indeed given a strong voice to developing countries is worth considering. The positive contributions of OECD initiatives to developing countries are well documented. These include such countries benefiting from reform proposals championed by their allies who are powerful OECD or G20 members, benefiting from inputs from influential individuals such as Secretariat staff and delegates from more powerful countries, collaboration among lower-income countries, and with other countries with common interests, and benefiting from having people with expertise, personal experience and networks representing them at the negotiation table.[124]

However, this chapter argues that, despite the OECD's salutary work on the international tax system, the IF and indeed the entire OECD regime has not provided any 'equal footing'. Instead, the OECD serves as an impediment to the establishment of a truly participatory and universally inclusive tax regime. OECD's current multiple and overlapping international tax standards have hampered the development of 'a genuinely global international tax body… in the international economic system' and this lacuna is a huge 'disadvantage for developing countries, which are unable to participate in international tax standard setting as full and equal participants'.[125]

From a TWAIL standpoint, OECD was created to have a Eurocentric outlook. Its occidental agenda was not accidental but well strategised from the very beginning of its existence. For example, the first Secretary-General that the OECD ever had clearly stated that

> The industrial countries with market economies have a definite mission in the world during the present phase of history. They have been the forerunners in economic development; and they will remain for a long time the pioneers in a number of fields because their structures are more refined and their national economies more interwoven … They can, therefore, develop certain techniques of economic policy-making that can later be transferred to other parts of the world … that are less highly developed.[126]

So, from the beginning, OECD set out to develop and impose its initiatives and techniques, including the ones on taxation, on developing countries. Although the body has sought to carry out some reforms (such as the IF) owing to criticism against its Eurocentric position, the fact remains that those reforms have not been able to completely address the deep-rooted systemic imbalances infused into the OECD system from the beginning.

While not countenancing harmful tax practices in developing countries, this chapter argues that OECD should be quick to call developed countries to order when they engage in harmful tax practices, just as the organisation is often quick to classify powerless and small island countries as tax havens.[127] After all, it was the US which started the use of tax incentives, tax holidays and tax-free zones which have now snowballed into tax haven activities in developing countries, yet OECD has not targeted the US.[128] The US itself seems to have confirmed this point when its Treasury Secretary recently conceded that in

> the popular imagination, the money laundering capitals of the world are small countries with histories of loose and secretive financial laws. But there's a good argument that, right now, the best place to hide and launder ill-gotten gains is actually the United States.[129]

This concession might have emboldened the Bahamas (a much-touted tax haven) to rise to the occasion of voting in favour of a 2023 UN resolution for UN-regulated tax cooperation mechanisms.[130] The resolution and mechanisms are discussed further down the line in this chapter.

In addition, the current decision-making configuration of the OECD on tax matters is G20-centric in outlook. For instance, apart from requiring payment of huge fees to join the IF and the Global Forum,[131] OECD's IF document also ensures that non-OECD members joining the IF do not enjoy universal or full rights. Thus, their participation right comes with a condition of being bound by already existing OECD standards. For example, developing countries which joined BEPS under the 2016 IF are required to implement the four minimum standards (that is, BEPS action 5 on harmful tax practices, action 6 on prevention of tax treaty abuse, action 13 on MNEs' country by Country Report and action 14 on mutual dispute resolution) which OECD/G20 members had finalised in 2013.[132]

The problem with the above condition is that the core standard setting on tax cooperation had been negotiated and concluded by OECD/G20 members before 2016 when the IF opened the door for non-OECD members. A similar position applies under the Global Forum where OECD requires developing countries which are joining the Forum to commit to implementing the Exchange of Information on Request Standard and the Common Reporting Standard, even though they never contributed to the framing of those standards.

While it could be argued that developing countries could resile from those pre-existing standards on the basis that, in international law, agreements are not binding on a state unless it consents to them,[133] one also must consider the exception to this hallowed international law rule. It is settled law that customary international law (CIL) rules are an exception to the consensus element of international law. CIL finds its roots in the widespread, consistent and uniform practice of states, whether internationally or regionally,[134] which the states have explicitly or implicitly recognised as binding.[135] It has been observed that the OECD tax treaties have acquired such popularity that they can easily pass for CIL rules, and thus an exception to the consensus requirement in international law.[136]

However, there is another question whether treaties produced by a non-state actor such as OECD (though made up of states) can constitute CIL. It could be argued that nothing stops such treaties from being recognised as CIL. As Baker notes,

> multilateral treaties [such as OECD treaties] can transform into sources of customary international law, binding on all states in the international system, whether they are parties to the particular treaty or not, if a large enough portion of non-signatory states in the international system adheres to their provisions out of a sense of legal obligation.[137]

It could also be argued that the high number of OECD members signing up for its treaties might satisfy this test of adherence.[138] However, a better argument would be that OECD treaties do not form part of CIL, because they are 'model' treaties which means states have not universally recognised them as binding, and where they are discreetly imposed (e.g., through G20 loan conditionalities), they would lose the imprimatur of being referred to as 'practice'.

Viewed through the lens of TWAIL, what the foregoing suggests is that developing countries' participation in tax cooperation design is only on the periphery, the substantive standards having been set before they were invited. This practice 'is inconsistent with the procedural criteria that all countries should be involved in agenda-setting'.[139] It leads to a situation where

> African countries as capital importing countries have had little bargaining power in these processes and bilateral relations. For years, OECD and G/20 countries have set the standards for international taxation while their member countries have simultaneously been some of the biggest perpetrators of tax abuse.[140]

This practice suggests that OECD/G20 members frame tax policies that align only with their 'mutually agreeable norms',[141] not universally agreeable norms. As an empirical study reveals,

> The IF's expansion has made little difference to the number of lower-income countries attending meetings at which the practical technical policy work is done, and that most members are fairly silent participants. This is partly because of well-documented structural obstacles not unique to the IF, but is exacerbated by some aspects of the OECD's decision-making processes, such as the pace and intensity of discussions, the culture of policymaking, the costs of attending regular meetings in Paris, and the absence of routine and timely translation of documents and meetings. This can make the OECD a daunting environment for member state delegates, but especially for those from lower-income countries. In addition, many have joined with no intention of influencing standards, but rather in pursuit of technical assistance or prestige, or under coercion from the European Union.[142]

The above point finds corroboration in other reports which suggest that OECD outputs are not user-friendly to most developing countries which have not received technical training to unravel the complexities of the outputs. For example, the International Bureau of Fiscal Documentation states that the OECD tax guidance is more popular among developed countries than developing countries.[143] The UN traces this popularity concern to the

> complexity of the provisions and administration, lack of capacity in developing countries and some missed opportunities in the context of the base erosion and profit shifting project to address comprehensively the key issues that are regarded as most pressing for developing countries.[144]

Another demonstration of the G20-centric colouration of the IF is that OECD's IF reports on BEPS are approved only by OECD and G20 members, making non-members of the bodies to play second fiddle.[145] This situation presents 'a paradox that the rich countries whose professional services firms are responsible for most of the world's cross-border tax abuse also write global tax rules'.[146] The fact that IF primarily 'reports only to the OECD and G20 countries', and that 'its Secretariat, which has played an increasingly powerful role, is provided by the OECD',[147] raises questions about the independence of thoughts and action among OECD non-members and begs the question of whether the IF has indeed given a strong voice to developing countries. Even the UN Secretary-General (UNSG) agrees that OECD's recent 'two-pillar solution', though laudable in addressing global tax injustice, 'would not fully address a broader discontent rooted in the long-standing conviction, held by many countries and stakeholders, that existing tax treaty rules do not reserve sufficient taxing rights for countries hosting multinational enterprises and constituting markets for their products'.[148] Thus, it has been observed that the recent OECD's BEPS Two Pillar Solution in terms of taxing the digital economy, is too G20-centric, fuelling the 'G-77's renewed demand for a global tax body' as a matter of priority.[149] Empirical research also reveals that 'although individuals from non-OECD Inclusive Framework members can apply for a role at the OECD Secretariat, people in the important positions are all from OECD countries'.[150]

As the UN sets out to develop a tax cooperation mechanism which has a more global outlook, it should be intentional about considering other regional perspectives rather than just the Western perspective as represented by the OECD or G20. For example, just as the OECD and the African Union's initiatives contributed to the norm-setting for the UN Convention on Anti-corruption, the UN should also involve not only the OECD but also the African Tax Administration Forum and the Regional Platform for Tax Cooperation in Latin America and the Caribbean in its current efforts to set agenda and standards for an international tax cooperation regime.[151] Such a fusion of regional initiatives and ideas will create healthy 'regime complexes' which could produce fruitful outcomes for developed and developing contexts.[152] It will also promote geographical, economic and linguistic diversity which is missing in current global tax governance.[153]

However, a major concern is that developing countries have not mustered the capacity for regional agenda-setting on taxation. They 'are not well organised into caucuses, unlike the OECD, G7 and European Union, which all have a long tradition of working together to negotiate common positions'.[154] While it is true that 'ATAF and the Intergovernmental Group of 24 (G-24) have emerged as developing country blocs within the IF, it will take time and experience to build up a culture of effective caucusing'.[155] It is also worrying that empirical research reports a leader from a developing country to have stated that the

> challenge [for] most developing countries is that we have not been part of the agenda. We do not come to defend an agenda, but only try not to get ourselves into a worse position. In contrast with US, no African country currently has an agenda. There has not been a time that we sat together to discuss an agenda.[156]

It is, thus, pertinent for political leaders and technical experts from developing countries to brace up for setting agendas or taking a regional position. If the current UN efforts on tax cooperation will be of any benefit to developing countries, then their leaders must keep their feet on the ground and assert their position firmly and urgently. They need to 'draw on socio-technical resources – expertise and professional networks – as an alternative source of power in deeply technical policy-making processes'.[157] The next section considers the evolving international tax cooperation regime within the UN system.

4.6 Towards a UN Tax Cooperation Regime

Further to the foregoing, there is an urgent need to take ongoing UN tax cooperation talks and processes seriously. As far back as 2001, the UN noted the importance of international tax cooperation, insisting that such cooperation provides 'global public goods, meaning goods and services whose benefits accrue to humanity in general rather than to the residents of any single country'.[158] As the UN Addis Ababa Action Agenda provides, such tax cooperation '...should be universal in approach and scope and should fully take into account the different needs and capacities of all countries...'[159]

Prior to the Addis Ababa Action Agenda, the UN already had a body known as the Committee of Experts on International Cooperation in Tax Matters (Tax Committee), established pursuant to ECOSOC Resolution 2004/69 and as a replacement for the defunct UN Ad Hoc Group of Experts on International Cooperation in Tax Matters which drafted the yet-to-be adopted 1980 UN Model Taxation Convention (UN Tax Convention).[160] The Tax Committee is made up of tax experts appointed by the UNSG on the recommendation of national governments (and taking equitable geographical spread into account). It is charged with enhancing and promoting international tax cooperation among national tax authorities; and considering 'how new and emerging issues could affect international cooperation in tax matters and develop assessments, commentaries and appropriate recommendations'.[161]

Ideally, the Tax Committee should be more appealing than the OECD because it is a UN mechanism and has evidently promoted pro-developing countries' agenda. However, it is beset by several problems which make it unable to achieve its mandate. One such challenge is the fact that the Committee is not a UN intergovernmental body and thus lacks the institutional legitimacy and resources to achieve its mandate. Thus, G77 members have called for its upgrading to an intergovernmental body to cure its legitimacy concerns.[162]

The G20 members have resisted these calls because they see them as a threat to OECD's prominence on tax cooperation matters.[163] Despite the paltry budget (USD 2.4 million as of 2010) proposed for the logistics of converting the Tax Committee to an intergovernmental and thus more powerful body, politicisation botched the idea.[164] Instead, the UN resolved that the UNSG should explore 'how the Committee could be further strengthened, with the emphasis on more collaboration with other actors, namely the OECD and the Bretton Woods'.[165] To pursue this new goal that flies in the face of the original goal of upgrading, a new body, Platform for Collaboration on Tax was created to enable Bretton Woods institutions such as the International Monetary Fund to collaborate with OECD on tax matters, but this only confirmed and legitimised OECD's domination on tax norm-setting.[166]

Over the years, despite that it lacks an intergovernmental body status, the Tax Committee has shown that it is committed to promoting tax justice between developed countries and developing countries. For example, it has reviewed (in 2011, 2017 and 2021) the UN Tax Convention and keeps updating the UN Manual for the Negotiation of Bilateral Tax Treaties between Developed and Developing Countries. Both the Convention and the Manual have assisted developing countries in 'developing and articulating their own treaty policies in negotiations'.[167] One major attribute of the Committee's review is that the Convention has been adjusted to provide for the retention of greater host country taxation rights (that is, a departure from 'residence country taxation' rules to 'source country' rules).[168] This favours developing countries which usually host MNEs but are unable to tax them simply because they are headquartered in developed countries. Thus, it has been observed that the most important changes included in the Convention 'address concerns expressed by developing countries regarding tax treaty obstacles to the taxation of foreign enterprises on income from automated digital services and on gains on so-called "offshore indirect transfers"'.[169] The latest Model has also streamlined, in favour of developing countries, the meaning of concepts such as 'permanent establishment' and 'beneficial owner' as they relate to taxation.[170] It is hoped that the Model will become a binding treaty soon.

Indeed, the UN has begun to take steps towards the adoption of a real-world taxation Convention that may address global tax injustice. For example, on 23 November 2022, the African Group succeeded in moving the UN General Assembly (UNGA) Second Committee to pass a resolution that will pave 'the way for a UN convention on taxation and a new global tax body'.[171] The resolution seeks 'ways to strengthen the inclusiveness and effectiveness of international tax cooperation, including the possibility of developing an international tax cooperation framework or instrument'.[172] It should be noted that OECD members opposed the resolution and sought to amend it, arguing that it would amount to a needless duplication of OECD's work on tax cooperation.[173] Luckily for developing countries, the amendment sought was defeated when it was put to vote. The Second Committee subsequently referred the resolution to UNGA to begin intergovernmental discussions on it.[174]

Consequently, on 30 December 2022, UNGA considered and approved the Committee's report.[175] UNGA resolved that 'developing countries are particularly susceptible to the negative impact of illicit financial flows' which 'reduce fiscal space along with the availability of valuable resources for financing for development' while recognising 'the importance of cooperation at the national, regional and international levels in combating illicit financial flows and promoting financial transparency'.[176] By this resolution, UNGA also decided 'to begin intergovernmental discussions … on … international tax cooperation through the evaluation of additional options, including the possibility of developing an international tax cooperation framework…'[177] To achieve this goal, UNGA requested the UNSG to prepare a report on international tax cooperation.[178]

The UNSG submitted the requested report to UNGA on 26 July 2023.[179] The report noted that UNGA has taken, 'by consensus, a potentially path-breaking decision… to strengthen the inclusiveness and effectiveness of international tax cooperation'.[180] The report recommended a Convention that would serve as a regulatory framework, providing 'mandatory, preferably enforceable, obligations that are deemed essential for appropriate domestic resource mobilization…'[181] The Convention is also expected to establish an institutional body to monitor compliance and resolve disputes.[182] The efficacy of this Convention will depend on countries' political will, consensus and readiness to recognise tax justice as a global issue that requires globally coordinated attention.[183]

In furtherance of the UNSG's report, on 22 November 2023, the UNGA approved a resolution (by simple majority votes of 125 to 48 with 9 abstentions) in favour of developing an international tax convention. The African Group stated that the resolution 'resonates with our aspirations as outlined in both the AU [African Union] Agenda 2063 and 2030 Agenda [for Sustainable Development], reinforcing our commitment to strengthening tax systems and fostering tax equity'.[184] It noted that it was

> high time that the international community addresses this injustice in global taxing rights that is impoverishing millions, which goes back to the League of Nations, when most Member States were colonies and which has been perpetuated by the monopoly that rich country clubs have held over international tax rule-making.[185]

As usual, OECD members opposed the resolution. For example, the UK which was supported by the US preferred a framework rather than a convention, so as to attenuate the binding nature of the international tax cooperation instrument.[186] By seeking to block this significant resolution, OECD members were 'not only undermining a fair and effective global tax system, but also acting against the interests of their own citizens, who pay a high price when wealthy individuals and big corporations use international loopholes to dodge taxes'.[187]

The 22 November 2023 resolution is historic in terms of its potential for raising resources for SR across the globe. It comes with benefits for the people of developing and developed countries. As Nigeria stated when introducing the resolution for UNGA approval,

> By adopting a unified, UN-led framework convention for international tax cooperation, we open doors to significant economic advantages. For emerging economies, this means greater ability to mobilize domestic resources, directly fuelling development projects and social welfare programmes. For more developed nations, it promises a level playing field, reducing instances of tax evasion and avoidance that currently undermine economic fairness. Moreover, recent data from the International Monetary Fund suggests that improving international tax cooperation could significantly reduce illicit financial flows, a scourge that deprives economies, especially those in the developing world, of critical funding. For all countries, illicit flows can fuel crime, destabilizing societies.[188]

While the world awaits the direction these emerging UN developments will take in the law and practice of international tax cooperation, the current milestones within the UN system are worth celebrating. The fact that the Tax Committee also has a reviewed draft taxation Convention makes the potential for a speedy establishment of the UN legal and institutional frameworks real. However, this is not the time for too much celebration for developing countries. The task ahead of them now is, convincing or lobbying the powerful OECD members who voted against the resolution. The fact that the resolution sailed through without OECD members' support does not take away the fact that they still wield great influence. Their cooperation is highly needed as the UN proceeds into the next stage of developing the long-awaited Tax Convention which will, hopefully, democratise tax regimes and establish equitable intergovernmental mechanisms on tax cooperation.

This cooperation, as noted above, is fundamental. It will help to hold individuals and MNEs accountable for tax evasion. It can address tax havens whose activities impede SR realisation. Indeed, being a tax haven is a violation of a state's extraterritorial obligation to respect, protect and fulfil SR.[189] As the CESCR stated in its Concluding Observations to the UK, financial secrecy legislation and permissive rules on corporate tax affect the ability of the UK and other States to meet their obligation to mobilise the maximum available resources for realising SR.[190] A developing country's domestic tax reforms may, therefore, never be effective enough, to shore up resources for SR, without being 'complemented by reforms in the countries which receive illicit financial flows from tax evasion or other forms of economic crime such as corruption'.[191] Thus, the cooperation of all may be an effective way to arrest tax evasion and minimise tax avoidance, thereby shoring up resources for the realisation of SR.

As the UN develops an international tax cooperation regime, there is a need to embrace subaltern realism which seeks to centre weak or poor states in the international arena, having been 'largely ignored by the elitist historiography as popularised by both neorealism and neoliberalism'.[192] Neorealism (which emphasises the role of power politics in international relations) and neoliberalism (which promotes free market competition) both promote the interests of developed countries to the detriment of developing countries and the solution to these uncanny theories is embracing the subaltern realism theory. This theory problematises the widely differing economic conditions in developed countries and developing countries and advocates equity between these countries.[193]

4.7 Looking into the Future

One area where international cooperation is vital is tax evasion. Tax evasion and avoidance lead to a huge loss of revenue to developing countries which lack the institutional mechanisms to confront the challenges. Developed countries should refuse to be tax havens and resist other countries that serve as tax havens to the detriment of developing countries. According to Elson and colleagues,

> The existence of tax havens, with very low tax rates, facilitates tax avoidance and evasion. Multinational corporations take advantage of tax havens to reduce tax payments. By setting up headquarters in a tax haven, then manipulating the price of imports purchased from and exports shipped to other divisions and affiliates of the same company operating in different countries, corporations can show their profits as accruing in a tax haven rather than in a country with higher taxes.[194]

A UN report states that '[f]rom 2000 to 2015, the total illicit capital flight from Africa amounted to $836 billion. Compared to Africa's total external debt stock of $770 billion in 2018, this makes Africa a "net creditor to the world"'.[195] To address this problem, cooperation between African nations and developed countries is urgently required. African nations cannot tackle the problem of tax evasion and avoidance alone, owing to a lack of relevant institutional mechanisms, and more fundamentally because of the transboundary nature of the problem.

Trade liberalisation is another area where international cooperation is needed. In line with the international cooperation obligation created in article 2(1) of ICESCR and other legal instruments, developed countries are required to contribute at least 0.7% of their Gross Domestic Product (GDP) to the Official Development Assistance (ODA), which is then used to carry out SR developmental projects in developing countries. While making their contributions to ODA, some developed countries often require the benefiting developing countries to enter into trade liberalisation agreements with them.

These agreements seek to remove trade barriers, including revenue tariffs on goods and services from developed countries to developing countries. The removal of such tariffs, which serve as huge tax revenue, directly or indirectly reduces the resources domestically available to the developing countries to meet their SR obligations. For example, McKinley's study reveals that between the early 1990s and the early 2000s, trade liberalisation led to a 5% reduction of revenue tariffs in 25 low-income countries which led to insufficiency in locally mobilised resources for development needs.[196] The fact that ODA is not disbursed based on an objective assessment but on donor interests ranging from the maintenance of colonial ties, military alliances, the protection of spheres of influence, and trade and investment ties,[197] shows that it is not a dependable source of resources for SR realisation.

Therefore, this chapter calls for a halt to the imposition of trade liberalisation as a condition for international cooperation and assistance. Using ODA as a trade or economic tool negates its essence, which is to assist developing countries in meeting their development needs. Research reveals that although there are positive results (about 91% compliance as of 2017) towards untying ODA commitments whereby recipient countries are free to determine procurement partners regarding ODA projects, some donors still insist that procurements regarding projects funded by their ODA contribution must be contracted to companies in the donor countries, thereby fettering the discretion of the recipient country.[198] This ought not to be. Teleguiding recipient countries on procurement processes amounts to a contravention of the 2005 Paris Declaration on Aid Effectiveness and the 2008 Accra Agenda for Action. These documents which most countries willingly adopted have been recognised – even by the UN – as important commitment documents on aid utilisation. The documents emphasise the need to give recipient countries some 'breathing space' in their choice of suppliers of goods and services needed to complete ODA projects.

4.8 Conclusion

The globalised nature and compact dynamics of contemporary issues of concern, such as climate change and pandemics justify a call for an international cooperation approach to addressing the issues. This call is also relevant in SR realisation, because of the devastating impact which the activities of multinational entities and individuals may have on people living overseas. Thus, it is pertinent that nations cooperate internationally with a view to mobilising resources to address socioeconomic needs whenever and wherever they arise. Sadly, there has been a lack of international cooperation framework on using taxation as an effective tool for mobilising globally available resources for the realisation of these needs. This chapter has examined the link between an effective tax system and the realisation of SR. While it acknowledges the laudable efforts of the OECD on tax cooperation, it argues that such efforts have still not produced the desirable outcomes of a universal and participatory tax cooperation regime. The chapter considers the UN's recent enthusiasm and evolving efforts aimed at establishing a UN legal and institutional framework for international tax cooperation. It is hoped that states will cooperate with the UN and with one another to address global tax inequities which have created new and exacerbated existing systemic imbalances among developed countries and developing countries. While the evolving UN's initiative may not be a full-blown solution to 'every barrier to inclusive and effective international tax cooperation', it will most likely serve 'as a space in which these barriers can be accommodated and gradually reduced'.[199]

Notes

1 Ignacio Saiz, 'Resourcing Rights: Combating Tax Injustice from a Human Rights Perspective' in Aoife Nolan, Rory O'Connell & Colin Harvey (eds) *Human Rights and Public Finance: Budgets & the Promotion of Economic and Social Rights* (Hart Publishing, 2013) 77.
2 Tom Cardamone & Edith Nyabicha, 'Curbing Illicit Financial Flows to Enhance Domestic Resource Mobilisation: Leveraging Transfer Pricing Strategies to Close Tax Loopholes in Uganda' (November 2023 Policy Brief, Global Financial Integrity) 1.
3 Courtney Jung, Ran Hirschl & Evan Rosevear, 'Economic and Social Rights in National Constitutions' (2014) 62 Am J Comp L 1043–1094, 1053.
4 Art. 6.
5 Art. 7.
6 Art. 8.
7 Art. 9.
8 Art. 10.
9 Art 11.
10 Art. 12.
11 Arts. 13 & 14.
12 Nigeria's National Tax Policy(NTP), 2017, para 2.2.7., available at: https://www.firs.gov.ng/wp-content/uploads/2021/01/National-Tax-Policy-Revised-2017.pdf (accessed on 04/01/2024).
13 For example, arts. 19, 20 and 43 of the Kenyan Constitution 2010.
14 For example, chapter II of the Constitution of the Federal Republic of Nigeria, 1999.
15 Danwood Mzikenge Chirwa & Lilian Chenwi (eds) *The Protection of Economic, Social and Cultural Rights in Africa*, (CUP, 2016) xxi–xxii.
16 *Mitu-Bell Welfare Society v Kenya Airports Authority & Others* [2021] eKLR (Petition 3 of 2018), [2021] KESC 34 (KLR), ILDC 3265 (KE 2021), 11th January 2021, Supreme Court, para 149.
17 *Mitu-Bell Welfare Society v Kenya Airports Authority & Others* [2021] eKLR (Petition 3 of 2018), [2021] KESC 34 (KLR), ILDC 3265 (KE 2021), 11th January 2021, Supreme Court, para 153.
18 *Mitu-Bell Welfare Society v Kenya Airports Authority & Others* [2021] eKLR (Petition 3 of 2018), [2021] KESC 34 (KLR), ILDC 3265 (KE 2021), 11th January 2021, Supreme Court, para 149.
19 *Mitu-Bell Welfare Society v Kenya Airports Authority & Others* [2021] eKLR (Petition 3 of 2018), [2021] KESC 34 (KLR), ILDC 3265 (KE 2021), 11th January 2021, Supreme Court, para 149.
20 See Harun Rashid, Hussein Warsame & Shahid Khan, 'Tax Collections and Democracy in Developing and Developed Countries' in Ali Farazmand (ed) *Global*

Encyclopedia of Public Administration, Public Policy, and Governance (Springer, 2021); Roger Gordon & Wei Li, 'Tax Structures in Developing Countries: Many Puzzles and a Possible Explanation' (2009) 93 (7) *Journal of Public Economics 855.*

21 For a detailed discussion on this, see Philip Alston & Nikki R. Reisch (eds) *Tax, Inequality, and Human Rights* (OUP 2019).

22 Olivier De Schutter, 'Taxing for the Realization of Economic, Social, and Cultural Rights' in Alston & Reisch (n 21) 60.

23 Olivier De Schutter, 'Taxing for the Realization of Economic, Social, and Cultural Rights' in Alston & Reisch (n 21) 60.

24 Halim Abdul & Rahman Mominur, 'The effect of taxation on sustainable development goals: Evidence from emerging countries' (2022) 8 (9) *Heliyon* 3.

25 CESCR, 'General Comment No. 24 (2017) on State Obligations under the International Covenant on Economic, Social and Cultural Rights in the Context of Business Activities' para 23.

26 Saiz (n 1) 83; Deborah Brautigam, Odd-Helge Fjeldstad & Mick Moore (eds) *Taxation and State-Building in Developing Countries: Capacity and Consent* (CUP, 2008); Michael L Rose, 'Does Taxation Lead to Representation?' (2004) 34 British Journal of Political Science 229.

27 Diane Elson, Radhika Balakrishnan & James Heintz, 'Public Finance, Maximum Available Resources and Human Rights' in Nolan, O'Connell & Harvey (n 1) 26.

28 Brian Roach, 'Taxes in the United States: History, Fairness, and Current Political Issues', in *Global Development and Environment Institute* (Tufts University, 2010) 1.

29 Danilo Turk, 'Report of the Special Rapporteur on the Realisation of Economic, Social and Cultural Rights' (UN Doc E/CN.4/Sub.2/1992/16).

30 See generally Wilson Prichard, *Taxation, Responsiveness and Accountability in Sub-Saharan Africa: The Dynamics of Tax Bargaining* (CUP, 2015).

31 Mike Pfister, 'Taxation for Investment and Development: An Overview of Policy Challenges in Africa' (2009) 5, available at: https://www.oecd.org/investment/investmentfordevelopment/43966821.pdf (accessed on 03/01/2024).

32 CESCR, 'Concluding Observations on the Initial Report of Burundi' (15 October 2015) UN Doc E/C.12/BDI/CO/1, para 13f.

33 CESCR, 'Concluding Observations on the Sixth Periodic Report of the United Kingdom of Great Britain and Northern Ireland' (13 July 2016) UN Doc E/C.12/GBR/CO/6, para 16f.

34 Abdul Muheet Chowdhary & Sol Picciotto, 'Streamlining the Architecture of International Tax through a UN Framework Convention on Tax Cooperation' (2021) 21 Tax Cooperation Policy Brief 6.

35 See Robert E Robertson, 'Measuring State Compliance with the Obligation to devote the "Maximum Available Resources" to Realizing Economic, Social, and Cultural Right' (1994) 16(4) *Human Rights Quarterly* 693–714, 695–697; Geraldine Van Bueren, 'Of Floors and Ceilings: Minimum Core Obligations and Children' in Danie Brand & Sage Russell (eds) *Exploring the Core Content of Economic and Social Rights: South African and International Perspectives* (Protea Book House, 2002) 185.

36 See Principle 15 of the Principles.

37 See Principle 15 of the Principles.

38 Eghosa Ekhator, Chisa Onyejekwe & Newman Richards, 'Human Rights and Taxation in Developing Countries: A Case for Tax Justice and Accountability in Africa' in Damilola Olawuyi & Oyeniyi Abe (eds) *Business and Human Rights Law and Practice in Africa* (Edward Elgar Publishing, 2022) 135.

39 Committee on the Rights of the Child, 'Day of General Discussion – Resources for the Rights of the Child: Responsibility of States', 46th Session (2007) para 6.

40 Nigeria's NTP, para 1.2.

41 See *UBN Plc v Ifeoruwa Nig. (Ent.) Ltd* (2007) 7 NWLR (pt 1032) 71 where it was held that a policy document is not legally binding.
42 Cardamone & Nyabicha (n2) 1.
43 See Chapter II of the Nigerian Constitution.
44 Section 24(f) of the Nigerian Constitution which is domiciled under the chapter on Directive Principles imposes a duty on every citizen to 'declare his income honestly to appropriate and lawful agencies and pay his tax promptly'.
45 For example, see para 1.3 of Nigeria's NTP.
46 Ekhator, Onyejekwe, and Richards (n 38) 137.
47 See Shola Soleye, 'Group Appeals Judgment On Tax Condition For Lagos Public School Enrolment'(Channels TV, 09 October 2023) available at: https://www.channelstv.com/2023/10/09/group-appeals-court-judgment-on-access-to-public-schools (accessed on 04/01/2024).
48 *Incorporated Trustees of 1SH-16 Human Rights & Social Justice Initiative (for and on Behalf of Disadvantaged Children of Lagos State) v Lagos State Government & Ors* (Suit No. ID/14042MFHR/22).
49 This Charter has been legislatively domesticated and pronounced enforceable in Nigeria by the Supreme Court. It is superior to all domestic laws other than the Constitution. See *Fawehinmi v Abacha* (2000) 6 NWLR (pt 660)228; *Centre for Oil Pollution Watch v NNPC* [2019] 5 NWLR 518.
50 (2002)9 NWLR (Pt. 772)222, (2002)6 SC (Pt 1)1.
51 Philip E Oamen & Eunice O Erhagbe, 'The Impact of Climate Change on Economic and Social Rights Realisation in Nigeria: International Cooperation and Assistance to the Rescue?' (2021) 21 (2) African Human Rights Law Journal 1080–1111.
52 Section 1 of the Tertiary Education Trust Fund (Establishment, ETC) Act 2011.
53 Udochukwu B. Akuru, 'Taxes to finance tertiary education: lessons from Nigeria's TETFund' (Global Dev., 10 May 2023) available at: https://globaldev.blog/taxes-to-finance-tertiary-education-lessons-from-nigerias-tetfund/ (accessed on 01 April 2024).
54 Udochukwu B. Akuru, 'Taxes to finance tertiary education: lessons from Nigeria's TETFund' (Global Dev., 10 May 2023) available at: https://globaldev.blog/taxes-to-finance-tertiary-education-lessons-from-nigerias-tetfund/ (accessed on 01 April 2024).
55 Brett R. Wilkinson & Amy M. Hageman, 'The Role of Political Elites in Income Tax System Design and Tax Fairness' (2023) 55 (3) *The British Accounting Review* 101172.
56 Roach (n 28) 1.
57 Ekhator, Onyejekwe & Richards (n 38)127.
58 See generally Magdalena Sepulveda, *The Nature of the Obligations under the International Covenant on Economic, Social and Cultural Rights* (Intersentia, 2003).
59 Elson, Balakrishnan & Heintz (n27) 16.
60 See generally Philip Ebosetale Oamen, 'Realisation of Economic and Social Rights in Nigeria: The Role of National and International Cooperation' (PhD Thesis submitted and defended at the University of Birmingham, 2022).
61 Pfister (n31).
62 Pfister (n31).
63 See generally Newman U Richards, 'Sustainable Development Goals and Taxation in Nigeria' (2021) 47(3) Commonwealth Law Bulletin 570–588.
64 Emo Idornigie Pearce & Chisa Onyejekwe, 'Taxation and the Implementation of Sustainable Development Goals in Nigeria' in Eghosa O Ekhator, Servel Miller & Etinosa Igbinosa (eds) *Implementing the Sustainable Development Goals in Nigeria: Barriers, Prospects and Strategies* (Routledge, 2021) 145.

65 See Jia Liu & Olatunde Julius Otusanya, 'How Multinationals Avoid Taxes in Africa and What Should Change' in (*The Conversation*, 05 April 2022) available at: https://theconversation.com/how-multinationals-avoid-taxes-in-africa-and-what-should-change-179797; Olatunde Julius Otusanya, 'Anti-social Tax Practices and Social Economic Development in Nigeria: The Stakeholders' Perceptions' (2013) 2 (4) *AJAF* 360.
66 Jonathan Todres & Charlotte S Alexander, 'Bringing the Right to Education into the 21st Century' (2024) 42 *Berkeley Journal of International Law (BJIL)* available at SSRN: https://ssrn.com/abstract=4391829 (accessed on 03/01/2025).
67 Internal Revenue Service, 'Federal Tax Compliance Research: Tax Gap Estimates for Tax Years 2008–2010' Publication 1415 (Rev. 5-2016) Washington, DC, 6 available at: https://www.irs.gov/pub/irs-soi/p1415.pdf (accessed on 03/01/2025).
68 Pfister (n31).
69 Elson, Balakrishnan & Heintz (n 27) 27.
70 G77, 'Ministerial Declaration' (2020) para 64, available at https://www.g77.org/doc/Declaration2020.htm (accessed on 10/01/2024).
71 See Meghan Campbell, 'Cooperating to Continuously Improve Living Conditions' in Jessie Hohmann & Beth Goldblatt(eds) *The Right to Continuous Improvement of Living Conditions* (Hart 2021) 41.
72 See Hakeem Yusuf & Philip Oamen, 'Realising Economic and Social Rights Beyond COVID-19: The Imperative of International Cooperation' (2022) 32 (1) *Indiana International & Comparative Law Review* 43–68.
73 Josh Curtis & Shane Darcy 'The Right to a Social and International Order for the Realisation of Human Rights: Article 28 of the Universal Declaration and International Cooperation' in David Keane & Yvonne McDermott (eds) *The Challenge of Human Rights: Past, Present and Future*, (Edward Elgar Publishing: 2012) available at https://aran.library.nuigalway.ie/bitstream/handle/10379/2185/CURTIS%20AND%20DARCY%20Article%2028%20and%20International%20Coop.pdf?sequence=1&isAllowed=y (accessed on 08/01/2024) 12.
74 See Sigrun Skogly, *Beyond National Borders: States' Human Rights Obligations in International Cooperation*, (Intersentia, 2006) 85; Roland Burke, 'Some Rights Are More Equal than Others: The Third World and the Transformation of Economic and Social Rights (2014) 3 *Humanity Journal* 427–448, 439.
75 Curtis & Darcy (n73) 13.
76 Oamen (n 60) 159.
77 Oamen (n 60) 159.
78 Similarly, the Guidelines on Treaty-Specific Documents to be submitted by States Parties under Articles 16 and 17 ICESCR,24 March 2009, E/C.12/2008/2 also mandate States to indicate international cooperation and assistance rendered or given during a particular review period.
79 CESCR, 'General Comment No. 3: The Nature of States Parties' Obligations (Art. 2, Para. 1, of the Covenant)' 14 December 1990 (Document E/1991/23), Paras 13 & 14.
80 CESCR, 'General Comment No. 3: The Nature of States Parties' Obligations (Art. 2, Para. 1, of the Covenant)' 14 December 1990 (Document E/1991/23), para 14.
81 Maastricht Principles on Extraterritorial Obligations of States in the area of Economic, Social and Cultural Rights, art. 31.
82 Saiz (n 1) 80.
83 Fons Coomans, 'The Extraterritorial Scope of the International Covenant on Economic, Social and Cultural Rights in the Work of the United Nations Committee on Economic, Social and Cultural Rights' (2011) 11 (1) *Human Rights Law Review* 1–35, 5.

84 Sigrun I Skogly & Mark Gibney, 'Economic Rights and Extraterritorial Obligations' in Shareen Hertel & Lanse Minkler (eds) Economic *Rights: Conceptual, Measurement and Policy Issues* (Cambridge University Press,2007) 267.
85 Oamen & Erhagbe (n 51) 1080.
86 Philip Alston & Gerard Quinn, 'The Nature and Scope of States Parties Obligations Under ICESCR' (1987) 9 *Human Rights Quarterly* 156, 191.
87 Olivier De Schutter, 'The International Dimensions of the Right to Development: A Fresh Start towards Improving Accountability' Human Rights Council Working Group on the Right to Development Nineteenth session 23 – 27 April 2018, 3 available at: https://www.ohchr.org/sites/default/files/Documents/Issues/Development/Session19/A_HRC_WG.2_19_CRP.1.pdf (accessed on 03/01/2024).
88 Oamen (n 60).
89 See Alexander Hamilton, James Madison & John Jay, *The Federalist Papers*, 1969 Paper No. 33, 198.
90 C Gusy, 'Demokraticdefizite postnationaler Gemeinschaften unter Berucksichtigung der Europaischen Union' in H Brunkhorst & M Kettner (eds) Glosaliserung und Democratie, Wirtschaft, Recht. Medien 2000, 131, cited in Thomas Cottier & Maya Hertig, 'The Prospects of 21st Century Constitutionalism' (2003) 7 *Max Planck UNYB* 305.
91 Raymond Breton, 'Identification in Transnational Political Communities' in K Knop, et al (eds) *Rethinking Federalism: Citizens, Markets, and Governments in a Changing World* (UBS Press, 1995) 41.
92 Anne Peters, Elemente einer Theorie der Verfassung Europas, 2001, 214, cited in Cottier & Hertig (n 90) 309.
93 Aoife O'Donoghue, *Constitutionalism in Global Constitutionalisation* (CUP, 2014).
94 De Schutter (n 87) 16.
95 Bakhtiyar Aslanbayli, 'Different Aspects of Interstate Cooperation in the Elimination of Double Taxation' (2022) 8 (171) *Eurasian Law Journal* 45-51, 45.
96 Bakhtiyar Aslanbayli, 'Different Aspects of Interstate Cooperation in the Elimination of Double Taxation' (2022) 8 (171) *Eurasian Law Journal* 45-51, 45.
97 James Thuo Gathii, 'TWAIL: A Brief History of Its Origins, Its Decentralized Network, and a Tentative Bibliography' (2011) 3 *Trade Law & Development* 26, 34.
98 Obiora Chinedu Okafor, 'Critical Third World Approaches to International Law (TWAIL): Theory, Methodology, or Both?' (2008) 10 *International Community Law Review* 371, 377.
99 Makau Mutua, 'What is TWAIL?' (2000) 94 *American Society of International Law Proceedings* 31, 36.
100 Oamen (n 60).
101 Ibironke T Odumosu, 'Challenges for the (Present/) Future of Third World Approaches to International Law' (2008) 10 Int'l Comm L Rev 467, 468.
102 James Thuo Gathii, 'Third World Approaches to International Economic Governance' in Richard Falk, Balakrishnan Rajagopal, Jacqueline Stevens (eds) *International Law and the Third World: Reshaping Justice* (Routledge, 2008) 255.
103 Opeoluwa Adetoro Badaru, 'The Right to Food and the Political Economy of Third World States' (2014) 1 Transnat'l Hum Rts Rev. 106, 116.
104 Antony Anghie, 'TWAIL: Past and Future' (2008) 10 *International Community Law Review* 479, 480.
105 Obiora Chinedu Okafor, 'Newness, Imperialism and International Legal Reform in our Time: A TWAIL Perspective' (2005) 43 *Osgoode Hall Law Journal* 176–177.
106 Gathii (n 97) 259.
107 Gathii (n 97) 259.
108 Oamen (n 60).
109 Badaru (n 103) 121.

110 BS Chimni, 'Third World Approaches to International Law: A Manifesto' (2006) 8 *International Community Law Review* 1–27, 1.
111 Rasmus Corlin Christensen, Martin Hearson & Tovony Randriamanalina, 'At the Table, Off the Menu? Assessing the Participation of Lower-Income Countries in Global Tax Negotiations'(ICTD Working Paper 115, 2020) 5 available at https://opendocs.ids.ac.uk/opendocs/bitstream/handle/20.500.12413/15853/ICTD_WP115.pdf?sequence=9 (accessed on 12/01/2024).
112 Tax Justice Network Africa, 'RE: Tax Justice Network Africa's Inputs to the Tax Report 2023 on Promotion of Inclusive and Effective Tax Cooperation at the United Nations' (A submission to the UN) available at https://globaltaxjustice.org/libraries/letter-200-csos-and-trade-unions-support-un-draft-resolution-for-inclusive-tax-cooperation/ (accessed on 12/01/2024).
113 UN, 'Promotion of Inclusive and Effective International Tax Cooperation at the United Nations: Report of the Secretary-General' (A/78/235) para 31 available at https://documents-ddsny.un.org/doc/UNDOC/GEN/N23/220/39/PDF/N2322039.pdf?OpenElement.
114 *I* UN, 'Promotion of Inclusive and Effective International Tax Cooperation at the United Nations: Report of the Secretary-General' (A/78/235) para 31 available at https://documents-ddsny.un.org/doc/UNDOC/GEN/N23/220/39/PDF/N2322039.pdf?OpenElement. South Africa is just a key partner of the OECD.
115 Abosede Abidemi Oladiji, 'Global Tax Regulation and Developing Countries' (A Thesis submitted to the Faculty of Graduate Studies of the University of Manitoba in partial fulfilment of the requirements of the degree of Master of Law, 2018) 57.
116 Abosede Abidemi Oladiji, 'Global Tax Regulation and Developing Countries' (A Thesis submitted to the Faculty of Graduate Studies of the University of Manitoba in partial fulfilment of the requirements of the degree of Master of Law, 2018) 57.
117 Ruth Mason, 'The Transformation of International Tax' (2020) 114 (3) *American Journal of International Law* 353–402.
118 OECD, 'Putting an End to Offshore Tax Evasion' available at https://www.oecd.org/tax/transparency/ (accessed on 12/01/2024).
119 OECD, 'Tax Cooperation for Development: Progress Report on 2022' (2022) availableat:https://www.oecd.org/tax/tax-global/tax-co-operation-for-development-progress-report-on-2022.pdf (accessed on 12/01/2024).
120 OECD, 'Tax Cooperation for Development: Progress Report on 2022' (2022) availableat:https://www.oecd.org/tax/tax-global/tax-co-operation-for-development-progress-report-on-2022.pdf (accessed on 12/01/2024).
121 OECD, 'Tax Cooperation for Development: Progress Report on 2022' (2022) availableat:https://www.oecd.org/tax/tax-global/tax-co-operation-for-development-progress-report-on-2022.pdf (accessed on 12/01/2024).
122 OECD, 'Developing Countries and the OECD/G20 Inclusive Framework on BEPS' (OECD Report for the G20 Finance Ministers and Central Bank Governors, October 2021, Italy) available at https://www.oecd.org/tax/beps/developing-countries-and-the-oecd-g20-inclusive-framework-on-beps.pdf (accessed on 13/01/2024).
123 See OECD, 'Tax Co-operation for Development: Progress Report' (2020) available at http://www.oecd.org/tax/tax-global/tax-co-operation-for-development-progressreport.htm; Ben Dickinson, 'The Inclusive Framework is Considering Radical Proposals, but in *the Real World…' (18 November 2019) International Centre for Tax and Development (ICTD)* Blog Post available at https://www.ictd.ac/blog/oecd-inclusive-framework-tax-proposals-negotiation/ (accessed on 13/01/2024).
124 Christensen, Hearson & Randriamanalina (n 111) 7.
125 Chowdhary & Picciotto (n34).
126 Thorkil Kristensen, 'Five Years of O.E.C.D' (1967) 13 European Yearbook 100–109, 103–104, cited in Tony Porter & Michael Webb, 'The Role of the OECD

in the Orchestration of Global Knowledge Networks' (2007) 3 available at https://www.cpsa-acsp.ca/papers-2007/Porter-Webb.pdf (accessed on 13/01/2024).

127 Oladiji (n115) 61.

128 Javier G. Salinas, 'The OECD Tax Competition Initiative: A Critique of its Merits in the Global Marketplace' (2003) 25 (3) *Houston Journal of International Law* 532, 550–559.

129 US Department of Treasury, 'Remarks by Secretary of the Treasury Janet L. Yellen at the Summit for Democracy' (09 December 2021), available at https://home.treasury.gov/news/press-releases/jy0524.

130 The Guardian, 'The Guardian View on a UN Treaty: Stop Rich Nations acting like the Tax Havens they condemn' (Editorial, 09 December 2023).

131 See UN (n 113) footnote 28 ('In 2022, the annual fee to join the Inclusive Framework was €21,500 (approximately $24,000). In 2016, the minimum annual fee for the Global Forum was €15,300 (just under $17,000 at the time)').

132 Chowdhary & Picciotto (n34).

133 Besson Samantha, 'State Consent and Disagreement in International Law-Making. Dissolving the Paradox' (2016) 29 (2) *Leiden Journal of International Law* 289–316.

134 *Asylum (Columbia v. Peru)* [1950] ICJ Rep 266.

135 International Law Association, 'London Conference Final Report of Commission on Formation of Customary (General) International Law, Statement of Principles Applicable to the Formation of General Customary International Law' (2000) 8; *North Sea Continental Shelf case (Germany v. Denmark and Germany v. the Netherlands)*, Judgment of 20 February 1969, [1969] ICJ Rep. 1969, 3; Thomas Buergenthal & Sean D Murphy, *Public International Law* (3rd edn, 2002) 18.

136 Oladiji (n 115) 58.

137 Roozbeh (Rudy) B Baker, 'Customary International Law in the 21st Century: Old Challenges and New Debates' (2010) 21(1) *European Journal of International Law* 173–204, 177.

138 For a detailed discussion on this, see Irma Johanna Mosquera Valderrama, 'BEPS Principal Purpose Test and Customary International Law' (2020) 33 Leiden Journal of International Law 745–766.

139 UN (n 113) para 42.

140 Tax Justice Network Africa (n 112) 3.

141 Allison Christians, 'Global Trends and Constraints on Tax Policy in the Least Developed Countries' (2010) Legal Studies Research Paper Series (Paper No. 1086) 3.

142 Christensen, Hearson & Randriamanalina (n111) 7.

143 International Bureau of Fiscal Documentation, 'Promotion of Inclusive and Effective Tax' (forthcoming), cited in UN (n113) para 33.

144 International Bureau of Fiscal Documentation, 'Promotion of Inclusive and Effective Tax' (forthcoming), cited in UN (n113) para 33.

145 See, for example, OECD, 'OECD/G20 Inclusive Framework on BEPS Progress Report September 2022 – September 2023' available at https://www.oecd.org/tax/beps/oecd-g20-inclusive-framework-on-beps-progress-report-september-2022-september-2023.pdf (accessed on 12/01/2024).

146 The Guardian (n 130).

147 Chowdhary & Picciotto (n34).

148 UN (n113) para 5.

149 UN (n113) para 5.

150 Lucinda Cadzow, *Et al*, ' Inclusive and Effective International Tax Cooperation: Views From the Global South' (Institute of Development Studies, August 2023) 10 available at https://opendocs.ids.ac.uk/opendocs/bitstream/handle/20.500.12413/18097/ICTD_WP_172_FINAL.pdf?sequence=1&isAllowed=y (accessed on 01 April 2024).

151 Cadzow, et al. (n 150) 19.
152 Thomas Gehring & Benjamin Faude, 'The Dynamics of Regime Complexes: Microfoundations and Systemic Effects' (2013) 19 *Global Governance* 119–130.
153 Cadzow, et al., (n 150) 8.
154 Martin Hearson, 'Corporate Tax Negotiations at the OECD: What's at Stake for Developing Countries in 2020?' (Summary Brief No. 2, 2020) 4 available at https://africaportal.org/wp-content/uploads/2023/05/Corporate_tax_negotiations1.pdf (accessed on 01 April 2024).
155 Martin Hearson, 'Corporate Tax Negotiations at the OECD: What's at Stake for Developing Countries in 2020?' (Summary Brief No. 2, 2020) 4 available at https://africaportal.org/wp-content/uploads/2023/05/Corporate_tax_negotiations1.pdf (accessed on 01 April 2024).
156 Cadzow, et al. (n 150) 19.
157 Martin Hearson, et al., 'Developing Influence: The Power of "The Rest" in Global Tax Governance' (2023) 30 (3) *Review of International Political Economy* 841–864, 842.
158 UN, 'Technical Report of the High-Level Panel on Financing for Development' (2001), para 4 available at https://www.iatp.org/documents/technical-report-of-the-high-level-panel-on-financing-for-development-0; 'Preparatory Committee for the International Conference on Financing for Development' (A/AC.257/23) 13, available at https://digitallibrary.un.org/record/439479?ln=en (accessed on 12/01/2024).
159 UN, 'The Addis Ababa Action Agenda of the Third International Conference on Financing for Development' (2015) para 28, available at: https://sustainabledevelopment.un.org/frameworks/addisababaactionagenda (accessed on 12/01/2024).
160 See https://www.un.org/en/ecosoc/docs/2004/resolution%202004-69.pdf (accessed on 12/01/2024).
161 See https://www.un.org/en/ecosoc/docs/2004/resolution%202004-69.pdf (accessed on 12/01/2024).
162 For example, in 2010, Yemen submitted a draft resolution to the ECOSOC (E/2010/L.10)7 on behalf of the G77 calling for the upgrading of the Committee into an intergovernmental body. See https://documents-dds-ny.un.org/doc/UNDOC/LTD/N10/436/28/PDF/N1043628.pdf?OpenElement; Jose Antonio Ocampo & Heidemarie Wieczorek-Zeulan, 'Intergovernmental Tax Body at the United Nations Implementation Note on FACTI Panel on Recommendation 14b' (FACTI Panel 2021) available at https://factipanel.org/docpdfs/Implementation%20Note%20-%20Intergovernmental%20tax%20body%20-%2014B.pdf (accessed on 12/01/2024). Also see Chowdhary & Picciotto (n 34).
163 See generally Chowdhary & Picciotto (n 34).
164 See generally Chowdhary & Picciotto (n 34) 4.
165 See generally Chowdhary & Picciotto (n 34) 4. Also see ECOSOC (E/RES/2012/33) para 5 available at: https://financing.desa.un.org/sites/default/files/2023-03/N1242145.pdf (accessed on 14/01/2024).
166 Chowdhary & Picciotto (n 34) 4.
167 UN (n113) para 25.
168 UN, 'United Nations Model Double Taxation Convention between Developed and Developing Countries 2021'(2021) iii available at https://financing.desa.un.org/sites/default/files/2023-05/UN%20Model_2021.pdf (accessed on 13/01/2024).
169 UN, 'United Nations Model Double Taxation Convention between Developed and Developing Countries 2021'(2021) iii available at https://financing.desa.un.org/sites/default/files/2023-05/UN%20Model_2021.pdf (accessed on 13/01/2024).
170 UN, 'United Nations Model Double Taxation Convention between Developed and Developing Countries 2021'(2021) iii available at https://financing.desa.un.org/sites/default/files/2023-05/UN%20Model_2021.pdf (accessed on 13/01/2024).

171 Anna Isaac, 'UN agrees Global Tax Rules Resolution giving Developing Nations Greater Say' (The Guardian, 23 November 2022) available at https://www.theguardian.com/world/2022/nov/23/un-agrees-global-tax-rules-resolution-giving-developing-nations-greater-say (accessed on 13/01/2024).
172 UN, 'Promotion of Inclusive and Effective International Tax Cooperation at the United Nations' (document A/C.2/77/L.11/Rev.1) available at Concluding Its Session, Second Committee Approves 11 Draft Resolutions, Including Texts on Women's Development, Global Tax Cooperation, Entrepreneurship | UN Press (accessed 09/01/2024).
173 UN, 'Promotion of Inclusive and Effective International Tax Cooperation at the United Nations' (document A/C.2/77/L.11/Rev.1) available at Concluding Its Session, Second Committee Approves 11 Draft Resolutions, Including Texts on Women's Development, Global Tax Cooperation, Entrepreneurship | UN Press (accessed 09/01/2024).
174 UN, 'Promotion of Inclusive and Effective International Tax Cooperation at the United Nations' (document A/C.2/77/L.11/Rev.1) available at Concluding Its Session, Second Committee Approves 11 Draft Resolutions, Including Texts on Women's Development, Global Tax Cooperation, Entrepreneurship | UN Press (accessed 09/01/2024).
175 A/RES/77/244 available at https://digitallibrary.un.org/record/3999979 (accessed on 12/01/2024).
176 A/RES/77/244 available at https://digitallibrary.un.org/record/3999979 (accessed on 12/01/2024).
177 A/RES/77/244 available at https://digitallibrary.un.org/record/3999979 (accessed on 12/01/2024) para 2.
178 A/RES/77/244 available at https://digitallibrary.un.org/record/3999979 (accessed on 12/01/2024) para 3.
179 UN (n 114).
180 UN (n 114) para 6.
181 UN (n 114) para 53.
182 UN (n 114) para 53.
183 UN (n 114) para 54.
184 UN, 'Second Committee Approves Nine Draft Resolutions, Including Texts on International Tax Cooperation, External Debt, Global Climate, Poverty Eradication' (GA/EF/3597) available at https://press.un.org/en/2023/gaef3597.doc.htm.
185 UN, 'Second Committee Approves Nine Draft Resolutions, Including Texts on International Tax Cooperation, External Debt, Global Climate, Poverty Eradication' (GA/EF/3597) available at https://press.un.org/en/2023/gaef3597.doc.htm.
186 UN, 'Second Committee Approves Nine Draft Resolutions, Including Texts on International Tax Cooperation, External Debt, Global Climate, Poverty Eradication' (GA/EF/3597) available at https://press.un.org/en/2023/gaef3597.doc.htm.
187 Tove Ryding, 'Historic Tax Vote paves the Way for a UN Tax Convention' (22 November 2023) available at https://www.eurodad.org/historic_tax_vote_paves_the_way_for_a_un_tax_convention (accessed on 13/01/2024).
188 AU, 'PRESS RELEASES: UN General Assembly Member States Have Voted with a Majority of 125 in Favor of Adopting a Convention on International Tax Cooperation' (22 November 2023) available at https://au.int/en/pressreleases/20231122/un-general-assembly-member-states-have-voted-majority-125-favor-adopting (accessed on 13/01/2024).
189 Saiz (n 1) 102; Nicholas Lusiani, 'Only the Little People Pay Tax: Tax Evasion and the Switzerland's Extraterritorial Obligations to Economic, Social and Cultural Rights in Zambia' in Mark Gibney & Wouter Vandenhole (eds) *Litigating Transnational Human Rights Obligations: Alternative Judgments* (Routledge Press, 2014).
190 CESCR (n 33) para 16–17.

191 De Schutter (n 23) 67.
192 Ronald Chipaike & Matarutse H Knowledge, 'The Question of African Agency in International Relations' (2018) 4(1) *Cogent Social Sciences* 1–16, 3.
193 Mohammed Ayoob, 'Inequality and Theorizing in International Relations: The Case for Subaltern Realism' (2002) 4 (3) *International Studies Review* 27–48.
194 Elson, Balakrishnan & Heintz (n 27) 27.
195 UN, 'Illicit Capital Robbing Africa and its People of their Future: UN Trade and Development Chief' (September 2020) available at https://news.un.org/en/story/2020/09/1074052 (accessed on 05/01/2024); UN Conference on Trade and Development, 'Tackling Illicit Financial Flows for Sustainable Development in Africa' (Economic Development in Africa Report 2020) available at https://unctad.org/system/files/official-document/aldcafrica2020_en.pdf (accessed on 05/01/2024).
196 Terry McKinley, *Why Have Tax Reforms Hampered MDG Financing?* (Brasilia, UNDP International Poverty Centre, 2007) 42.
197 Thad Dunning, 'Conditioning the Effects of Aid: Cold War Politics, Donor Credibility, and Democracy in Africa' (2004) 58(2) International Organization 409–423.
198 OECD, '2020 Report on the DAC Recommendation on Untying ODA' (DCD/DAC(2020)54/FINAL) available at https://one.oecd.org/document/DCD/DAC(2020)54/FINAL/en/pdf (accessed on 08/01/2024); Elson, Balakrishnan & Heintz (n 27) 31–32; Edward J Clay, Matthew Geddes & Luisa Natali, 'Aid Untying: Is it working?' (Overseas Development Institute, 2009) available at https://www.oecd.org/development/evaluation/dcdndep/44549932.pdf (accessed on 17/01/2024).
199 Lucinda Cadzow, et al. (n 150) 24.

Bibliography

Halim Abdul and Rahman Mominur, 'The Effect of Taxation on Sustainable Development Goals: Evidence from Emerging Countries' (2022) 8 (9) *Heliyon*. e10512

Udochukwu B. Akuru, 'Taxes to Finance Tertiary Education: Lessons from Nigeria's TETFund' (Global Dev., 10 May 2023) available at: https://globaldev.blog/taxes-to-finance-tertiary-education-lessons-from-nigerias-tetfund/ (accessed on 01 April 2024).

Philip Alston and Gerard Quinn, 'The Nature and Scope of States Parties Obligations Under ICESCR' (1987) 9 *Human Rights Quarterly*. 156–229.

Philip Alston and Nikki R. Reisch (eds), *Tax, Inequality, and Human Rights* (OUP, 2019).

Antony Anghie, 'TWAIL: Past and Future' (2008) 10 *International Community Law Review*. 479–481.

Bakhtiyar Aslanbayli, 'Different Aspects of Interstate Cooperation in the Elimination of Double Taxation' (2022) 8 (171) *Eurasian Law Journal*. 45–51

AU, 'PRESS RELEASES: UN General Assembly Member States Have Voted with a Majority of 125 in Favor of Adopting a Convention on International Tax Cooperation' (22 November 2023) available at https://au.int/en/pressreleases/20231122/un-general-assembly-member-states-have-voted-majority-125-favor-adopting (accessed on 13/01/2024).

Mohammed Ayoob, 'Inequality and Theorizing in International Relations: The Case for Subaltern Realism' (2002) 4 (3) *International Studies Review*. 27–48.

Opeoluwa Adetoro Badaru, 'The Right to Food and the Political Economy of Third World States' (2014) 1 *Transnational Human Rights Review*. 106–134.

Roozbeh (Rudy) B. Baker, 'Customary International Law in the 21st Century: Old Challenges and New Debates' (2010) 21 (1) *European Journal of International Law*. 173–204.

Deborah Brautigam, Odd-Helge Fjeldstad and Mick Moore (eds), *Taxation and State-Building in Developing Countries: Capacity and Consent* (CUP, 2008).

Raymond Breton, 'Identification in Transnational Political Communities' in K Knop, et al. (eds), *Rethinking Federalism: Citizens, Markets, and Governments in a Changing World* (UBS Press, 1995).

Roland Burke, 'Some Rights Are More Equal than Others: The Third World and the Transformation of Economic and Social Rights' (2014) 3 *Humanity Journal*. 427–448.

Lucinda Cadzow, et al., 'Inclusive and Effective International Tax Cooperation: Views From the Global South' (Institute of Development Studies, August 2023) 10 available at https://opendocs.ids.ac.uk/opendocs/bitstream/handle/20.500.12413/18097/ICTD_WP_172_FINAL.pdf?sequence=1&isAllowed=y (accessed on 01/04/2024).

Meghan Campbell, 'Cooperating to Continuously Improve Living Conditions' in Jessie Hohmann and Beth Goldblatt (eds) *The Right to Continuous Improvement of Living Conditions* (Hart, 2021).

Tom Cardamone and Edith Nyabicha, 'Curbing Illicit Financial Flows to Enhance Domestic Resource Mobilisation: Leveraging Transfer Pricing Strategies to Close Tax Loopholes in Uganda' (November 2023 Policy Brief, Global Financial Integrity). https://gfintegrity.org/report/curbing-illicit-financial-flows-to-enhance-domestic-resource-mobilization-leveraging-transfer-pricing-strategies-to-close-tax-loopholes-in-uganda/

B S Chimni, 'Third World Approaches to International Law: A Manifesto' (2006) 8 *International Community Law Review*. 47–73.

Ronald Chipaike and Matarutse H Knowledge, 'The Question of African Agency in International Relations' (2018) 4 (1) *Cogent Social Sciences*. 1487257.

Danwood Mzikenge Chirwa and Lilian Chenwi (eds), *The Protection of Economic, Social and Cultural Rights in Africa*, (CUP, 2016).

Abdul Muheet Chowdhary and Sol Picciotto, 'Streamlining the Architecture of International Tax through a UN Framework Convention on Tax Cooperation' (2021) 21 *Tax Cooperation Policy Brief*. 1–12.

Rasmus Corlin Christensen, Martin Hearson and Tovony Randriamanalina, 'At the Table, Off the Menu? Assessing the Participation of Lower-Income Countries in Global Tax Negotiations' (ICTD Working Paper 115, 2020) 5 available at https://opendocs.ids.ac.uk/opendocs/bitstream/handle/20.500.12413/15853/ICTD_WP115.pdf?sequence=9 (accessed on 12/01/2024).

Allison Christians, 'Global Trends and Constraints on Tax Policy in the Least Developed Countries' (2010) Legal Studies Research Paper Series (Paper No. 1086) https://papers.ssrn.com/sol3/papers.cfm?abstract_id=1445433

Edward J. Clay, Matthew Geddes and Luisa Natali, 'Aid Untying: Is It Working?' (Overseas Development Institute, 2009) available at https://www.oecd.org/development/evaluation/dcdndep/44549932.pdf (accessed on 17/01/2024).

Fons Coomans, 'The Extraterritorial Scope of the International Covenant on Economic, Social and Cultural Rights in the Work of the United Nations Committee on Economic, Social and Cultural Rights' (2011) 11 (1) *Human Rights Law Review*. 1–35.

Thomas Cottier and Maya Hertig, 'The Prospects of 21st Century Constitutionalism' (2003) 7 *Max Planck UNYB*. 216–328.

Josh Curtis and Shane Darcy, 'The Right to a Social and International Order for the Realisation of Human Rights: Article 28 of the Universal Declaration and International Cooperation' in David Keane and Yvonne McDermott (eds) *The Challenge of Human Rights: Past, Present and Future* (Edward Elgar Publishing, 2012).

Olivier De Schutter, 'The International Dimensions of the Right to Development: A Fresh Start towards Improving Accountability' Human Rights Council Working Group on the Right to Development Nineteenth session 23–27 April 2018, 3 available at: https://www.ohchr.org/sites/default/files/Documents/Issues/Development/Session19/A_HRC_WG.2_19_CRP.1.pdf (accessed on 03/01/2024).

Olivier De Schutter, 'Taxing for the Realization of Economic, Social, and Cultural Rights' in Philip G. Alston & Nikki R. Reisch (eds.) *Tax, Inequality, and Human Rights*, (Oxford University Press, 2019) 59–80.

Ben Dickinson, 'The Inclusive Framework is Considering Radical Proposals, but in *the Real World…*' (18 November 2019) *International Centre for Tax and Development (ICTD)* Blog Post available at https://www.ictd.ac/blog/oecd-inclusive-framework-tax-proposals-negotiation/ (accessed on 13/01/2024).

Thad Dunning, 'Conditioning the Effects of Aid: Cold War Politics, Donor Credibility, and Democracy in Africa' (2004) 58 (2) *International Organization*. 409–423.

Eghosa Ekhator, Chisa Onyejekwe and Newman Richards, 'Human Rights and Taxation in Developing Countries: A Case for Tax Justice and Accountability in Africa' in Damilola Olawuyi and Oyeniyi Abe (eds) *Business and Human Rights Law and Practice in Africa* (Edward Elgar Publishing, 2022).

Diane Elson, Radhika Balakrishnan and James Heintz, 'Public Finance, Maximum Available Resources and Human Rights' in Nolan, O'Connell & Colin Harvey (eds.) *Human Rights and Public Finance: Budgets and the Promotion of Economic and Social Rights* (Hart Publishing 2013)

James Thuo Gathii, 'Third World Approaches to International Economic Governance' in Richard Falk, Balakrishnan Rajagopal and Jacqueline Stevens (eds) *International Law and the Third World: Reshaping Justice* (Routledge, 2008).

James Thuo Gathii, 'TWAIL: A Brief History of Its Origins, Its Decentralized Network, and a Tentative Bibliography' (2011) 3 *Trade, Law and Development*. 26–64

Thomas Gehring and Benjamin Faude, 'The Dynamics of Regime Complexes: Microfoundations and Systemic Effects' (2013) 19 *Global Governance*. 119–130.

Roger Gordon and Wei Li, 'Tax Structures in Developing Countries: Many Puzzles and a Possible Explanation' (2009) 93 (7) *Journal of Public Economics*. 855–866.

C Gusy, 'Demokraticdefizite postnationaler Gemeinschaften unter Berucksichtigung der Europaischen Union' in H Brunkhorst and M Kettner (eds) *Glosaliserung und Democratie* (Wirtschaft, Rech tMedien, 2000).

Alexander Hamilton, James Madison and John Jay, *The Federalist Papers*, 1969 Paper No. 33. https://guides.loc.gov/federalist-papers/full-text

Martin Hearson, 'Corporate Tax Negotiations at the OECD: What's at Stake for Developing Countries in 2020?' (Summary Brief No. 2, 2020) 4 available at https://africaportal.org/wp-content/uploads/2023/05/Corporate_tax_negotiations1.pdf (accessed on 01/04/2024).

Martin Hearson, et al., 'Developing Influence: The Power of "The Rest" in Global Tax Governance' (2023) 30 (3) *Review of International Political Economy*. 841–864.

Anna Isaac, 'UN agrees Global Tax Rules Resolution giving Developing Nations Greater Say' (*The Guardian*, 23 November 2022) available at https://www.theguardian.com/world/2022/nov/23/un-agrees-global-tax-rules-resolution-giving-developing-nations-greater-say (accessed on 13/01/2024).

Courtney Jung, Ran Hirschl and Evan Rosevear, 'Economic and Social Rights in National Constitutions' (2014) 62 *American Journal of Comparative Law*. 1043–1094.

Thorkil Kristensen, 'Five Years of O.E.C.D' (1967) 13 European Yearbook 100–109, 103–104, cited in Tony Porter & Michael Webb, 'The Role of the OECD in the Orchestration of Global Knowledge Networks' (2007) 3 available at https://www.cpsa-acsp.ca/papers-2007/Porter-Webb.pdf (accessed on 13/01/2024).

Jia Liu and Olatunde Julius Otusanya, 'How Multinationals Avoid Taxes in Africa and what Should Change' in (*The Conversation*, 05 April 2022) https://theconversation.com/how-multinationals-avoid-taxes-in-africa-and-what-should-change-179797

Nicholas Lusiani, 'Only the Little People Pay Tax: Tax Evasion and the Switzerland's Extraterritorial Obligations to Economic, Social and Cultural Rights in Zambia' in Mark Gibney and Wouter Vandenhole (eds) *Litigating Transnational Human Rights Obligations: Alternative Judgments* (Routledge Press, 2014).

Ruth Mason, 'The Transformation of International Tax' (2020) 114 (3) *American Journal of International Law*. 353–402.
Terry McKinley, *Why Have Tax Reforms Hampered MDG Financing?* (Brasilia, UNDP International Poverty Centre, 2007).
Makau Mutua, 'What is TWAIL?' (2000) 94 *American Society of International Law Proceedings*. 31–38.
Aoife O'Donoghue, *Constitutionalism in Global Constitutionalisation* (CUP, 2014).
Philip E. Oamen and Eunice O. Erhagbe, 'The Impact of Climate Change on Economic and Social Rights Realisation in Nigeria: International Cooperation and Assistance to the Rescue?' (2021) 21 (2) *African Human Rights Law Journal*. 1080–1111.
Philip Ebosetale Oamen, 'Realisation of Economic and Social Rights in Nigeria: The Role of National and International Cooperation' (PhD Thesis submitted and defended at the University of Birmingham, 2022).
Jose Antonio Ocampo and Heidemarie Wieczorek-Zeulan, 'Intergovernmental Tax Body at the United Nations Implementation Note on FACTI Panel on Recommendation 14b' (FACTI Panel 2021) available at https://factipanel.org/docpdfs/Implementation%20Note%20-%20Intergovernmental%20tax%20body%20-%2014B.pdf (accessed on 12/01/2024).
Ibironke T. Odumosu, 'Challenges for the (Present/) Future of Third World Approaches to International Law' (2008) 10 *International Community Law Review*. 467–477.
OECD, '2020 Report on the DAC Recommendation on Untying ODA' (DCD/DAC(2020a)54/FINAL) available at https://one.oecd.org/document/DCD/DAC(2020)54/FINAL/en/pdf (accessed on 08/01/2024).
OECD, 'Tax Co-operation for Development: Progress Report' (2020b) available at http://www.oecd.org/tax/tax-global/tax-co-operation-for-development-progressreport.htm
OECD, 'Developing Countries and the OECD/G20 Inclusive Framework on BEPS' (OECD Report for the G20 Finance Ministers and Central Bank Governors, October 2021, Italy) available at https://www.oecd.org/tax/beps/developing-countries-and-the-oecd-g20-inclusive-framework-on-beps.pdf (accessed on 13/01/2025).
OECD, 'Tax Cooperation for Development: Progress Report on 2022' (2022) available at: https://www.oecd.org/tax/tax-global/tax-co-operation-for-development-progress-report-on-2022.pdf (accessed on 12/01/2025).
OECD, 'OECD/G20 Inclusive Framework on BEPS Progress Report September 2022–September 2023' (n.d.-a) available at https://www.oecd.org/tax/beps/oecd-g20-inclusive-framework-on-beps-progress-report-september-2022-september-2023.pdf (accessed on 12/01/2025).
OECD, 'Putting an End to Offshore Tax Evasion' (n.d.-b) available at https://www.oecd.org/tax/transparency/ (accessed on 12/01/2025).
Obiora Chinedu Okafor, 'Newness, Imperialism and International Legal Reform in Our Time: A TWAIL Perspective' (2005) 43 *Osgoode Hall Law Journal* 145–161.
Obiora Chinedu Okafor, 'Critical Third World Approaches to International Law (TWAIL): Theory, Methodology, or Both?' (2008) 10 *International Community Law Review*. 371–378.
Abosede Abidemi Oladiji, 'Global Tax Regulation and Developing Countries' (A Thesis submitted to the Faculty of Graduate Studies of the University of Manitoba in partial fulfilment of the requirements of the degree of Master of Law, 2018).
Olatunde Julius Otusanya, 'Anti-social Tax Practices and Social Economic Development in Nigeria: The Stakeholders' Perceptions' (2013) 2 (4) *AJAF*. 360–381.
Emo Idornigie Pearce and Chisa Onyejekwe, 'Taxation and the Implementation of Sustainable Development Goals in Nigeria' in Eghosa O Ekhator, Servel Miller and Etinosa Igbinosa (eds) *Implementing the Sustainable Development Goals in Nigeria: Barriers, Prospects and Strategies* (Routledge, 2021).
Anne Peters, Elemente einer Theorie der Verfassung Europas, (2013).

Mike Pfister, 'Taxation for Investment and Development: An Overview of Policy Challenges in Africa' (2009) 5, available at: https://www.oecd.org/investment/investmentfordevelopment/43966821.pdf (accessed on 03/01/2024).

Wilson Prichard, *Taxation, Responsiveness and Accountability in Sub-Saharan Africa: The Dynamics of Tax Bargaining* (CUP, 2015).

Harun Rashid, Hussein Warsame and Shahid Khan, 'Tax Collections and Democracy in Developing and Developed Countries' in Ali Farazmand (ed) *Global Encyclopedia of Public Administration, Public Policy, and Governance* (Springer, 2021).

Newman U. Richards, 'Sustainable Development Goals and Taxation in Nigeria' (2021) 47 (3) *Commonwealth Law Bulletin*. 570–588.

Brian Roach, 'Taxes in the United States: History, Fairness, and Current Political Issues' in *Global Development and Environment Institute* (Tufts University, 2010).

Robert E. Robertson, 'Measuring State Compliance with the Obligation to devote the "Maximum Available Resources" to Realizing Economic, Social, and Cultural Right' (1994) 16 (4) *Human Rights Quarterly*. 693–714.

Michael L. Rose, 'Does Taxation Lead to Representation?' (2004) 34 *British Journal of Political Science*. 229–249.

Tove Ryding, 'Historic Tax Vote paves the Way for a UN Tax Convention' (22 November 2023) available at https://www.eurodad.org/historic_tax_vote_paves_the_way_for_a_un_tax_convention (accessed on 13/01/2025).

Ignacio Saiz, 'Resourcing Rights: Combating Tax Injustice from a Human Rights Perspective' in Aoife Nolan, Rory O'Connell and Colin Harvey (eds) *Human Rights and Public Finance: Budgets & the Promotion of Economic and Social Rights* (Hart Publishing, 2013).

Javier G. Salinas, 'The OECD Tax Competition Initiative: A Critique of its Merits in the Global Marketplace' (2003) 25 (3) *Houston Journal of International Law*. 531–560.

Besson Samantha, 'State Consent and Disagreement in International Law-Making. Dissolving the Paradox' (2016) 29 (2) *Leiden Journal of International Law*. 289–316.

Magdalena Sepulveda, *The Nature of the Obligations under the International Covenant on Economic, Social and Cultural Rights* (Intersentia, 2003).

Sigrun Skogly, *Beyond National Borders: States' Human Rights Obligations in International Cooperation* (Intersentia, 2006).

Sigrun I Skogly and Mark Gibney, 'Economic Rights and Extraterritorial Obligations' in Shareen Hertel and Lanse Minkler (eds) *Economic Rights: Conceptual, Measurement and Policy Issues* (Cambridge University Press,2007).

Tax Justice Network Africa, 'RE: Tax Justice Network Africa's Inputs to the Tax Report 2023 on Promotion of Inclusive and Effective Tax Cooperation at the United Nations' (A submission to the UN) (11 April 2023) available at https://www.taxjusticeafrica.net/resources/blog/tjnas-inputs-tax-report-2023-promotion-inclusive-and-effective-tax-cooperationn/ (accessed on 12/01/2025).

The Guardian, 'The Guardian View on a UN Treaty: Stop Rich Nations acting like the Tax Havens They Condemn' (Editorial, 09 December 2023). https://www.theguardian.com/commentisfree/2023/dec/20/the-guardian-view-on-a-un-treaty-stop-rich-nations-acting-like-the-tax-havens-they-condemn#:~:text=31-,Guardian%20Pick,in%20which%20it%20is%20earned

Jonathan Todres and Charlotte S. Alexander, 'Bringing the Right to Education into the 21st Century' (2024) 42 *Berkeley Journal of International Law (BJIL)* available at SSRN: https://ssrn.com/abstract=4391829 (accessed on 13/01/2024).

Trade and Development, 'Tackling Illicit Financial Flows for Sustainable Development in Africa' (Economic Development in Africa Report 2020) available at https://unctad.org/system/files/official-document/aldcafrica2020_en.pdf (accessed on 05/01/2024).

UN, 'Technical Report of the High-Level Panel on Financing for Development' (2001), available at https://www.iatp.org/documents/technical-report-of-the-high-level-panel-on-financing-for-development-0

UN, 'The Addis Ababa Action Agenda of the Third International Conference on Financing for Development' (2015), available at: https://sustainabledevelopment.un.org/frameworks/addisababaactionagenda (accessed on 12/01/2024).

UN, 'Illicit Capital Robbing Africa and its People of their Future: UN Trade and Development Chief' (September 2020) available at https://news.un.org/en/story/2020/09/1074052 (accessed on 05/01/2025).

UN, 'United Nations Model Double Taxation Convention between Developed and Developing Countries 2021'(2021) available at https://financing.desa.un.org/sites/default/files/2023-05/UN%20Model_2021.pdf (accessed on 13/01/2025).

UN, 'Promotion of Inclusive and Effective International Tax Cooperation at the United Nations: Report of the Secretary-General' (A/78/235) (2023) available at https://documents-ddsny.un.org/doc/UNDOC/GEN/N23/220/39/PDF/N2322039.pdf?OpenElement

UN, 'Second Committee Approves Nine Draft Resolutions, Including Texts on International Tax Cooperation, External Debt, Global Climate, Poverty Eradication' (GA/EF/3597) (2023) available at https://press.un.org/en/2023/gaef3597.doc.htm

UN, 'Promotion of Inclusive and Effective International Tax Cooperation at the United Nations' (document A/C.2/77/L.11/Rev.1) (2022) available at Concluding Its Session, Second Committee Approves 11 Draft Resolutions, Including Texts on Women's Development, Global Tax Cooperation, Entrepreneurship | UN Press (accessed 09/01/2025). https://digitallibrary.un.org/record/3999979?v=pdf

US Department of Treasury, 'Remarks by Secretary of the Treasury Janet L. Yellen at the Summit for Democracy' (09 December 2021) available at https://home.treasury.gov/news/press-releases/jy0524

Irma Johanna Mosquera Valderrama, 'BEPS Principal Purpose Test and Customary International Law' (2020) 33 *Leiden Journal of International* Law. 745–766.

Geraldine Van Bueren, 'Of Floors and Ceilings: Minimum Core Obligations and Children' in Danie Brand and Sage Russell (eds) *Exploring the Core Content of Economic and Social Rights: South African and International Perspectives* (Protea Book House, 2002).

Brett R. Wilkinson and Amy M. Hageman, 'The Role of Political Elites in Income Tax System Design and Tax Fairness' (2023) 55 (3) *The British Accounting Review*. 101172.

Hakeem Yusuf and Philip Oamen, 'Realising Economic and Social Rights Beyond COVID-19: The Imperative of International Cooperation' (2022) 32 (1) *Indiana International & Comparative Law Review*. 43–68.

Part B

Role of Stakeholders in Taxation

5 Supporting Infrastructure Development Initiatives Using Tax Frameworks in Emerging Economies

Augustine Edobor Arimoro and Habiba Musa†*

5.1 Introduction

For emerging economies, infrastructure development is critical for enabling economic growth and improving overall quality of life.[1] However, massive deficits in infrastructure plague many developing nations. Traditional roads, power grids, sanitation systems and telecommunications networks are often inadequate or absent in these countries.[2] This severely hampers economic productivity and global competitiveness.[3] The human impact is also profound, as a lack of basic infrastructure impedes health, education and other aspects central to human development. Bridging the infrastructure gap is thus an urgent priority across the developing world.[4]

Infrastructure development requires enormous capital investment. Many emerging economies lack the public funding needed to support such large-scale projects. This necessitates private-sector financing and participation. However, attracting sufficient private investment faces challenges. Investors and contractors perceive major risks in emerging markets, including political instability, weak legal frameworks and possibilities of expropriation.[5] Returns on investment are also uncertain. This can inhibit the private sector's enthusiasm for infrastructure projects.[6]

Tax policy potentially provides powerful tools to help overcome these barriers. Taxation has traditionally been viewed narrowly to generate revenue for government budgets.[7] However, increasingly, taxation plays a broader developmental role. Thoughtfully designed tax policies and incentives can achieve economic and social objectives beyond just funding the state.[8] With infrastructure deficits being a key constraint for emerging economies, taxation presents an underutilised lever to spur private sector development.

This chapter argues that emerging economies should utilise taxation measures to incentivise and accelerate private infrastructure development. Targeted

* Senior Lecturer in Law, School of Law, University of West London, augustine.arimoro@uwl.ac.uk.
† Professor, Faculty of Law, Nasarawa State University, Keffi E: habibahmusa@nsuk.edu.ng.

DOI: 10.4324/9781003432890-7

tax breaks and exemptions can lower risks and increase returns for investors in major road, power and other projects. Tax incentives can take various forms – including subsidised financing, accelerated depreciation, import duty waivers and tax holidays.[9] The overall aim is to make infrastructure investment more commercially attractive for private developers and contractors.

When framed appropriately, tax incentives can support infrastructure development in avoiding negative impacts on overall tax revenue. Safeguards can ensure investors deliver on commitments and do not abuse generous tax benefits. Compliance regimes can be strengthened alongside offering tax breaks to mitigate any losses. The developmental impact generated through growth in infrastructure makes the trade-off economically and socially beneficial for emerging economies.[10]

There are successful precedents for utilising tax policy tools to catalyse infrastructure progress. For example, India has granted 10-year tax holidays on profits earned on infrastructure projects meeting certain criteria.[11] South Africa, on its part, exempts qualifying infrastructure bond interest income from taxes to lower financing costs.[12] In Latin America, Colombia and Peru have enacted tax incentives targeting transport, energy and other infrastructure.[13] Where efficiently implemented, such policies have mobilised private capital flows into urgent national infrastructure priorities.

This chapter highlights these and other case studies demonstrating the effective deployment of tax incentives for infrastructure. It will analyse incentive design, implementation and impact across countries. Challenges and lessons around balancing developmental aims and fiscal prudence will be examined. Most critically tailored recommendations will be presented for how emerging economies can best leverage tax policy to attract greater private investment into roads, utilities, telecoms and other foundational infrastructure.

Infrastructure is crucial for unlocking productivity, growth, jobs and services – but requires major capital outlays. For developing countries facing large infrastructure gaps, private sector involvement augurs hope for progress. Tax incentives can catalyse this private participation. This paper will illuminate how emerging economies can strategically employ targeted tax measures to accelerate infrastructure advancement. With thoughtful implementation, taxation policy can extend far beyond funding the government, to enabling national development.[14]

5.2 Traditional View of Taxation as Revenue Generation

Historically, taxation has been conceived narrowly as a means for governments to raise revenue to fund public budgets and state operations. In this conventional perspective, the core purpose of taxation is fiscal – to provide finances for government expenditure.[15] Taxation provides states the income needed to deliver public services, administer justice, provide defence and carry out other governing functions entailing financial costs. This traditional revenue-centric view of taxation emerged alongside the rise of centralised governance and persists as an influential framing in modern times.[16]

The origins of organised taxation can be traced back over five millennia to ancient Mesopotamian and Egyptian societies. Rulers imposed various forms of taxes on subjects – in grain, other goods or labour to finance the administrative apparatus of early states.[17] Over 2000 years ago, the political theorist Kautilya wrote in the Arthashastra that revenue collection enables the king to maintain law and order, underscoring taxation's budgetary role.[18] Subsequent philosophers and economists emphasised this fiscal purpose. Ibn Khaldun described tax revenues as necessary to fund soldiers and state functions.[19] David Hume called taxes essential for security provision.[20] To Adam Smith, taxes pay for public goods like infrastructure.[21] John Stuart Mill linked taxes to state responsibilities like education.[22] Adolph Wagner connected taxes to the growing financial needs of modern governments.[23] These and other prominent scholars endorsed taxation as chiefly a revenue tool.

Modern states have expansive financial requirements that necessitate substantial taxation. Major budgetary expenditures include public sector salaries, defence, infrastructure, healthcare, education, pensions, social welfare programmes and more. On average across OECD countries, government spending equals 33% of GDP.[24] Tax revenue pays for most of this outlay. In Denmark, for example, it is about 80%.[25] This intertwined relationship between taxation and state budgets underlies the traditional perspective of its core purpose as fiscal.

However, this conventional viewpoint exhibits limitations. First, it overlooks taxation's potential to shape economic incentives and outcomes beyond mere revenue generation. Tax design can further additional goals such as reducing inequality, improving healthcare access and so on.[26] Second, standard fiscal thinking ignores how tax regimes distribute burdens unevenly based on political and philosophical principles. Tax policy embodies judgments on equitable contributions reflecting the ability to pay.[27] Finally, the typical framework unduly narrows taxation into a technocratic exercise, obscuring the profound social contract it represents between state and citizen.

A purely fiscal approach poorly equips tax policy to address complex modern challenges. Concerns like technology disruption, climate change, ageing populations and inequality require taxation to play a more versatile role.[28] Expanding its purpose enables leveraging tax tools to drive inclusive growth, sustainable development and other public aims.[29] Hence, while financing government remains critical, contemporary perspectives recognise taxation's wider potential for achieving economic and social policy objectives. This multidimensional view better harnesses taxation to promote national progress.[30]

5.3 Expanding the Role of Taxation in Development

While revenue generation remains an essential function, taxation in modern times is recognised as having immense potential beyond fiscal purposes. Thoughtfully designed tax policies can achieve broader economic, social and environmental objectives. This represents an expanding perspective on taxation's role in enabling multidimensional development.

Taxation possesses powerful mechanisms to shape behaviours and incentives. Taxes inherently induce individuals and firms to adjust to minimise burdens. This response can be leveraged by policymakers to further non-revenue goals aligned with national priorities. As former International Monetary Fund (IMFP chief, Christine Lagarde summarised, 'Tax is about more than just raising revenues. It is also a powerful tool for governments to affect people's lives.'[31]

One major dimension is using tax policy to drive economic development and growth. Tax reforms aimed at attracting investment, stimulating business activity, promoting exports and enhancing competitiveness accelerate development.[32] Strategic tax incentives and credits also foster growth sectors, innovation and human capital foundations for advancement.[33] Beyond direct economic impacts, taxation also increasingly serves equity and social welfare objectives including reducing poverty and inequality.[34]

Additionally, tax policy is gaining recognition as an instrument to achieve environmental aims like emission reductions, energy efficiency and conservation. Charging industries for pollution created via carbon taxes or emission permit auctions incentivises mitigation actions. Tax preferences for clean energy and 'green' products spur environmental transitions. Thus, from economic, social and environmental perspectives, thought leaders now advocate broadening taxation's scope beyond simple revenue raising.[35]

5.3.1 Tax Policy for Development

Taxation possesses multiple mechanisms to accelerate economic development in developing countries. Lower corporate and individual income tax rates encourage greater investment, entrepreneurship and effort. Allowances, credits and exemptions can stimulate priority sectors with spillovers like manufacturing, agriculture and tourism. Customs and import tariff structures affect trade competitiveness. Adjusting these tax settings in a development-friendly manner fosters growth and investment.

In India, targeted tax incentives promoted rapid expansion in IT services, automobile manufacturing and biopharmaceuticals – catalysing rising prosperity.[36] South Korea aggressively utilised tax policies to drive export competitiveness across industries critical for its development success.[37] Tax measures also play a role in Singapore's strategy to develop as a prime investment and business hub. Its tax regime offers generous incentives for multinational activities and nurtures advanced manufacturing.[38]

Empirical evidence shows that thoughtfully designed tax reforms in developing countries positively impact economic growth. A study found average GDP gains of 0.5–0.9 percentage points from tax changes that flattened and simplified rates while broadening bases.[39] Cross-country analysis also demonstrates the growth dividends from tax policy that lowers and stabilises marginal rates, increases neutrality across sectors and enhances administration.[40] Hence, developmental tax design goes beyond revenue performance to actively spurring investment, innovation and progress.

5.3.2 Taxation for Equity and Social Development

Tax systems inherently involve value judgments on distributing financial burdens equitably across society. Progressive income taxes that charge higher marginal rates on the affluent embody principles of vertical equity and ability to pay. Transfer schemes and social security contributions reflect caring for disadvantaged groups.[41] As such, tax policy principles also serve social objectives like inclusive development, poverty alleviation and reducing income inequality.[42]

Developing countries can harness tax mechanisms to finance healthcare, education, social protection, housing and other programmes that improve standards of living.[43] Effectively taxing the better off expands resources for pro-poor spending. South Africa's tax regime consciously aims to reduce inequality, especially racial disparities dating from apartheid.[44] Property taxes help finance decentralised service delivery in diverse countries like Indonesia, Colombia and Tunisia.[45] Strategically designed tax policies thus promote equity alongside revenue gains.

5.3.3 Environmental Taxation

Pigouvian taxes that make polluters pay for negative environmental externalities they generate are a classic economic policy prescription.[46] Carbon taxes, congestion charges, plastic levies and other environmental taxation tools incentivise mitigating pollution and waste. They also mobilise revenues for environmental protection and climate adaptation – fiscal benefits alongside behavioural impacts.[47]

Emerging economies face heightened climate risks along with sustainable development financing needs. Over 75 countries now employ some form of carbon pricing, with emerging economies like Chile, Mexico and China adopting carbon taxes.[48] Environmental tax reforms also benefit development – a 10% revenue-neutral swap from tabour taxes to pollution taxes increased GDP by over 2% in the modelling of archetype developing economies.[49] Thus, environmental taxation aligns with economic, social and climate goals.

In totality, taxation's portfolio has expanded tremendously from its historical origins as simply financing states. Tax policy in the modern era represents a versatile instrument for progress across economic, social and environmental dimensions.[50] This modern perspective envisages an active developmental role for taxation in enabling prosperity.

5.4 Infrastructure Needs in Emerging Economies

Infrastructure represents the fundamental physical backbone necessary for economic activity and improved living standards. Roads, power grids, telecom networks, water supply, sanitation systems, public transit, ports and airports constitute economic infrastructure vital for production, commerce, mobility and efficient functioning of markets.[51] Social infrastructure like schools, hospitals, courts, public housing and amenities support human development.[52] For both economic progress and social welfare, quality infrastructure represents a crucial prerequisite. However, massive deficits in infrastructure accessibility and quality plague the developing world – a critical obstacle to advancement that strategic tax incentives can help overcome.

5.4.1 Infrastructure as an Enabler of Growth and Development

Extensive empirical evidence demonstrates that infrastructure availability, affordability and quality crucially determine developmental outcomes. Macroeconomic studies have found that infrastructure stock and investment explain over half of cross-country per capita income and productivity differences.[53] World Bank econometric analysis indicates that infrastructure contributes at least 1% directly to annual per capita GDP growth across developing countries and enhances productivity further by enabling other drivers like education and urbanisation.[54]

At the macroeconomic level, multiple studies highlight how infrastructure slashes input costs and trading costs for firms, expands market access possibilities, allows exploiting economies of scale and enables specialisation.[55] For African manufacturing firms, power shortages alone were found to reduce annual sales growth by 8.7% on average.[56] In India, paved road access boosted plant productivity by around 15% in affected districts.[57] Across Latin American countries, electricity scarcity hindered total factor productivity significantly.[58]

For national economies, increased public infrastructure investment expands aggregate output and demand through multiplier effects, crowding in additional private investment.[59] The macroeconomics modelling suggests that a sustained increase in public infrastructure spending of just 1% of GDP could boost a developing country's GDP by over 2.5% in a decade.[60] The macro development payoffs from transport, power, ICT and social infrastructure expansion are thus substantial, making addressing deficits a high priority.

Infrastructure also unlocks massive welfare and social benefits, particularly for lower-income groups. Access to clean water, sanitation, electricity and all-weather road connectivity crucially enables improved health outcomes, education, nutrition, poverty reduction and gender equality across the developing world.[61] Piped water access reduces infant mortality substantially by curbing waterborne infectious diseases.[62] Electricity facilitates proper healthcare delivery, powering lifesaving equipment and vaccines.[63] Better district road connectivity cuts maternal mortality rates by enabling access to hospitals during childbirth.[64] Hence quality infrastructure underpins human development alongside economic growth.

Therefore, the economic growth and welfare case for urgently expanding infrastructure investment and access in developing countries is unequivocal. As the African Development Bank emphasised, 'Infrastructure is a precondition for …achieving many of the SDGs [Sustainable Development Goals].'[65]

5.4.2 *Infrastructure Deficits in the Developing World*

Despite compelling needs, infrastructure remains highly inadequate and scarce across most emerging economies. Sub-Saharan Africa's electricity access rate is just 43% leaving over 600 million unconnected.[66] South Asia performs somewhat better at 75% electrification but still 150 million are deprived.[67] Only 34% of Africa's Road networks are paved, making transport slow and costly.[68] Just 20% of South Asians have access to safely managed sanitation.[69] While individual country and regional pictures show variation, overall; the developing world severely lags in infrastructure provision across the board.

Quantifying the exact extent of the deficit is complex but various indicators confirm the stark picture. The World Bank's Relative Access Index measuring availability across power, paved roads, telephony, sanitation and other infrastructure rated South Asia at 0.4 and Sub-Saharan Africa at 0.3 against high-income OECD economies averaging 0.820 UNCTAD's infrastructure development index had a similar over 50 percentage point differential between developed and developing country categories.[70] Similarly, the African Infrastructure Development Index, covering power, ICT, transport, water and sanitation, scored the continent at just 0.34/1 overall as of 2019.[71]

These large infrastructure gaps impose heavy costs and constrain inclusive development. Harvard economist Ricardo Hausmann emphasised infrastructure deficits as a key factor explaining the productivity gap between developing and advanced economies even for countries at similar income levels.[72] For African countries, inadequate transport, power, water and ICT infrastructure slashes national competitiveness and adds 30–40% to business costs.[73] At the human level, lack of water, sanitation and electricity access causes millions of preventable deaths each year across low-income countries.[74]

Therefore, powering past these constraints by expanding quality, sustainable infrastructure represents an urgent economic and moral imperative for the developing world. As the World Bank has stressed, 'Infrastructure is critical to enable developing countries to significantly improve productivity, growth and quality of life.'[75] Tax incentives can play a catalytic role by helping mobilise finance and expertise to advance high-priority infrastructure projects serving the greatest needs.

5.4.3 *Economic Infrastructure*

In terms of specific categories, transport and power infrastructure represent fundamental pillars for almost all productive economic activity and thus merit priority focus:

- *Roads* – All-weather road access crucially enables firms to get goods and inputs to markets, facilitates trade and mobility and integrates national economies.[76] However, Africa has just 204 km of paved roads per 1000 km^2 of land compared to 944 in the EU.[77] Some 60% of rural Africans lack access to an all-season road.[78] Better road connectivity expands markets, reduces costs and drives productivity for agriculture and non-farm enterprises.[79]

- *Electricity* – Modern economic activity is impossible without reliable, affordable electricity. However, 25 Sub-Saharan countries face regular power shortages and outages.[80] Manufacturing enterprises across Africa report losing on average 8% of sales due to power inadequacy.[81] Manufacturing enterprises across Africa report losing on average 8% of sales due to power inadequacy.[82] Transport and cold storage also depend on electricity. Shortages hence curtail productivity.
- *Rail, ports, air transport* – Efficient rail and port infrastructure facilitate trade competitiveness, particularly for landlocked developing countries. Airport connectivity enables tourism exports and participation in global value chains.[83] Africa's handling costs and container ship turnaround times are uncompetitive, reflecting infrastructure gaps.[84]
- *Telecom/ICT* – Broadband and mobile access allow firms to coordinate supply chains, reach customers and leverage digital tools. However, Africa has just 80% mobile coverage against 98% in Europe.[85]
- *Water/sanitation* – Water is essential for agriculture, industry and power generation.[86] Inadequate supply inhibits industrial zones and other enterprises reliant on water access.[87] Safely managed sanitation also crucially enables workforce health and productivity.[88]

5.4.4 Social Infrastructure

While economic infrastructure supports commerce, social infrastructure in education, healthcare and housing underpins human capital development and welfare:

- *Healthcare* – Functioning clinics and hospitals connected by roads are essential to reduce maternal and child mortality and infectious diseases and to enable a healthy productive workforce.[89] However, hospital bed density in South Asia is just 7 per 10,000 against 34 in Europe.[90]
- *Schools* – Quality education depends on adequate infrastructure like buildings, electricity, sanitation and ICT. Sub-Saharan Africa averages 34 primary students per classroom, hindering learning.[91]
- *Housing* – Affordable housing options and public transit enable the creation of economically dynamic urban clusters.[92] However, with massive urban housing deficits, nearly 1 billion global slum dwellers lack durable housing, power or sanitation.[93]
- *Public amenities* – Shared infrastructure like public parks, sports complexes, community halls and libraries support social cohesion, recreation and cultural development.[94] However, many developing country urban areas lack liveable public spaces and amenities.

Overall, advancing infrastructure across transport, power, ICT, water, sanitation, healthcare, education, housing and public goods represents a multivariate

challenge. However, given its fundamental role in unlocking development, one that developing nations must urgently overcome. Tax incentives can serve as a valuable catalyst.

5.5 Private Sector Partnerships in Infrastructure Development

Given the enormous financing and expertise requirements for addressing developing county infrastructure deficits, public investment alone is insufficient.[95] Mobilising private sector resources and capabilities through public–private partnerships (PPPs) offers greater promise for tackling infrastructure gaps sustainably. Tax incentives can help drive this private involvement by improving project returns.

5.5.1 Limitations of Traditional Public Procurement

Historically, infrastructure in most countries was built primarily through direct procurement funded by the state budget and implemented by state-owned entities.[96] However, this conventional model faces constraints in meeting the vast needs of developing economies today.[97]

Public funding is inadequate – competing priorities like health, education and social spending limit budgets available for capital-intensive infrastructure projects. Limited public financing risks infrastructure investments falling behind population and economic growth needs.[98] Also, developing country governments face tighter fiscal constraints than advanced economies in mobilising large-scale capital.

Public capacity is also often overstretched, leading to inefficiencies in project design, delays and cost overruns. Many developing countries lack sufficient technical personnel across ministries and public agencies to design, implement and operate major complex infrastructure systems to global standards.[99] Weak institutions and governance can exacerbate matters.[100]

A fundamental constraint is that public provision lacks market discipline and commercial orientation. State entities may have weak incentives to control project costs, optimise efficiency and prioritise maintenance. Political interference and corruption can also affect public procurement.[101]

5.5.2 PPP as an Infrastructure Development Model

PPPs thus emerged as an alternative model to attract private financing and technical expertise to deliver quality infrastructure efficiently. PPPs take diverse contractual forms but fundamentally involve greater private participation in infrastructure financing, construction and operation, while the asset ownership remains public.[102]

Private partners bring capital, share risks, introduce technologies and best practices, and inject commercial orientation. PPP projects are also more insulated from political pressures. Studies show that PPPs reduce delay and costs compared to traditional procurement in contexts like India, Mexico and Brazil.[103]

However, PPPs face their own challenges in emerging markets. Investors and financiers still perceive major risks including weak regulation, lack of dispute resolution frameworks and policy instability. Returns may be insufficient given high costs and uneasy revenue models. Developing countries also often lack the capacity to structure complex deals.[104] Therefore, for their potential to be realised, PPPs require an enabling framework including governance reforms, clear policies, capable institutions and – critically – targeted tax incentives as this chapter focuses on.[105]

5.5.3 Tax Incentives to Catalyse Private Participation

Thoughtfully designed tax incentives can better align private partner returns with infrastructure projects' significant development benefits and positive externalities. Tax breaks reduce costs and risks that deter investors. Countries like Turkey, India, Colombia and South Africa have successfully employed tax incentives to enable PPPs in priority infrastructure sectors.[106] Common tax policy tools include[107] the following:

- *Tax holidays* – Full profit tax exemptions for an initial number of years improve project cash flows. It is used across sectors like roads, ports, and hospitals. Tax holidays were effective in drawing investors to major port and road PPPs in countries like India, Vietnam and Nigeria.
- *Accelerated depreciation* – Allows faster write-offs on capital equipment to reduce taxable income early on. This lowers financing costs and improves early cash flows. For example, the Philippines provided accelerated depreciation for its first PPP toll roads.
- *Import duty concessions* – Waivers on imported construction materials and equipment reduce capital outlays. This is used to lower infrastructure costs.
- *Withholding tax exemptions* – Removing taxes on dividends, interest payments and equipment leasing improves cash flows.
- *Loss carryforwards* – Permitting losses to offset future tax bills lowers risks for initial years. This is available for Indian infrastructure projects.
- *Investment tax credits* – Direct reductions in tax liability on qualifying infrastructure investments. Available in countries like Turkey, Egypt and Colombia.
- *Sales tax incentives* – Exemptions on local/VAT taxes improve operational viability. Colombia exempts PPPs from property taxes for 20 years.
- *Special zones* – Geographically targeted tax incentives like SEZs and economic zones enable infrastructure. This is successful in countries like China, the UAE and Mauritius.

Developing countries should assess local conditions and priorities in designing combinations of such incentives for PPPs.[108] Indonesia provided a 10-year tax holiday, import duty relief and land-use incentives for its first PPP toll road. South Africa exempts qualifying infrastructure bond interest income from taxes to lower financing costs. Such policies succeeded in catalysing private investment that otherwise faced hurdles. However, incentives warrant careful design considering fiscal impacts. Time limits, qualifying criteria and recapture provisions on underperformance can safeguard public revenues. However, the development gains from unlocking infrastructure justify limited revenue sacrifice, provided governance is strong.

In total, PPPs enabled by prudent tax incentives offer excellent promise for emerging economies to harness private sector resources. PPPs guided by incentives can accelerate sustainable infrastructure to meet critical economic and social needs. With their large deficits and financing constraints, developing nations stand to benefit greatly. Tax policy thus holds powerful tools to leverage infrastructure PPPs and drive development.

5.6 Tax Incentives to Attract Private Investment

Developing countries can design a range of targeted tax incentives to help overcome investor risks and uncertainties holding back greater involvement in infrastructure. Tax breaks and credits that lower costs and improve returns help mobilise finance and expertise needed for major roads, power, water and other projects. Where prudently implemented, tax incentives succeeded in catalysing private capital for high-priority national infrastructure goals.

5.6.1 Tax Policy Tools to Incentivise Infrastructure Investment

Tax incentives take diverse forms but fundamentally serve to improve the risk-return profile of infrastructure projects to attract investors and lenders. By reducing tax burdens, they enhance post-tax returns, lower financing costs and mitigate losses if projects underperform. The incentives also signal government commitment to enabling private infrastructure participation.

5.6.2 Prudent Design Considerations

It is important to state that tax incentives warrant careful design considering fiscal impacts. Revenue losses can be substantial if incentives are over-generous or not complemented by tax administration reforms. Common features to balance benefits versus costs include the following:

- The inclusion of sunset clauses limits incentives to the first 5–10 years of projects to support initial investments and de-risk but avoid indefinite loss.
- Having qualifying criteria such as minimum investment size, priority locations and sectors helps to limit the scope of projects benefiting.
- It might be helpful to insert clawback provisions. In this case, recapturing future benefits if investors fail to meet commitments like pre-agreed infrastructure quality standards.

- Ringfencing clauses can help to ensure that tax losses in initial years only offset profits of the infrastructure project, not other investments by the company.
- The state might require investors to submit accounts, costs and progress reports to regulators to monitor implementation. This is referred to as transparent reporting.
- There could also be a need to put a cap on incentives that are claimable by project companies in order to contain public revenue sacrifice.
- More importantly, there must be a structure in place to mitigate the risk of abuse.

Essentially, with prudent design considering trade-offs, developing countries can craft targeted tax incentives that serve their infrastructure goals while maintaining fiscal sustainability. The overall gains for growth and welfare make limited revenue sacrifices worthwhile, provided governance mechanisms are robust.[109] Within appropriate frameworks, tax incentives proved successful in mobilising infrastructure investment across emerging economies. See Table 5.1.[110,111]

It can be argued, and rightly so, that appropriately designed tax incentives can catalyse infrastructure development through PPPs by improving risk-adjusted returns. However, complementary policy reforms across regulation, dispute resolution and governance are also crucial to realise the full benefits. Tax measures are most effective when part of a comprehensive enabling framework for infrastructure investment.

Table 5.1 Country examples of tax incentives for infrastructure

Country	*Example of tax incentives for infrastructure*
Malaysia	10-year tax holiday on profits, import duty exemptions, accelerated depreciation for privatised highways, ports, airports and rail. This helped make Malaysia, a leading PPP model.
Turkey	15-year exemption from corporate tax and duties for build–operate–transfer projects over $50 million. This drove $100 billion in projects.
Colombia	A 10-year corporate income tax holiday for qualifying road concessions and exemption from property taxes for 20 years helped to enable major highway expansions.
India	A 10-year tax holiday for profits of infrastructure projects like roads, ports and airports as well as import duty relief on equipment helped to mobilise over $21 billion.
South Africa	A 15% investment deduction on qualifying infrastructure as well as interest income exemption on bonds for clean energy, transport and social infrastructure PPPs.

5.7 Recommendations and Conclusion

Drawing on analysis so far, this section provides tailored recommendations for how emerging economies can best leverage tax policy tools and incentives to boost private infrastructure investment. A strategic focus on incentives for PPP project companies and contractors and strengthening enabling frameworks can help mobilise greater finance and expertise towards national development goals.

Countries should provide targeted tax incentives to improve returns and lower risks for private companies undertaking major PPP infrastructure projects in priority sectors with big development payoffs. For private contractors, beyond PPPs, incentives should also target contractors undertaking government infrastructure contracts to expand their involvement.

In conclusion, infrastructure development is vital but requires major financing and expertise. Emerging economies face huge deficits but have limited public capacity alone. Private sector participation enabled by targeted tax incentives offers excellent promise. When carefully designed and prudently implemented, tax measures can catalyze infrastructure PPPs and contractors to accelerate development.

Tax incentives like holidays, accelerated depreciation and import duty relief improve the risk-return profile of infrastructure projects to attract investors and lenders. By lowering costs and uncertainty, thoughtful tax policies enable the mobilisation of private commercial capital and skills. This expands infrastructure access and quality faster than traditional public mechanisms. The spillovers into economic growth, social welfare and quality of life are immense.

Taxation policy thus represents an underutilised but potent tool for emerging economies. Beyond raising revenue, it can strategically mobilise resources aligned to national priorities. Infrastructure is a prime example where fiscal incentives can unlock finance to fill yawning deficits constraining growth and prosperity.

With prudent design minimising abuses and revenue losses, the gains warrant temporary and targeted tax incentives. The policy and institutional environment also need to be strengthened in parallel to fully leverage private sector infrastructure capabilities. However, overall, taxation flexibility focused on development goals serves emerging economies far better than overly rigid regimes.

Unleashing infrastructure and national development ultimately requires expanding taxation's role. Rather than just funding the government, it must enable private resources to be catalysed for the public good. By doing so strategically, emerging economies can drive inclusive growth and better living standards. Taxation designed for development goals, not just revenues, represents the future.

Notes

1 Augustine Edobor Arimoro, *Public-Private Partnerships in Emerging Economies* (New York and London: Routledge 2020) 1.
2 Jeffrey Delmon, *Public-Private Partnership Projects in Infrastructure: An Essential Guide for Policy Makers* (Cambridge: Cambridge University Press, 2011) 1.

3 ER Yescombe, *Public-Private Partnerships in Sub-Saharan Africa: Case Studies for Policymakers* (Dar es Salaam: Uongozi Institute, 2017) 3.
4 Augustine Edobor Arimoro, 'Legal Framework for Public Private Partnership: South Africa and Nigeria in Focus' (2018) 5 (2) *University of Maiduguri Journal of Public Law* 89–111. See also, Augustine Edobor Arimoro, 'Private Sector Investment in Infrastructure in Sub-Saharan Africa Post COVID-19: The Role of Law' (2022) 27(2) *Public Works Management & Policy* 108–126.
5 Augustine Arimoro, 'Public-Private Partnership and the Right to Property in Nigeria' (2019) 19(2) *African Human Rights Law Journal* 763–778.
6 World Bank, 'Annual PPI Database Global Report' (2019) available at https://ppi.worldbank.org/content/dam/PPI/documents/private-participation-infrastructure-annual-2019-report.pd accessed 10 March 2025.
7 William D Samson, 'History of Taxation' in A Lymer and J Hasseldine (eds), *The International Taxation System* (Boston MA: Springer, 2002) 21-41 DOI:10.1007/978-1-4615-1071-0_2.
8 OECD, *Tax Policy Reforms 2023: OECD and Selected Partner Economies* (2023) available at https://www.oecd-ilibrary.org/sites/d8bc45d9-en/index.html?itemId=/content/publication/d8bc45d9-en accessed 21 September 2023.
9 Shafik Hebous, 'Money at the Docks of Tax Havens: A Guide' (2014) 70(3) *FinanzArchiv: Public Finance Analysis* 458–485.
10 Zsolt Darvas, 'The Economic Growth and Income Distribution Implications of Public Spending and Tax Decisions' (2020) available at https://www.bruegel.org/sites/default/files/wp-content/uploads/2020/10/WP-2020-05-FINAL1.pdf accessed 21 September 2023.
11 Infrastructure Today, 'Income Tax Holiday: Eligibility for Infra Developers Demystified' (2011) available at https://infrastructuretoday.co.in/income-tax-holiday-eligibility-for-infra-developers-demystified/ accessed 21 September 2023.
12 African Centre for Cities, 'Infrastructure Financing in Africa: Overview, Research Gaps and Research Agenda' (2021) available at https://www.africancentreforcities.net/wp-content/uploads/2021/08/AH_SUSINFRA_report_1809.pdf accessed 21 September 2023.
13 Geraldine Ang and Virginie Marchal, 'Mobilising Private Investment in Sustainable Transport: The Case of Land-Based Infrastructure' (2013) OECD Environment Working Papers available at https://doi.org/10.1787/5k46hjm8jpmv-en accessed 12 March 2025.
14 OECD (n 8).
15 Deborah Brautigam, Odd-Helge Fjeldstad and Mick Moore, 'Taxation and State Building in Developing Countries' (2008) available at https://www.cmi.no/publications/file/2598-taxation-and-state-building-in-developing.pdf accessed 21 September 2023.
16 Salvador Carmona and Mahmoud Ezzamel, 'Ancient Accounting' in John Richard Edwards and Stephen Walker (eds) *The Routledge Companion to Accounting History* (Routledge 2020) DOI: 10.4324/9781351238885.
17 Rhyne King, 'Trips to the King, Taxation, and the New Year in the Persepolis Fortification Archive' (2022) *Iran, Journal of the British Institute of Persian Studies* https://doi.org/10.1080/05786967.2022.2101936.
18 Dipak Basu and Victoria Miroshnik, *Imperialism and Capitalism, Volume II* (Cham: Palgrave Macmillan, 2020) 1–14.
19 Ibn Khaldun, *The Muqaddimah: An Introduction to History – Abridged Edition* (Princeton: Princeton University Press, 1967).
20 David Hume, *Essays, Moral, Political and Literary* (Cosimo Classics, 2007).
21 Adam Smith, *The Wealth of Nations* (Modern Library, 2000).
22 John Stuart Mill, *Principles of Political Economy* (Prometheus Books, 2004).

23 Richard A Musgrave, Peggy B Musgrave and Richard M Bird, *Public Finance in Theory and Practice* (McGraw-Hill, 1987).
24 OECD, *Revenue Statistics* (OECD, 2019) available at https://www.oecd.org/en/publications/2019/12/revenue-statistics-2019_816e4552.html accessed 12 March 2025.
25 OECD (n 24).
26 Jialu L Streeter, 'How=Do Tax Policies Affect Individuals and Business' (2022) available at https://siepr.stanford.edu/publications/policy-brief/how-do-tax-policies-affect-individuals-and-businesses accessed 12 March 2025.
27 Thomas Piketty, *Capital and Ideology* (Cambridge: Harvard University Press, 2020).
28 Marcin Pawel Jarzebsiki et al., 'Ageing and Population Shrinking: Implications for Sustainability in the Urban Century' (2021) 1(17) *Urban Sustain* https://doi.org/10.1038/s42949-021-0002.
29 UNDP, 'UNDP Launches a New Initiative to Help Countries Leverage Taxation to Make Progress on Sustainable Development Goals' (2022) available at https://www.undp.org/press-releases/undp-launches-new-initiative-help-countries-leverage-taxation-make-progress-sustainable-development-goals accessed 24 September 2023.
30 Simon James, 'The Future International Tax Environment' in A Lymer and J Hasseldine (eds) *The International Taxation System* (Springer 2002) DOI: 10.1007/978-1-4615-1071-0_6.
31 Gita Bhatt, 'How Talent Fuels Growth' (2025) available at https://www.imf.org/en/Blogs accessed 12 March 2025.
32 Annet Wanyana Oguttu, 'Tax Base Erosion and Profit Shifting in Africa – Part 1: What Should Africa's Response be to the OECD BEPS Action Plan?' (2015) 48 *The Comparative and International Law Journal of Southern Africa* 516.
33 Oguttu (n 7).
34 R Hagemann, 'Tax Policies for Inclusive Growth' (2018) OECD Policy Paper No. 24 (December 2018) available at https://www.oecd.org/content/dam/oecd/en/publications/reports/2018/12/tax-policies-for-inclusive-growth_4df639c9/09ba747a-en.pdf accessed 12 March 2025.
35 See generally, Ehtisham Ahmad and Giorgio Brosio (eds), *Handbook of Multilevel Finance* (Edward Elgar, 2015).
36 Alex Gray, 'How India is Harnessing Technology to Lead the Fourth Industrial Revolution' (2018) available at https://www.weforum.org/agenda/2018/10/how-india-is-harnessing-technology-to-lead-the-fourth-industrial-revolution/ accessed 24 September 2023.
37 Kang-Kook Lee, 'Korea's Economic Growth and the Growth Model in the Changing Global Economy' (2024) 50(2) *The Japanese Political Economy* 161–184 DOI:10.1080/2329194X.2024.2325981.
38 K Martins et al, 'The Role of Tax Heavens and Offshore Financial Centers in Asia-Pacific Networks: Evidence from Firm Subsidiary Connections' (2019) 18 *Asian Bus Manage* 389-411 DOI: 10.1057/s41291-018-00051-1.
39 Era Dabla-Norris et al., 'Tax Policy for Inclusive Growth' (IMF Staff Discussion Note SDN/15/06, 2015). Staff Discussion Notes available at https://www.imf.org/en/Publications/Staff-Discussion-Notes/Issues/2016/12/31/Causes-and-Consequences-of-Income-Inequality-A-Global-Perspective-42986 accessed 12 March 2025.
40 Vito Tanzi and Howell Zee, 'Tax Policy for Emerging Markets: Developing Countries' (2000) available at https://www.imf.org/external/pubs/ft/wp/2000/wp0035.pdf accessed 12 March 2025.
41 Richard M Bird and Eric M Zolt, 'Tax Policy in Emerging Countries' (2008) 26 *Environment and Planning C: Government and Policy* 73.
42 Khaled Abdel-Khader and Ruud De Mooij, 'Tax Policy' in Valerie Cerra, and others (eds), *How to Achieve Inclusive Growth* available at https://doi.org/10.1093/oso/9780192846938.003.0012 accessed 10 March 2025.

43 Committee of Experts on International Cooperation in Tax Matters, 'The Role of Taxation and Domestic Resource Mobilisation in the Implementation of Sustainable Development Goals' (2018) available at https://www.un.org/esa/ffd/wp-content/uploads/2018/08/CRP19-The-Role-of-Taxation-and-Domestic-Resource-Mobilization-in-the-Implementation-of-the-Sustainable-Development-Goals.pdf#:~:text=Taxation%20is%20a%20powerful%20tool%20to%20help%20finance,reducing%20inequalities%20and%20promoting%20positive%20sustainable%20development%20patterns accessed 25 September 2023.

44 Ingrid Woolard et al., 'How Much is Inequality Reduced by Progressive Taxation and Government Spending?' (2015) available at http://www.econ3x3.org/article/how-much-inequality-reduced-progressive-taxation-and-government-spending#:~:text=Through%20progressive%20taxation%20and%20pro-poor%20social%20spending%2C%20the,than%20in%20twelve%20comparable%20middle-income%20countries%20measured%20similarly accessed 25 September 2023.

45 Roy Kelly, 'Property Taxation in Indonesia: Challenges from Decentralisation' (2003) available at https://www.lincolninst.edu/publications/working-papers/property-taxation-indonesia accessed 10 March 2025.

46 Nahid Asianbeugui and Guy Oakes, 'The 'Pigouvian Tradition' in Externality Analysis: Reconsiderations' (2023) available at https://ipl.econ.duke.edu/seminars/system/files/seminars/3737_slides.pdf accessed 10 March 2025.

47 PWC, 'Environment and Green Taxes' available at https://www.pwc.com/gx/en/services/tax/tax-policy-administration/environmental-and-green-taxes.html accessed 12 March 2025.

48 World Bank, 'Carbon Pricing Dashboard' (2023) available at https://carbonpricingdashboard.worldbank.org/ accessed 25 September 2023.

49 Gilbert Metcalf and David Weisbach, 'The Design of Carbon Tax' (2009) 33 *Harvard Law Review* 499.

50 OECD, 'Tax and Development' (2024) available at https://www.oecd.org/en/topics/policy-issues/tax-and-development.html accessed 12 March 2024.

51 Marianne Fay et al, *Rethinking Infrastructure in Latin America and the Caribbean: Spending to Achieve More* (Washington DC: The World Bank, 2017) available at https://documents1.worldbank.org/curated/pt/676711491563967405/114110-REVISED-Rethinking-Infrastructure-Low-Res.pdf accessed 12 March 2025.

52 DF Bryceson, 'African Urban Economies: Viability, Vitality or Vitiation?' (2011) available at http://ndl.ethernet.edu.et/bitstream/123456789/45121/1/187.pdf accessed 12 March 2025.

53 Cesar Calderon and Lusis Serven, 'The Effects of Infrastructure Development on Growth and Income Distribution' (2004) 3 *World Bank Policy Research Working Paper* 3400. available at https://openknowledge.worldbank.org/entities/publication/62471bf1-a785-5b41-b42b-f8cb689bdf33 accessed 12 March 2025.

54 Fay (n 51).

55 Andrew Crudgington, 'State of the Nation 2022: Improving Infrastructure Productivity' (2022) available at https://www.ice.org.uk/areas-of-interest/productivity/state-of-the-nation-2022-improving-infrastructure-productivity accessed 12 March 2025.

56 JL Blanco et al, 'Improving Infrastructure Outcomes through Better Capital Allocation' (2017) available at https://www.mckinsey.com/capabilities/operations/our-insights/improving-infrastructure-outcomes-through-better-capital-allocation accessed 12 March 2025.

57 Ejaz Ghani et al, 'Highway to Success: The Impact of Golden Quadrilateral Project for the Location and Performance of Indian Manufacturing' (2014) available at https://www.worldbank.org/content/dam/Worldbank/document/Development%20Research%20Group/Highway%20to%20Success%20The%20Impact%20of%20the%20Golden%20Quadrilateral.pdf accessed 12 March 2025.

58 Caldron and Serven (n 53).

59 David Alan Aschauer, 'Is Public Expenditure Productive?' (1989) 23 *Journal Monetary Economics* 177.
60 Marianne Fay et al (n 51).
61 PS Mukoki, 'Infrastructure Financing and Bond Market' (2022) available at https://bankseta.org.za/wp-content/uploads/2024/10/INFRASTRUCTURE-FINANCING-AND-BOND-MARKETS-DEVELOPMENT-IN-SUB-SAHARAN-AFRICA.pdf accessed 12 March 25.
62 Maoyong Fan and Guojun He, 'Clean Water and Infant Health: Evidence from Piped Water Provision in China' (2023) 10(1) *Journal of the Association of Environmental and Resource Economists* 159-193 DOI: 10.1086/721418.
63 Gordon McGranahan and David Satterthwaite, 'Urbanisation Concepts and Trends' (2014) available at https://www.iied.org/10709iied accessed 30 September 2023.
64 Sean Kaisser Shaeen et al., 'Maternal Mortality in Pakistan: Challenges, Efforts, and Recommendations' (2022) *Annals of Medical Surgery (London)* available at https://www.ncbi.nlm.nih.gov/pmc/articles/PMC9420499/ accessed 30 September 2023.
65 African Development Bank Group, 'Categories Annual Development Effectiveness Review' (2019) available at https://www.afdb.org/en/topics-and-sectors/topics/quality-assurance-results/development-effectiveness-reviews/development-effectiveness-reviews-2019/annual-development-effectiveness-reviews-2019 accessed 30 September 2023.
66 International Energy Agency, 'SDG7: Data and Projections' (2021) available at https://www.iea.org/reports/sdg7-data-and-projections accessed 30 September 2023.
67 International Energy Agency (n 66).
68 International Energy Agency (n 66).
69 WHO/UNICEF, Progress on household drinking water, sanitation and hygiene 2000–2020(2021). https://data.unicef.org/resources/progress-on-household-drinking-water-sanitation-and-hygiene-2000-2020/.
70 See UNCTADstat, 'Infrastructure Development Index' available at https://unctad.org/statistics accessed 30 September 2023.
71 See African Development Bank, 'Africa Infrastructure Development Index' (2019) available at https://www.afdb.org/en/documents/economic-brief-africa-infrastructure-development-index-aidi-2020-july-2020 accessed 30 September 2023.
72 Ricardo Hausmann, 'Final Recommendations of the International Panel on ASGISA' (Centre for International Development, Harvard Kennedy School, 2008). available at https://growthlab.hks.harvard.edu/files/growthlab/files/161.pdf accessed 12 March 2015.
73 Alan Gelb and Julia Clark, 'Identification for Development: The Biometrics Revolution – Working Paper 315' (2013) available at https://www.cgdev.org/publication/identification-development-biometrics-revolution-working-paper-315 accessed 30 September 2023.
74 World Health Organisation, 'Global Health Estimates: Life Expectancy and Leading Causes of Death and Disability' (2019) available https://www.who.int/data/gho/data/themes/mortality-and-global-health-estimates accessed 30 September 2023.
75 Fay et al (n 51).
76 Ken Gwilliam et al., 'Africa Infrastructure Country Diagnostic: Roads in Sub-Saharan Africa' (2008) available at https://documents.worldbank.org/en/publication/documents-reports/documentdetail/938171468194345853/africa-infrastructure-country-diagnostic-roads-in-sub-saharan-africa accessed 30 September 2023.
77 Cesar Calderon et al., Infrastructure Development in Sub-Saharan Africa: A Scorecard' (2018) available at. https://openknowledge.worldbank.org/entities/publication/e9b72ad5-9163-50b1-b0ac-4aa852b1ee0b accessed 30 September 2023.
78 United Nations Economic Commission for Africa, 'African Regional Review of Twenty-Five Years of Implementation of the Beijing Declaration and Platform for

Actions (BPfA): Generation Equality' (2019) available at https://repository.uneca.org/handle/10855/43171 accessed 30 September 2023.

79 Patricia Macchi, 'Transport Prices and Costs: The Need to Revisit Donors' Policies in Transport in Africa' (2009) available at https://papers.ssrn.com/sol3/papers.cfm?abstract_id=1511190 accessed 30 September 2023.

80 Anton Eberhard et al., *Africa's Power Infrastructure: Investment, Integration, Efficiency* (Washington DC: The World Bank, 2011).

81 Anton Eberhard et al., *Africa's Power Infrastructure: Investment, Integration, Efficiency* (Washington DC: The World Bank, 2011).

82 Mwangi S Kimenyi et al, *The African Lions: Kenya Country Study* (2016) available at https://www.brookings.edu/wp-content/uploads/2016/07/kenya-country-case.pdf accessed 12 March 2025.

83 Gee Hee Hong et al., 'China and Asia in Global Trade Slowdown' (2016) *IMF Working Paper* WP/16/105 available at https://www.imf.org/en/Publications/WP/Issues/2016/12/31/China-and-Asia-in-Global-Trade-Slowdown-43925 accessed 1 October 2023.

84 Nuno Limao and Anthony J Venables, 'Infrastructure, Geographical Disadvantage, Transport Costs, and Trade' (2001) 15(3) *The World Bank Economic Review* 451–457availableathttps://openknowledge.worldbank.org/entities/publication/e8f79737-65d9-591e-9f9e-a882ff8f1971 accessed 12 March 2025.

85 Broadband Commission for Sustainable Development, 'The State of Broadband 2021: People-Centred Approaches for Universal Broadband Connectivity' (2021) available at https://www.itu.int/itu-d/reports/broadbandcommission/state-of-broadband-2021/#:~:text=This%20report%20details%20the%20current,achieving%20universal%20connectivity%20by%202030.&text=This%20interactive%20report%20is%20an%20abridged%20version accessed 1 October 2023.

86 Augustine Arimoro and Habibah Musa, 'Toward Sustainable Water Resource Management in Rural Nigeria: The Role of Communities' (2020) 11(1) *The Journal of Sustainable Development Law* 1–17.

87 Augustine Arimoro and Habibah Musa, 'Toward Sustainable Water Resource Management in Rural Nigeria: The Role of Communities' (2020) 11(1) *The Journal of Sustainable Development Law* 1–17.

88 World Health Organisation, 'Global Costs and Benefits of Drinking-Water Supply and Sanitation Interventions to Reach the MDG Target and Universal Coverage' (2012) available at https://www.who.int/publications/i/item/WHO-HSE-WSH-12.01 accessed 1 October 2023.

89 Augustine Edobor Arimoro, 'The Corona Virus (COVID-19) Pandemic and the Challenge of Healthcare Infrastructure in Nigeria: What Role for Public-Private Partnerships?' (2020) 3 *Theoretical and Applied Law* 19–35.

90 The World Bank, 'World Bank Development Indicators' (2020) available at https://datatopics.worldbank.org/world-development-indicators/ accessed 1 October 2023.

91 UNESCO, 'Mapping of SDG Indicators in Learning Assessments' (2017) available https://gaml.uis.unesco.org/dashboard/ accessed 1 October 2023.

92 Sule Akkoyunlu, 'The Potential of Rural-urban Linkages for Sustainable Development and Trade' (2013) available at https://www.researchgate.net/publication/259577244_The_Potential_of_Rural-urban_Linkages_for_Sustainable_Development_and_Trade accessed 1 October 2023.

93 UN Habitat, Slum Almanac 2015/2016 (2015) available at https://landportal.org/library/resources/slum-almanac-2015-2016 accessed 10 March 2025.

94 Alessandro Rigolon and Jeremy Nemeth, '"We're Not in the Business of Housing:" Environmental Gentrification and the Nonprofitization of Green Infrastructure Projects' (2018) 81 *Cities* 71–80.

95 Augustine Edobor Arimoro, 'Legal Framework for Public Private Partnership: South Africa and Nigeria in Focus' (2018) 5(2) *University of Maiduguri Journal of Public Law* 89–111. See also, Augustine Edobor Arimoro, 'Institutional Framework

for Public-Private Partnerships in Nigeria: Is it a Case of Too Many Cooks for One Pot of Broth?' (2019) 40(2) *Business Law Review* 73–79.

96 Augustine Edobor Arimoro, 'Institutional Framework for Public-Private Partnerships in Nigeria: Is it a Case of Too Many Cooks for One Pot of Broth?' (2019) 40(2) *Business Law Review* 73–79.

97 Clive Harris, 'Private Participation in Infrastructure in Developing Countries: Trends, Impacts, and Policy Lessons' (2003) World Bank Working Paper available at https://documents.worldbank.org/en/publication/documents-reports/documentdetail/877581468762634492/private-participation-in-infrastructure-in-developing-countries-trends-impacts-and-policy-lessons accessed 1 October 2023.

98 Fernanda Ruiz-Nunez and Zichao Wei, 'Infrastructure Investment Demands in Emerging Markets and Developing Economies' (2015) Brookings Policy Paper available at https://openknowledge.worldbank.org/entities/publication/7549e243-f658-586a-8849-1da81072eb82 accessed 1 October 2023.

99 Mona Hammanmi et al., 'Determinants of Public-Private Partnerships in Infrastructure' (2006) IMF Working Paper available at https://www.imf.org/external/pubs/ft/wp/2006/wp0699.pdf accessed 1 October 2023.

100 Augustine Edobor Arimoro, 'Institutional Framework for Public-Private Partnerships in Nigeria: Is it a Case of Too Many Cooks for One Pot of Broth?' (2019) 40(2) *Business Law Review* 73–79.

101 Eduardo Engel et al., 'Public-Private Partnerships to Revamp U.S. Infrastructure' (2011) Brookings Policy Paper available at https://www.brookings.edu/articles/public-private-partnerships-to-revamp-u-s-infrastructure/ accessed 1 October 2023.

102 Robert Osei-Kyei and Albert PC Chan, 'Review of Studies on the Critical Success Factors for Public-Private Partnership (PPP) Projects from 1990 to 2013' (2015) 33 *International Journal of Project Management* 1335–1346.

103 OECD, 'Good Governance for Latin America and the Caribbean: Representing the Interest of All' (2020) available at https://www.oecd-ilibrary.org/sites/4f292bd2-en/index.html?itemId=/content/component/4f292bd2-en accessed 1 October 2023.

104 The World Bank, 'Independent Power Projects in Sub-Saharan Africa – Lessons from Five Key Countries' (2016) available at https://www.worldbank.org/en/topic/energy/publication/independent-power-projects-in-sub-saharan-africa accessed 1 October 2023.

105 The United Nations, 'Developing Successful Public-Private Partnerships for Increased Transport Connectivity: Case Studies, Experiences and Learning Materials' (2020) available at https://www.un.org/ohrlls/sites/www.un.org.ohrlls/files/training_materials_ppps_botswana_9_oct_rev.pdf accessed 1 October 2023.

106 Manabu Nose, 'Enforcing Public-Private Partnership Contract: How Do Fiscal Institutions Matter? (2017) available at https://www.imf.org/en/Publications/WP/Issues/2017/11/15/Enforcing-Public-Private-Partnership-Contract-How-do-Fiscal-Institutions-Matter-45353 accessed 1 October 2023.

107 ESCAP, 'A Guidebook on Public-Private Partnership in Infrastructure' (2011) available at https://www.unescap.org/resources/guidebook-public-private-partnership-infrastructure accessed 1 October 2023.

108 Robert Osei-Kyei and Albert PC Chan, 'Implementing Public-Private Partnership (PPP) Policy for Public Projects in Ghana: Critical Success Factors and Policy Implications' (2017) 17(2) *International Journal of Construction Management* 113-123 DOI: 10.1080/15623599.2016.1207865.

109 Ruiz-Nunez and Wei (n 98).

110 H Hashim et al., 'Review of Issues and Challenges for Public Private Partnership in Malaysia'(2017)availableathttps://pubs.aip.org/aip/acp/article/1891/1/020051/887012/Review-of-issues-and-challenges-for-public-private accessed 1 October 2023.

111 Ekin Tas and Erkan Erdii, 'Effectiveness of R & D Tax Incentives in Turkey' (2023) *Journal of the Knowledge Economy*. DOI: 10.1007/s13132-023-01326-5.

Bibliography

Abdel-Khader K and De Mooij R, 'Tax Policy' in Valerie Cerra, et al. (eds), *How to Achieve Inclusive Growth* (2021) available at https://doi.org/10.1093/oso/9780192846938.003.0012 accessed 10 March 2025.

African Centre for Cities, 'Infrastructure Financing in Africa: Overview, Research Gaps and Research Agenda' (2021) available at https://www.africancentreforcities.net/infrastructure-financing-in-africa-overview-research-gaps-and-research-agenda/ accessed 21 September 2023.

African Development Bank, 'Africa Infrastructure Development Index' (2019) available at https://www.afdb.org/en/documents/economic-brief-africa-infrastructure-development-index-aidi-2020-july-2020 accessed 30 September 2023.

African Development Bank Group, 'Categories Annual Development Effectiveness Review' (2019) available at https://www.afdb.org/en/topics-and-sectors/topics/quality-assurance-results/development-effectiveness-reviews/development-effectiveness-reviews-2019/annual-development-effectiveness-reviews-2019 accessed 30 September 2023.

Ahmad E and Brosio G (eds), *Handbook of Multilevl Finance* (Edward Elgar, 2015).

Akkoyunlu S, 'The Potential of Rural-urban Linkages for Sustainable Development and Trade' (2013) available at https://www.researchgate.net/publication/259577244_The_Potential_of_Rural-urban_Linkages_for_Sustainable_Development_and_Trade accessed 1 October 2023.

Arimoro A, 'Public-Private Partnership and the Right to Property in Nigeria' (2019a) 19(2) *African Human Rights Law Journal* 763–778.

Arimoro A and Musa H, 'Toward Sustainable Water Resource Management in Rural Nigeria: The Role of Communities' (2020) 11(1) *The Journal of Sustainable Development Law* 1–17.

Arimoro AE, 'Legal Framework for Public Private Partnership: South Africa and Nigeria in Focus' (2018) 5(2) *University of Maiduguri Journal of Public Law* 89–111.

Arimoro AE, 'Institutional Framework for Public-Private Partnerships in Nigeria: Is it a Case of Too Many Cooks for One Pot of Broth?' (2019b) 40(2) *Business Law Review* 73–79.

Arimoro AE, 'The Corona Virus (COVID-19) Pandemic and the Challenge of Healthcare Infrastructure in Nigeria: What Role for Public-Private Partnerships?' (2020a) 3 *Theoretical and Applied Law* 19–35.

Arimoro AE, *Public-Private Partnerships in Emerging Economies* (Routledge 2020b).

Arimoro AE, 'Private Sector Investment in Infrastructure in Sub-Saharan Africa Post COVID-19: The Role of Law' (2022) 27(2) *Public Works Management & Policy* 108–126.

Ang G and Marchal V, 'Mobilising Private Investment in Sustainable Transport: The Case of Land-Based Infrastructure' (2013) OECD Environment Working Papers available at https://doi.org/10.1787/5k46hjm8jpmv-en accessed 12 March 2025.

Aschauer DA, 'Is Public Expenditure Productive?' (1989) 23 *Journal Monetary Economics* 177.

Asianbeugui N and Oakes G 'The 'Pigouvian Tradition' in Externality Analysis: Reconsiderations' (2023) available at https://ipl.econ.duke.edu/seminars/system/files/seminars/3737_slides.pdf accessed 10 March 2025.

Basu D and Miroshnik V, *Imperialism and Capitalism, Volume II* (Palgrave Macmillan, 2020).

Bhatt G, 'How Talent Fuels Growth' (2025) available at https://www.imf.org/en/Blogs accessed 12 March 2025.

Bird RM and Zolt EM, 'Tax Policy in Emerging Countries' (2008) 26 *Environment and Planning C: Government and Policy* 73.

Blanco JL et al, 'Improving Infrastructure Outcomes through Better Capital Allocation' (2017) available at https://www.mckinsey.com/capabilities/operations/our-insights/improving-infrastructure-outcomes-through-better-capital-allocation accessed 12 March 2025.

Brautigam D, Fjeldstad O and Moore M, 'Taxation and State Building in Developing Countries' (2008) available at https://www.cmi.no/publications/file/2598-taxation-and-state-building-in-developing.pdf accessed 21 September 2023.

Broadband Commission for Sustainable Development, 'The State of Broadband 2021: People-Centred Approaches for Universal Broadband Connectivity' (2021) available at https://www.itu.int/itu-d/reports/broadbandcommission/state-of-broadband-2021/#:~:text=This%20report%20details%20the%20current,achieving%20universal%20connectivity%20by%202030.&text=This%20interactive%20report%20is%20an%20abridged%20version accessed 1 October 2023.

DF Bryceson, 'African Urban Economies: Viability, Vitality or Vitiation?' (2011) available at http://ndl.ethernet.edu.et/bitstream/123456789/45121/1/187.pdf accessed 12 March 2025.

Calderon C and Serven L, 'The Effects of Infrastructure Development on Growth and Income Distribution' (2004) 3 *World Bank Policy Research Working Paper* 3400.https://openknowledge.worldbank.org/entities/publication/62471bf1-a785-5b41-b42b-f8cb689bdf33

Calderon C et al., 'Infrastructure Development in Sub-Saharan Africa: A Scorecard' (2018) available at https://openknowledge.worldbank.org/entities/publication/e9b72ad5-9163-50b1-b0ac-4aa852b1ee0b accessed 30 September 2023.

Committee of Experts on International Cooperation in Tax Matters, 'The Role of Taxation and Domestic Resource Mobilisation in the Implementation of Sustainable Development Goals' (2018) available at https://www.un.org/esa/ffd/wp-content/uploads/2018/08/CRP19-The-Role-of-Taxation-and-Domestic-Resource-Mobilization-in-the-Implementation-of-the-Sustainable-Development-Goals.pdf#:~:text=Taxation%20is%20a%20powerful%20tool%20to%20help%20finance,reducing%20inequalities%20and%20promoting%20positive%20sustainable%20development%20patterns accessed 25 September 2023.

Crudgington A, 'State of the Nation 2022: Improving Infrastructure Productivity' (2022) available at https://www.ice.org.uk/areas-of-interest/productivity/state-of-the-nation-2022-improving-infrastructure-productivity accessed 12 March 2025.

Dabla-Norris E et al., 'Tax Policy for Inclusive Growth' (IMF Staff Discussion Note SDN/15/06, 2015). Staff Discussion Notes available at https://www.imf.org/en/Publications/Staff-Discussion-Notes/Issues/2016/12/31/Causes-and-Consequences-of-Income-Inequality-A-Global-Perspective-42986

Darvas Z, 'The Economic Growth and Income Distribution Implications of Public Spending and Tax Decisions' (2020) available at https://www.bruegel.org/sites/default/files/wp-content/uploads/2020/10/WP-2020-05-FINAL1.pdf accessed 21 September 2023.

Delmon J, *Public-Private Partnership Projects in Infrastructure: An Essential Guide for Policy Makers* (Cambridge University Press, 2011).

Eberhard A et al., *Africa's Power Infrastructure: Investment, Integration, Efficiency* (The World Bank, 2011).

Engel E et al., 'Public-Private Partnerships to Revamp U.S. Infrastructure' (2011) Brookings Policy Paper available at https://www.brookings.edu/articles/public-private-partnerships-to-revamp-u-s-infrastructure/ accessed 1 October 2023.

ESCAP, 'A Guidebook on Public-Private Partnership in Infrastructure' (2011) available at https://www.unescap.org/resources/guidebook-public-private-partnership-infrastructure accessed 1 October 2023.

Carmona S and Ezzamel M, 'Ancient Accounting' in John Richard Edwards and Stephen Walker (eds) *The Routledge Companion to Accounting History* (Routledge 2020) 10.4324/9781351238885

Fan M and He G, 'Clean Water and Infant Health: Evidence from Piped Water Provision in China' (2023) 10(1) *Journal of the Association of Environmental and Resource Economists* 159–193 doi:10.1086/721418

Fay M et al., *Rethinking Infrastructure in Latin America and the Caribbean: Spending to Achieve More* (The World Bank, 2017).available at https://documents1.worldbank.org/curated/pt/676711491563967405/114110-REVISED-Rethinking-Infrastructure-Low-Res.pdf accessed 12 March 2025.

Gelb A and Clark J, 'Identification for Development: The Biometrics Revolution – Working Paper 315' (2013) available at https://www.cgdev.org/publication/identification-development-biometrics-revolution-working-paper-315 accessed 30 September 2023.

Ghani E et al., 'Highway to Success: The Impact of Golden Quadrilateral Project for the Location and Performance of Indian Manufacturing' (2014) https://www.worldbank.org/content/dam/Worldbank/document/Development%20Research%20Group/Highway%20to%20Success%20The%20Impact%20of%20the%20Golden%20Quadrilateral.pdf

Gray A, 'How India is Harnessing Technology to Lead the Fourth Industrial Revolution' (2018) available at https://www.weforum.org/agenda/2018/10/how-india-is-harnessing-technology-to-lead-the-fourth-industrial-revolution/ accessed 24 September 2023.

Gwilliam K et al., 'Africa Infrastructure Country Diagnostic: Roads in Sub-Saharan Africa' (2008) available at https://documents.worldbank.org/en/publication/documents-reports/documentdetail/938171468194345853/africa-infrastructure-country-diagnostic-roads-in-sub-saharan-africa accessed 30 September 2023.

Hagemann R, 'Tax Policies for Inclusive Growth' (2018) OECD Policy Paper No. 24 (December 2018) available at https://www.oecd.org/content/dam/oecd/en/publications/reports/2018/12/tax-policies-for-inclusive-growth_4df639c9/09ba747a-en.pdf accessed 12 March 2025.

Harris C, 'Private Participation in Infrastructure in Developing Countries: Trends, Impacts, and Policy Lessons' (2003) World Bank Working Paper available at https://documents.worldbank.org/en/publication/documents-reports/documentdetail/877581468762634492/private-participation-in-infrastructure-in-developing-countries-trends-impacts-and-policy-lessons accessed 1 October 2023.

Hashim H et al., 'Review of Issues and Challenges for Public Private Partnership in Malaysia'(2017)availableathttps://pubs.aip.org/aip/acp/article/1891/1/020051/887012/Review-of-issues-and-challenges-for-public-private accessed 1 October 2023.

Hausmann R, *Final Recommendations of the International Panel on ASGISA* (Centre for International Development, Harvard Kennedy School, 2008). available at https://growthlab.hks.harvard.edu/files/growthlab/files/161.pdf accessed 12 March 2015.

Hebous S, 'Money at the Docks of Tax Havens: A Guide' (2014) 70(3) *FinanzArchiv: Public Finance Analysis* 458–485.

Hong GH et al., 'China and Asia in Global Trade Slowdown' (2016) *IMF Working Paper* WP/16/105 available at available at https://www.imf.org/en/Publications/WP/Issues/2016/12/31/China-and-Asia-in-Global-Trade-Slowdown-43925 accessed 1 October 2023.

Hume D, *Essays, Moral, Political and Literary* (Cosimo Classics, 2007).

Infrastructure Today, 'Income Tax Holiday: Eligibility for Infra Developers Demystified' (2011) available at https://infrastructuretoday.co.in/income-tax-holiday-eligibility-for-infra-developers-demystified/ accessed 21 September 2023.

International Energy Agency, 'SDG7: Data and Projections' (2021) available at https://www.iea.org/reports/sdg7-data-and-projections accessed 30 September 2023.

James S, 'The Future International Tax Environment' in A Lymer and J Hasseldine (eds) *The International Taxation System* (Springer 2002) DOI:10.1007/978-1-4615-1071-0_6
Jarzebsiki MP et al., 'Ageing and Population Shrinking: Implications for Sustainability in the Urban Century' (2021) 1(17) *Urban Sustain* https://doi.org/10.1038/s42949-021-0002
Streeter JL, 'How Do Tax Policies Affect Individuals and Business' (2022) available at https://siepr.stanford.edu/publications/policy-brief/how-do-tax-policies-affect-individuals-and-businesses accessed 12 March 2025.
Kelly R 'Property Taxation in Indonesia: Challenges from Decentralisation' (2003) availableathttps://www.lincolninst.edu/publications/working-papers/property-taxation-indonesia accessed 10 March 2025.
Khaldun I, *The Muqaddimah: An Introduction to History – Abridged Edition* (Princeton University Press, 1967).
Lee, KK 'Korea's Economic Growth and the Growth Model in the Changing Global Economy' (2024) 50(2) *The Japanese Political Economy* 161–184 doi:10.1080/2329194X.2024.2325981
Mwangi S, Kimenyi MS, et al., *The African Lions: Kenya Country Study* (2016) available at https://www.brookings.edu/wp-content/uploads/2016/07/kenya-country-case.pdf accessed 12 March 2025.
King R, 'Trips to the King, Taxation, and the New Year in the Persepolis Fortification Archive' (2022) *Iran, Journal of the British Institute of Persian Studies*. https://doi.org/10.1080/05786967.2022.2101936
Limao N and Venables AJ, 'Infrastructure, Geographical Disadvantage, Transport Costs, and Trade' (2001) 15(3) *The World Bank Economic Review* 451–457 available at https://openknowledge.worldbank.org/entities/publication/e8f79737-65d9-591e-9f9e-a882ff8f1971 accessed 12 March 2025.
Macchi P, 'Transport Prices and Costs: The Need to Revisit Donors' Policies in Transport in Africa' (2009) available at https://papers.ssrn.com/sol3/papers.cfm?abstract_id=1511190 accessed 30 September 2023.
Martins K. et al., 'The Role of Tax Heavens and Offshore Financial Centers in Asia-Pacific Networks: Evidence from Firm Subsidiary Connections' (2019) 18 *Asian Bus Manage* 389–411 doi:10.1057/s41291-018-00051-1
McGranahan G and Satterthwaite D, 'Urbanisation Concepts and Trends' (2014) available at https://www.iied.org/10709iied accessed 30 September 2023.
Metcalf G and Weisbach D, 'The Design of Carbon Tax' (2009) 33 *Harvard Law Review* 499.
Mill JS, *Principles of Political Economy* (Prometheus Books, 2004).
Hammanmi M et al., 'Determinants of Public-Private Partnerships in Infrastructure' (2006) IMF Working Paper available at https://www.imf.org/external/pubs/ft/wp/2006/wp0699.pdf accessed 1 October 2023.
Mukoki PS, 'Infrastructure Financing and Bond Market' (2022) available at https://bankseta.org.za/wp-content/uploads/2024/10/INFRASTRUCTURE-FINANCING-AND-BOND-MARKETS-DEVELOPMENT-IN-SUB-SAHARAN-AFRICA.pdf accessed 12 March 25.
Musgrave RA, Musgrave PB and Bird RM, *Public Finance in Theory and Practice* (McGraw-Hill, 1987).
Nose M, 'Enforcing Public-Private Partnership Contract: How Do Fiscal Institutions Matter?' (2017) available at https://www.imf.org/en/Publications/WP/Issues/2017/11/15/Enforcing-Public-Private-Partnership-Contract-How-do-Fiscal-Institutions-Matter-45353 accessed 1 October 2023.
OECD, *Revenue Statistics* (OECD, 2019). available at https://www.oecd.org/en/publications/2019/12/revenue-statistics-2019_816e4552.html accessed 12 March 2025.

OECD, 'Tax and Development' (2024) available at https://www.oecd.org/en/topics/policy-issues/tax-and-development.html accessed 12 March 2024.
OECD, 'Good Governance for Latin America and the Caribbean: Representing the Interest of All' (2020) available at https://www.oecd-ilibrary.org/sites/4f292bd2-en/index.html?itemId=/content/component/4f292bd2-en accessed 1 October 2023.
OECD, *Tax Policy Reforms 2023: OECD and Selected Partner Economies* (2023) available at https://www.oecd-ilibrary.org/sites/d8bc45d9-en/index.html?itemId=/content/publication/d8bc45d9-en accessed 21 September 2023.
Oguttu AW, 'Tax Base Erosion and Profit Shifting in Africa – Part 1: What Should Africa's Response be to the OECD BEPS Action Plan?' (2015) 48 *The Comparative and International Law Journal of Southern Africa* 516.
Osei-Kyei R and Chan APC, 'Implementing Public-Private Partnership (PPP) Policy for Public Projects in Ghana: Critical Success Factors and Policy Implications' (2017) 17(2) *International Journal of Construction Management* 113–123 doi:10.1080/15623599.2016.1207865
Piketty T, *Capital and Ideology* (Harvard University Press, 2020).
PWC, 'Environment and Green Taxes' available at https://www.pwc.com/gx/en/services/tax/tax-policy-administration/environmental-and-green-taxes.html accessed 12 March 2025.
Rigolon A and Nemeth J, '"We're Not in the Business of Housing:" Environmental Gentrification and the Nonprofitization of Green Infrastructure Projects' (2018) 81 *Cities* 71–80.
Ruiz-Nunez F and Wei Z, 'Infrastructure Investment Demands in Emerging Markets and Developing Economies' (2015) Brookings Policy Paper available at https://openknowledge.worldbank.org/entities/publication/7549e243-f658-586a-8849-1da81072eb82 accessed 1 October 2023.
Samson WD, 'History of Taxation' in A Lymer and J Hasseldine (eds), *The International Taxation System* (Boston, MA: Springer, 2002) 21–41. doi:10.1007/978-1-4615-1071-0_2
Shaeen SK et al., 'Maternal Mortality in Pakistan: Challenges, Efforts, and Recommendations' (2022) *Annals of Medicine and Surgery (London)* available at https://www.ncbi.nlm.nih.gov/pmc/articles/PMC9420499/ accessed 30 September 2023.
Smith A, *The Wealth of Nations* (Modern Library, 2000).
Tanzi V and Zee H, 'Tax Policy for Emerging Markets: Developing Countries' (2000) available at https://www.imf.org/external/pubs/ft/wp/2000/wp0035.pdf
Tas E and Erdii E, 'Effectiveness of R & D Tax Incentives in Turkey' (2023) *Journal of the Knowledge Economy*. doi: 10.1007/s13132-023-01326-5
The United Nations, 'Developing Successful Public-Private Partnerships for Increased Transport Connectivity: Case Studies, Experiences and Learning Materials' (2020) available at https://www.un.org/ohrlls/sites/www.un.org.ohrlls/files/training_materials_ppps_botswana_9_oct_rev.pdf accessed 1 October 2023.
World Bank, 'Annual PPI Database Global Report' (2019) available at https://ppi.worldbank.org/content/dam/PPI/documents/private-participation-infrastructure-annual-2019-report.pdf accessed 10 March 2025.
The World Bank, 'Independent Power Projects in Sub-Saharan Africa – Lessons from Five Key Countries' (2016) available at https://www.worldbank.org/en/topic/energy/publication/independent-power-projects-in-sub-saharan-africa accessed 1 October 2023.
The World Bank, 'World Bank Development Indicators' (2020) available at https://datatopics.worldbank.org/world-development-indicators/ accessed 1 October 2023.
UN Habitat, Slum Almanac 2015/2016 (2018). available at https://landportal.org/library/resources/slum-almanac-2015-2016 accessed 10 March 2025.
UNCTADstat, 'Infrastructure Development Index' available at https://unctad.org/statistics accessed 30 September 2023.

UNDP, 'UNDP Launches a New Initiative to Help Countries Leverage Taxation to Make Progress on Sustainable Development Goals' (2022) available at https://www.undp.org/press-releases/undp-launches-new-initiative-help-countries-leverage-taxation-make-progress-sustainable-development-goals accessed 24 September 2023.

UNESCO, 'Mapping of SDG Indicators in Learning Assessments' (2017) available https://gaml.uis.unesco.org/dashboard/ accessed 1 October 2023.

United Nations Economic Commission for Africa, 'African Regional Review of Twenty-Five Years of Implementation of the Beijing Declaration and Platform for Actions (BPfA): Generation Equality' (2019) available at https://repository.uneca.org/handle/10855/43171 accessed 30 September 2023.

WHO/UNICEF, 'Progress on Household Drinking Water, Sanitation and Hygiene 2000–2020'(2021).https://data.unicef.org/resources/progress-on-household-drinking-water-sanitation-and-hygiene-2000-2020/

Woolard I et al., 'How Much is Inequality Reduced by Progressive Taxation and Government Spending?' (2015) available at http://www.econ3x3.org/article/how-much-inequality-reduced-progressive-taxation-and-government-spending#:~:text=Through%20progressive%20taxation%20and%20pro-poor%20social%20spending%2C%20the,than%20in%20twelve%20comparable%20middle-income%20countries%20measured%20similarly accessed 25 September 2023.

WorldBank,'CarbonPricingDashboard'(2023)availableathttps://carbonpricingdashboard.worldbank.org/ accessed 25 September 2023.

World Health Organisation, 'Global Costs and Benefits of Drinking-Water Supply and Sanitation Interventions to Reach the MDG Target and Universal Coverage' (2012) available at https://www.who.int/publications/i/item/WHO-HSE-WSH-12.01 accessed 1 October 2023.

World Health Organisation, 'Global Health Estimates: Life Expectancy and Leading Causes of Death and Disability' (2019) available at https://www.who.int/data/gho/data/themes/mortality-and-global-health-estimatesaccessed 30 September 2023.

Yescombe ER, *Public-Private Partnerships in Sub-Saharan Africa: Case Studies for Policymakers* (Uongozi Institute, 2017).

6 Unpacking the Mobile Money Tax Conundrum

Insights from Case Studies of Kenya, Uganda and Tanzania

Marie-Louise F. Aren and Magalie Masamba†*

6.1 Introduction

The digitalisation of financial services has facilitated the growth of innovative business models for reaching the unbanked.[1] Africa now boasts mobile penetration that has risen by 3200% in over 20 years,[2] and now has over 110 money mobile systems with a user base of more than 30 million subscribers.[3] Mobile money service partnerships between banks and telecommunication network providers have facilitated the faster and cheaper transfer of money, despite geographical barriers.[4] The introduction and growth of mobile money services constitute a critical tool for financial inclusivity and a potential tool for achieving the goal of expanding intra-African trade and investment envisaged in the African Continental Free-Trade Area (AfCFTA).[5]

Despite the growth of the money services sector, the opportunities to expand the tax base from the massive revenue gained by digital companies are challenging. Chronic tax avoidance from sophisticated tax planning strategies of multinational corporations, obsolete tax rules, difficulty in taxing the digital-derived profits, and exploiting Base Erosion and Profit Shifting (BEPS) gaps have instead led to Mobile Money Taxation.[6]

Against the setting of global tax events and to supplement shrinking tax bases from the Covid-19 pandemic, many African countries introduced or are planning to introduce mobile money taxes as a key domestic resource mobilisation (DRM) strategy. Some countries have taken steps ahead of the finalisation of the BEPS proposed measures in taxing their elusive digital economy firms over and above value-added taxes (VAT). While it helps to hold a subset of digital operators accountable for the benefits of using public goods in the production of wealth and contributing to the revenue purse, it is also a dicey move. As governments strive to capitalise on the potential income streams provided by this digital financial environment, the application of mobile money taxes has proven controversial as they appear to detract from the hard gains

* Marie-Louise Fehun Aren is an International Lawyer and currently a concluding doctoral candidate (International Tax Law) at the University of Pretoria, South Africa.

† Dr Magalie Masamba is an Extraordinary Lecturer at the Centre for Human Rights, University of Pretoria and a legal and policy consultant specialising on sovereign debt, global economic governance, climate finance, and development finance.

DOI: 10.4324/9781003432890-8

made in the trajectory of digital innovation and financial inclusion due to its regressive nature. These taxes raise concerns about the cost and accessibility of financial services and the promotion of financial inclusion. Mobile money users would likely be subject to increased transaction costs implemented across various African countries, including Uganda, Tanzania, Lesotho, Zambia and Cameroon which have introduced mobile money taxes.[7]

This chapter analyses the factors motivating the emergence of these taxes and uncovers some of the consequences for mobile money users. In the following sections, we examine how the growth of mobile money services has contributed to development and human rights and argue that taxation within the context of DRM pressures may impact potential gains. We conduct case studies of Kenya, Uganda and Tanzania to demonstrate the issue and provide high-level policy recommendations.

6.2 Mobile Money as a Gamechanger for Development, Human Rights and Social Justice in Africa

Mobile Money is the supply of financial services using mobile networks and SIM-enabled devices, primarily mobile phones.[8] Three forms of services occur using mobile money—mobile finance, mobile banking and mobile payments.[9] The technology behind mobile money requires a cash flow infrastructure and cash flows through a network of cash issuers or merchants.[10] Cash merchants, depending on regulations, could be independent mobile network operators, a financial institution, another licensed third-party provider or a mix of these providers.

The use of mobile money payments in Africa commenced in 2000, however, the success story of mobile money began with M-PESA in 2007, which gained 2.37 million subscribers in about a year and quickly spread into other African countries.[11] Its proliferation prompted the exponential growth of mobile money platforms.[12] In 2020, the African e-payments industry generated US$24 billion in revenues, with almost half of the revenues generated from 47 billion individual domestic transactions.[13] This could be attributed to the Covid-19 pandemic national lockdowns that created a shift in consumer payment patterns from traditional payment platforms to digital platforms. Africa's domestic e-payments market revenues are predicted to grow annually by 20%, culminating in an overall revenue base of US$40 billion by 2025.[14] The benefits of this proliferation are both macroeconomic and microeconomic and include the following.

6.2.1 The Local Business Environment

Mobile money platforms support an ecosystem of businesses that can promote increased economic activities. Mobile money aids businesses to gain access to more customers and new services. These businesses, in turn, create employment that increases the tax base through expanded savings, and investments in the formal and informal economy.[15] At a household level, mobile money increases household savings and consumption which drives production in the larger economy. In many African countries, mobile money has contributed to socio-economic growth and productivity by facilitating entrepreneurship leading to more MSMEs. For example, the Kenyan economy witnessed a 14% per capita real income growth between 2006 and 2013 after the emergence of M-Pesa.[16]

6.2.2 *Financial and Digital Inclusion*

Mobile Money platforms serve as the desired instrument that may help Africa meet its economic goals of transformation into a cashless society by bringing MSMEs in the informal sector into the formal sector.[17] Consequently, MSMEs can improve payment collection with faster transactions and access to digital loans.

The International Finance Corporation's (IFC) study of Madagascar reveals that since the introduction of mobile money services, digital inclusion stands at 81%.[18] Madagascar has over 10 million mobile money accounts. Between 2016 and 2020, mobile money transactions reached a value of US$639 million. A study conducted by Evans on mobile money usage and financial inclusion in 44 African countries shows a significant positive relationship between mobile money usage and financial inclusion.[19] Greater penetration of mobile money and the increased access to financial services has also been vital for the financial inclusion gains of African countries like Kenya, South Africa, Nigeria and others over the past years.[20]

6.2.3 *Cross-Border and Regional Trade*

Financial inclusion and access provided by mobile money services, its affordability and ubiquity support cross-border transactions for international trade. Mobile money services may foster regional trade, particularly with the AfCFTA as a machinery to facilitate traditional and digitally enabled intra-African trade.[21] Mobile Money provides a platform for MSMEs and individuals across Africa to easily make payments. The role of small-scale cross-border trading activities cannot be underestimated, as they account for about 40% of Africa's regional trade.[22] The trade facilitation needs of this group remain high, and mobile money services can become critical to facilitate trade in this context. Notably, a study carried out by Sawadogo and Wandaogo shows that African countries with good mobile money services adoption registered a greater goods trade share in GDP of about 0.6% in comparison to non-adopters.[23]

6.2.4 *Development, Human Rights and Women's Empowerment*

Access to affordable financial services is critical for poverty reduction and economic growth. Mobile money has been used for person-to-person services (P2Ps), business-to-business services (B2Bs), business-to-person services (B2Ps) and government-to-person services (G2Ps).[24] Mobile money has contributed to financial access and inclusivity by ensuring the swift processing of large sizes of small transactions where infrastructure is non-existent or inadequate.[25] Additionally, marginalised groups have greater access to financial services. Accordingly, Adaba *et al* posit that mobile money has provided its users with the freedom and agency to accomplish their welfare goals.[26]

Mobile money permeation has direct and indirect impacts on the Sustainable Development Goals (SDGs) and human rights.[27] The use of mobile money as a developmental and human rights tool brings to life the idea that

> The power of digital technology to support the promise of human rights lies in the potential to finally reach those who have been, and remain, underserved throughout much of history—a promise that goes back to the Charter of the United Nations.[28]

Accordingly, from a capacity perspective, mobile money contributes to providing access to public services such as education, financial services and other social protections. Increased access to services reduces inequality and poverty. Mobile money has also helped in improving the gender gap for account ownership, which tends to be low for the usual bank account ownership. A study conducted in Senegal showed that over 55% of women in Senegal own a mobile money account.[29]

6.3 Mobile Money in Africa and Its Taxation: The Case of Kenya, Uganda and Tanzania

With the growing prevalence of the use of mobile money as a payment option among the unbanked population, an increasing number of African countries impose mobile money taxes for a variety of economic and regulatory reasons. By taxing this vast volume of financial transactions, governments hope to capitalise on this lucrative revenue source. In addition, formalising the unofficial sector of the economy has the potential to both increase the rate of tax compliance and broaden the revenue base.

Although several African countries have introduced mobile money taxes, three countries from the East African sub-region have been selected as case studies for this chapter—Kenya, Uganda and Tanzania. The case studies delve into the integration of mobile money tax in the national tax systems of these countries and explore their reception and impacts. They have been selected due to the significant mobile money penetration in these countries, and because they demonstrate the potential social and economic consequences of mobile money taxation. These case studies emphasise the significance of striking a balance between DRM and the financial inclusion of marginalised communities and individuals with lower incomes.

6.3.1 Mobile Money Taxes in Kenya

Kenya has several tax provisions on digital products. Beginning with the implementation of the excise tax on airtime in 2003, Kenya has subsequently revised its taxation policies on digital goods, including mobile phones and computer gadgets.[30] However, in 2018 the Kenyan government through its Finance Act, introduced stronger taxes on mobile money transactions.[31] The Finance Act increased the excise tax on money transfer services by banks from 10% to 20%; airtime taxes from 10% to 15%; mobile financial transactions from 10% to 12%; and a 15% excise tax on internet data services and fixed-line telephone services.[32] Prior to the introduction of the mobile money tax, Kenya had experienced significant growth in mobile money services, with Safaricom's M-Pesa being the predominant market participant.[33] M-Pesa had revolutionised financial services in Kenya, allowing millions of people to send and receive money, pay bills, and access other financial services through their mobile phones.[34] Recognising the potential of this sector, the government saw an opportunity for DRM by taxing mobile money transactions.

The mobile money tax was initially set at a rate of 10% on all mobile money transfers, including person-to-person transactions and payments for goods and services.[35] The introduction of the mobile money tax resulted in criticism from various stakeholders, including mobile money service providers, consumers and civil society organisations. Critics argued that the tax would increase the cost of using mobile money services, potentially discouraging usage and hindering financial inclusion.[36] They also raised concerns about the potential negative impact on small businesses and the overall economy. In response to the public outcry, the government made several changes to the mobile money tax policy. In the financial year of 2013/2014, the tax rate was reduced from 10% to 10 Kenyan shillings (approximately 0.1 US$) per transaction.[37] This move aimed to alleviate the burden on consumers and promote the affordability of mobile money services. However, the reduction in the tax rate did not fully address the concerns raised by the public and stakeholders.

The 2018 amendment to the Finance Act, resulted in reduced transaction volumes from 1.5 billion transactions per annum in 2017 to 1.3 billion transactions per annum in 2018.[38] This may hinder the use of mobile phone-based transactions and incentivise consumers to return to previous alternatives of cash transactions to evade taxes, which frustrates the revenue generation intent of introducing mobile money taxes in the first place.[39] Additionally, the trend of increased mobile money taxes since the beginning of the Covid-19 pandemic may adversely impact the digital economy, small businesses and the overall economy.

The evolution of mobile money tax in Kenya, which is the pioneer for mobile money services in Africa, reflects the challenges surrounding the taxation of mobile money transactions. While the government's intention was to generate revenue and formalise the sector, it has instead hindered financial inclusion, particularly for low-income individuals who heavily relied on mobile money for their financial transactions. Diouf *et al* studies using country-level data to assess the impact of mobile money tax in the use of mobile money transaction amounts and volume provide reduced changes in the use of mobile money services.[40] Mobile money taxes fostered a significant reduction in the volume of the use of mobile money services in sending and receiving money, but not the amount of the transaction. In addition, users who send and receive money within households use mobile money services less regularly. Overall, using disaggregated values, the introduction of mobile money taxes had a more detrimental effect on poorer and large households with prior difficulty in financial inclusion before the tax.[41]

The effect of a mobile money tax depends on variable factors including the size of the household, policy design, the business climate, the purpose of using mobile services tax, among others. Policymakers should not view the mobile money industry as easy to tax due to the high turnover of transactions, without considering its level of regression and the tougher impact on poorer populations. Instead, they need to carefully consider the implications of these taxes. Some of these implications may include assessing how mobile money taxes may hamper regular usage of mobile services which detracts from efforts for financial inclusivity.[42] Other policy implications considerations include the elasticity of mobile money tax revenue and mobile money taxes, obliteration of the gains made in digital payments adoption due to rising costs and tax burden in favour of cash-based payment which has little to no transaction costs, adverse impact of investment attraction and innovations in mobile money services industry, and other implications which should be considered in designing the right mobile money policy.

6.3.2 Mobile Money Taxes in Uganda

The proliferation of mobile money taxes in Uganda has been characterised by controversy and public outcry, mirroring the experience in Kenya. The introduction of this tax in 2018 sparked significant opposition, leading to several revisions in the tax policy. As is also the case with Kenya, the debates surrounding the taxation of mobile money transactions in Uganda also reflect the challenges of balancing revenue generation with promoting affordability and financial inclusion.

In 2018 the Ugandan government introduced the Excise Duty (Amendment) Act,[43] which imposed a tax on mobile money transactions. Before the introduction of the mobile money tax, Uganda had witnessed the increased popularity of mobile money platforms such as MTN Mobile Money and Airtel Money, for transfers, paying bills and accessing financial services.[44] Recognising the potential of this sector, the government saw an opportunity for DRM by taxing these transactions. Initially, the mobile money tax was set at a rate of 1% on all transactions, including deposits, withdrawals and transfers.[45]

The introduction of the mobile money tax led to widespread protests and opposition from various stakeholders, including mobile money service providers, civil society organisations and the public.[46] Many stakeholders maintained that the tax would increase the cost of using mobile money services, potentially discouraging usage and hindering financial inclusion. In response, in July 2018, just a few weeks after the tax was introduced, the tax rate was reduced from 1% to 0.5% on withdrawals.[47] This reduction aimed to alleviate the burden on consumers and promote the affordability of mobile money services. However, the revised tax policy still faced significant opposition. Critics argued that the tax was regressive and disproportionately affected low-income individuals who relied heavily on mobile money for their financial transactions.[48] The revised tax policy was seen by the government as a positive step towards addressing the public's concerns.[49] However, some critics argue that the tax remains a burden for low-income individuals and still hinders financial inclusion.[50]

6.3.3 Mobile Money Taxes in Tanzania

In 2013, the Tanzanian government introduced a Data Card Tax as part of its efforts to increase revenue and promote financial inclusion.[51] The tax was imposed on mobile money transactions, which, as is the case with other countries in the region, were becoming increasingly popular. At the time, mobile money services were rapidly growing in Tanzania, with millions of people using their mobile phones to send and receive money.[52] Recognising the potential of this technology, the government saw an opportunity to generate revenue by taxing these transactions.

The rationale behind Tanzania's mobile taxes is to finance development projects, applied in addition to an 18% VAT, and a 10% excise duty on mobile money transfer and withdrawal fees.[53] This tax applied to both P2P transactions and payments for goods and services. Mobile money service providers were responsible for collecting the tax on behalf of the government and remitting it to the Tanzania Revenue Authority. The introduction of the mobile money tax was met with mixed reactions. Critics of the tax raised concerns that it would hinder financial inclusion and burden low-income individuals who heavily relied on mobile money. Others believed that it was a necessary measure to increase government revenue for public services and development projects and ensure a fairer tax system by helping to formalise the informal economy. Resultantly, the government introduced measures to mitigate the impact of the tax on low-income individuals by exempting transactions below a certain threshold and thus enabling small transactions to remain tax-free to not disproportionately affect the poor.

In 2016, the government further expanded the mobile tax system by introducing the Mobile Phone Tax. This tax was imposed on airtime purchases, with a rate of 10%.[54] Similar to the mobile money tax, mobile network operators were responsible for collecting and remitting the tax to the government. In 2021, the Tanzanian Government also introduced a series of Electronic Communication Levies, including the Mobile Money Transaction Levy. These taxes also faced criticism from various stakeholders, including mobile network operators and consumers who argued that the tax would increase the cost of communication. The Mobile Phone Tax also raises concerns about its potential impact on the telecommunications industry.[55] These taxes may impact investments in network infrastructure and slow down digitalisation.

Mobile money services in Tanzania have served as a key driver of socio-economic growth by generating employment, enabling savings, improving business productivity and investments and so on.[56] The assessment above however demonstrates that the introduction of the various mobile money taxes in Tanzania appears to be gradually reversing digital financial gains made, indicating a policy incongruence which may impact financial services expansion gains. The GSMA Impact Analysis Report indicates that following the initiation of the mobile money levy, a lower growth trajectory of mobile money P2P transfers and cash-out transactions, especially in July and August 2021.[57] Specifically, between the months of June to September 2021, mobile money transfer volume fell from 30 to 18 million for P2P transactions per month and from 33 to 25 million for cash-out transactions per month.[58]

6.4 Unintended Outcomes of Mobile Money Tax on E-commerce in Africa

The widespread trend of new mobile money taxes as a languid attempt at DRM in the Aftermath of the Covid-19 pandemic may create issues for African countries, which are still at a nascent stage in Africa and not fully developed for global competition. Some of the intended issues of mobile money tax include the following.

6.4.1 Conflict with the Canons and Principles of Taxation

Efficient tax systems are a product of deliberate adherence to principles that aid the administration of optimal and equitable taxes. According to Murphy, taxes are not only an economic consideration, but they are also more of a political tool that gauges the ability of governments to exercise economic control and citizens to demand representation.[59] Most tax policies are based on principles called the canons of taxation, that prevent the arbitrariness of taxes that created unrest and inefficiency in his time. These are the canons of equality—arising from taxpayers' ability to contribute to the support of the government in proportion to their respective abilities; the Canon of Certainty—where time, manner, the quantity of taxes paid must be clear; the Canon of Convenience—where the time of tax levy must be convenient for the payer and canon of the economy—where the collection of taxes must be cost-sensitive with little possibility of leakages, complexity and corruption.[60] From the four canons, an efficient tax system should be based on the ability of the taxpayer to pay the tax while subsequently benefiting from public services. Also, a tax system from the canon principles must not interfere with the market, i.e., increasing production that generates more revenue. So far, the mobile money taxes appear not to meet a good number of these criteria.

The imposition of mobile money taxes violates the fiscal horizontal equity principle where persons in similar positions are subject to the same tax liability. Therefore, the implication may be that business decisions should be motivated by purely tax considerations, rather than economic ones. For, example, there is evidence that these taxes lowered domestic tax revenue.[61] Using the ability-to-pay principle, mobile money taxes affect marginalised consumers because the tax burden may not be fairly distributed among taxpayers. It detracts from the previous economic policy of digital financial inclusion and its activities. Mobile money consumption and purchasing patterns, especially for cross-border e-commerce trade with an intra-African trade consequence. This arises from the impact of mobile money tax on individual decisions who may return to traditional payment methods, which creates automatic discrimination against traditional payment system users and mobile money platform users. Under the benefit principle, it is unclear how the tax policy behind mobile money taxes justifies the taxes and how the mobile money industry would benefit from these taxes. So far, it appears that the mobile money tax interferes with the market's allocation of economic resources, violating the efficiency canon of taxation.

The principle of neutrality is affected by the imposition of mobile money taxation. Mobile money taxes impose an excessive burden that might distort the production and consumption economic decisions of taxpayers and business decisions.[62] Imposing taxes that are not at par with marginal increases in overall taxation may foster a public perception of preferential tax treatment that may lead to rising discontent as seen in the case of Cameroon in 2022.[63] A completely proper and fair deduction that is permitted to the group may be perceived by many others to be improper, because according to Kahn, in the world of taxes, public perception is reality.[64] Under the Ottawa Framework for Taxation, taxation of e-commerce is based on the same principles as taxation for other commercial activities: neutrality, efficiency, certainty and simplicity, effectiveness and fairness and flexibility.[65] So far, mobile money taxes do not meet some of these principles, especially the principles of certainty and simplicity, where tax rules should be clear and simple to understand. Mobile Money tax rules appear to be designed in such a manner that taxpayers cannot easily anticipate the tax consequences in advance of a mobile transaction. The principle of fairness is also undermined. There is a high likelihood that mobile money taxes may generate sufficient taxes based on the sheer volume of transactions based on mobile subscription and mobile account ownership. However, the potential for tax evasion and avoidance is relatively high because of the elasticity of mobile money services.

On the policy front, besides expanding the tax base for revenue mobilisation, there is no future justification for imposing mobile money taxes. The reason for this is not farfetched, because many African countries generally announce public policies based on political motives rather than sound economic or tax principles.[66] Mobile money taxes are justified by a lack of understanding and political over-confidence in the internet value chain in Africa, which is relatively young. Mobile money taxes appear to compound the connectivity and supportive infrastructural barriers faced in segments of the internet value chain.

6.4.2 Promotes Economic Double Taxation and Tax Avoidance

Increasing domestic revenue from the back-to-back global economic setbacks in the past couple of years has African lawmakers resorting to all forms of tax tactics that may be counter-productive to its development interests.

Some scholars have described mobile money tax as a thoughtless tax with the potential to increase the tax burden on industry stakeholders and consumers. Mobile money tax beyond conflicting with the principles of taxation, may also promote economic double taxation based on the Haig-Simons income taxation concept. Under the concept, income mobile money taxes may promote economic double taxes in two ways, using the present consumption and the present value of a mobile money taxpayer's future consumption. Personal income in the hands of the taxpayer is taxed. Subsequent savings of the taxed income, especially if deposited in the bank become present money saved for future purposes.

When the money is saved at its present value for consumption at a future date (mobile money), it will ordinarily not incur a tax because it was taxed in the (previous) year in which it was earned. The justification for taxing the saved money in the year it was earned is to capture the present value of the money (which will ultimately be expended on consumption at a later indeterminable date). However, the imposition of mobile money tax appears thus to tax the (discounted) value of savings that would be spent in a future year as well as the income earned on the savings (now an investment income arising from say interest paid on the savings). Therefore, to tax the income in a previous year and tax it again on its consumption date amounts to double taxation on savings. Double taxation irrespective of its form impedes trade and investment and contributes to tax avoidance.

Whereas mobile money offers a convenience value for its users, it may erroneously be taken as an essential service. A high pricing adjustment triggers a negative consumer reaction—where consumers abandon traditional payment alternatives. Using the Laffer curve, it is unclear how mobile money taxes may be the salvation of DRM challenges for African countries.[67]

This is because the premise of mobile services demand or consumption explosion is not strong enough to impose taxes on its consumption. In addition to other forms of consumption taxes like VATs, imposing mobile money tax may make the overall consumption taxes too high. High tax rates or excessive consumption taxes in this case may discourage mobile money producers from producing more output, and households are reluctant to transact, unless necessary, as Figure 6.1 depicts. Ndung'u justifies the Laffer principle that the operation of mobile money tax could, in theory, raise market alterations from imposing taxes, which would lead to tax revenue decline once the optimal tax rate threshold is exceeded.[68] The vagueness of mobile money taxation and its policy justification can weaken the enforcement capabilities of implementing authorities like the revenue office.[69] This is because tax revenue is affected by a myriad of variables, not just the average tax rate. Tax avoidance considerations may encourage a trend where mobile money service providers will limit investment and reduce mobile money penetration. In turn, a lack of investment interest may lead to lower customers and, consequently, the loss of the socio-economic benefits derived from this mobile money usage.

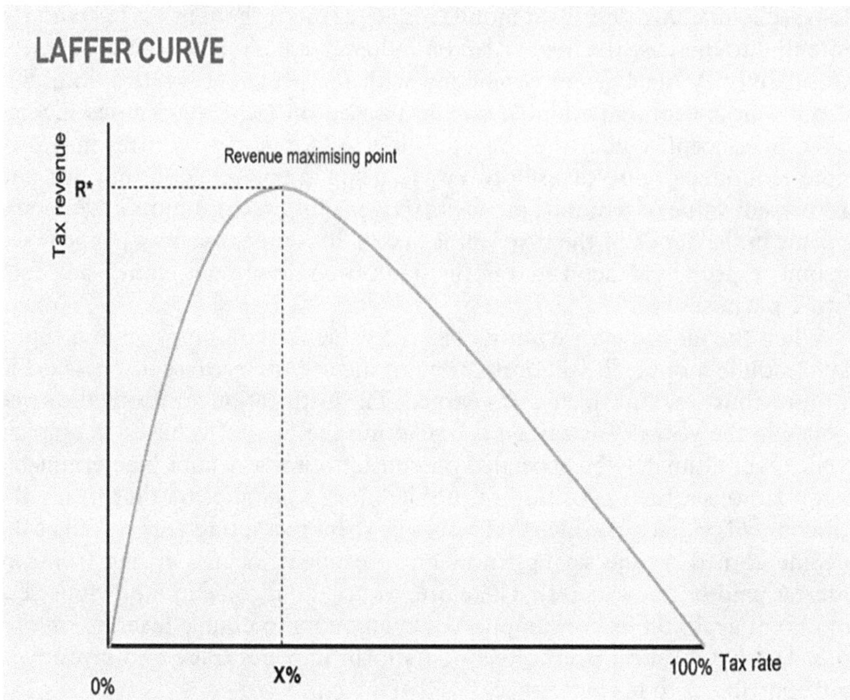

Figure 6.1 Laffer Curve on Optimal Tax for Mobile Money.

6.4.3 Contributes to Mobile Money Flight

Political and legal certainty is one of the primary indicators for foreign investment considerations. Incidentally, it is one of the reasons sustainable foreign investment flows into Africa are not at an optimal level. Investors are apprehensive about the risks that come from frequent and incoherent legal, policy and political changes. The mobile money tax as it stands now goes against the government's policy direction of expanding financial inclusion. The burden bearers of the mobile money tax are the poor, who do not have the financial capability to cope with the infrequent and increased changes made to the tax system from widening the tax base. There is also some level of uncertainty on how mobile money tax improves the delivery of social benefits. For example, in Uganda, since the introduction of the mobile money tax, 44% of survey respondents transacted less in July of the year it was introduced and 47% stopped using mobile money completely.[70]

The introduction of mobile money tax as an easy channel for DRM disrupts the years of private and public efforts made for the digital inclusion of African MSMEs, especially in inaccessible regions. While mobile money taxation helps governments meet their revenue generation responsibilities to finance development and recover from economic losses from the Covid-19 pandemic on one hand, it encourages mobile money flight on the other hand. Generally, mobile money taxes considerably challenge the sustainability of the mobile money services ecosystem.

6.5 Policy Recommendations

Policies towards advancing mobile money usage have improved business productivity, easier access to trade finance, and economic growth. However, the imposition of mobile money taxes in the medium to long term has increased transaction costs, deterring its value as a financial inclusion tool. This impacts its utility as a tool for broadening the tax base and threatens the African Union Agenda 2063 goals and the SDGs. This section makes recommendations on policy considerations in the future development of a mobile money taxation approach by policymakers, as well as directions for raising revenue beyond mobile money taxation.

6.5.1 Striking a Balance: Policy Considerations for Developing Mobile Money Taxation Policy and Reforms

This chapter has sought to demonstrate that mobile money tax policies are often aimed at generating DRM and fostering economic development, but the consequences of such policies extend far beyond fiscal considerations. Mobile money tax is not the most progressive approach to driving the digital economy and promoting tax compliance. More innovative approaches can be used to encourage a move away from cash-based payments and rather incentivise digital transactions. However, where this taxation approach is preferred, it needs to be balanced and equitable and should mitigate the various potential negative impacts on financial inclusion, economic growth and even human rights. In so doing, best practices should be considered. Among the key considerations or actions that may catalyse changes to the formulation of a regulatory framework.

a *Policymakers need to thoroughly assess the potential consequences of tax policy in the financial service sector*: This chapter has both explored the developmental consequences of the proliferation of mobile money services, as well as the potential threats of the taxation of these services. While mobile money taxes are becoming more prevalent, policymakers exploring DRM options, should not merely join the bandwagon, but should, conduct a comprehensive assessment of its potential consequences prior to implementing this tax approach. These assessments should include the consideration of impacts on (1) the growth of the digital economy, (2) financial inclusion broadly, (3) low-income households and individuals and (4) vulnerable groups like women and persons with disabilities. At the core of policy development should be stakeholder engagement, which can include engagement with network operators. This collaborative approach will help incorporate the concerns of the relevant stakeholders.

b *Should a mobile money tax approach be chosen, policymakers need to instate thorough monitoring and evaluation on impacts*: As part of the robust monitoring and evaluation mechanisms needed to assess the impact of mobile money tax policies, policymakers need to (1) conduct regular reviews of the effectiveness of the tax structure in achieving the DRM objectives and (2) conduct impact assessments that evaluate the socio-economic ramifications of the tax policy. This ensures that the policy remains pertinent, equitable and in line with the changing demands of both the economy and society.

c *Financial inclusion should be at the core of the policy approach chosen*: Policymakers must prioritise the promotion of financial inclusion in formulating any mobile money tax policy. Mobile money has proven instrumental in extending financial services to unbanked individuals, making it crucial for tax structures to be designed in a manner that minimizes the impact on the affordability and accessibility of mobile money services, particularly for vulnerable communities.

d *Design mobile money tax policies to ensure a balanced tax system*: To achieve this, it is necessary to implement an effective burden-sharing mechanism that places more responsibility on higher-value transactions or individuals with greater wealth, while providing exemptions or reduced rates for smaller transactions or low-income earners. The objective of this approach is to promote financial inclusion and ensure affordability for all.

6.5.2 Exploring Alternative DRM Approaches: Curtail Wasteful Fiscal Spending and Tax High-Net-Worth Persons

Taxes are relevant to enable the government to provide essential public services through social spending on education, critical infrastructure and others. However, public approval and cooperation in the introduction of new tax types is essential to the success of these taxes. Taxpayers have repetitively witnessed a lack of accountability with many African governments in the use of taxes, evidence of a problem of wasteful fiscal spending. Governments are notorious for creating new programmes and agencies, leading to financial pressures on a lean revenue purse. Wasteful spending has been a contributing factor to the deteriorating fiscal strength. Therefore, it is recommended that national governments review and reorganise tax revenues received against clear and pro-development programmes and initiatives. This can be achieved by eliminating duplicative programs and conducting oversight and periodic reviews of tax revenues and their resulting spending categories, their socio-economic development contribution and sharing this information with the public. This will help in setting the basis for public trust and transparency that ensure public approval for new tax types. In addition, the government can focus and create other tax forms that do not overstretch the tax burden of marginalised groups like women and the poor which the mobile money tax does. Instead, the government can meet its urgent revenue needs by creating taxes for high-net-worth individuals and corporations whose effective tax rates are unjustified and creating specialised units within the revenue offices to tax this subset of taxpayers whose effective taxes are usually not commensurate with the benefits received from using public goods and services.

6.6 Conclusion

The rapid expansion of mobile money in Africa has encouraged the adoption of a regressive taxation strategy for mobile money services. While mobile money taxes have their pros and cons, it becomes crucial to refine taxation approaches to achieve a balance between generating revenue and promoting financial inclusion. As economic and regulatory landscapes continue to evolve, policymakers should play a crucial role in monitoring and adjusting tax frameworks to facilitate the sustainable expansion of mobile money services. It is essential to strike a balance that promotes a fair and favourable environment for e-commerce and financial inclusion in Africa. By tackling the challenges discussed in this chapter and embracing creative solutions, African nations can unleash the complete potential of mobile money as a catalyst for economic growth and enhanced financial inclusivity among their populations.

Notes

1 R Mishra & S Bvuma, 'Conceptualising the relationship between mobile money banking and financial inclusion to support sustained economic growth' (2022) 13 *African Journal of Public Affairs* 54–78.
2 J Aron, 'Mobile money and the economy: A review of the evidence' (2018) 33. World Bank Research Observer 135–188.
3 As of 2018, there were 132 Mobile Money Platforms owned by Mobile Network Operators in Sub-Sahara Africa. These platforms recorded a total of 395.7 million registered accounts. See GSMA, *State of the Industry Report on Mobile Money State of the Industry Report* (2018) 2–15. Kenyan M-PESA is the most popular, with over 50 million users in over six countries. See Vodacom, What is M-Pesa, https://www.vodafone.com/about-vodafone/what-we-do/consumer-products-and-services/m-pesa.
4 J Lepoutre & A Oguntoye, 'The (non-) emergence of mobile money systems in Sub-Saharan Africa: A comparative multilevel perspective of Kenya and Nigeria' (2018) 131 *Technological Forecasting and Social Change* 262–275.
5 AH Ahmad, C Green & F Jiang. 'Mobile money, financial inclusion and development: A review concerning African experience' (2020) 34 (4) *Journal of Economic Surveys* 753–792.
6 OECD, Programme of Work to Develop a Consensus Solution to the Tax Challenges Arising from the Digitalisation of the Economy, OECD/G20 Inclusive Framework on BEPS (2019) 1–4 www.oecd.org/tax/beps/programme-of-work-to-develop-aconsensussolution-to-the-tax-challenges-arising-from-the-digitalisation-of-the-economy.htm.
7 Research ICT Africa, Multifaceted challenges of digital taxation in Africa Policy Brief (2020) 1–7 https://researchictafrica.net/wp/wp-content/uploads/2020/11/Final-Tax-PB_30112020.pdf accessed 8 November 2024.
8 Research ICT Africa, Multifaceted challenges of digital taxation in Africa Policy Brief (2020) 1–7 https://researchictafrica.net/wp/wp-content/uploads/2020/11/Final-Tax-PB_30112020.pdf accessed 8 November 2024.

9 Such as peer-to-peer transfers), finance (such as insurance products) and banking (such as account balance inquiries). Also, see K Donovan, 'Mobile money for financial inclusion' (2012) 61 (1) *Information and Communications for Development* 61–73.

10 N Hughes & S Lonie, 'M-PESA: mobile money for the "unbanked" turning cellphones into 24-hour tellers in Kenya' (2007) 2 *Innovations: Technology, Governance, Globalization* 63–81.

11 Vodacom (n 3).

12 McKinsey, The future of payments in Africa, 7 September 2022 https://www.mckinsey.com/industries/financial-services/our-insights/the-future-of-payments-in-africa accessed 8 November 2024.

13 Mobile money transactions in Africa are valued at $836.5bn, which is about two-thirds of the global value. See GSMA, *The State of The Industry Report on Mobile Money* (2023) 7–10.

14 McKinsey (n 12).

15 These include Mobile network operators, banks, payment card companies, mobile money agents and liquidity management firms and so on. See FY Mpofu, 'Industry 4.0 in Financial Services: Mobile Money Taxes, Revenue Mobilisation, Financial Inclusion, and the Realisation of Sustainable Development Goals (SDGs) in Africa' (2022) 14 *Sustainability* 8667.

16 Vodacom (n 3). See also J Aron, 'Mobile money and the economy: a review of the evidence' (2018) 33. World Bank Research Observer 135–188.

17 A Tsemane, 'The impact of mobile money on financial inclusion in Lesotho' A field study submitted to the UFS Business School in the Faculty of Economic and Management Sciences in November 2015.

18 O Monnier, Madagascar's Mobile Money Boom, 15 February 2023, *IFC Insights*. https://www.ifc.org/wps/wcm/connect/news_ext_content/ifc_external_corporate_site/news+and+events/news/insights/madagascars-mobile-money-boom accessed 8 November 2024.

19 O Evans, 'Connecting the poor: The internet, mobile phones and financial inclusion in Africa' (2018) 20 *Digital Policy, Regulation and Governance* 568–581.

20 FY Mpofu & D Mhlanga, 'Digital financial inclusion, digital financial services tax and financial inclusion in the fourth industrial revolution era in Africa' (2022) 10 *Economies* 184.

21 F Sawadogo & A Wandaogo, 'Does mobile money services adoption foster intra-African goods trade' (2021) 119 *Economics Letters 109681.*

22 Simonetta Zarrilli, 'What future for women small-scale and informal cross-border traders when borders close?' UNCTAD (8 May 2020) https://unctad.org/news/what-future-women-small-scale-and-informal-cross-border-traders-when-borders-close accessed 8 November 2024; Kimberley Nyajeka, 'How can the AfCFTA assist Small Scale Traders?' TRALAC (28 Jul 2021) https://www.tralac.org/blog/article/15301-how-can-the-afcfta-assist-small-scale-traders.html accessed 8 November 2024.

23 F Sawadogo & Wandaogo (n 21).

24 LP Sekantsi, 'Digital financial services uptake in Africa and its role in financial inclusion of women' (2019) 4 *Journal of Digital Bank* 161–174.

25 For a discussion on the growth and social impacts of mobile money see T Suri & W Jack, 'The long-run poverty and gender impacts of mobile money' (2016) 354 (6317) *Science* 1288–1292.

26 GB Adaba, DA, Young & DY Abbott, 'Exploring the contribution of mobile money to well-being from a capability perspective (2019) 85 *The Electronic Journal of Information Systems in Developing Countries* 11.

27 Mobile money has been seen to directly facilitate 13 of the SDGs, including SDG1 (No Poverty), SDG 2 (Zero Hunger), SDG 3 (Good Health and Wellbeing), SDG 4 (Quality Education) SDG 8 (Decent Work and Economic Growth), SDG 9

(Industry, Innovation and Infrastructure) and SDG 10 (Reduce Inequalities), See GSMA, 'The impact of mobile money on the UN Sustainable Development Goals'. (6 October 2016) https://www.gsma.com/mobilefordevelopment/uncategorized/the-impact-of-mobile-money-on-the-un-sustainable-development-goals/ accessed 8 November 2024.

28 Mariana Lopez & Karima Wardak 'The digital last mile: Where the achievement of human rights, sustainable development and women's empowerment meet' United Nations (23 March 2023) https://www.un.org/en/un-chronicle/digital-last-mile-where-achievement-human-rights-sustainable-development-and-women%E2%80%99s accessed 8 November 2024.

29 A Delaporte & N Naghavi, 'The promise of mobile money for further advancing women's financial inclusion' (2019) *GSMA Connected Women Mobile Money* 1–12.

30 For an assessment of the evolution and the more recent amendments of the Excise Duty Act, see A. Diouf, M Carreras & F Santoro, Taxing Mobile Money in Kenya: Impact on Financial Inclusion' Working ICTD Paper 168 https://opendocs.ids.ac.uk/opendocs/bitstream/handle/20.500.12413/18005/ICTD_WP168.pdf?sequence=1&isAllowed=y accessed 8 November 2024.

31 S. 32 (2) Kenyan Finance Act 2018. The Act has amended Section 10 of the *Excise Duty Act, 2015*. The Excise Act provides for the adjustment of the excise duty rates every two years. Also see A Kanyi et al., 'Kenya budget speech 2023/24 analysis' CDH Analysis 2023 https://www.cliffedekkerhofmeyr.com/news/publications/2023/Practice/Tax/tax-and-exchange-control-alert-16-june-2023-kenya-budget-speech-edition accessed 8 November 2024.

32 A Kanyi et al., 'Kenya budget speech 2023/24 analysis' CDH Analysis 2023 https://www.cliffedekkerhofmeyr.com/news/publications/2023/Practice/Tax/tax-and-exchange-control-alert-16-june-2023-kenya-budget-speech-edition accessed 8 November 2024.

33 E Nyamongo & LN Ndirangu, 'Financial innovations and monetary policy in Kenya' (2013) 52387 *MPRA Paper Series* https://www.nber.org/system/files/working_papers/w17129/w17129.pdf accessed 8 November 2024.

34 I Mbiti & DN Weil, "Mobile banking: The impact of M-Pesa in Kenya' (2011) 17129 *Nber Working Paper Series* 1–5.

35 J Fehling, 'How did the introduction of a mobile money tax in Kenya influence the usage of mobile money?' (2019) *Lund University Master Dissertation* 3–14 https://lup.lub.lu.se/luur/download?func=downloadFile&recordOId=8990690&fileOId=8990691 accessed 8 November 2024.

36 AH Ahmad, C Green & F Jiang, 'Mobile money, financial inclusion and development: A review with reference to African experience (2020) 34 (4) *Journal of Economic Surveys* 753–792 and R Mugume & EWN Bulime, 'Post-COVID-19 recovery for African economies: Lessons for digital financial inclusion from Kenya and Uganda' (2022) 34 *African Development Review* S161–S176.

37 NS Ndung'u, 'Taxing mobile phone transactions in Africa: Lessons from Kenya' *AGI* (2019) 3.

38 FSD Kenya, Financial Access Kenya https://www.fsdkenya.org/finaccess/finaccess/, accessed 8 November 2024.

39 K Mensah & N Bhalla, 'Africa's mobile money taxes risk driving poor out of digital economy' Reuters (25 May 2022) https://news.trust.org/item/20220525132730-c7nyf/ accessed 8 November 2024.

40 A Diouf, AM Carreras & F Santoro, 'Taxing mobile money in Kenya: Impact on financial inclusion' (2023) 168 ICTD Working Paper 1–52.

41 A Diouf, AM Carreras & F Santoro, 'Taxing mobile money in Kenya: Impact on financial inclusion' (2023) 168 ICTD Working Paper 27–28. However, the effect of mobile money was non-significant at the macroeconomic level on aggregated values.

42 F Pobee, AB Jibril & E Owusu-Oware, 'Does taxation of digital financial services adversely affect the financial inclusion agenda? Lessons from a developing country' 3 (2) (2023) *Digital Business* 1–5.
43 Ugandan Excise Duty (Amendment) Act 2018.
44 A Ndiwalana, O Morawczynski & O Popov, 'Mobile money use in Uganda: A preliminary study' 2 https://www.gsma.com/mobilefordevelopment/wp-content/uploads/2012/06/m4dmobilemoney.pdf accessed 8 November 2024.
45 PWC, What 1% new tax on mobile money transactions means, https://www.pwc.com/ug/en/press-room/what-new-tax-on-mobile-money-transactions-means.html accessed 15 August 2023.
46 S Asiimwe, Controversy over Uganda mobile money taxes, *The East African* 7 July 2023 accessed 15 August 2023.
47 PWC (n 45).
48 UNCDF, *The Impact of Mobile Money Taxation in Uganda* (2021) 1–14 and UNCDF, *Understanding the Consequences of Mobile Money Taxes in Uganda* (2018) https://www.uncdf.org/article/3892/understanding-the-consequences-of-mobile-money-taxes-in-uganda accessed on 31 July 2023.
49 Joyce Aheebwa, *Taxes not Responsible for High Cost of Mobile Money, says Finance Minister*, Monitor (2023) https://www.monitor.co.ug/uganda/business/finance/taxes-not-responsible-for-high-cost-of-mobile-money-says-finance-minister--4131542 accessed on 31 July 2023.
50 ICTD, 'There and Back Again: The making of Uganda's Mobile Money tax' (2021) 123 Working Paper, 1–7 https://www.ictd.ac/publication/there-back-again-uganda-mobile-money-tax/, accessed 15 August 2021.
51 PWC, Tanzania tax datacard 2013/2014 (2014) 1–6.
52 I Gaddisisis, G Wane & J Morisset, *How Can the Mobile Revolution Lift Up Tanzania's Poor?* World Bank Blog (2012) https://blogs.worldbank.org/africacan/how-can-the-mobile-revolution-lift-up-tanzania-s-poor accessed 8 November 2024.
53 I Gaddisisis, G Wane & J Morisset, *How Can the Mobile Revolution Lift Up Tanzania's Poor?* World Bank Blog (2012) https://blogs.worldbank.org/africacan/how-can-the-mobile-revolution-lift-up-tanzania-s-poor accessed 8 November 2024.
54 E Wainaina, Tanzania's 10% tax on Mobile Money Transactions Criticized, *Techweez* 16 June 2016, https://techweez.com/2016/06/13/tax-on-mobile-money-tanzania/ accessed 8 November 2024.
55 E Bermeo, Re-evaluating the taxation of mobile money, *Global Dev* 3 May 2023 https://globaldev.blog/re-evaluating-the-taxation-of-mobile-money/ accessed 8 November 2024.
56 The United Republic of Tanzania, *National Financial Inclusion Framework 2018–2022* (2018) 15–16.
57 GSMA, *Tanzania Mobile Money Levy Impact Analysis* (2021).
58 GSMA, *Tanzania Mobile Money Levy Impact Analysis* (2021) 9–10.
59 R Murphy, *The Joy of Tax* (Random 2015) 18–30.
60 O Soyode & GE Oyedokun, 'Relevance of Adam Smith canons of taxation to the modern tax system' (2019) 18 *Journal of Taxation and Economic Development*, 12–34. See also, A Smith, *The Wealth of Nations* Vol. 2 (1776). Online Library of Liberty. http://lf-oll.s3.amazonaws.com/titles/119/Smith_0206-02_EBk_v6.0.pdf.
61 FY Mpofu & T Moloi, 'Direct digital services taxes in Africa and the canons of taxation' (2022) 11 *Laws* 57.
62 HC Simons, 'Personal income taxation: The definition of income as a problem of fiscal policy' (1938) 7–15. See also RM Haig, 'The concept of income—economic and legal aspects' in Dean GW and Wells MC, *Forerunners of Realizable Values Accounting in Financial Reporting* (Garland 1982) 140–167. Simons defined 'personal income' as the increase in a taxpayer's wealth over a specified period (typically a period of a year) plus the market value of the taxpayer's consumption during that period.

63 Quentin Velluet, 'Tough times: MTN, Orange, Camtel: Cameroon's operators suffer financial pressures' (The Africa Report 23 June 2023) https://www.theafricareport.com/313829/mtn-orange-camtel-cameroons-operators-suffer-financial-pressures/ accessed 8 November 2024.
64 DA Kahn, 'The two faces of tax neutrality: Do they interact or are they mutually exclusive?' (1990) 18 *Northern Kentucky Law Review* 1–19.
65 OECD, 'Implementing the Ottawa Taxation Framework Conditions: Progress Since 2001 Report' 2003 https://www.oecd.org/tax/administration/20499630.pdf.
66 J Frieden, The Political Economy of Economic Policies (2020) *IFC Finance & Development* 3–7.
67 The Laffer curve shows the relationship between tax rates and total tax revenue. The Laffer curve states that total tax revenue is most likely not maximized when tax rates are at 100%, as this disincentives workers from earning wages. When rates are too low, government tax revenues are less maximized. The government has the opportunity to raise tariffs and increase revenue. But, if it is too high, it burdens the taxpayer and, in the end, leads to less tax revenue. See AB Laffer, 'The Laffer curve: Past, present, and future' (2004) 1765 *Backgrounder* 1–16.
68 NS Ndung'u, 'Taxing mobile phone transactions in Africa: Lessons from Kenya' (2019) *Brookings Africa Growth Initiative Policy Brief* 11–12.
69 X Pedros & MSivakumaran, 'Rethinking mobile taxation to improve connectivity' (2019) *GSMA* 1–5.
70 CM Okello, P Yourougou & JC Munene, 'Digital financial innovations in the twenty-first century: Do transaction tax exemptions promote mobile money services for financial inclusion in developing countries?' 36 *Journal of Economic and Administrative Sciences* 185–203.

Bibliography

A Smith, *The Wealth of Nations* Vol. 2 (1776). Online Library of Liberty. http://lf-oll.s3.amazonaws.com/titles/119/Smith_0206-02_EBk_v6.0.pdf

GB Adaba, DA Young & DY Abbott, 'Exploring the contribution of mobile money to well-being from a capability perspective' (2019) 85 *The Electronic Journal of Information Systems in Developing Countries* 11.

Joyce Aheebwa, *Taxes Not Responsible for High Cost of Mobile Money, says Finance Minister*, Monitor (2023) https://www.monitor.co.ug/uganda/business/finance/taxes-not-responsible-for-high-cost-of-mobile-money-says-finance-minister--4131542 accessed 31 July 2023.

AH Ahmad, C Green & F Jiang, 'Mobile money, financial inclusion and development: A review concerning African experience' (2020) 34 (4) *Journal of Economic Surveys* 753–792.

J Aron, 'Mobile money and the economy: a review of the evidence' (2018) 33 *World Bank Research Observer* 135–188.

S Asiimwe, 'Controversy over Uganda mobile money taxes' *The East African* 7 July 2023 accessed 15 August 2023.

E Bermeo, 'Re-evaluating the taxation of mobile money' *Global Dev* 3 May 2023 https://globaldev.blog/re-evaluating-the-taxation-of-mobile-money/ accessed 8 November 2024.

A Delaporte & N Naghavi, 'The promise of mobile money for further advancing women's financial inclusion' (2019) *GSMA Connected Women Mobile Money* 1–12. https://www.gsma.com/solutions-and-impact/connectivity-for-good/mobile-for-development/blog/the-promise-of-mobile-money-for-further-advancing-womens-financial-inclusion/

A Diouf, M Carreras & F Santoro, 'Taxing mobile money in Kenya: Impact on financial inclusion' Working ICTD Paper 168 (2023) https://opendocs.ids.ac.uk/opendocs/

bitstream/handle/20.500.12413/18005/ICTD_WP168.pdf?sequence=1&isAllowed=y accessed 8 November 2024.

K Donovan, 'Mobile money for financial inclusion' (2012) 61 (1) *Information and Communications for Development* 61–73.

O Evans, 'Connecting the poor: The internet, mobile phones and financial inclusion in Africa' (2018) 20 *Digital Policy, Regulation and Governance* 568–581.

J Fehling, 'How did the introduction of a mobile money tax in Kenya influence the usage of mobile money?' (2019) *Lund University Master Dissertation* 3–14 https://lup.lub.lu.se/luur/download?func=downloadFile&recordOId=8990690&fileOId=8990691 accessed 8 November 2024.

J Frieden, 'The political economy of economic policies' (2020) *IFC Finance & Development*.https://www.imf.org/en/Publications/fandd/issues/2020/06/political-economy-of-economic-policy-jeff-frieden

FSD Kenya, 'Financial access Kenya' https://www.fsdkenya.org/finaccess/finaccess/, accessed 8 November 2024.

I Gaddisisis, G Wane & J Morisset, 'How can the mobile revolution lift up Tanzania's poor?' World Bank Blog (2012) https://blogs.worldbank.org/africacan/how-can-the-mobile-revolution-lift-up-tanzania-s-poor accessed 8 November 2024.

GSMA, 'The impact of mobile money on the UN Sustainable Development Goals' (6 October 2016) https://www.gsma.com/mobilefordevelopment/uncategorized/the-impact-of-mobile-money-on-the-un-sustainable-development-goals/ accessed 8 November 2024.

GSMA, *State of the Industry Report on Mobile Money State of the Industry Report* (2018) 2–15. https://www.gsma.com/r/wp-content/uploads/2019/05/GSMA-State-of-the-Industry-Report-on-Mobile-Money-2018-1.pdf

GSMA, *Tanzania Mobile Money Levy Impact Analysis* (2021). https://www.gsma.com/r/wp-content/uploads/2019/05/GSMA-State-of-the-Industry-Report-on-Mobile-Money-2018-1.pdf

RM Haig, 'The concept of income—economic and legal aspects' (in Dean GW and Wells MC, *Forerunners of Realizable Values Accounting in Financial Reporting* (Garland 1982) 140–167.

N Hughes & S Lonie, 'M-PESA: mobile money for the "unbanked" turning cellphones into 24-hour tellers in Kenya' (2007) 2 *Innovations: Technology, Governance, Globalization* 63–81.

ICTD, 'There and back again: The making of Uganda's mobile money tax' (2021) 123 *Working Paper* 1–7 https://www.ictd.ac/publication/there-back-again-uganda-mobile-money-tax/, accessed 15 August 2021.

DA Kahn, 'The two faces of tax neutrality: Do they interact or are they mutually exclusive?' (1990) 18 *Northern Kentucky Law Review* 1–19.

A Kanyi et al., 'Kenya budget speech 2023/24 analysis' CDH Analysis 2023 https://www.cliffedekkerhofmeyr.com/news/publications/2023/Practice/Tax/tax-and-exchange-control-alert-16-june-2023-kenya-budget-speech-edition accessed 8 November 2024.

AB Laffer, 'The Laffer curve: Past, present, and future' (2004) 1765 *Backgrounder* 1–16.

J Lepoutre & A Oguntoye, 'The (non-) emergence of mobile money systems in Sub-Saharan Africa: A comparative multilevel perspective of Kenya and Nigeria' (2018) 131 *Technological Forecasting and Social Change* 262–275.

Mariana Lopez & Karima Wardak 'The digital last mile: Where the achievement of human rights, sustainable development and women's empowerment meet' United Nations (23 March 2023) https://www.un.org/en/un-chronicle/digital-last-mile-where-achievement-human-rights-sustainable-development-and-women%E2%80%99s accessed 8 November 2024.

I Mbiti & DN Weil, 'Mobile banking: The impact of M-Pesa in Kenya' (2011) 17129 *Nber Working Paper Series* 1–5.

McKinsey, 'The future of payments in Africa' 7 September 2022 https://www.mckinsey.com/industries/financial-services/our-insights/the-future-of-payments-in-africa accessed 8 November 2024.

K Mensah & N Bhalla, 'Africa's mobile money taxes risk driving poor out of digital economy' Reuters (25 May 2022) https://news.trust.org/item/20220525132730-c7nyf/ accessed 8 November 2024.

R Mishra & S Bvuma, 'Conceptualising the relationship between mobile money banking and financial inclusion to support sustained economic growth' (2022) 13 *African Journal of Public Affairs* 54–78.

O Monnier, 'Madagascar's Mobile Money Boom' 15 February 2023, *IFC Insights* https://www.ifc.org/wps/wcm/connect/news_ext_content/ifc_external_corporate_site/news+and+events/news/insights/madagascars-mobile-money-boom accessed 8 November 2024.

FY Mpofu, 'Industry 4.0 in financial services: Mobile money taxes, revenue mobilisation, financial inclusion, and the realisation of Sustainable Development Goals (SDGs) in Africa' (2022) 14 *Sustainability* 8667.

FY Mpofu & D Mhlanga, 'Digital financial inclusion, digital financial services tax and financial inclusion in the fourth industrial revolution era in Africa' (2022) 10 *Economies* 184.

FY Mpofu & T Moloi, 'Direct digital services taxes in Africa and the canons of taxation' (2022) 11 *Laws* 57.

R Mugume & EWN Bulime, 'Post-COVID-19 recovery for African economies: Lessons for digital financial inclusion from Kenya and Uganda' (2022) 34 *African Development Review* S161–S176.

R Murphy, *The Joy of Tax* (Random House, 2015).

A Ndiwalana, O Morawczynski & O Popov, 'Mobile money use in Uganda: A preliminary study' (2010) https://www.gsma.com/mobilefordevelopment/wp-content/uploads/2012/06/m4dmobilemoney.pdf accessed 8 November 2024.

NS Ndung'u, 'Taxing mobile phone transactions in Africa: Lessons from Kenya' (2019) *Brookings Africa Growth Initiative Policy Brief*. https://www.brookings.edu/articles/taxing-mobile-phone-transactions-in-africa-lessons-from-kenya/#:~:text=A%20higher%20tax%20rate%20on,and%20so%20less%20tax%20revenue

Kimberley Nyajeka, 'How can the AfCFTA assist small scale traders?' TRALAC (28 July 2021) https://www.tralac.org/blog/article/15301-how-can-the-afcfta-assist-small-scale-traders.html accessed 8 November 2024.

E Nyamongo & LN Ndirangu, 'Financial innovations and monetary policy in Kenya' (2013) 52387 *MPRA Paper Series* https://www.nber.org/system/files/working_papers/w17129/w17129.pdf accessed 8 November 2024.

OECD, 'Implementing the Ottawa taxation framework conditions: Progress since 2001 report' (2003) https://www.oecd.org/tax/administration/20499630.pdf accessed 8 November 2024.

OECD, 'Programme of work to develop a consensus solution to the tax challenges arising from the digitalisation of the economy, OECD/G20 inclusive framework on BEPS' (2019) 1–4www.oecd.org/tax/beps/programme-of-work-to-develop-aconsensussolution-to-the-tax-challenges-arising-from-the-digitalisation-of-the-economy.htm accessed 8 November 2024.

CM Okello, P Yourougou & JC Munene, 'Digital financial innovations in the twenty-first century: Do transaction tax exemptions promote mobile money services for financial inclusion in developing countries?' (2019) 36 *Journal of Economic and Administrative Sciences* 185–203.

X Pedros & M Sivakumaran, 'Rethinking mobile taxation to improve connectivity' (2019) *GSMA* https://www.gsma.com/solutions-and-impact/connectivity-for-good/public-policy/gsma_resources/rethinking-mobile-taxation-to-improve-connectivity/

F Pobee, A B Jibril & E Owusu-Oware, 'Does taxation of digital financial services adversely affect the financial inclusion agenda? Lessons from a developing country' 3 (2) (2023) *Digital Business* 1–5.

PWC, 'Tanzania tax datacard 2013/2014' (2014) 1–6. https://www.pwc.co.tz/assets/pdf/tanzania-tax-datacard-2013-2014.pdf

PWC, 'What 1% new tax on mobile money transactions means' https://www.pwc.com/ug/en/press-room/what-new-tax-on-mobile-money-transactions-means.html accessed 15 August 2023.

Research ICT Africa, 'Multifaceted challenges of digital taxation in Africa Policy Brief' (2020) 1–7 https://researchictafrica.net/wp/wp-content/uploads/2020/11/Final-Tax-PB_30112020.pdf accessed 8 November 2024.

F Sawadogo & A Wandaogo, 'Does mobile money services adoption foster intra-African goods trade' (2021) 119 *Economics Letters* 109681.

LP Sekantsi, 'Digital financial services uptake in Africa and its role in financial inclusion of women' (2019) 4 *Journal of Digital Banking* 161–174.

HC Simons, 'Personal income taxation: The definition of income as a problem of fiscal policy' (1938) 7–15. https://archive.org/details/in.ernet.dli.2015.224813

O Soyode & GE Oyedokun, 'Relevance of Adam Smith Canons of taxation to the modern tax system' (2019) 18 *Journal of Taxation and Economic Development*, 12–34.

T Suri & W Jack, 'The long-run poverty and gender impacts of mobile money' (2016) 354 (6317) *Science* 1288–1292.

The United Republic of Tanzania, *National Financial Inclusion Framework 2018–2022* (2018).https://www.fsdt.or.tz/wp-content/uploads/2019/01/National-Financial-Inclusion-Framework-NFIF-2018-2022.pdf

A Tsemane, 'The impact of mobile money on financial inclusion in Lesotho' A field study submitted to the UFS Business School in the Faculty of Economic and Management Sciences in November 2015. https://scholar.ufs.ac.za/items/4bf91ee6-bf52-4097-8598-439d4896500c

Ugandan Excise Duty (Amendment) Act 2018. https://www.uncdf.org/article/7313/the-impact-of-mobile-money-taxation-in-uganda

UNCDF, *The Impact of Mobile Money Taxation in Uganda* (2021) https://www.uncdf.org/article/7313/the-impact-of-mobile-money-taxation-in-uganda

UNCDF, *Understanding the Consequences of Mobile Money Taxes in Uganda* (2018) https://www.uncdf.org/article/3892/understanding-the-consequences-of-mobile-money-taxes-in-ugandahttps://www.uncdf.org/article/3892/understanding-the-consequences-of-mobile-money-taxes-in-uganda accessed on 31 July 2023.

Quentin Velluet, 'Tough times: MTN, Orange, Camtel: Cameroon's operators suffer financial pressures' (The Africa Report 23 June 2023) https://www.theafricareport.com/313829/mtn-orange-camtel-cameroons-operators-suffer-financial-pressures/ accessed 8 November 2024.

Vodacom, 'What is M-Pesa' https://www.vodafone.com/about-vodafone/what-we-do/consumer-products-and-services/m-pesa accessed 8 November 2024.

E Wainaina, 'Tanzania's 10% tax on mobile money transactions criticized' *Techweez* 16 June 2016 https://techweez.com/2016/06/13/tax-on-mobile-money-tanzania/ accessed 8 November 2024.

Simonetta Zarrilli, 'What future for women small-scale and informal cross-border traders when borders close?' UNCTAD (8 May 2020) https://unctad.org/news/what-future-women-small-scale-and-informal-cross-border-traders-when-borders-close accessed 8 November 2024.

7 The South African Revenue Service's Role in Providing Access to Justice to Taxpayers

Carika Keulder[*]

7.1 Introduction

The South African Revenue Service (SARS) is tasked with effectively and efficiently collecting taxes in South Africa,[1] whilst at the same time it must respect taxpayers' rights.[2] An important piece of legislation that aims to balance these two interests, the Tax Administration Act 28 of 2011 (TAA), came into operation just over a decade ago on 1 October 2012.[3] Added to this important milestone in South African tax administration, the Commission of Inquiry into Tax Administration and Governance by SARS Report in 2018 and the 2022 Judicial Commission of Inquiry into State Capture Report[4] have shown that there has been '[a] [m]assive [f]ailure of [i]ntegrity and [g]overnance'[5] at SARS during the period 1 April 2014 to 31 March 2018.[6] Resultantly, SARS forms part of the government institutions which 49 per cent of South Africans do not trust.[7] In accordance with the political legitimacy theory, being perceived as untrustworthy impacts the trust in the revenue authority and taxpayers are then less inclined to pay their taxes.[8] Thus, at this time it is important to assess how SARS should balance these two competing interests.

In this chapter, the focus is on examining the role of SARS in facilitating access to justice for taxpayers. The central argument put forward is that the rule of law, in conjunction with the pertinent legislation, establishes the necessary framework to enable taxpayers to seek and obtain justice. Accordingly, the initial objective is to analyse the key principles and rights within the South African context that must be upheld and respected to ensure access to justice for taxpayers. Subsequently, the chapter proceeds to demonstrate that SARS should not exceed the requirements stipulated by this framework to foster access to justice. Finally, drawing from case law, this chapter identifies what upholding this framework entails.

* Carika Keulder, Professor School of Law, University of the Witwatersrand, South Africa.

DOI: 10.4324/9781003432890-9

7.2 Access to Justice Framework

Goal 16.3 of The United Nations' Sustainable Development Goals (SDGs) requires the promotion of the rule of law and ensuring equal access to justice for all. The rule of law forms the basis for access to justice as it ensures legal certainty and deter the arbitrary use of revenue powers.[9] Bentley remarks that adhering to the rule of law requires revenue authorities to respect taxpayers' rights in their daily operations.[10]

As the South African Constitution entrenches the rule of law as a core principle in South Africa,[11] it also forms the basis of providing access to justice to taxpayers in South Africa. At its core, the rule of law requires the government and organs of states, such as SARS, to adhere to 'pre-announced, clear and general rules'.[12]

Assuming that the framework adequately provides for access to justice, when SARS, as a creature of statute, acts within the four corners of the law by upholding legislation and administrative procedures, a taxpayer will have access to justice.[13] In the recent matter of *C:SARS v Esibonga Investment (Pty) Ltd*[14] the court reaffirmed the role of the rule of law in tax matters when it indicated that '[i]n the battle for the soul of SARS, the rule of law must trump shekel'.[15]

The first important component in the access to justice framework is s 195 of the Constitution. SARS as an organ of state within the public administration,[16] must provide services in an impartial, fair, equitable and unbiased manner,[17] be accountable[18] and act in a transparent manner.[19] Moreover, SARS must use resources in an efficient, economic and effective manner.[20] These basic values establish the basis of how SARS should conduct itself and they filter through to rights contained in the Bill of Rights, which SARS should respect.[21] Additionally, by adhering to these values, SARS contributes to achieving Goal 16.6 of the United Nations' SDGs, which emphasises effective, accountable and transparent institutions.

Turning to the rights in the Bill of Rights, the two foremost rights that provide access to justice are the rights of access to courts[22] and to just administrative action.[23] As regards the former, s 34 of the Constitution stipulates that '[e]veryone has the right to have any dispute that can be resolved by the application of law decided in a fair public hearing before a court or, where appropriate, another independent and impartial tribunal or forum'. This right prevents persons from taking the law into their own hands[24] and consequently gives effect to the *nemo iudex in propria causa est* (no one may be a judge in his or her own case),[25] one of the principles of natural justice.[26] In the South African tax context the right to access to courts is embodied in the tax dispute resolution procedure, which provides avenues for taxpayers to resolve their tax disputes.[27]

The right to access to courts also provides a party with the opportunity to have his or her side of the case heard. Kokott and Pistone remark that, in turn, the right to be heard requires revenue authorities to provide reasons.[28] This remark links to a component of the right to just administrative action as provided for in s 33 of the Constitution. Specifically, s 33(2) stipulates that written reasons must be provided to a person 'whose rights have been adversely affected by administrative action'.

Another component of the right to just administrative action, as contained in s 33(1) of the Constitution, is that '[e]veryone has the right to administrative action that is lawful, reasonable and procedurally fair'. The Promotion of Administrative Justice Act 3 of 2000 (PAJA) gives effect to the rights in s 33 of the Constitution[29] and provides 'for the review of administrative action by a court or, where appropriate, an independent and impartial tribunal'.[30]

Central to this right is the concept of 'administrative action', which is defined in s 1 of PAJA as

> any decision taken, or any failure to take a decision, by—
> (*a*) an organ of state, when—
> (i) exercising a power in terms of the Constitution or a provincial constitution; or
> (ii) exercising a public power or performing a public function in terms of any legislation; …
> which adversely affects the rights of any person, and which has a direct, external legal effect.[31]

Generally, when SARS exercises discretion (or fails to do so) in terms of the TAA, it would be of an administrative nature[32] and in terms of an empowering provision.[33] Accordingly, the two most contentious elements when determining if SARS' discretion is 'administrative action' are if the decision had adversely affected the rights of a person and if it has a direct, external legal effect.[34] The former requires one to consider the consequence of the administrative action.[35] If the decision places a burden on a person to, for instance, do or tolerate something, or when a person's right is taken away, it would be a decision that adversely affects the rights of a person.[36] In terms of the latter, the decision should be final[37] and affect someone other than the organ of the state who made this decision.[38]

Once a decision constitutes administrative action, SARS needs to ensure that it is lawful, reasonable and procedurally fair as per s 33 of the Constitution. In this respect, 'lawful' denotes that the administrative action should be done within the confines of the empowering provision.[39] Thus, lawful means one needs to adhere to the rule of law.[40]

'Reasonable' means that the decision should be rational.[41] As such there should be an 'objective basis justifying the connection made by the administrative decision-maker between the material properly available to him and the conclusion he or she eventually arrived at'.[42] In this regard, s 6 of PAJA, which provides that the grounds of judicial review, indicates that administrative action can be taken on review when irrelevant factors were taken into account or relevant factors were not taken into account.[43]

Finally, procedurally fair administrative action entails *inter alia* that a clear statement regarding the administrative action is provided and notice of the nature and purpose of the proposed administrative given to the person who will be affected by the action.[44]

Section 33 of the Constitution, together with PAJA and the TAA, provides access to justice in relation to administrative action in several ways. One, in terms of s 33(2) of the Constitution and s 5 of PAJA when a person's rights have been adversely affected by administrative action, the relevant administrator needs to provide reasons. In a similar vein, the TAA requires SARS in some instances to provide reasons or state the grounds upon which a decision was made. For instance, a taxpayer can request reasons for an assessment,[45] SARS is required to state the grounds upon which an objection has been rejected[46] and in a letter of audit findings SARS must indicate the grounds for the proposed assessment.[47] Requiring reasons ensures that a person can establish if the administrative action occurred in a manner that is lawful and procedurally fair.[48]

Baxter highlights the importance of providing reasons as follows:

> In the first place, a duty to give reasons entails a duty to *rationalize* the decision. Reasons therefore help to structure the exercise of discretion, and the necessity of explaining *why* a decision is reached requires one to address one's mind to the decisional referents which ought to be considered. Secondly, furnishing reasons satisfies an important desire on the part of the affected individual to know why a decision was reached. This is not only fair: it is also conducive to public confidence in the administrative decision-making process. Thirdly – and probably a major reason for the reluctance to give reasons – rational criticism of a decision may only be made when the reasons for it are known. This subjects the administration to public scrutiny, and it also provides an important basis for appeal or review. Finally, reasons may serve a genuine educative purpose, for example where an applicant has been refused on grounds which he is able to correct for the purpose of future applications.[49]

Two, access to justice is further promoted as s 6(2)(*a*)(iii) of PAJA encapsulates the *nemo iudex in propria causa* rule. This is the case as this section provides that bias on the side of an administrator is a ground for review. Thus, when an administrator, in this case, SARS, was not objective in exercising its discretion, a taxpayer has recourse. As s 195(1)(*d*) of the Constitution requires SARS to be impartial, fair, equitable and act in an unbiased manner,[50] PAJA gives effect thereto and provides appropriate recourse when SARS fails to fulfil this constitutional obligation.

Three, PAJA incorporates the principle of *audi alteram partem* as s 3(2)(*b*)(ii) of PAJA stipulates that a person should be granted a reasonable opportunity to state his or her case in relation to the administrative action.

The above discussion has shown the legislative framework that provides access to justice for taxpayers. The focus of the chapter now shifts towards examining how SARS applies or should apply the framework.

7.3 Sars' Role in Foster Access to Justice for Taxpayers

What role does SARS play in ensuring that taxpayers' access to justice is respected? To answer this question, I first highlight that SARS should not go beyond the provisions contained in the framework to ensure access to justice. Thereafter, I evaluate the courts' approach when SARS did not respect the protections afforded to taxpayers in terms of the framework.

7.3.1 Upholding Legislation without Exceeding Obligation to Respect Taxpayers' Rights

In a chapter focussing on taxpayers' rights, it appears almost inconceivable to indicate that SARS should do no more than adhere to legislation in relation to taxpayers' access to justice. However, it is important to place SARS' duties and obligations in the right context. As stated earlier, SARS does not only have an obligation to respect taxpayers' rights, but it must also effectively and efficiently collect taxes.[51] The latter is essential as collected taxes are used to realise socio-economic rights, which include the right to food and water,[52] health care,[53] and education.[54] Realising these socio-economic rights also addresses the United Nations' SDGs to end hunger, achieve food security and improved nutrition (goal 2) and to ensure availability and sustainable management of water (goal 6), healthy lives and promote well-being (goal 3) and inclusive and equitable quality education (goal 4).

SARS' task in fulfilling both obligations can be described as 'so plucking the goose as to procure the largest quantity of feathers with the least amount of hissing'.[55] Legislation should establish the parameters of the 'plucking' (how to proceed with tax collection) and the adequate amount of 'hissing' (infringement of taxpayers' rights) allowed. When the parameters of this balance are established in legislation, SARS merely needs to adhere to these provisions in line with the rule of law.

The matter of *Arena Holdings (Pty) Ltd t/a Financial Mail v SARS*,[56] is an example of how SARS' upholding of the rule of law ensures the protection of taxpayers' rights. This matter dealt with SARS' obligation to treat taxpayers' information confidential.[57] In this respect, s 69(1) of the TAA stipulates that a SARS official 'must preserve the secrecy of taxpayer information and may not disclose taxpayer information to a person who is not a SARS official'. Nonetheless, there are occasions where information provided by a taxpayer or obtained by SARS in respect of the taxpayer[58] may be disclosed.[59] These occasions are for instance when it is 'in the course of performance of duties under a tax Act or customs and excise legislation'[60] or when an Act expressly provides that the information should be disclosed.[61] SARS' duty to uphold taxpayer secrecy is further emphasised in s 35(1) of Promotion of Access to Information Act 2 of 2000 (PAIA) as it prohibits SARS from disclosing information obtained or held by SARS for tax collection purposes.[62]

In this matter, the applicants approached the court after SARS refused to disclose the tax information of the former president of the Republic of South Africa, Mr Jacob Zuma.[63] SARS argued that it is in the public interest to have access to the information as it would reveal 'a substantial contravention of the law'.[64]

SARS, in line with the relevant provisions, did not disclose the taxpayer's information and the third party had to approach the court to challenge the relevant provisions. As such, this case is an example of where SARS adhered to the rule of law as it remained within the four corners of the law. This fosters taxpayer certainty and trust in SARS to act in a non-arbitrary manner. Hence, the taxpayer was afforded access to justice by SARS adhering to the provisions in the TAA and PAIA, which were drafted to protect their right to privacy. While respecting taxpayers' rights and adhering to the law, SARS also ensured the proper functioning of tax collection.[65] By maintaining taxpayer confidentiality, SARS encouraged taxpayers to feel secure in providing full details of their tax affairs.[66]

The importance of the rule of law is highlighted in this matter as the taxpayer's rights were respected even though the taxpayer in question, Zuma, did not initially oppose the application.[67] The fact that both the High Court and the Constitutional Court held that the provisions under consideration did not strike the required balance[68] and that the legislator should make the necessary amendments[69] accentuate that the courts and legislature are tasked with ensuring that the required balance is achieved – not SARS who as a creature of statute should simply adhere to the legislative provisions.

Another case that demonstrates that SARS should rely on the legislation to respect taxpayers' rights as opposed to 'reading-in' protective measures on its own, is the case of *Bechan v SARS Customs Investigations Unit*.[70] In this matter, which deals with SARS' power to conduct searches and seizures, the court had to decide if SARS' conduct was unlawful when it searched Mr Bechan's vehicle, which was parked in the general parking area outside the office that was subject to a search and seizure warrant. Mr Bechan reasoned that a warrant must be construed narrowly to only refer to persons (such as a specific taxpayer) and items mentioned in the warrant itself.[71] According to Mr Bechan, a broader interpretation will affect numerous of his constitutional rights such as human dignity (s 10), privacy (s 14), not to be arbitrarily deprived of property (s 25(1)) and access to courts (s 34).[72]

Nonetheless, the court supported SARS' conduct because the warrant itself allowed SARS to conduct the search and seizure at the specified physical address where Mr Bechan's vehicle was parked. A more restrictive interpretation of the warrant would seriously hamper SARS' ability to gather the relevant information required to fulfil its mandate.[73]

Furthermore, the court held that even if the warrant could not be construed to include vehicles and property of persons other than the taxpayer at the specified premises, SARS conduct would be lawful in terms of s 62 of the TAA. Section 62 allows SARS to extend its search and seizure beyond the scope of the warrant if there is an imminent threat that the goods may be removed or destroyed and as such the time it will take to obtain the warrant would defeat the purpose of the search and seizure.

Thus, SARS' duty to respect constitutional rights does not stretch beyond what is provided in terms of legislation. Moving beyond the parameters of the framework would mean that SARS is neglecting its duty to collect taxes efficiently and effectively.

7.3.2 Upholding Legislation – Correct Application Required

7.3.2.1 Ensure That the Purpose of Peremptory Provisions Is Achieved

Just as SARS should not exceed the parameters of the framework, it should not fall foul of the framework. Accordingly, SARS should apply the legislation correctly and fulfil the requirements established in the TAA.

One such requirement is that when SARS issues an assessment, as opposed to the taxpayer determining the liability, SARS *must* provide a notice of assessment,[74] which fosters engagement between SARS and an informed taxpayer.[75] This notice of assessment includes the date of the assessment, the relevant tax period and the date by which the assessed amount should be paid.[76] In the event of SARS estimating the assessment, in terms of s 95 of the TAA, the notice of assessment must also include a statement regarding the grounds for the assessment.[77] These grounds should make it possible for the taxpayer to determine the factual and legal basis for the assessment.[78] Consequently, including the grounds of assessment in the notice of assessment assists taxpayers in making an informed decision as to whether to dispute the assessment, which forms part of the access to justice framework discussed above.

In the matter of *Nondabula v C:SARS*,[79] SARS failed to deliver a notice of assessment stipulating the grounds for the assessment, which was required as it was an estimated assessment. The court held that SARS must adhere to peremptory provisions and consequently SARS could not proceed with enforcement actions.[80] In this regard, one must be careful of falling into the trap of interpreting a provision by simply relying on a catchword such as 'must'.[81] Instead, the purposive approach dictates that one should determine the purpose of the provision and ascertain whether a literal interpretation would obstruct the identified purpose.[82] If the purpose would be obstructed by a literal interpretation, an interpretation should be used that fosters this purpose.[83]

Applying the purposive approach to s 96 of the TAA, which requires the notice of assessment, the purpose of this notice is to inform taxpayers and ensure engagement between SARS and the informed taxpayer. Thus, if this purpose was achieved in another way, for instance, by having a meeting with the taxpayer and discussing the grounds of assessment during the meeting, failure by SARS to serve the notice of assessment would not lead to subsequent actions being null and void. In *Nondabula*, the purpose was not achieved in an alternative manner and consequently, if such an interpretation was followed, the court would still have reached the same conclusion – the subsequent actions are null and void.

Not only did the court declare SARS' subsequent enforcement actions null and void, but it also highlighted that SARS' conduct was unconstitutional as it violated s 195(1) of the Constitution. This is because SARS' failure to comply with legislative provisions points to SARS' inability to act in an accountable manner, as required in terms of s 195(1)(*f*) of the Constitution. Moreover, s 195(1) of the Constitution was violated as SARS did not provide 'timely, accessible and accurate information' to the taxpayer, which is contrary to s 195(1)(*g*) of the Constitution.[84] It is commendable the court drew specific attention to SARS' unconstitutional behaviour as this emphasises that SARS should fulfil its obligations within the parameters of the Constitution and in adherence to the rule of law.[85]

Another important observation from this case is that the court emphasised the potential impact of SARS' conduct. In this matter, the taxpayer employed other people and proceeded with enforcement actions when SARS was not authorised to do so, which will reach further than just the taxpayer and his family.[86] Thus, when SARS fails to adhere to the four corners of the law, it could have a ripple effect.[87]

Section 179(5) of the TAA is another peremptory provision in the TAA, which stipulates that SARS *must* serve a notice on a taxpayer. This notice is a final demand to a taxpayer setting out the recovery steps that SARS may take in case of non-compliance of the taxpayer and the debt relief mechanisms available to the taxpayer. Once a taxpayer has received this final demand, the taxpayer may request a reduction of the amount owed to SARS due to financial circumstances. As such, s 179(5) of the TAA facilitates engagement with a taxpayer as regards its financial circumstances, the powers of SARS and a taxpayer's options in relation to the tax debt. SARS may only proceed with appointing a third party who holds or owes money to the taxpayer[88] after 10 business days have passed since the final demand was delivered to the taxpayer.[89] In terms of the appointment notice, SARS can instruct such a third party to pay over that money to SARS.

In line with the purposive approach discussed above, the court in *SIP Project Managers (Pty) Ltd v C:SARS*[90] held that even when the wording is peremptory,[91] the purpose of the requirement should be considered.[92] In this respect, the court held that s 179(5) of the TAA curtails SARS' third-party appointment power[93] and a failure by SARS to deliver the required notice means that SAR is disregarding a restriction that is imposed by law.[94] Consequently, the third-party appointment was declared null and void.[95]

WPD Fleetmas CC v C:SARS[96] also dealt with a s 179(5) notice. SARS was able to provide proof that the final demand letter was served, yet the taxpayer could show that on their side there was no such letter.[97] Granting that much of this case focussed on a factual dispute when a taxpayer disputes the delivery of a s 179(5) notice, SARS should verify if the delivery did in fact take place and not simply proceed with its enforcement powers.[98] In fact, when it comes to SARS' attention that a notice has not been delivered to the taxpayer and this will cause material disadvantage to the taxpayer, SARS must withdraw the notice and deliver a new notice to the taxpayer.[99] This suggested approach would be more in line with the values of acting fair, equitable and accountable as espoused in s 195(1) of the Constitution. SARS' failure to verify whether the required notice was indeed served when allegations to the contrary are made, also means that it is forsaking its duty to use resources in an efficient, economic and effective manner as required in terms of section 195.[100] SARS is in reality wasting time and money when a matter proceeds to court, simply for the court to rule that SARS has not complied with a requirement. Time in court and fees for legal representation should rather be preserved for instances that require more than simply verifying whether something has occurred or not.

Legwaila, commenting on *WPD Fleetmas CC v C:SARS* and SARS proceeding with enforcement actions when the notice is not showing on the taxpayer's profile, opines that SARS' conduct 'points to sheer professional negligence if not malice, and/or incompetence on the part of the SARS's officials issuing these third party notices'.[101] Whilst one might argue that this criticism is too harsh as there was a dispute as to whether the notice was served on the taxpayer, two subsequent third-party appointment cases, *Ferrari Logistics South Africa (Pty) Ltd v C:SARS*[102] and *Autumn Skies Trading 94 CC v C:SARS*,[103] show that this criticism is well-deserved. The reason being that in these two cases SARS' failure to comply with the relevant provisions did not only relate to a failure to serve a final demand, but also in these cases there were not even an outstanding tax debt.[104] This means there was no basis for SARS to even embark with any tax enforcement measures.

What does this approach of SARS with regard to third-party appointments mean for access to justice? This approach points to a disregard for the rule of law and the constitutional values contained in s 195 of the Constitution. Furthermore, by proceeding (or trying to proceed) with enforcement actions without notifying taxpayers of the possible enforcement actions and avenues at the taxpayer's disposal and an opportunity to engage with SARS about its financial circumstances, a taxpayer is devoid of the opportunity to engage with SARS. As is apparent from *Ferrari Logistics South Africa (Pty) Ltd v C:SARS* and *Autumn Skies Trading 94 CC v C:SARS*, SARS could erroneously appoint a third party when there is no tax debt and this could have been avoided if the taxpayer was made aware of SARS' (incorrect) view that there is an outstanding tax debt.

7.3.2.2 Avoid Ex Post Facto Adherence to Legislation

In addition, to ensure that the purpose of peremptory provisions is achieved, SARS should not adhere to legislation *ex post facto*. An example of such *ex post facto* adherence can be detected in *Rappa (Pty) Ltd v C:SARS*.[105] In this matter, SARS withheld paying a refund to the taxpayer in terms of s 190(2) of the TAA. This section stipulates that 'SARS need not authorise a refund' pending verification, inspection or audit. This dispute centred on the fact that SARS withheld a refund due for a period that was not subject to an audit.[106]

Although, s 190(2) does not provide legislative guidance in this respect, Van Zyl and Fritz remark that if SARS was able to suspend the payment of all refunds, irrespective of to which period it relates, when conducting an audit, it would be contrary to the spirit and purpose of the TAA.[107] Correspondingly, the court held that SARS should not use an audit to suspend paying out all refunds but could only withhold a refund for the period subject to an audit.[108]

After the taxpayer complained that the withholding included refunds for periods that were not subject to audit, SARS issued audit notices for the periods of assessment for which it had already withheld the refunds.[109] SARS claimed that it issued these notices for the other tax periods as the suspected fraudulent activities were ongoing and thus all the periods should be subject to audit.[110]

Withholding a tax refund and justifying this action with a notice of audit after the fact, is contrary to the Constitution. This is because SARS did not operate with impartiality, fairness, equity and unbiased.[111] Moreover, the constitutional values of being accountable[112] and acting in a transparent manner[113] are absent in this instance.

SARS' conduct in this matter should also be seen in the broader context of refunds, as '[t]axpayers have over the years been complaining that SARS unduly delays the payment of verified refunds'.[114] In this respect, the Office of the Tax Ombud has identified the delay in paying out refunds as a systemic issue,[115] which means that this office has identified the delay of refunds to have a negative impact on many taxpayers.[116] Taking this broader context, SARS' conduct in Rappa, which denied the taxpayer access to justice should not be seen as an isolated incident and leads one to question whether SARS was acting in good faith.

7.3.2.3 Exercising Discretion with Due Consideration

As discussed in the framework above, just administrative action requires administrative action that is reasonable. If SARS took irrelevant factors into consideration to reach its decision or failed to take relevant factors into consideration, that would be a ground for review. Thus, factors provided in legislation ensure that taxpayers can gauge whether SARS has acted reasonably when SARS furnishes the reasons for the administrative action.

In *Peri Formwork Scaffolding Engineering (Pty) Ltd v C:SARS*,[117] SARS levied a percentage-based penalty in terms of s 213 of the TAA.[118] Nonetheless, s 217(3) of the TAA stipulates that SARS *may* remit a penalty if the penalty relates to a first incidence of non-compliance or involves an amount of less than R2000, there are reasonable grounds for the non-compliance; and 'the non-compliance in issue has been remedied'.[119]

When determining if there are reasonable grounds for non-compliance, the taxpayer's behaviour after it realised it would be unable to pay the outstanding tax debt by the due date is important.[120] In the current matter, once the taxpayer realised that it would be unable to pay the taxes by the payment date, it applied for an overdraft.[121] However, the payment was made after the required date.[122] As the taxpayer acted in good faith and SARS did not suffer any prejudice, the court found that SARS had unreasonably exercised its discretion when it decided not to remit the penalty.[123]

The discretion to remit a penalty in terms of s 217(3) of the TAA constitutes 'administrative action' because this decision clearly has the potential to have a lasting detrimental impact on taxpayers.[124] Accordingly, SARS must exercise this discretion in a lawful, reasonable and procedurally fair manner,[125] by considering relevant considerations.[126] In this specific case, SARS failed to provide administrative justice to the taxpayer. On the one hand, it has been speculated that SARS failed to consider why there was non-compliance to ensure maximum tax collection close to its financial year-end.[127] Such speculation points to SARS' inability to act objectively – a requirement that is essential to ensure administrative justice. On the other hand, and a more favourable interpretation for SARS, the judgment can be seen as clarifying how SARS should exercise its discretion on the remittance of penalties.[128] Unfortunately, it is difficult to view SARS' conduct in this case in such a favourable light as one of the factors to consider remittance is specifically listed to be whether the non-compliance has been remedied. Evidently, SARS' conduct in this case falls short of the access to justice framework as discussed above.

7.4 Conclusion

This chapter has demonstrated the critical role of the rule of law in protecting a taxpayer's right to tax justice. The rule of law, together with relevant legislation, establishes the essential framework that allows taxpayers to seek and obtain tax justice. When SARS upholds this framework, taxpayers are guaranteed access to justice. However, SARS must carefully balance its duty to collect taxes with its obligation to respect taxpayers' rights. It should neither exceed nor fall short of what the framework mandates.

This means that SARS must ensure full compliance with peremptory provisions, avoid retroactive adherence to legislation and exercise proper discretion when required. As discussed in Section 7.3.2, case law reveals instances where SARS has failed to correctly apply the framework, leading to serious consequences. As an organ of state, SARS has an obligation to prevent matters from reaching the courts when it is evident that it did not follow proper procedures. This failure not only contradicts its legal obligations but also imposes unnecessary financial burdens on taxpayers, which can have far-reaching effects on their dependents and employees. Therefore, it is imperative that SARS reflect on previous judgments and educate itself on how to effectively ensure access to justice by consistently adhering to the framework.

Moreover, adherence to the rule of law is crucial in supporting the United Nations' SDG of fostering effective, accountable and transparent institutions.

Notes

1 In South Africa, the duty to collect taxes effectively and efficiently is provided for in s 3(a) of the South African Service Act 34 of 1997 (SARS Act).
2 The Constitution of the Republic of South Africa 1996 (the Constitution) s 8(1).
3 The TAA s 2.
4 The full set of reports can be accessed at https://www.statecapture.org.za/site/information/reports accessed 2 May 2023. Volume I of the reports specifically dealt with SARS and can be accessed at https://bit.ly/3Oe7hvT accessed 26 April 2023.
5 Commission of Inquiry into Tax Administration and Governance by SARS, *Final Report* (2018) 197.
6 Commission of Inquiry into Tax Administration and Governance by SARS, *Final Report* (2018) 21.
7 Edelman, '2023 Edelman Trust Barometer' (2023) 9 https://bit.ly/3pHdsyu accessed 2 May 2023.
8 See TR Tyler, 'Psychological Perspectives on Legitimacy and Legitimation' [2005] *Annual Review of Psychology* 375, 393; O-H Fjeldstad, C Schulz-Herzenberg and IH Sjursen 'People's Views of Taxation in Africa: A Review of Research on Determinants of Tax Compliance' [2012] CMI Working Paper 7. See also F Moosa, 'Protecting the Public Purse with Moral Tax Administration' [2023] Business Tax & Company Law Quarterly 23, 25 regarding the South African perspective.
9 J Kokott and P Pistone, *Taxpayers in International Law* (Bloomsbury Publishing 2022) 493.
10 D Bentley, 'The Rise of "Soft Law" in Tax Administration – Good News for Taxpayers?' (2008) January/February Asia-Pacific Tax Bulletin 32, 38.
11 Constitution s 1(c).
12 *Dawood v Minister of Home Affairs; Shalabi v Minister of Home Affairs; Thomas v Minister of Home Affairs* [2000] 5 BCLR 837 CC 842; *Affordable Medicines Trust v Minister of Health of the RSA* [2005] 6 BCLR 529 CC [108].
13 C Fritz, 'An Appraisal of Selected Tax-Enforcement Powers of The South African Revenue Service in the South African Constitutional Context' (LLD thesis, University of Pretoria 2017) 35–36.
14 Case no: 16177/(29 July 2022).
15 Case no: 16177/(29 July 2022).
16 The SARS Act s 2.
17 The Constitution s 195(1)(*d*).
18 The Constitution s 195(1)(*f*).
19 The Constitution s 195(1)(*g*).
20 The Constitution s 195(1)(*b*).
21 The Constitution s 8(1).
22 The Constitution s 34.
23 The Constitution s 33(1).
24 *Chief Lesapo v North West Agricultural Bank* [1999] (1 2) BCLR 1420 CC 1429.
25 Y Burns and M Beukes, *Administrative Law under the 1996 Constitution* (LexisNexis Butterworths 2003) 197.
26 *Chief Lesapo v North West Agricultural Bank* [13].
27 See Chapter 9 of the TAA in this regard.
28 Kokott and Pistone (n 9) 496.
29 The Constitution s 33(3); PAJA Preamble.

30 The Constitution s 33(3).
31 For a discussion of 'administrative action' in general, see C Hoexter 'Administrative Action' in I Currie and J De Waal (eds), *The Bill of Rights Handbook* (6th edn, Juta & Co Ltd 2013) 654–666. For a discussion of 'administrative action, in the context of SARS' powers, see Fritz (n 12) 44–48.
32 In *The President of the Republic of South Africa v South African Rugby Football Union* [2000] 1 SA CC [141] it was held that 'administrative in nature' is concerned with whether the task itself is administrative. As such, the focus is on the function and not on the functionary.
33 In terms of PAJA s 1, 'empowering provision' is 'a law, a rule of common law, customary law or an agreement, instrument or other document'.
34 See *Carte Blanche Marketing CC v C:SARS* [2020] 6 SA 463, *Wingate-Pearse v C:SARS* [2019] 6 SA 196 in this regard.
35 I Currie and J Klaaren, *The Promotion of Administrative Justice Act Benchbook* (Siber Ink 2001) 75.
36 I Currie and J Klaaren, *The Promotion of Administrative Justice Act Benchbook* (Siber Ink 2001) 75.
37 Currie and Klaaren (n 34) 82; Burns and Beukes (n 24) 30.
38 Currie and Klaaren (n 34) 82; Burns and Beukes (n 24) 30.
39 JR De Ville *Judicial Review of Administrative Action in South Africa* (LexisNexis: Durban 2003) 99.
40 Fritz (n 12) 49.
41 *Metcash Trading Ltd v Commissioner of SARS* 2001 1 SA 1109 (CC) 1134.
42 *Carephone Ltd v Marcus* 1998 11 BLLR 1093 (LAC) [37].
43 PAJA s 6(2)(*e*)(iii).
44 PAJA s 3(2)(b).
45 The TAA s 103, read with regulation 6 of the Rules Promulgated under Section 103 of the Tax Administration Act, 2011 (Act No. 28 Of 2011), Prescribing the Procedures to be Followed in Lodging an Objection and Appeal Against an Assessment or a Decision Subject to Objection and Appeal Referred to in Section 104(2) of that Act, Procedures for Alternative Dispute Resolution, the Conduct and Hearing of Appeals, Application on Notice Before a Tax Court and Transitional Rules.
46 The TAA s 106(5).
47 The TAA s 42(2)(*b*).
48 *Transnet v Goodman Brothers* [2001] 1 SA 853 SCA [12].
49 L Baxter Administrative Law (Juta and Co 1984) 228.
50 The Constitution s 195(1)(*d*).
51 The SARS Act s 3(*a*).
52 The Constitution s 26.
53 The Constitution s 27.
54 The Constitution s 29.
55 'Jean-Baptiste Colbert Quotes' https://www.azquotes.com/author/20137-Jean_Baptiste_Colbert accessed 1 June 2023.
56 *Arena Holdings (Pty) Ltd t/a Financial Mail v SARS* (ZAGPPHC) (unreported High Court case number 88359/2019, 16 November 2021) (HC); unreported Constitutional Court Case CCT 365/21, 30 May 2023 (CC).
57 See the TAA ch 6 in this regard.
58 The TAA s 1, read with s 67(1)(*b*).
59 The TAA s 69(2).
60 The TAA s 69(2)(*a*). A witness in court proceedings under a tax Act (s 69(2)(*a*)(ii) or to the South African Police Service (s 69(2)(*a*)(i) are examples of when it will be during the performance of duties.
61 The TAA s 69(2)(*b*).

62 B Croome and L Olivier, *Tax Administration* (2nd edn, Juta & Co, 2015) 620.
63 *Arena Holdings (Pty) Ltd t/a Financial Mail v SARS* (HC) [1–2]. Financial Mail requested the taxpayer information based on allegations that Zuma failed to pay tax in respect of security upgrades, received donations from illegal sources and did not file tax returns for the period during which he was the president (*Arena Holdings (Pty) Ltd t/a Financial Mail v SARS* (HC) [5.1]). These allegations were made in the book *The President's Keepers* written by Jacques Pauw, an investigative journalist. Some corroboration of these allegations can be found in the evidence of the Nugent Commission and the Commission of Enquiry into State Capture (also known as the Zondo Commission) (*Arena Holdings (Pty) Ltd t/a Financial Mail v SARS* (HC) [5.2]).
64 *Arena Holdings (Pty) Ltd t/a Financial Mail v SARS* (HC) [1–2]. Whilst both the High Court and Constitutional Court's decisions on how to balance a taxpayer's right to privacy, thus the protection of taxpayer information, vis-à-vis the right to freedom of expression (s 16) and right of access to information (s 32) are interesting, the focus in this chapter falls on SARS' approach.
65 See Fritz and Van Zyl (n 61) 591–597 where the authors express a contrary view.
66 *Arena Holdings (Pty) Ltd t/a Financial Mail v SARS* (HC) [7.2].
67 *Arena Holdings (Pty) Ltd t/a Financial Mail v SARS* (HC) [2.3]; *Arena Holdings (Pty) Ltd t/a Financial Mail v SARS* (CC) [204].
68 *Arena Holdings (Pty) Ltd t/a Financial Mail v SARS* (HC)[11]; *Arena Holdings (Pty) Ltd t/a Financial Mail v SARS* (CC) [198].
69 *Arena Holdings (Pty) Ltd t/a Financial Mail v SARS* (CC) [205].
70 84 SATC 413 (28 April 2022) (initial application).
71 *Bechan* v *SARS Customs Investigations Unit* (initial application) [24].
72 *Bechan v SARS Customs Investigations Unit* 19626/2022 [2022] ZAGPPHC 525 (25 July 2022) [4]. The applicant only advanced the argument regarding the violation of constitutional rights in the subsequent application for leave to appeal the dismissal of the initial application.
73 *Bechan* v *SARS Customs Investigations Unit* (initial application) [25–26].
74 The TAA s 96(1).
75 Fritz '*Nondabula v Commissioner: SARS* (2018 (3) SA 541 (ECM) (27 June 2017)) "Victory" for taxpayer after SARS fails to fulfil its duties' [2019] De Jure Law Journal 181, 182.
76 The TAA s 96(1).
77 The TAA s 96(2)(*a*).
78 SARS 'SARS Dispute Resolution Guide' (28 October 2014) 31.
79 79 SATC 333.
80 *Nondabula v C:SARS* [26].
81 L Du Plessis 'Interpretation' in S Woolman and M Bishop (eds), Constitutional Law of South Africa (2nd edition, Juta & Co Ltd 2013) 32–54.
82 *African Christian Democratic Party v Electoral Commission* 2006 3 SA 305 CC.
83 W Le Roux, 'Directory provisions, section 39(2) of the Constitution and the ontology of statutory law' (2006) 21 *Southern Africa Public Law* 382,386.
84 *Nonadabula v C:SARS* [24].
85 Fritz (n 75) 185.
86 *Nondabula v C:SARS* [25].
87 C Fritz, 'Old Habits Die Hard – The South African Revenue Service's Inability to Comply With Its Own Legislation *SIP Project Managers (Pty) Ltd v C:SARS* Case number: 11521/2020 Gauteng Division, Pretoria' (30 April 2020) Obiter 436, 442.
88 The TAA s 179(1).
89 The TAA s 179(5).
90 Case number: 11521/2020 Gauteng Division, Pretoria (30 April 2020) [8].

91 *SIP Project Managers v C:SARS* [22].
92 *SIP Project Managers v C:SARS* [24].
93 *SIP Project Managers v C:SARS* [26].
94 *SIP Project Managers v C:SARS* [23].
95 *SIP Project Managers v C:SARS* [27].
96 Case no: 31339 2020 (unreported) 19-08-2020 (GNP).
97 *WPD Fleetmans CC v C:SARS* [24–25].
98 Fritz (n 83) 441.
99 *Siphayi v C:SARS* 34975/2019 [2019] ZAGPJHC 455 [25 October 2019] [10].
100 The Constitution s 195(1)(*b*).
101 T Legwaila, 'Third-party Appointments – May the Tax Collector Please Comply?' [2021] *Journal of South African Law* 136, 143.
102 GNP unreported case no: 62914/2020 [8 December 2020].
103 Unreported case no: 28987/2020 [14 July 2020] GNP.
104 *Ferrari Logistics South Africa (Pty) Ltd v C:SARS* [17]; *Autumn Skies Trading 94 CC v C:SARS* [14].
105 Case no: 20/18875 [5 November 2020].
106 *Rappa (Pty) Ltd v C:SARS* [47]. See SP Van Zyl and C Fritz 'Withholding a Tax Refund: Did the High Court Apply Section 190 of the Tax Administration Act 28 of 2011 Correctly? – *Rappa (Pty) Ltd v Commissioner for the South African Revenue Service* (20/18875) [2020] ZAGPPHC (5 Nov 2020)' [2021] Journal for Contemporary Roman Dutch Law 239 for a detailed discussion of the various issues that arose in Rappa.
107 Van Zyl and Fritz (n 108) 246.
108 *Rappa (Pty) Ltd v C:SARS* [47].
109 *Rappa (Pty) Ltd v C:SARS* [47–48].
110 *Rappa (Pty) Ltd v C:SARS* [55].
111 The Constitution s 195(1)(*d*).
112 The Constitution s 195(1)(*f*).
113 The Constitution s 195(1)(*g*).
114 Office of the Tax Ombud 'Tax Ombud's Report on the Investigation in Terms of Section 16(1)(b) of the Tax Administration Act 28 of 2011 into Alleged Delayed Payment of Refunds as a Systemic and Emerging Issue' [2017] 9.
115 Office of the Tax Ombud 'Open Systemic Issues' https://www.taxombud.gov.za/systemic-issues-2/ accessed 1 June 2023.
116 Office of the Tax Ombud 'Systemic Issues' https://www.taxombud.gov.za/systemic-issues/ accessed 1 June 2023.
117 Case number A67/2020, Western Cape Division [23 August 2021].
118 *Peri Formwork Scaffolding Engineering (Pty) Ltd v C:SARS* [1].
119 The TAA s 217(3)(a)-(c).
120 *Peri Formwork Scaffolding Engineering (Pty) Ltd v C:SARS* [66].
121 *Peri Formwork Scaffolding Engineering (Pty) Ltd v C:SARS* [6]; [67].
122 *Peri Formwork Scaffolding Engineering (Pty) Ltd v C:SARS* [67].
123 *Peri Formwork Scaffolding Engineering (Pty) Ltd v C:SARS* [73].
124 C Fritz 'Prosecution of Tax Offences by the South African Revenue Service: Time to Take Stock [2022] Journal for Contemporary Roman Dutch Law 233, 236.
125 The Constitution s 33.
126 PAJA s 6(2)(*e*)(iii).
127 B Curson 'SARS Behaving Badly: Revenue Service Exercised "Unreasonable Discretion" in Disallowing Penalty' (9 September 2021) *Moneyweb* https://bit.ly/3DSpwhM accessed 1 June 2023.
128 A Visser 'Ruling Highlights SARS's Discretionary Powers to Remit Penalties' (7 November 2021) *Business Day* https://bit.ly/3EViie6 accessed 1 June 2023.

Bibliography

A Visser 'Ruling Highlights SARS's Discretionary Powers to Remit Penalties' (7 November 2021) *Business Day* https://bit.ly/3EViie6 accessed 1 June 2023.

Affordable Medicines Trust v Minister of Health of the RSA [2005] 6 BCLR 529 CC [108]. https://www.saflii.org/za/cases/ZACC/2005/3.html

African Christian Democratic Party v Electoral Commission 2006 3 SA 305 CC. https://www.saflii.org/za/cases/ZACC/2006/1.html

Arena Holdings (Pty) Ltd t/a Financial Mail v SARS (ZAGPPHC) (unreported High Court case number 88359/2019, 16 November 2021) (HC); unreported Constitutional Court Case CCT 365/21, 30 May 2023 (CC). https://www.concourt.org.za/index.php/judgement/511-arena-holdings-pty-limited-t-a-financial-mail-and-others-v-south-african-revenue-service-and-others-cct365-21

Bechan v SARS Customs Investigations Unit 19626/2022 [2022] ZAGPPHC 525 (25 July 2022). https://www.saflii.org/za/cases/ZAGPPHC/2022/525.html

D Bentley, 'The Rise of "Soft Law" in Tax Administration – Good News for Taxpayers?' (2008) 14 (1) *Asia-Pacific Tax Bulletin* 32.

Y Burns and M Beukes, *Administrative Law under the 1996 Constitution* (LexisNexis Butterworths 2003).

Carephone Ltd v Marcus 1998 11 BLLR 1093 (LAC). https://www.saflii.org/za/cases/ZALAC/1998/11.html

Carte Blanche Marketing CC v C:SARS [2020] 6 SA 463. https://www.saflii.org/za/cases/ZAGPJHC/2020/202.html

Chief Lesapo v North West Agricultural Bank [1999] (1 2) BCLR 1420 CC 1429. https://www.saflii.org/za/cases/ZACC/1999/16.html

Commission of Inquiry into Tax Administration and Governance by SARS, *Final Report* (2018). https://www.thepresidency.gov.za/commission-inquiry-tax-administration-and-governance-sars

B Croome and L Olivier, *Tax Administration* (2nd edn, Juta & Co 2015).

I Currie and J Klaaren, *The Promotion of Administrative Justice Act Benchbook* (Siber Ink 2001).

B Curson 'SARS Behaving Badly: Revenue Service Exercised "Unreasonable Discretion" in Disallowing Penalty' (9 September 2021) *Moneyweb* https://bit.ly/3DSpwhM accessed 1 June 2023.

Dawood v Minister of Home Affairs; Shalabi v Minister of Home Affairs; Thomas v Minister of Home Affairs [2000] 5 BCLR 837 CC 842. https://www.saflii.org/za/cases/ZACC/2000/8.html

JR De Ville, *Judicial Review of Administrative Action in South Africa* (Durban 2003).

L Du Plessis 'Interpretation' in S Woolman and M Bishop (eds), *Constitutional Law of South Africa* (2nd edn, Juta & Co Ltd 2013).

'Edelman Trust Barometer' (2023) https://bit.ly/3pHdsyu accessed 2 May 2023.

O-H Fjeldstad, C Schulz-Herzenberg and IH Sjursen 'People's Views of Taxation in Africa: A Review of Research on Determinants of Tax Compliance' [2012] CMI Working Paper 7. https://www.cmi.no/publications/4577-peoples-views-of-taxation-in-africa

C Fritz, 'An Appraisal of Selected Tax-Enforcement Powers of The South African Revenue Service in the South African Constitutional Context' (LLD thesis, University of Pretoria 2017).

C Fritz '*Nondabula v Commissioner: SARS* (2018 (3) SA 541 (ECM) (27 June 2017)) "Victory" for taxpayer after SARS fails to fulfil its duties' (2019) 52 (1) *De Jure Law Journal* 181.

C Fritz, 'Old Habits Die Hard – The South African Revenue Service's Inability to Comply With Its Own Legislation *SIP Project Managers (Pty) Ltd v C:SARS* Case number: 11521/2020 Gauteng Division, Pretoria' 42 (2) (30 April 2020) *Obiter* 436.

C Fritz 'Prosecution of Tax Offences by the South African Revenue Service: Time to Take Stock' (2022) 85 *Journal for Contemporary Roman Dutch Law* 233.
C Hoexter 'Administrative Action' in I Currie and J De Waal (eds), *The Bill of Rights Handbook* (6th edn, Juta & Co Ltd 2013).
In The President of the Republic of South Africa v South African Rugby Football Union [2000] 1 SA CC. https://www.saflii.org/za/cases/ZACC/1999/11.html
J Kokott and P Pistone, *Taxpayers in International Law* (Bloomsbury Publishing 2022)
L Baxter Administrative Law (Juta and Co 1984).
W Le Roux, 'Directory provisions, section 39(2) of the Constitution and the ontology of statutory law' (2006) 21 *Southern Africa Public Law* 382.
T Legwaila, 'Third-party Appointments – May the Tax Collector Please Comply?' (2021) 1 *Journal of South African Law* 136.
Metcash Trading Ltd v Commissioner of SARS 2001 1 SA 1109 (CC) 1134. https://www.saflii.org/za/cases/ZACC/2000/21.html#:~:text=This%20case%20concerns%20the%20constitutional,section%2034%20of%20the%20Constitution
F Moosa, 'Protecting the Public Purse with Moral Tax Administration' (2023) 14 (3) *Business Tax & Company Law Quarterly* 23.
Office of the Tax Ombud 'Systemic Issues' https://www.taxombud.gov.za/systemic-issues/ accessed 1 June 2023.
SARS 'SARS Dispute Resolution Guide' (28 October 2014). https://www.sars.gov.za/wp-content/uploads/Ops/Guides/LAPD-TAdm-G05-Dispute-Resolution-Guide.pdf
Siphayi v C:SARS 34975/2019 [2019] ZAGPJHC 455 (25 October 2019). https://www.saflii.org/za/cases/ZAGPJHC/2019/455.html
Transnet v Goodman Brothers (2001) 1 SA 853 SCA https://www.saflii.org/za/cases/ZASCA/2000/62.html#:~:text=Transnet%20Ltd.-,v%20Goodman%20Brothers%20(Pty)%20Ltd%20(373%2F98),(SCA)%20(9%20November%202000)&text=Duty%20to%20give%20reasons%20to,or%20interest%20to%20obtain%20reasons
TR Tyler, 'Psychological Perspectives on Legitimacy and Legitimation' (2005) 57 (1) *Annual Review of Psychology* 375.
SP Van Zyl and C Fritz 'Withholding a Tax Refund: Did the High Court Apply Section 190 of the Tax Administration Act 28 of 2011 Correctly? – *Rappa (Pty) Ltd v Commissioner for the South African Revenue Service* (20/18875) [2020] ZAGPPHC (5 Nov 2020)' (2021) 84 *Journal for Contemporary Roman Dutch Law* 239.
Wingate-Pearse v C:SARS [2019] 6 SA 196. https://www.saflii.org/za/cases/ZAGPJHC/2019/218.html

8 Refuting Its "Tax Haven" Characterisation

The BVI's Offshore Financial Services Industry and Its Right to Economic Self-Determination

Antonius R. Hippolyte[*]

8.1 Introduction

International law[1] enshrines peoples' right to self-determination. This is defined as peoples' right to determine their political prospects and pursue their economic, social and cultural development,[2] and is recognised as a fundamental human right. Self-determination is an important principle on which broader rights realisation is based. A key aspect of self-determination is economic self-determination, referring to people's right to exploit their natural resources in accordance with democratic decisions and to arrange their economies without outside interference.[3] Economic self-determination empowers people to control and use mineral resources to foster their development, for instance, by deciding how natural resources are exploited. They also have the freedom to tax incoming goods and services and other economic activities within their territory to fund their development. However, in practice, this principle has not translated into rights for many people, especially economically vulnerable developing economies.[4] The parameters of their freedom to freely manage their economic affairs depend, *inter alia*, on how their policies impact developed countries' tax revenue collection. One such developing economy which developed countries often criticise is the British Virgin Islands (BVI).[5] The BVI is a small player in the offshore financial services business, accounting for less than 1%. Yet, its zero corporate tax regime has attracted many businesses seeking to capitalise on its offerings.[6] Although accounting for less than 1% of the global financial services industry, in 2017 the BVI was the seventh-largest source of foreign direct investment globally.[7]

The road to becoming an offshore finance powerhouse has been daunting.[8] Since the 1970s, the BVI has been accused of impeding effective tax collection through its creation of an offshore regime that facilitates the aggressive tax planning strategies of MNCs and other high-net-worth individuals.[9] Developed countries such as the United States,[10] the United Kingdom,[11] France,[12] and the

* Antonius R. Hippolyte, Dean (Interim), Lecturer in International Investment Law, Faculty of Law, University of the West Indies, Cave Hill Campus, Barbados; Email: antonius.hippolye@cavehill.uwi.edu.

DOI: 10.4324/9781003432890-10

Netherlands[13] argue it provides opportunities for their citizens to evade their tax obligations by providing extraterritorial tax neutrality. Consequently, the BVI has long been viewed as a "tax haven" and defined as a jurisdiction with either low or non-existent tax rates, lack of transparency, bank secrecy, information sharing and minimal economic activity for entities to obtain legal status.[14] The Netherlands[15] and France[16] blacklisted the BVI in December 2018 and January 2020 respectively. The Organisation for Economic Cooperation and Development (OECD) and the European Union (EU), which have both developed definitions of "tax havens",[17] to combat MNCs' aggressive tax planning strategies, have also either blacklisted or threatened to blacklist the BVI, which they consider a "tax haven".[18] This often results in heavy withholding taxes being levied on businesses with companies registered in such jurisdictions. Civil society organisations such as the Tax Justice Network[19] and the International Consortium of Investigative Journalist[20] have also condemned the BVI due to its characterisation as a "tax haven".

Criticisms of the territory's offshore industry such as the suggestion that companies are incorporated in the BVI merely to facilitate crimes, arguably fail to depict the reality of the BVI financial services product adequately and accurately. Moreover, it asserts condemnation of the BVI's financial services industry fails to reveal the laws which BVI companies violate.[21] Cases decided in domestic law systems, such as *WT Ramsay Ltd v IRC*[22] and *IRC v Burmah Oil Co Ltd*[23] decided by courts in England and Wales, and which underpin the current position in this area of law, in that jurisdiction, do not provide adequate reasoning to sustain the illegality of corporate tax planning resulting in tax avoidance as they were decided partly on public policy grounds and therefore take on moral underpinnings.[24] In today's rapidly changing commercial environment, whereby businesses are constantly innovating ways to enhance profitability, it is difficult to determine whether a decision has no commercial purpose apart from the avoidance of tax.[25] It is unreasonable to hold jurisdictions accountable for individuals' legal tax planning strategies in open economies. Rather, states should close the international tax regime's loopholes used to facilitate tax avoidance.

Notwithstanding, the BVI has made significant strides aimed at improving regulation of its financial services industry, addressing the OECD's 1998 "tax haven" characterisation.[26] This includes the establishment of the Financial Services Commission (FSC), International Tax Authority (ITA) and Financial Investigations Agency (FIA). It has also ratified 28 Tax Information Exchange Agreements (TIEAs),[27] the Mutual Administrative Assistance in Tax Matters Convention 1988 and the OECD's Multilateral Competent Authority Agreement (MCAA) on automatic exchange of financial account information. Other key legislation such as the Beneficial Ownership Secure Search System Act 2017 was enacted to fulfil its international obligations. In 2019, the Economic Substance (Companies and Limited Partnerships) Act, 2018, came into force, requiring companies and partnerships to demonstrate adequate economic substance in the BVI. The ITA also published a draft Economic Substance Code, which seeks to ensure compliance with international standards on economic substance for entities in zero or nominal tax jurisdictions. This was replaced by the Rules on Economic Substance.[28] Thus, despite the territory's continued portrayal as a "tax haven", it continues to regulate its offshore business to position itself as a transparent and cooperative jurisdiction.

Thus, this chapter challenges the BVI's classification as a "tax haven", arguing it has the right to arrange its economy in ways that promote sustainable development and improve its socio-economic condition consistent with its peoples' right to economic self-determination – a fundamental feature of their human rights. It examines the doctrine of economic self-determination and the historical origin of the BVI financial services industry. The chapter examines the legality of corporate tax planning, distinguishing tax avoidance from tax evasion. It also examines the BVI's numerous regulatory initiatives, concluding that the territory's commitment to cooperation, good governance and transparency has led to significant strides in policy enactments, agencies and technology development. The chapter concludes that the BVI's portrayal as a "tax haven" does not reflect its status as an offshore financial centre in 2024.

8.2 Economic Self-Determination as a Fundamental Human Right

A fundamental human right is the right of peoples to self-determination. Self-determination denotes people's right to decide their own destiny. Self-determination is a core principle of international law, arising from customary international law, but also recognised as a general principle of law and enshrined in several international treaties.[29] For instance, self-determination is protected in the UN Charter and the International Covenant on Civil and Political Rights (ICCPR) as a right of all peoples.[30] As outlined in Article 55 of the UN Charter, Universal Declaration of Human Rights (UDHR) and International Covenant on Economic, Social and Cultural Rights (ICESCR), governments have socio-economic obligations to citizens.[31] These obligations aim to enhance citizens' development and contribute to peoples' socio-economic standing.[32] Key responsibilities include access to food, healthcare, housing, education and employment.[33]

Therefore, it is fundamental that peoples are freely able to utilise their resources and organise their economies in ways which seek to enhance their future development.[34] Thus, a sub-category of self-determination is what academics describe as economic self-determination. This is an expression used in the study of international law to refer to peoples' capacity, unreservedly, to dispose of their natural resources in accordance with democratically taken decisions.[35] It refers to the idea that peoples are empowered to freely regulate their economies without outside interference.[36] Economic self-determination is a fundamental principle that underpins broader rights realisation. It allows people to control their mineral resources and use them for their development, including the harvesting and selling of resources like water, minerals, oil, metals, timber and produce.[37] This principle also allows people to generate revenue from the national or foreign exploitation of their natural resources, tax incoming goods and services and fund their socio-economic development. This international law principle grants people the authority to plan their future economic development and act in ways aimed at augmenting their living standards.

Thus, by virtue of the right of its people to self-determination, the BVI, with very little natural resources, has a right in international law to arrange its economy in ways aimed at securing its future economic, social and cultural development. In this vein, beginning in the 1970s, the BVI sought to transform its relatively poor economy.[38]

8.3 A Brief History of the BVI's Financial Services Industry

The BVI signed its first international tax treaty in 1959, after the United Kingdom extended the 1945 US–UK double taxation treaty to the BVI.[39] However, the modern offshore sector was established in 1976 when Paul Butler, a US lawyer, incorporated a BVI company, paving the way for the modern BVI financial services industry.[40] In 1981, the US government raised concerns about the BVI's double taxation agreements with what the United States deemed "tax havens".[41] In 1982, the United States unilaterally terminated the 1959 treaty due to the BVI's reluctance to renegotiate it.[42]

The termination of the 1959 treaty led to the birth of the BVI's modern offshore sector. The idea was to create an extraterritorial corporate vehicle not subject to US regulation. Paul Butler, Michael Riegels, Neville Westwood, Richard Peters and Attorney General Lewis Hunte sought an alternative offshore model, leading to the International Business Companies Act. This Act became law in 1984 and it grew into an industry which has provided local employment and contributed to poverty reduction globally.[43] The BVI International Business Company (IBC) faced an initial slow start, with few new companies incorporated under the 1984 Act. However, as the 1980s progressed, it gained popularity, particularly among Hong Kong Chinese businesspeople. Sir Li Kai-Shing, Asia's richest man in 2014, used a BVI IBC as his holding company during the corporate restructuring of his shipping business Hutchison Whampoa in the 1980s.[44]

Today, the BVI offshore industry generates over USD $1.5 trillion in investment and employs 2.2 million people.[45] With over 350,000 international business companies,[46] it ranks as one of the largest sources of foreign direct investment globally.[47] Since 2006, BVI companies have been the second-largest investors in mainland China.[48] The BVI is also a leading player in offshore investment into Russia, with the share of outward FDI stocks structured through the BVI increasing from almost zero in 1990 to $123.5 billion in 2006.[49] However, the BVI has long faced challenges due to its "tax haven" characterisation.

8.4 Examining the Legality of Corporate Tax Planning Resulting in Tax Avoidance

In examining the legality of tax avoidance, the distinction between tax evasion and avoidance is paramount. The distinction between tax evasion and tax avoidance is clear. It is well established that tax evasion is illegal. The US Internal Revenue Service (IRS) defines tax evasion as the failure to pay or deliberate underpayment of taxes.[50] Tax avoidance is legal and seeks to reduce tax liability and maximise after-tax income.[51] In 2012, Margaret Hodge, Chair of the United Kingdom's Public Accounts Committee, questioned Google UK's Matt Brittin about Google's aggressive tax planning strategies. Hodge's questioning focused on Google's economic activities in the United Kingdom before migrating to Ireland in the early 2000s, while Brittin's answers focused on Google's post-migration Irish operations. If Google UK profited from economic activity from its early UK clients and did not pay taxes on these profits before migrating, this would be tax evasion. If Google migrated its operations to Ireland, taking its UK clients with it, it would be tax avoidance.[52] Shaxson, however, argues tax avoidance often involves activities that cannot be considered legal. He cites Germany's collection of €83 billion in additional taxes from corporations that had underpaid between 2013 and 2017, which he believes taxpayers tried to claim for themselves but were found to have transgressed the law. Shaxson also criticises multinationals for potentially unlawfully dodging billions in taxes.[53] Sol Piciottto has argued creating complex structures involving intermediary entities and exploiting loopholes is not just a matter of choosing jurisdictions to avoid inconvenient rules, especially tax.[54]

International law has failed to identify the illegality of multijurisdictional tax planning resulting in decreased tax liability. Conversely, the OECD has been largely reactive in its approach to combatting tax avoidance by promulgating treaties, in response to tax avoidance strategies and coercing jurisdictions worldwide into compliance. Domestic judicial decisions are conflicting and those which have reasoned certain tax planning strategies are unlawful have been driven by public policy.[55] In England and Wales, up until the 1980s, there was a clear distinction between tax evasion and avoidance. In *Lumsden v IRC*, [56] Viscount Haldane in the House of Lords said judges were under a duty to adhere to the literal construction in interpreting statutes, especially in cases of statutes which impose taxation, unless the context made it plain the words could not so be interpreted. In *IRC v Duke of Westminster*,[57] Lord Tomlin held:

> Every man is entitled if he can to arrange his affairs so that the tax attaching under the appropriate Acts is less than it otherwise would be. If he succeeds in ordering them so as to secure that result, then, however unappreciative the Commissioners of Inland Revenue or his fellow taxpayers may be of his ingenuity, he cannot be compelled to pay an increased tax.[58]

Lord Tomlin's reasoning in *IRC v Duke of Westminster*[59] was ahead of its time as it reflects the contemporary world of business and free market economics since World War II. It suggests persons should not have to account to the taxman for employing the best tax planners to reduce their tax liability. Free market economics advocates for free trade, open markets, privatisation and deregulation. The regulatory scope of governments should be limited according to free market economics rules. If an entity operates within the law, taking advantage of loopholes in the tax system is not unlawful, reflecting the significance of economic liberalisation in recent decades.

In the early 1980s, around the time which so-called "tax haven" abuses started garnering global attention, the House of Lords adopted a purposive approach in statutory interpretation, aimed at closing legislative loopholes taxpayers had previously enjoyed, such as in *WT Ramsay Ltd v IRC*,[60] where Lord Wilberforce ruled, courts were not obliged to stand still in the face of sophisticated tax avoidance techniques aimed at reducing a person's tax liability. This marked a significant change in the law. In *IRC v Burmah Oil Co Ltd*,[61] Lord Diplock argued it would be disingenuous to suggest that *WT Ramsay Ltd v IRC*[62] did not mark a significant change in the House of Lords' judicial role to a pre-ordained series of transactions with inserted steps merely aimed at avoiding tax liability. However, a literal interpretation of tax legislation at the time suggests the reasoning in these cases was based on public policy grounds. The Court's intention in adopting a purposive interpretation was to restrain tax avoidance which it deemed a moral wrong.

In *Cadbury Schweppes plc and Cadbury Schweppes Overseas Ltd v. Commissioners of Inland Revenue*[63] and subsequent cases, the European Court of Justice (ECJ), held that controlled foreign company rules and tax provisions applicable to cross-border transactions that seek to prevent tax avoidance must specifically target wholly artificial arrangements whose only purpose is to obtain a tax advantage. So, while tax avoidance is not illegal, it is the right of EU member states to enact domestic laws to tackle wholly artificial arrangements aimed at decreasing taxpayers' tax liability.[64] The ECJ's reasoning implies a clear distinction between tax avoidance and evasion.

Given the difficulties which Courts and policymakers have faced in identifying tax avoidance as being somehow illegal, due to the myriad innovative strategies employed by tax planners, it is arguable that tax avoidance is legal. It is merely the navigation of loopholes in local and international laws, to secure tax advantages. In today's rapidly evolving commercial environment, whereby MNCs innovate ways to enhance profitability, it is difficult to determine whether their decisions are merely aimed at avoiding taxes.[65] However, notwithstanding the legality of tax planning aimed at the reduction of tax liability, the BVI has demonstrated its commitment to cooperation, good governance and transparency.

8.5 Demonstrating the BVI's Commitment to Cooperation, Good Governance and Transparency

The Territory's competent authorities and law enforcement agencies, such as the FSC, FIA and ITA, continue to facilitate international cooperation with international partners to ensure the BVI is not used as a hub for crime.

8.5.1 The Financial Services Commission

The FSC is the BVI's primary regulator, established under the Financial Services Commission Act 2001. It regulates, monitors and supervises all BVI financial services, including insurance and banking. The FSC also hosts the company registry, ensuring the registration of companies, limited partnerships and intellectual property.[66]

The FSC enjoys regulatory and operational autonomy, despite reporting lines between it and the BVI government.[67] It participates in international and regional financial services regulatory initiatives, including the Group of International Finance Centre Supervisors (GIFCS),[68] which regulates nearly 10% of global international banking assets.[69] GIFCS is a leading authority on Trust and Company Service Providers (TCSPs) regulation, promoting compliance with Basel Core Principles for Effective Banking Supervision and the Financial Action Task Force (FATF) 49 Recommendations on AML/CFT. The BVI is ahead of its peers in TCSP regulation, having enacted the Banks and Trust Companies Act 1990 and the Company Management Act 1990.[70]

The FSC, a regulator of insurance businesses, subscribes to the International Association of Insurance Supervisors (IAIS) Insurance Core Principles. Established in 1994, the IAIS is responsible for developing and implementing insurance principles for effective supervision of the insurance industry globally. The IAIS has over 200 member jurisdictions and regulates 97% of the world's insurance premiums.[71] The BVI has been a member since 1997.[72]

The FSC has been a member of the International Organisation of Security Commissions (IOSCO) since 2007. IOSCO, established in 1983, sets global standards for securities market regulation and works with the G20 and Financial Stability Board (FSB) on regulatory reform.[73] With a membership of over 115 jurisdictions, IOSCO regulates over 95% of the world's securities markets, ensuring transparency and accountability in the industry. IOSCO also works along with the G20 and the FSB on the global regulatory reform agenda.[74]

Arguably, the BVI has demonstrated its commitment to good governance and effective supervision. The FSC has been instrumental in establishing an effective supervisory regime and engaging on an international level.[75] It has strengthened the territory's position on international cooperation, wielding enforcement powers over regulated entities and assisting requests from international partners.[76] The International Cooperation Handbook issued by the FSC is a hallmark of international cooperation initiatives. International cooperation requests are processed through the FSC's Legal and Enforcement Division, with statistics recorded from regulators to regulators and through member organisations. From 2014 to 2018, the FSC processed 594 formal requests for information from foreign regulatory counterparts and local authorities. This highlights the BVI's commitment to good governance and cross-border cooperation.

8.5.2 The International Tax Authority

The ITA is another competent authority established in 2018 under the International Tax Authority Act 2018. Its origins can be traced back to the early 2000s when the Territory enacted the Mutual Legal Assistance (Tax Matters) Act in 2003. Section 4 of this Act made the Financial Secretary the competent authority in the Virgin Islands for international tax matters.[77] The Commissioner of Inland Revenue handled requests for assistance on these matters. In 2012, the financial secretary delegated his duties to the ITA, who has since overseen the territory's international tax matters.[78] In 2018, the ITA became its own agency. Today, it is primarily responsible for processing requests made through the TIEAs signed by the territory.

8.5.2.1 Tax Information Exchange Agreements (TIEAs)

The BVI is a signatory to various TIEAs, providing a framework for information exchange between signatory governments.[79] It entered its first TIEA in 2002 with the United States. In 2003, a new regime was established by the Ministry of Finance to assist in tax-related matters based on negotiated TIEAs. By 2009, the Territory had signed 19 agreements.[80] Today the BVI is party to 28 TIEAs. These include TIEAs with Aruba, Australia, Canada, China (People's Republic), Curacao, Czech Republic, Denmark, Faroe Islands, Finland, France, Germany, Greenland, Guernsey, Iceland, India, Ireland, Isle of Mann, Japan, New Zealand, Norway, Poland, Portugal, Sint Martin, South Korea, Sweden, The Netherlands, the United Kingdom and the United States.

The Mutual Legal Assistance Tax Matters Act, 2003, is the basis for all BVI TIEAs. These agreements are enforced by the Minister of Finance and outline strict criteria to prevent phishing expeditions. Any information sought under a TIEA must be relevant to the taxpayer's tax affairs in the requesting jurisdiction.[81] BVI TIEAs generally cover corporate income tax, personal income tax, payroll tax and property tax.[82] They also outline guidelines for information exchange upon request,[83] tax examinations abroad,[84] declining requests,[85] and confidentiality.[86] The agreements with Guernsey, Isle of Mann and the United Kingdom contain Automatic Exchange of Information (AEOI) provisions, allowing cross-border information exchange without any party having to request it.

8.5.2.2 FATCA, UK FACTA and CRS

In addition to its TIEAs, the BVI subscribes to several other tax information exchange mechanisms including Inter-Governmental Exchange Agreements (IGAs) with the US FATCA, UK FATCA and the Common Reporting Standards (CRS).

8.5.2.2.1 FATCA

The US Foreign Account Tax Compliance Act 2010 (FATCA) is a framework for the AEOI on financial accounts and assets held by US citizens, both on the US mainland and offshore. It requires citizens to file annual reports on their foreign account holdings and foreign financial institutions to sign individual agreements with the US government. FATCA was endorsed as part of the Hiring Incentives to Restore Employment (HIRE) Act in 2010, aiming to provide incentives for businesses to hire more unemployed individuals and decrease unemployment rates. One way in which this was done was through the provision of a business tax credit per each newly hired employee retained for 52 weeks or more. To fund these initiatives, Congress included revenue-generating provisions in the HIRE Act through FATCA, collecting more taxes for assets held by US citizens abroad.[87] In 2014, the BVI signed a Model 1B Intergovernmental Agreement (IGA) with the US in relation to FATCA, demonstrating their willingness to comply with FATCA and support the US in ensuring its citizens holding assets abroad pay their fair share of taxes.[88]

8.5.2.2.2 UK FATCA

In 2013, the United Kingdom entered into agreements with its Crown Dependencies and Overseas Territories to provide financial account details to UK tax residents or passive investment companies. These agreements, known as the CDOT agreements or UK FATCA, were triggered by the US FATCA. Each jurisdiction required permission from the United Kingdom to enter an IGA to implement FATCA.[89] Accordingly, it was agreed equivalent information to that being sent to the United States would also be sent to the United Kingdom. As with FATCA, IGAs require the respective revenue authorities to collect information from financial institutions which have a permanent establishment (including branches and subsidiaries of entities headquartered elsewhere) in that jurisdiction.[90] The UK CDOT builds upon the US FATCA agreements and is based on tax residency rather than citizenship.[91] It is designed to improve the United Kingdom's international tax compliance regime in its Crown Dependencies and Overseas Territories. The exception is Bermuda, where financial institutions report directly to UK HMRC.[92]

8.5.2.2.3 COMMON REPORTING STANDARDS

The CRS, approved by the OECD Council in 2014, mandates jurisdictions to exchange financial information with other jurisdictions annually.[93] It requires financial institutions to identify customer tax residencies and report all local and foreign financial accounts held by foreign tax residents.[94] The CRS aims to prevent tax evasion by outlining the information to be exchanged, the institutions required to report, the types of accounts and taxpayers covered and common due diligence procedures. The standard consists of a model Competent Authority Agreement, the CRS, commentaries and a CRS XML Schema User

Guide. The CRS is applicable for individuals and legal entities alike and aims to give participating countries transparency on the financial assets residents hold offshore.[95]

The BVI was an early adopter of the CRS, having ratified the MCAA on Automatic Exchange of Financial Account Information in 2014 and the Multilateral Convention on Mutual Administrative Assistance in Tax Matters in 2013.[96] The BVI also amended local legislation, particularly the Mutual Legal Assistance (Tax Matters) (Amendment) (No. 2) Act 2015, to implement the CRS. To ensure compliance, the BVI Government created the BVI Financial Accounts Reporting System (BVIFARS), a web-based portal, to provide a secure environment for BVI financial institutions to fulfil their obligations under the US FATCA, UK FATCA/UK CDOT and CRS. The BVIFARS, launched in 2015, is administered by the ITA.[97] This rigorous regulatory regime has led to functional overlap between different instruments, such as the UK FATCA regime and the CRS, with the BVI/UK FATCA regime largely subsumed.

Between 2012 and 2017, the BVI received 1,750 tax information requests and responded to 1,215 of these requests. During that period, the ITA, itself, made 535 requests. Thus, ratification of multiple TIEAs and participation in several initiatives to limit tax avoidance/evasion demonstrates the BVI's commitment to cooperation, tax transparency and compliance with international financial standards.[98]

8.5.2.3 The Beneficial Ownership Secure Search System (BOSSS)

The Beneficial Ownership Secure Search System (BOSSS) is a private Register of beneficial ownership information, administered by the BVI ITA. It enables the timely retrieval of beneficial ownership information for exchange among UK authorities. The system was created in response to the BVI and UK governments signing an exchange of notes for the purpose of exchanging information on the beneficial owners of corporate structures incorporated in the BVI, in 2016, facilitating the United Kingdom's ability to tax its citizens' BVI-held assets. The BOSSS Act was enacted in 2017, to ensure compliance with the agreement and establish a legal basis for the system.[99] It facilitates the effective storage and retrieval of beneficial ownership information for all BVI companies and legal entities using the BOSSS. While administered by the ITA, the information in the BOSSS is accessible to other BVI competent authorities, aimed at ensuring the BVI complies with its international obligations. However, this information is not available to the public.[100]

8.5.2.4 Economic Substance

In 2017, the EU placed several jurisdictions on its grey list, including the BVI, due to concerns about "economic substance" within these jurisdictions. The phrase "economic substance" refers to whether corporate activities are managed within their jurisdiction of domiciliation and if core-income-generating activities are conducted within their jurisdiction.[101] The BVI and other grey-listed jurisdictions were given a deadline of 31 December 2018 to pass legislation addressing this issue. In response, the BVI Government passed the Economic Substance (Companies and Limited Partnership) Act, 2018, which introduced increased economic substance requirements for certain BVI-resident legal entities.[102] The legislation applies to banking, insurance, fund management, finance and leasing, headquarters, shipping, holding, intellectual property, and distribution and service centre businesses. The enactment of the 2018 Act and amendments to the Beneficial Ownership Secure Search System Act, 2017, again demonstrates the BVI's commitment to complying with global standards and the EU's Code of Conduct Group's requirements for jurisdictions which were then on the EU's "grey list".

The BVI is a member of the OECD's Inclusive Framework on BEPS. Enactment of economic substance legislation brings the BVI in compliance with BEPS Action 5.[103] According to the authors of "Creating Value: The BVI's Global Contribution",

> The BVI is not a material centre for corporate profit shifting.[104] Multinational companies seeking to optimise their tax position would presumably look to conduct any "profit shifting" through jurisdictions giving them protection from double taxation, and where they are exempt from withholding charges.[105]

8.5.3 The Financial Investigation Agency (FIA)

Since tax evasion is a predicate offence to money laundering, it is necessary to include the BVI's FIA and its anti-money laundering (AML) and terrorist financing (CFT) initiatives in the discussion on tax transparency. Since 1992, through the enactment of the Drugs Trafficking Offences Act, the BVI has pursued policies demonstrating its commitment to the global fight against money laundering and the financing of terrorism and has strived to combat cross-border financial crimes.[106]

In 2003, the BVI established the Financial Investigation Unit under the Financial Investigation Agency Act. This Unit was succeeded by the FIA in 2004. The FIA is an autonomous competent authority, supported by other authorities like the Attorney General's Chambers. It is integral to the Territory's AML/CFT machinery. It is responsible for processing Suspicious Activity Reports (SARs) and Suspicious Transaction Reports (STRs), which involve receiving, obtaining, investigating, analysing and disseminating information related to financial offences or requests for legal assistance from foreign jurisdictions.[107] The FIA works closely with local law enforcement to fulfil its investigative role and may exchange information spontaneously.[108]

The FIA became an operational member of the Egmont Group in 2004. The Egmont Group is a global network of circa 164 FIUs and is considered by some as the "operational arm of the international AML/CFT apparatus", "...and provides for the secure exchange of expertise and financial intelligence to combat money laundering and terrorist financing".[109] In addition to its investigative responsibilities, the FIA has oversight of designated non-financial businesses and professions (DNFBPs) and non-profit organisations (NPOs), which have been identified as targets for criminals for the purposes of money laundering and terrorist financing.[110]

The FATF is the global standard setter for AML, terrorist financing and proliferation financing measures. It urges countries to implement effective measures to comply with its 49 recommendations on money laundering and terrorist financing. Regional bodies, such as the Caribbean Financial Action Task Force (CFATF), assist the FATF in addressing specific regional needs. The CFATF is an organisation of Caribbean jurisdictions that agree to implement common countermeasures against money laundering, enjoying associate membership of the FATF.[111]

The BVI is a founding member of the CFATF and has been an active contributor. The BVI assumed vice chairmanship from 2012 to 2013 and chairmanship from 2015 to 2016. The most recent Mutual Evaluation of the BVI for compliance with AML/CFT was conducted by the CFATF in 2008. This evaluation included three follow-up rounds which produced reports in 2010, 2011 and 2012. The 2008 evaluation saw the territory emerge with compliant ratings against the FATF's 40+9 Recommendations, 15 largely compliant (LC); 18 compliant (C); 15 partially compliant (PC); and 1 non-compliant (NC). By the third follow-up round in 2011, the compliance ratings saw 12 PC ratings improve to LC, demonstrating the territory's continuous commitment to regulatory improvement. For instance, with regards to conducting and collecting due diligence on clients, the BVI was an early adopter of the FATF's requirements to verify and identify clients as well as taking steps to determine whether a client or beneficial owner was a politically exposed person. According to the report by Capital Economics, "Creating Value: The BVI's Global Contribution",

> with regards to anti-money laundering, the territory is ahead of most in terms of complying with procedures set out by the FATF with the BVI now meeting 40 of the 49 Recommendations for effectively combatting money laundering and terrorist financing, measurably better than many of its peers.[112]

The BVI's commitment to establishing an effective regulatory regime is evidenced in the ongoing initiatives aimed at improving. The regulation of trust and corporate service providers, the immobilisation of bearer shares, the establishment of an AML and terrorist financing regime which includes mandatory reporting obligations for suspicious activity and the establishment of relevant institutions to address these, demonstrates the BVI's commitment to best practices in the international financial arena.

8.5.4 The Attorney General's Chambers (AGC)

The AGC is another BVI competent authority responsible for responding to international cooperation requests made under various Acts, including the Evidence (Proceedings in Foreign Jurisdictions) Act 1988, Mutual Legal Assistance (United States of America) Act 1990, Drug Trafficking Offences Act 1992 and Proceeds of Criminal Conduct Act 1997. These requests typically have an average response time of three to four days. The AGC aims to facilitate clear information exchange among international counterparts. From 2015 to 2018, it received 495 international cooperation requests, fulfilling its obligations under relevant international agreements. This demonstrates the cooperative spirit of BVI regulators.

8.6 The BVI's Right to Self-Determination and Economic Development

Unqualified criticisms of the BVI's offshore sector, reveal a profound lack of understanding of the offshore finance sector generally and an even greater lack of understanding of the operation of the territory's financial services sector. Criticisms suggest a total lack of regulation since the term "offshore" has come to attract pejorative connotations. In the minds of many casual observers, the term offshore sparks ideas about profit-obsessed MNCs, gangsters and narcotic traffickers sipping cocktails beneath palm trees, lax to non-existent regulations and trifling tax rates.[113] For instance, Robert Barrington, director of Transparency International UK, which lobbies against "tax havens", believed the fine imposed on Mossack Fonseca following the Panama Papers leak, was inadequate.[114] To him, since it took a leak for BVI regulators to uncover Mossack Fonseca's activities, the BVI's own abilities as a regulator were questionable.[115] Such statements are unfair. They infer ineffectiveness on the part of regulators and an absence of true regulation, however, discount the innovative concealment strategies often employed by wrongdoers. In measuring its response, the regulator's resources must also be considered. Surely the United States, the United Kingdom, New Zealand and Singapore, also implicated in the Panama Papers leak, all have more resources than the BVI and were better placed, resources-wise, to discover nefarious activity, yet like the BVI, it took an inside leak to reveal such nefarious activity.

Moreover, the BVI IBC, despite its condemnation, is rarely cited as being heavily influenced by Delaware's low corporate tax rate of 8.7% at the time, while the federal corporate tax rate stood at 35%.[116] Instead, the BVI continues to face criticism.[117] Such criticisms, discount that there are genuine commercial reasons unrelated to tax avoidance for incorporation in foreign jurisdictions. For instance, the home country laws of the parent company may make it more difficult to employ foreign staff, own property or borrow money. Therefore, research such as the TJN's financial secrecy index does not provide a comprehensive overview of the sector. This is a disturbing trend, especially as it is yet to be established that corporate tax planning resulting in tax avoidance is illegal. There is an absence of a grounding of the illegality of multijurisdictional tax avoidance strategies. This is a key reason why the OECD has reacted to such tax avoidance strategies by promulgating treaties and imposing rules promoting transparency and cooperation on economically weaker jurisdictions with threats of blacklisting and sanctions. It should not be discounted that the integration of national economies and markets has increased substantially in recent years, putting a strain on the international tax rules, which were designed more than a century ago. It is due to loopholes in the current rules, that tax avoidance opportunities are created.[118] Therefore, it is unreasonable to hold jurisdictions, whose economies are a fraction of the GDP of some multinationals, accountable for their tax planning strategies. It is therefore important to examine the legal implications of multijurisdictional corporate tax planning strategies resulting in tax avoidance, especially as it relates to the international image of offshore financial centres, such as the BVI, who are portrayed as facilitating financial crimes on a global scale. This is placing too great a burden on small economies – a standard with which developed countries themselves have struggled, as seen in the United States' failure, so far, to implement the OECD's CRS.[119] This issue is especially important in relation to MNCs given the fact that it is the open economies and free trade, as advocated by developed countries, that caused these entities to grow to their current size. Considering the above legal argument, arguably the BVI has demonstrated commitment to regulation as required by the international tax regime, by its implementation of the numerous initiatives described above.

Moreover, as aforementioned, a fundamental human right is the right of peoples to self-determination. Self-determination denotes the legal right of people to decide their own destiny in the international order. A key facet of self-determination is economic self-determination i.e. a people's use of their resources to further their sustainable development objectives. This is particularly important in the case of economically vulnerable territories such as the BVI with little to no natural resources as the creation and implementation of sustainable development models will determine the future existence of such societies. As aforementioned, it refers to the idea that peoples are empowered to freely regulate their economies without outside interference.[120]

Economic self-determination is a fundamental principle that underpins broader rights realisation. It allows people to control their mineral resources and use them for their development, including the harvesting and selling of resources like water, minerals, oil, metals, timber and produce.[121] This principle also allows people to generate revenue from the national or foreign exploitation of their natural resources, tax incoming goods and services and fund their socio-economic development. Thus, consistent with its right to economic self-determination and its right to development, in the 1970s, the BVI mobilised its resources to transform its economy. This has been particularly important considering that the BVI is a Small Island Developing State (SIDS) harbouring all the vulnerabilities frequently associated with poorer SIDs i.e. economic volatility, sea level rise, climate change, desertification, food insecurity, notwithstanding its economic success. Today, the BVI can be regarded as an example of an economic success story. In the 1960s, the BVI's GDP per capita, which stood at $1,183 in 1973 was comparable to that of today's least developed countries (LDCs).[122] Today it enjoys a GDP per capita of $46,997, which is comparable to Portugal, a developed country.[123] Being natural resources-poor, it was able to achieve this largely through the success of its financial services industry, which is a key pillar of its economy.

Considering the issues, it is fundamental that any international regulation suggested by international society, aimed at combatting the aggressive tax avoidance strategies employed by MNCs, take into consideration the right to self-determination and economic development of the BVI. It is fundamental that such regulations are consistent with or at the very least do not constrain the BVI's ability to achieve its development goals.

8.7 Conclusion

A fundamental human right in international law is the right of peoples to economic self-determination. This refers to the right of a people to arrange their economic affairs in ways best suited to achieving their economic goals.[124] By virtue of its right to economic self-determination, the BVI has the right to arrange its economy in ways best suited to achieve its future economic goals. However, this has not translated into practice for many jurisdictions. Duplicity in the international tax regime means that developed countries have demanded standards from developing countries that they refuse to apply to themselves. This is particularly true of the unrelenting criticisms of the BVI financial services industry by developed countries and the international organisations dominated by them. Blacklisting and threats of blacklisting have forced the BVI to adopt measures and implement policies demonstrating its commitment to a transparent and cooperative offshore financial services industry. The BVI has implemented various regulatory initiatives, which demonstrate its commitment to transparency and cooperation. The BVI is now better regulated than larger economies. The BVI has demonstrated commitment to fulfilling its obligations vis-à-vis its foreign counterparts and condemnation of its financial services sector is misleading. The territory has not received due acknowledgement for its efforts to develop a highly regulated financial services industry. Moreover, the BVI has a right to arrange its economic affairs in the ways best suited to achieving its economic goals. Thus, it is important that any international regulations suggested by developed countries aimed at combatting tax avoidance, take into consideration the BVI's right to economic self-determination and sustainable development. It is fundamental that such regulations are consistent with or at the very least do not constrain the BVI's ability to achieve its development goals.

Notes

1 Article 1(2) of the UN Charter 1945 [1945] ATS 1/59 Stat. 1031; TS 993; 3 Bevans 1153. Article 1(2) of UNGA Resolution 2200, International Covenant on Economic, Social and Cultural Rights UN GAOR, 21st Sess., Supp. No. 16 at 49, UN Doc. A/6316 (1966) and Article 1(2) UNGA Resolution 2200A(XXI), International Covenant on Civil and Political Rights, UN 21st Sess., UN Doc. A/RES/ (1966).

2 Robert Mccorquodale, 'Self-Determination: A Human Rights Approach' (1994) 43(4) *International and Comparative Law Quarterly* 857–858.

3 Oji U. Umozurike, 'Nationalization of Foreign Owned Property and Self-Determination' (1970) 6 *East Africa Law Journal* 79–99.

4 Hedley Bull, 'The Revolt Against the West,' in Bull and Watson (eds), *The Expansion of the International Society* (Clarendon 1992) 227.

5 David Leigh, 'David Cameron urged to act over British Virgin Islands' (2013) *The Guardian* www.theguardian.com/uk/2013/apr/04/david-cameron-british-virgin-islands Accessed on 5 May 2019. See also Tax Justice Network, Financial Secrecy Index2018, NarrativeReport on the British Virgin Islands www.financialsecrecyindex.com/PDF/BritishVirginIslands.pdf accessed 3 May 2019. See also Youtube, Tax Heavens: How to loot a country (and get away with it) www.youtube.com/watch?v=VDcce4KnLNs accessed 5 May 2019.

6 BVI-Liquidations.com, BVI Company Statistics [Online] Available from: https://bvi-liquidations.com/bvi-company-statistics/#:~:text=There%20are%20366%2C050%20BVI%20Business,as%20of%2030th%20June%202023 accessed 1 September 2024. As of 30 June 2024, there were 366, 050 companies registered on the BVI's company register.

7 World Finance's Youtube Channel, How BVI Business Companies power $1.5tr of investment worldwide www.youtube.com/watch?v=OMfa3UkR_W0 accessed on 5 May 2023.

8 Harneys, The International Business Companies Act: The Building of a Nation www.harneys.com/files/the-ibc-act-the-building-of-a-nation-(2).pdf accessed 9 May 2024.

9 Stephen Platt, 'Criminal Capital: How the Finance Industry Facilitates Crime' (2015) Palgrave MacMillan p. 53.

10 Jeff Gerth, 'U.S. is Opening Talks on Tax Haven Treaty' (1982) *New York Times* www.nytimes.com/1982/01/15/business/us-is-opening-talks-on-tax-haven-treaty.html accessed 3 May 2024.

11 David Leigh, 'David Cameron urged to act over British Virgin Islands' (2013) *The Guardian* www.theguardian.com/uk/2013/apr/04/david-cameron-british-virgin-islands accessed on 5 May 2024.

12 Vanessa Houlder and Hugh Carnegy, 'France Steps Up Assault on Tax Havens' (2013) *Financial Times* www.ft.com/content/bf0e889e-10ca-11e3-b291-00144feabdc0 accessed on 5 May 2024.

13 Cristian Angeloni, The Netherlands creates its own tax haven blacklist (2019) International Adviser https://international-adviser.com/the-netherlands-creates-its-own-tax-haven-blacklist/ 5 May 2024.

14 Platt (n 9) 53.

15 Helen Burggraf Netherlands quietly unveils its own tax haven 'blacklist' American Expat Financial News Journal (2018) https://americanexpatfinance.com/news/item/85-netherlands-quietly-unveils-its-own-tax-haven-blacklist accessed on 9 May 2019. See also Cristian Angeloni, The Netherlands creates its own tax haven blacklist (2019) International Adviser https://international-adviser.com/the-netherlands-creates-its-own-tax-haven-blacklist/ accessed 5 May 2023.

16 Michael Klein, 'France Blacklists BVI, Bahamas' (Cayman Compass 14th January 2020). Availablefrom:https://www.caymancompass.com/2020/01/14/france-blacklists-bvi-bahamas/ accessed on 18 February 2023.

17 The Report was approved by the OECD Council, with abstentions from Luxembourg and Switzerland, on 9th April 1998, and was presented to Ministers on 27/28 April 1998. Tax havens should be distinguished from preferential tax regimes. Preferential tax regimes are generally part of the tax legislation of countries with a standard corporate income tax design. The preferential tax regime offers a benefit in comparison to the standard tax rules in that relevant country.
18 Vanessa Houlder and Hugh Carnegy, 'France Steps Up Assault on Tax Havens' (2013) *Financial Times* www.ft.com/content/bf0e889e-10ca-11e3-b291-00144feabdc0 accessed 5 May 2019.
19 Tax Justice Network, financial Secrecy Index 2018, Narrative Report on the British Virgin Islands www.financialsecrecyindex.com/PDF/BritishVirginIslands.pdf p. 1.
20 Hamish Boland-Rudder, BVI Hits Mossack Fonseca With Largest Fine Ever After Panama Papers Investigation (2016) *International Consortium of Investigative Journalist* www.icij.org/investigations/panama-papers/20161116-bvi-mossack-fonseca-penalty/ accessed 11 May 2024.
21 M. B. Angell, 'Tax Evasion and Tax Avoidance' (1938) 80 *Columbia Law Review* 80.
22 [1982] AC 300.
23 1982 SC (HL) 114.
24 WT Ramsay Ltd v IRC [1982] AC 300 326.
25 IRC v Burmah Oil Co Ltd 1982 SC (HL) 114.
26 The Report was approved by the OECD Council, with abstentions from Luxembourg and Switzerland, on 9 April 1998, and was presented to Ministers on 27/28 April 1998.
27 Government of the Virgin Islands, Tax Information Exchange Agreements www.bvi.gov.vg/tiea accessed 9 May 2019.
28 Deloitte, 'Economic Substance Rules Published' (10 November 2019). Available from: www.taxathand.com/article/12345/British-Virgin-Islands/2019/Economic-substance-rules-published accessed 11 December 2019.
29 Umozurike (n 3) 79–99.
30 Cornell Law School Legal Information Institute, Self-Determination (International Law), Available from: https://www.law.cornell.edu/wex/self_determination_(international_law) accessed 23 May 2024.
31 Article 1(2) of UNGA Resolution 2200, International Covenant on Economic, Social and Cultural Rights UN GAOR, 21st Sess., Supp. No. 16 at 49, UN Doc. A/6316 (1966).
32 Daniel Muriu Wanjau, 'Third World Resistance to International Economic and Structural Constraints: Assessing the Utility of the Right to Health in the Context of the TRIPS Agreement' (2009) International Community Law Review 409, 429.
33 Daniel Muriu Wanjau, 'Third World Resistance to International Economic and Structural Constraints: Assessing the Utility of the Right to Health in the Context of the TRIPS Agreement' (2009) International Community Law Review 409, 429.
34 Alice Farmer, 'Towards a Meaningful Rebirth of Self-Determination: Human Rights Realization in Resources-Rich Countries' (2006) 39 *Journal of International Law and Politics* 418.
35 Anthony Carty, 'From the Right to Economic Self-Determination to the Right to Development: A Crisis in Legal Theory' (1984) *Third World Legal Studies* 86.
36 Umozurike (n 3) 79–99.
37 Carty, (n. 35) 86.
38 Harneys (n. 8).
39 Jeff Gerth, 'U.S. is Opening Talks on Tax Haven Treaty' (1982) *New York Times* www.nytimes.com/1982/01/15/business/us-is-opening-talks-on-tax-haven-treaty.html accessed 3 May 2024.
40 Tax Justice Network (n.19) 2.
41 Gerth (n. 39).
42 Gerth (n. 39).
43 Tax Justice Network (n.19) 3.

44 Harneys (n. 8).
45 World Finances, Youtube Channel (n. 7).
46 BVI-Liquidations.com (n. 6).
47 World Finance's Youtube Channel (n 7).
48 Business BVI 'Emerging Opportunities in Asia for BVI Products' (2015) www.businessbvi.com/business/.../559-emerging-opportunities-in-asia-for-bvi-products Accessed 5 May 2019. See also Tax Justice Network 'China Leaks: how the BVI became China's foreign tax haven of choice'. Available from: www.taxjustice.net/2014/01/22/china-leaks-bvi-became-chinas-tax-haven-choice/ accessed 5 May 2019.
49 Simon Pascoe and Kristian Wilson, 'British Virgin Islands: The BVI: Stepping-Stone to Russia' (2015) Mondaq. www.mondaq.com/x/392642/offshore+financial+centres/The+BVI+Stepping+Stone+To+Russia accessed 5 May 2019. See also Settles, International Investment Activities of Russian Corporations, https://gdex.dk/ofdi/35%20Settles%20Alex.pdf.
50 United States Internal Revenue Services, Worksheet Solutions: The Difference Between Tax Avoidance and Tax Evasion [Online] Available from: https://apps.irs.gov/app/understandingTaxes/whys/thm01/les03/media/ws_ans_thm01_les03.pdf accessed 20 February 2024.
51 United States Internal Revenue Services, Worksheet Solutions: The Difference Between Tax Avoidance and Tax Evasion [Online] Available from: https://apps.irs.gov/app/understandingTaxes/whys/thm01/les03/media/ws_ans_thm01_les03.pdf accessed 20 February 2024.
52 Angell (n. 21) 80.
53 Nick Shaxson 'No, corporate tax avoidance is not 'legal" (16 May 2019) Network, www.taxjustice.net/2019/05/16/no-corporate-tax-avoidance-is-not-legal/ accessed 12 May 2024.
54 Sol Picciotto, 'Why Tax Avoidance Is Illicit' (10 May 2018) International Centre for Tax and Development www.ictd.ac/blog/why-tax-avoidance-is-illicit/ accessed 12 May 2024.
55 Angell (n. 21) 80.
56 [1914] AC 877.
57 [1936] AC 1.
58 [1936] AC 1 at 19–20.
59 [1936] AC 1.
60 [1982] AC 300 326.
61 [1982] STC 30.
62 [1982] AC 300 326.
63 Cadbury Schweppes plc and Cadbury Schweppes Overseas Ltd v. Commissioners of Inland Revenue, C-196/04.
64 See Itelcar – Automóveis de Aluguer Lda. v. Fazenda Pública, Case C-282/12 (3 October 2013).
65 IRC v Burmah Oil Co Ltd 1982 SC (HL) 114.
66 British Virgin Islands Financial Services Commission, "About Us" Available from: www.bvifsc.vg/content/about-us accessed 1 December 2024.
67 British Virgin Islands Financial Services Commission, "About Us" Available from: www.bvifsc.vg/content/about-us accessed 1 December 2024.
68 "British Virgin Islands Handbook on International Co-operation and Information Exchange: A Guide for Regulators and Judicial and Law Enforcement Officials"., p.11.
69 "Purpose and Objectives" Group of International Financial Centres Supervisors", Available from: https://www.groupgifcs.org/about/purpose-and-objectives accessed 20 November 2019.
70 Paul Byles, s Offshore Financial Services: A BVI Text (BVI Financial Services Commission, 2014) 204.
71 International Association of Insurance Supervisors. Available from www.iaisweb.org/home accessed 1 September 2024.

72 British Virgin Islands: Handbook on International Co-operation and Information Exchange- A Guide for Regulators and Judicial and Law Enforcement Officials.
73 International Organization of Securities Commissions 'About'. Available from: www.iosco.org/about/??subsection=about/?_iosco accessed 20 November 2023.
74 Terry Dwyer, "Is Tax Competition even "harmful" – The OECD Dogma" Visiting Fellow, Asia Pacific School of Economics and Management, Australian National University, Canberra, Australia. Available from: www.aph.gov.au/DocumentStore.ashx?id=cf8646db-4cea-4567-8b17-2a7d1a6e5ea1&subId=404023 Accessed 4 December 2023.
75 Terry Dwyer, "Is Tax Competition even "harmful" – The OECD Dogma" Visiting Fellow, Asia Pacific School of Economics and Management, Australian National University, Canberra, Australia. Available from: www.aph.gov.au/DocumentStore.ashx?id=cf8646db-4cea-4567-8b17-2a7d1a6e5ea1&subId=404023 Accessed 4 December 2023.
76 Byles (n. 70) 204.
77 Section 4 of the Mutual Legal Assistance (Tax Matters) Act 2003.
78 Byles (n. 70) 204.
79 Government of the British Virgin Islands (n. 27).
80 Byles (n. 70) 204.
81 Government of the British Virgin Islands (n. 27).
82 Agreement Between the Portuguese Republic and The Government of the British Virgin Islands for the Exchange of Information Relating to Taxes. Available from: https://bvi.gov.vg/sites/default/files/TIEA%20between%20Portugal%20and%20BVI.pdf accessed 5 December 2023. See Article 3.
83 I Article 5 of the Agreement Between the Portuguese Republic and The Government of the British Virgin Islands for the Exchange of Information Relating to Taxes. Available from: https://bvi.gov.vg/sites/default/files/TIEA%20between%20Portugal%20and%20BVI.pdf Accessed on 5th December 2023.
84 Article 6 of the Agreement Between the Portuguese Republic and The Government of the British Virgin Islands for the Exchange of Information Relating to Taxes. Available from: https://bvi.gov.vg/sites/default/files/TIEA%20between%20Portugal%20and%20BVI.pdf Accessed on 5th December 2023.
85 Article 7 of the Agreement Between the Portuguese Republic and The Government of the British Virgin Islands for the Exchange of Information Relating to Taxes. Available from: https://bvi.gov.vg/sites/default/files/TIEA%20between%20Portugal%20and%20BVI.pdf Accessed on 5th December 2023.
86 Article 8 of the Agreement Between the Portuguese Republic and The Government of the British Virgin Islands for the Exchange of Information Relating to Taxes. Available from: https://bvi.gov.vg/sites/default/files/TIEA%20between%20Portugal%20and%20BVI.pdf Accessed on 5th December 2023.
87 Foreign Account Tax Compliance Act (FATCA): Investopedia. Available from: www.investopedia.com/terms/f/foreign-account-tax-compliance-act-fatca.asp accessed 1 December 2019.
88 Competent Authority Arrangement between the Competent Authorities of the United States of America and the Government of the British Virgin Islands. Available from: https://bvi.gov.vg/sites/default/files/competent_authority_arrangement_between_the_competent_authorities_of_the_usa_and_the_bvi.pdf accessed on 25 November 2019.
89 Lexis Nexis, 'UK Crown Dependency/Overseas Territory Agreements (CDOT)—FAQs' Available from: www.lexisnexis.co.uk/legal/guidance/uk-crown-dependency-overseas-territory-agreements-cdot-faqs accessed 5 December 2023.
90 Lexis Nexis, 'UK Crown Dependency/Overseas Territory Agreements (CDOT)—FAQs' Available from: www.lexisnexis.co.uk/legal/guidance/uk-crown-dependency-overseas-territory-agreements-cdot-faqs accessed 5 December 2023.

91 Yair Zorea and Katya Weiner 'FATCA, UK CDOT and CRS Overview of Due Diligence and Reporting (2015) Pricewater Coopers. Available from: www.pwc.com/il/he/events/assets/2017/1-10-us-tax/fatca_crs_reporting.pdf accessed 5 December 2023.
92 Pinsent Masons 'UK FATCA' – The Disclosure to HMRC of Information about Reportable Accounts held by UK Taxpayers in the Crown Dependencies and Overseas Territories (1 April 2016). Available from: www.pinsentmasons.com/out-law/guides/uk-fatca---the-disclosure-to-hmrc-of-information-about-reportable-accounts-held-by-uk-taxpayers-in-the-crown-dependencies-and-overseas-territories accessed 6 November 2023.
93 OECD, 'What is the CSR?' Available from: www.oecd.org/tax/automatic-exchange/common-reporting-standard/ accessed 15 November 2023.
94 ING 'Common Reporting Standard' Available from: www.ingwb.com/rules-regulations/common-reporting-standard accessed 2 September 2019.
95 ING 'Common Reporting Standard' Available from: www.ingwb.com/rules-regulations/common-reporting-standard accessed 2 September 2019.
96 Gosling, J., Davies, A., Penn-Lettsome L. and Waldron P., 'British Virgin Islands and The CRS' 8th January 2016. Available from: www.mondaq.com/x/456476/Financial+Services/British+Virgin+Islands+and+the+CRS accessed 15 June 2019.
97 Government of the Virgin Islands, 'BVI Financial Account Reporting System'. Available from: www.bvi.gov.vg/fatca accessed 14 November 2015.
98 The relevant statistics are on file with the author.
99 "Still Not in the Clear: More updates to BOSSs laws as BVI eludes EU blacklist" BVINews, 2nd August 2019. Available from: https://bvinews.com/still-not-in-the-clear-more-updates-to-bosss-laws-as-bvi-eludes-eu-blacklist/ accessed 5 December 2023.
100 Vistra, 'BVI Beneficial Ownership Secure Search System Act' Available from: www.vistra.com/beneficial-ownership-secure-search-system-act-2017 accessed 15 November 2023.
101 Collis, G.B.R., "Bermuda: Economic Substance – What does it Mean for International Financial Centers?" Available from www.mondaq.com/x/781246/Fund+Management+REITs/Economic+Substance+What+Does+It+Mean+For+International+Financial+Centres accessed 13 February 2024.
102 Government of the Virgin Islands Legislation Passed to Address EU Economic Substance Concerns, 2nd January 2019. Available from: www.bvi.gov.vg/media-centre/legislation-passed-address-eu-economic-substance-concerns accessed 2 December 2023.
103 Government of the Virgin Islands Legislation Passed to Address EU Economic Substance Concerns, 2nd January 2019. Available from: www.bvi.gov.vg/media-centre/legislation-passed-address-eu-economic-substance-concerns accessed 2 December 2023.
104 Byles (n. 70) 204.
105 David Collins, Ashley Davies, Andy Randall, Rowena Lawrence, John Rogers, 'Creating Value: The BVI's Global Contribution'. Mondaq.com. Available from: www.mondaq.com/x/607926/offshore+financial+centres/Creating+Value+The+BVIs+Global+Contribution accessed 5 December 2023.
106 Byles (n. 70) 204.
107 Virgin Islands-Financial Investigation Agency Act, 2003, s.4 (19 of 2003).
108 The exchange of information spontaneously is facilitated among domestic competent authorities and members of the Inter-Governmental Committee on AML/CFT through the *Memorandum of Understanding between Authorities of the Inter-governmental Committee on AML/CFT"*.
109 The Egmont Group 'About Us' Available from: https://egmontgroup.org/en/content/about accessed 4 December 2019.

110 "Recommendation 28" Financial Action Task Force & "FATF Report: Risk of Terrorist Abuse in Non-Profit Organisations" June 2014. Available from: www.fatf-gafi.org/media/fatf/documents/reports/Risk-of-terrorist-abuse-in-non-profit-organisations.pdf accessed 5 November 2019.
111 Caribbean Financial Action Task Force. Available from: www.fatf-gafi.org/pages/caribbeanfinancialactiontaskforcecfatf.html accessed 8 December 2019. CFATF members include Anguilla, Aruba, Bahamas, Barbados, Belize, Bermuda, British Virgin Islands, Cayman Islands, Curaçao, Dominica, El Salvador, Grenada, Guyana, Haiti, Jamaica, Montserrat, St. Kitts & Nevis, St. Lucia, St. Maarten, St. Vincent & the Grenadines, Suriname, Trinidad & Tobago, Turks & Caicos Islands and Venezuela.
112 Byles (n. 70) 204.
113 Platt (n. 9) 53.
114 Juliette Garside, 'Mossack Fonseca fined $440,000 in British Virgin Islands' (2016) *The Guardian* www.theguardian.com/business/2016/nov/15/mossack-fonseca-fined-british-virgin-islands-panama-papers accessed 11 May 2024.
115 Juliette Garside, 'Mossack Fonseca fined $440,000 in British Virgin Islands' (2016) *The Guardian* www.theguardian.com/business/2016/nov/15/mossack-fonseca-fined-british-virgin-islands-panama-papers accessed 11 May 2024.
116 Tax Justice Network (n.19) 3.
117 'Offshore financial centres grey listed by EU' (2017) Economist http://country.eiu.com/article.aspx?articleid=1336224117&Country=Bermuda&topic=Economy&subtopic=Forecast&subsubtopic=Policy+trends accessed 5 May 2024.
118 OECD (2015), Designing Effective Controlled Foreign Company Rules, Action 3 – 2015 Final Report, OECD/G20 Base Erosion and Profit Shifting Project, OECD Publishing, Paris. http://doi.org/10.1787/9789264241152-en.
119 Bloomberg's Editorial Board, 'The U.S. is Becoming the World's New Tax Haven' (2017) www.bloomberg.com/opinion/articles/2017-12-28/the-u-s-is-becoming-the-world-s-new-tax-haven accessed 12 May 2024.
120 Umozurike (n 3) 79–99.
121 Carty, (n. 35) 86.
122 UN Data, Per Capita GDP of the British Virgin Islands [Online] Available from: https://data.un.org/Data.aspx?d=SNAAMA&f=grID%3A101%3BcurrID%3AUSD%3BpcFlag%3A1%3BcrID%3A92 accessed 5 August 2024.
123 UN Data, Per Capita GDP of the British Virgin Islands [Online] Available from: https://data.un.org/Data.aspx?d=SNAAMA&f=grID%3A101%3BcurrID%3AUSD%3BpcFlag%3A1%3BcrID%3A92 accessed 5 August 2024.
124 Mccorquodale (n. 2) 857–858.

Bibliography

Angell, Montgomery B. 'Tax Evasion and Tax Avoidance' (1938) 80 *Columbia Law Review* 80.

Angeloni, Cristian, 'The Netherlands Creates Its Own Tax Haven Blacklist' (2019) International Adviser https://international-adviser.com/the-netherlands-creates-its-own-tax-haven-blacklist/ accessed 5 May 2024.

Boland-Rudder, Hamish, 'BVI Hits Mossack Fonseca with Largest Fine Ever After Panama Papers Investigation' (2016) International Consortium of Investigative Journalist,https://www.icij.org/investigations/panama-papers/20161116-bvi-mossack-fonseca-penalty/ accessed 11 May 2024.

Bull, Hedley 'The Revolt Against the West,' in Bull H and Watson A (eds), *The Expansion of the International Society* (Clarendon 1992) 227.

Byles, Paul '*Offshore Financial Services: A BVI Text* (BVI Financial Services Commission, 2014)

Carty, Anthony 'From the Right to Economic Self-Determination to the Right to Development: A Crisis in Legal Theory' (1984) 3 *Third World Legal Studies* 73.

Collins, David Ashley Davies, Randall, Andy, Lawrence, Rowena and Rogers, John, 'Creating Value: The BVI's Global Contribution' (2017) Mondaq.com. https://www.mondaq.com/x/607926/offshore+financial+centres/Creating+Value+The+BVIs+Global+Contribution accessed 5 December 2023.

Deloitte, 'Economic Substance Rules Published' (10 November 2019). Available from: https://www.taxathand.com/article/12345/British-Virgin-Islands/2019/Economic-substance-rules-published accessed 11 December 2023.

Farmer, Alice 'Towards a Meaningful Rebirth of Self-Determination: Human Rights Realization in Resources-Rich Countries' (2006) 39 *Journal of International Law and Politics* 418.

Garside, Juliette 'Mossack Fonseca fined $440,000 in British Virgin Islands' (2016) *The Guardian* www.theguardian.com/business/2016/nov/15/mossack-fonseca-fined-british-virgin-islands-panama-papers accessed 11 May 2024.

Gerth, Jeff 'U.S. Is Opening Talks on Tax Haven Treaty' (1982) *New York Times* https://www.nytimes.com/1982/01/15/business/us-is-opening-talks-on-tax-haven-treaty.html accessed 3 May 2024.

Houlder, Vanessa and Hugh Carnegy, 'France Steps Up Assault on Tax Havens' (2013) *Financial Times* https://www.ft.com/content/bf0e889e-10ca-11e3-b291-00144feabdc0 accessed 5 May 2024.

Klein, Michael 'France Blacklists BVI, Bahamas' (Cayman Compass 14 January 2020). Available from: https://www.caymancompass.com/2020/01/14/france-blacklists-bvi-bahamas/ accessed 18 February 2023.

Leigh, David 'David Cameron urged to act over British Virgin Islands' (2013) *The Guardian* https://www.theguardian.com/uk/2013/apr/04/david-cameron-british-virgin-islands accessed 5 May 2019.

Mccorquodale, Robert 'Self-Determination: A Human Rights Approach' (1994) 43(4) *International and Comparative Law Quarterly* 857–858.

Piciotto, Sol 'Why Tax Avoidance Is Illicit' (10 May 2018) International Centre for Tax and Development https://www.ictd.ac/blog/why-tax-avoidance-is-illicit/ accessed 12 May 2024.

Platt, Stephen 'Criminal Capital: How the Finance Industry Facilitates Crime' (2015) Palgrave MacMillan. https://link.springer.com/book/10.1057/9781137337306

Shaxson, Nick 'No, Corporate Tax Avoidance Is Not 'Legal'' (16 May 2019) Network, https://www.taxjustice.net/2019/05/16/no-corporate-tax-avoidance-is-not-legal/ accessed 12 May 2024.

Tax Justice Network, Financial Secrecy Index, 2018 'Narrative Report on the British Virgin Islands' https://www.financialsecrecyindex.com/PDF/BritishVirginIslands.pdf accessed 3 May 2019.

Umozurike, Oji U. 'Nationalization of Foreign Owned Property and Self-Determination' (1970) 6 *East Africa Law Journal* 79–99.

Wanjau, Daniel Muriu 'Third World Resistance to International Economic and Structural Constraints: Assessing the Utility of the Right to Health in the Context of the TRIPS Agreement' (2009) 11 (4) *International Community Law Review* 409.

Zorea, Yair and Weiner, Katya 'FATCA, UK CDOT and CRS Overview of Due Diligence and Reporting' (2015) Pricewater Coopers https://www.pwc.com/il/he/events/assets/2017/1-10-us-tax/fatca_crs_reporting.pdf accessed 5 December 2023.

9 IMF, World Bank, and Fossil Fuel Subsidies

*Emeka Duruigbo**

9.1 Introduction

International financial institutions, notably the International Monetary Fund (IMF) and the World Bank support reform of fossil fuel subsidy policies across the world.[1] More precisely, they advocate removing or reducing production and consumption subsidies for coal, oil, and natural gas. The expectation is that these reforms will modify the behavior of producers and consumers desirably, foster economic growth, and usher in environmental gains. The expectation of behavior modification has a sound basis when situated within the context of the modalities of regulation.

Human behavior can be regulated by the modalities of law, markets, architecture, and social norms. Leaving fuel prices largely to the dictates of the market, and not the influence of government subsidies, will ensure proper pricing of energy products and services, leading to adjustments of consumer behavior. Yet, this outcome is not assured if people at the lower rungs of the economic ladder are left with fewer choices to transport themselves to work or heat and cool their homes. Thus, subsidy reforms could result in the unsavory consequence of further squeezing the poor financially with little environmental benefits or possibly worse environmental outcomes.

Avoiding this unpalatable destination requires the accompanying removal of petrol subsidies, for instance, with the provision of good public transportation systems and cash compensation for the economically marginalized segments of the society to cushion the impact of high energy costs. Otherwise, fossil fuel subsidy reforms in the Global South would undermine sustainable development goals of addressing poverty, ensuring equitable access to energy, and fostering economic development without exacerbating environmental degradation. Accordingly, this chapter advances the notion that while subsidy reforms are necessary for economic and environmental reasons, they must be carefully planned and implemented to avoid negative social impacts.

* Emeka Duruigbo, Roberson King Professor of Law, Thurgood Marshall School of Law, Texas Southern University. I am grateful for the excellent research assistance of Thurgood Marshall School of Law student, Edgar Ramon.

DOI: 10.4324/9781003432890-11

This chapter is organized into four sections. Section 9.2 discusses the four regulatory modalities of law, markets, architecture, and social norms and the role played by each of them separately and in interaction with one another in regulating behavior. Section 9.3 examines the concept of subsidies, focusing on their advantages and disadvantages that underpin their existence in the policy toolkit in advanced and developing economies alike. Section 9.4 focuses on approaches to subsidy reforms by the IMF and the World Bank. Section 9.5 includes observations on the subsidy reform approaches of the noted international financial institutions. The chapter concludes by observing that bad subsidy programs are unsustainable for government budgets and unfavorable to the environment, but subsidy reforms require careful planning and faithful implementation. While this chapter encompasses a general discussion of subsidies, primary emphasis is placed on consumer subsidies.

9.2 Modalities of Regulation

Legal theorists have identified four modalities that regulate or constrain human behavior. Human beings respond to the constraints of law, architecture, social norms, and markets. This section elaborates on the operation of these modalities and their interactions with one another in regulating human conduct.

9.2.1 Modalities

Law refers to explicit mandates enforceable by public authorities. The law stipulates behaviors, disobedience to which threatens legal sanctions and whose obedience avoids punishment by the government.

Social norms are often difficult to identify.[2] Indeed, the term, 'social norm,' is used in ordinary language to refer to many different kinds of behavior'[3] and so may change in meaning depending on the context in which it is used. Suffice it to state that a social norm is a non-state obligation that evolved through years of usage or was created by privately organized groups. They are social conventions that people generally feel compelled to follow.[4] Social norms have been defined as 'informal social regularities that individuals feel obligated to follow because of an internalized sense of duty, because of a fear of external non-legal sanctions, or both.'[5] In general, social norms may be understood as 'social attitudes of approval and disapproval, specifying what ought to be done and what ought not to be done.'[6] Social norms are enforced by the community.[7] The regulatory role of social norms is more visible where law or government barely exists.[8]

Architecture refers to the biological, geographical, physical, or technical constraints on activities. Human beings respond to their environment. The government can seek to prohibit speeding on public roads and resulting accidents by specifying speed limits and imposing punishment for their breach, deploying a battery of police officers to enforce them. But the same result may be accomplished at lower costs to the public treasury by placing speed bumps and generally designing the roads in ways that inhibit speeding.[9]

Architecture may also be deployed to prevent or address more serious offenses or crimes. The placement of streetlights and the design of public spaces to make them very visible can affect the behavior of those intending to engage in criminal behavior.[10]

Markets are used in reference to economic forces. A market can be defined as a '[c]ollection of buyers and sellers that, through their actual or potential interactions, determine the price of a product or set of products.'[11] Through supply and demand, markets set a price on various items. The cost of an item affects a buyer's behavior. Therefore, 'Typically, a high financial cost would constrain users' behavior; these costs are termed market forces.'[12]

Smoking provides a helpful illustration of how these modalities regulate behavior. Smoking behavior is directed by laws that prescribe a minimum age for purchasing cigarettes and those that designate places where smoking is permitted.[13] Social norms also play a role in when and where to smoke or whether to smoke at all. Consequently, 'There are no smoking police, and smoking courts are quite rare. Rather, smokers in America are regulated by norms. Norms say that one doesn't light a cigarette in a private car without first asking permission of the other passengers.'[14]

Markets also regulate smoking behavior. The ability to smoke is affected by the price of cigarettes.[15] The higher the cost, the more likely a decision to limit the number of sticks to smoke in a given period. The quality of cigarettes supplied by the market is a key factor in the decision to reduce, increase, or stop smoking. Thus, 'If the market supplies a variety of cigarettes of widely varying quality and price, your ability to select the kind of cigarette you want increases; increasing choice here reduces constraint.'[16]

Architecture is another regulator of smoking behavior. The composition of a cigarette determines where it can be smoked. For instance, smokeless cigarettes can be smoked in more places.[17] On the other hand, there are fewer places where one can smoke cigarettes with a strong odor.[18] 'How the cigarette is, how it is designed, how it is built—in a word, its architecture—affects the constraints faced by the smoker.'[19]

9.2.2 Interaction

The modalities interact with one another in providing a comprehensive or wholistic regulatory framework.[20] If one constraint fails, another constraint provides an alternative means of regulation. Professor Lawrence Lessig explains the distinctiveness of each modality and their interplay as follows:

> The constraints are distinct, yet they are plainly interdependent. Each can support or oppose the others. Technologies can undermine norms and laws; they can also support them. Some constraints make others possible; others make some impossible. Constraints work together, though they function differently and the effect of each is distinct. Norms constrain through the stigma that a community imposes; markets constrain through the price that they exact; architectures constrain through the

> physical burdens they impose; and law constrains through the punishment it threatens. We can call each constraint a 'regulator,' and we can think of each as a distinct modality of regulation. Each modality has a complex nature, and the interaction among these four is also hard to describe.... But for now, it is enough to see that they are linked and that, in a sense, they combine to produce the regulation to which [every person] is subject in any given area.[21]

Law has an interesting relationship with social norms.[22] Some legal stipulations started out as social norms.[23] Law can change social norms.[24] In the same manner that

> regulations ideally correct failures in markets, laws ideally correct failures in social norms. No law is required when the "market" for social norms works, but when it fails, law may improve the situation by enforcing a beneficial social norm, suppressing a harmful social norm, or supplying a missing obligation.[25]

Law can change the regulation of architecture. Laws may be passed that change the designs of roads, buildings, and other structures to constrain or modify human behavior. Laws requiring speed bumps modify architecture and achieve the same purpose as a speed limit or a norm against excessive speeding.[26] Laws modifying architecture include bad laws. A city could build bridges to block buses so that a racial group that depends on public transportation will be prevented from getting to public beaches easily.[27]

Law can influence markets in various ways, including through taxes to reduce consumption of any product and subsidies to increase a product's supply.[28] Law also regulates elements of the market by enforcing contracts, establishing property, and regulating currency.[29] Undoubtedly, in many ways 'the constraint of law is used to change the constraints of the market.'[30]

The interaction of law and markets is visible in energy markets: 'There is a long history of government intervention in energy markets. Numerous energy subsidies exist in the U.S. tax code to promote or subsidize the production of cheap and abundant fossil energy.'[31]

With this background in mind, we can see the role of fossil fuel subsidies in regulating the behavior of energy producers and consumers. Governments intervene in energy markets by providing subsidies that promote the production and enhance the consumption of these fuels. Governments' decisions to subsidize fossil fuels and the implications of the subsidies are examined in the next section.

9.3 Subsidies

Subsidies denote '[a] payment by a government to a firm or household that provides or consumes a commodity.'[32] Fossil fuel subsidies have been defined as 'any government action that lowers the cost of fossil fuel energy production, raises the price received by energy producers, or lowers the price paid by energy consumers.'[33] While taxes increase the price of products, subsidies are primarily designed to keep the price of a product or commodity low, thereby increasing its availability and affordability.[34] Subsidies are usually categorized into two types, namely production (or producer) subsidies and consumption (or consumer) subsidies. They are discussed in Section 9.3.1.

9.3.1 *Types of Subsidies*

Subsidies, including those for fossil fuels, can exist on the production side or the consumption end.[35] Production subsidies reduce the cost of producing items to ensure that the producer conducts its business profitably while consumption subsidies aim at reducing the price of a product to make it more affordable to the consumer.[36] These subsidies include, but are not limited to, direct payments to individuals, groups, or industries.[37]

Production subsidies take various forms such as 'subsidized insurance, below-market credit, guaranteed loans, and below-market payments for access to publicly-owned resources.'[38] Thus, for fossil fuels in the United States, production subsidies include inexpensive leases and low royalty rates for oil and gas produced on government-owned lands.[39] They may also take the form of guarantees of a certain price to producers and 'accelerated tax depreciation allowances for capital equipment and tax exemptions for fossil-fuel producers' own energy use.'[40] In a nutshell, fossil fuel production subsidies 'are government support for fossil fuel production, including exploration, development, extraction, and transportation.'[41]

Consumption subsidies are generally computed 'based on the price-gap method, which measures the difference between domestic and international prices of fuels and electricity.'[42] If the price paid by consumers is lower than a market reference price, a subsidy exists.[43] A second type of classification defines consumption subsidies in terms of benefits that are conferred on a specific segment of society.[44] Consumption subsidies include fuel sold at below-market prices and reduced electricity prices.[45]

The distinction between a production and a consumption subsidy should, however, not be overstated. 'This distinction is a bit artificial, although it is commonly used in the literature. A subsidy for production can, of course, spur consumption by lowering prices. Likewise, if structured properly a consumption subsidy can spur production to meet increased demand.'[46]

Production and consumption subsidies are designed to achieve certain objectives. Section 9.3.2 discusses the function of subsidies.

9.3.2 *Purpose and Effect of Subsidies*

Production subsidies are meant to lower costs for producers, thereby increasing profitability and spurring economic growth.[47] Thus, it has been noted that 'the end purpose of subsidies is to overcome underinvestment in order to create growth by satisfying consumer preferences (and satisfying them better than they would be in the absence of the subsidy).'[48]

In general, subsidies make products artificially cheaper, leading to consumption levels that may be higher than what would have been the case if the product was priced properly.[49] On the other hand, taxes on raw materials or end products will usually affect consumption patterns negatively.[50]

Governments introduce consumption subsidies out of a genuine concern for their citizens' welfare or as an instrument to buy their political loyalty. 'For many governments, keeping consumer energy prices affordable is the top priority. That's why numerous countries, ranging from Japan to Brazil, last year imposed or increased subsidies to cushion consumers from skyrocketing prices.'[51]

Subsidies can be used as a tool to protect local industry against foreign competition.[52] Subsidy as a form of protectionism has been a source of conflicts in the area of trade policy.[53] Subsidies as a significant component of a protectionist strategy assume greater importance where the use of other tools such as tariffs and quotas has been restricted by international trade agreements.[54]

Subsidies can be presented as part of a solution to a problem of national or international significance. For instance, subsidies have been used to promote energy security by incentivizing production when imports have been difficult to obtain.[55] Similarly, subsidies to boost renewable energy production or consumption provide an additional tool for fighting global climate change.[56] In some cases, business survival and jobs may be riding on the level of support received from the government.[57] Subsidies are favored in some quarters on the basis that in certain instances, government support is needed to spur innovation.[58]

On the other hand, subsidies are viewed as orchestrating or at least encouraging technological stagnation as they divert resources away from productive use.[59] Products are made at a higher cost not borne by the producers and the consumers; thus, producers have little incentive to embark on Research and Development to drive down costs. At the same time, they spend energy lobbying for the continuation of subsidy programs.[60] Subsidies reward political connectedness, instead of sound economic ideas, thus elevating rent-seeking that distorts the economy and propels corruption in the political process.[61] Accordingly, opponents contend that subsidies for all energy sources should be removed to transform a country's energy economy into a competitive, market-oriented system.[62]

Regardless of the purpose of creating a subsidy program, subsidies have a wide range of effects. Subsidies 'could distort the allocation of resources within the economy. The trade-distorting effects of subsidies include overproduction, artificial competitiveness of subsidized commodities in domestic and external markets, and global price suppression with adverse revenue implications for the non-subsidizing countries.'[63]

The environmental consequences of subsidies appear in different ways. With cheaper prices for fossil fuels, overconsumption of carbon products that release more carbon dioxide into the atmosphere is a likely result. Consumers also have a reduced incentive to switch to cleaner, alternative sources of energy.[64]

Indeed, fossil fuel subsidies have 'environmental, fiscal, macroeconomic and distributive consequences.'[65] The environmental consequences include local air pollution and global climate change.[66] The fiscal consequences are evident in the fact that 'fossil fuel subsidies constitute public expenditure, either as direct spending or as revenue foregone (e.g. lower tax rates).'[67] The macroeconomic consequences are captured by the fact that subsidies distort the best allocation of resources in the society by facilitating over-consumption.[68] The environmental, fiscal, and macroeconomic consequences can be viewed as negative while the distributive consequences may be considered as both negative because they can be regressive, and positive because they can foster poverty reduction.[69]

The purpose and effect of energy subsidies are probably best understood when contrasted with energy taxes.[70] Taxes raise revenues for the government and generally may be used to discourage the use of a product. Subsidies take away money from the public coffers and are generally used to encourage the use of a product.[71] Both energy taxes and subsidies can distort prices and production. One scholar explores these differences as follows:

> Governments have various reasons for taxing energy, and such taxes will influence energy markets. An energy-producing country or state may find energy taxation a politically expedient source of revenues, particularly if a large part of the output is exported. They may tax an energy source to provide a public good related to energy consumption, such as gasoline taxes that are collected to fund roadways. They may use taxes to discourage energy use, such as passing a carbon tax to discourage the burning of high-carbon fossil fuels that influence our climate. They may use differential taxes on energy products to influence industrial behavior, such as Europe's high import taxes on oil products and low import taxes on crude oil imports. Historically, this encouraged refineries to be built in Europe rather than in the oil-producing countries. Alternatively, governments may subsidize rather than tax an energy product to encourage use, such as California subsidies on solar energy panels, or to protect a domestic industry and employment, such as Germany's subsidies to protect its domestic coal industry. Governments may subsidize energy products as part of an income redistribution scheme, such as Indonesian subsidies on kerosene to help poor residents who use kerosene for cooking and lighting. No matter the reason for their adoption, energy taxes and subsidies are likely to distort prices and production in energy markets. Such distortions may decrease efficiency in efficient markets, or they may increase efficiency in inefficient markets with externalities present.[72]

It is considering the above understanding that we examine the position of international economic organizations, particularly the IMF and World Bank on fossil fuel subsidies. This examination is conducted in the next section.

9.4 IMF and World Bank on Fossil Fuel Subsidies

Several international economic organizations, including the IMF, World Bank, Organisation for Economic Cooperation and Development (OECD), and the World Trade Organization (WTO) have taken a public stand on subsidies, including fossil fuel subsidies. In a nutshell, they advocate the phasing out of all kinds of subsidies.[73] This chapter's focus is on the IMF and the World Bank.

9.4.1 IMF

IMF can be said to be at the forefront of the fossil fuel subsidy reform discourse. Its stance stems from an understanding that taxes and subsidies can influence behavior: 'Underpinning the policy recommendations is the notion that taxation (or tax-like instruments) can influence behavior—in much the same way that taxes on cigarettes discourage their overuse, appropriate taxes can discourage overuse of environmentally harmful energy sources.'[74] Summarizing the purpose and content of its campaign for fossil fuel subsidy reform, the IMF states,

> Subsidies are intended to protect consumers by keeping prices low, but they come at a substantial cost. Subsidies have sizable fiscal consequences (leading to higher taxes/borrowing or lower spending), promote inefficient allocation of an economy's resources (hindering growth), encourage pollution (contributing to climate change and premature deaths from local air pollution), and are not well targeted at the poor (mostly benefiting higher income households). Removing subsidies and using the revenue gain for better targeted social spending, reductions in inefficient taxes, and productive investments can promote sustainable and equitable outcomes. Fossil fuel subsidy removal would also reduce energy security concerns related to volatile fossil fuel supplies.[75]

One of the most significant contributions of the IMF to the subsidy debate is the definition of subsidies.[76] The IMF breaks down the definition of the concept into explicit and implicit subsidies. Explicit subsidies refer to the generally understood meaning of subsidies as support that makes a product sell at a price below its actual cost. 'Explicit subsidies occur when the retail price is below a fuel's supply cost.'[77]

Implicit subsidies are defined to include external costs of a product that are not reflected in the price.[78] Furthermore, 'Implicit subsidies occur when the retail price fails to include external costs, inclusive of the standard consumption tax.'[79] The spectrum of external costs is wide and includes 'contributions to climate change through greenhouse gas emissions, local health damages (primarily pre-mature deaths) through the release of harmful local pollutants like fine particulates, and traffic congestion and accident externalities associated with the use of road fuels.'[80]

Combining these two categories of subsidies, the IMF notes that fossil fuel subsidies globally amounted to $7 trillion or 7.1% of GDP in 2022.[81] This number reflects a $2 trillion increase since 2020 attributable to support provided by governments in the face of mounting energy prices.[82] Of the 2022 numbers, 18% represents explicit subsidies while implicit subsidies account for 82%.[83]

Subsidy reforms do not always proceed without glitches. Riots or some forms of public protests have accompanied governments' plans to reduce or remove fossil fuel subsidies, including in Haiti in 2022.[84] Mindful of the fact that subsidy reforms may run into difficulty or fail woefully, and examining country experiences, the IMF has identified several critical elements for successful subsidy reform, as follows:

- A comprehensive energy sector reform plan with clear long-term objectives with an analysis of the impact of reforms;
- Transparent and extensive communication and consultation with stakeholders, including information on the size of subsidies and how they affect the government's budget;
- Price increases that are phased-in;
- Improving the efficiency in state-owned enterprises to reduce producer subsidies;
- Measures to protect the poor through targeted cash or near-cash transfers or, if this option is not feasible, a focus on existing targeted programs that can be expanded quickly; and
- Institutional reforms that depoliticize energy pricing, such as the introduction of automatic pricing mechanisms.[85]

A close examination of the above factors reveals why subsidy reforms have met with a brick wall in some places. For instance, proceeding to remove fuel subsidies without adequate engagement with those that would bear the brunt of the removal and not providing sufficient cushion for the hardship that will accompany the removal set an unfortunate and unnecessary stage for calamitous consequences.

9.4.2 World Bank

A brief overview of the World Bank's participation in the energy subsidy reform initiative is captured in the following words:

> The World Bank—through the Energy Sector Management Assistance Program—is supporting countries seeking to reform energy subsidies that can threaten their economic, fiscal, and environmental health. The Energy Subsidy Reform Facility (ESRF) offers a concrete guide to analyzing energy subsidies and developing pragmatic and effective reform strategies. Based on a wealth of country case studies and empirical

> evidence, it holds lessons that can help policy makers to navigate complex political economy challenges in several key areas.... Its recommendations are relevant beyond the energy sector—in particular, those related to mobilizing public support and protecting livelihood risks associated with subsidy removal.[86]

A recent publication by staff of The World Bank with external contributions provides a rich commentary on the purpose and effect of fossil fuel, agricultural and fisheries subsidies with cogent proposals for reform.[87] The publication's authors state the objective of the work as follows:

> This report identifies and quantifies known as well as new channels through which poorly designed subsidies in natural resource sectors, though often well intentioned, deepen inequality, diminish productivity, and drive the destruction of ecosystems. Especially in an era of fiscal constraints and degrading natural capital, reform and repurposing of perverse and harmful subsidies offer an opportunity to promote greater sustainability, inclusion, and shared prosperity.[88]

Accordingly, the authors remark that '[g]iven the scarcity of public funds and the challenges related to sustainability, reexamining and repurposing environmentally harmful subsidies are especially relevant.'[89] The goals of subsidy reform are clearly identified: 'Subsidy reform can have multiple objectives, from freeing up public budgets to reducing inefficiencies, achieving pro-poor redistribution, or addressing environmental externalities.'[90]

On the specific point of combating global change, the World Bank believes that subsidies are a notable part of the conversation on the design of public policy. Thus, the Bank observes that greenhouse gas 'emissions can also be indirectly priced through other policy instruments such as the removal of fossil fuel subsidies and energy taxation.'[91]

The World Bank staff in their 2023 publication also subscribe to the premise that taxes and subsidies play a crucial role in unleashing the economic forces of demand and supply. Additionally, 'A fundamental principle of economics is that lowering the price of a good tends to increase people's demand for it.'[92] As more demand and consumption of fossil fuels flow from lower prices, the result is an increase in the level of pollution from the use of these fuels.[93] It follows, therefore, that while fossil fuel subsidies may present some benefits in that they 'make energy goods more affordable to low-income households,'[94] they also simultaneously 'contribute to air pollution challenges, reinforcing inequality and perpetuating inefficient and obsolete technologies.'[95]

Subsidy reform is sometimes resisted because of the popular belief that subsidies benefit the poor; thus, subsidy reforms will place low-income segments of the society at a disadvantage. *Au contraire*, subsidy reforms could favor the poor and disadvantage the rich since the rich consume more energy by residing in bigger homes and owning more cars.[96] Furthermore, 'In Indonesia, for example, the World Bank found that the richest decile of households consumed 40% of subsidized gasoline, while the poorest decile consumed less than one percent.'[97] Nevertheless, it is important to incorporate in subsidy reforms measures that ameliorate the immediate impact of removal or reduction of subsidies on the poor.[98]

The World Bank staff note that subsidy reform success requires a comprehensive strategy encompassing six principles including a comprehensive assessment of existing subsidies, building public acceptance for the reform, and social protection and compensation where subsidy removal may negatively affect the livelihoods of vulnerable groups and lead to a rise in poverty.[99] Other principles include sound strategies on how to reinvest reform revenues, such as investments in health and education, targeted complementary measures to solve environmental externalities where subsidy removal or reduction or other price-based instruments would not be sufficient to solve them, and carefully sequencing and coordinating the reforms to enable firms and individuals adjust gradually rather than face disruption of their lives and operations from large price shocks.[100] Government agencies would need to coordinate their activities to avoid haphazardness and ensure that the various components of the reform are aligned and complement one another.[101]

9.5 Observations

Fossil fuel subsidy reform enjoys widespread support among economists and policy analysts.[102] The IMF and World Bank have made a formidable case for fossil fuel subsidy reform. As with many policy proposals, the challenge is often with proper implementation to ensure precise realization of the envisaged objectives.

Fossil fuel subsidy reform, including the total removal of consumption subsidies for carbon-based fuels, is justified on economic grounds. Payment of subsidies takes a good portion of a country's budget, leading to the accumulation of debts to fund them. Where a subsidy program is accompanied by large-scale corruption, the pressure on the budget becomes more intense and the justification for continuing with the subsidies gets harder to present.

Directing subsidy funds to targeted segments of the economy such as infrastructure development and investments in education and healthcare would lead to better outcomes for the society. In addition, the distortion created by subsidies can be inimical to economic growth and societal welfare.[103] Usually, market prices balance supply and demand, thereby ensuring or encouraging efficient production.[104] When subsidies are in play, this balance is disrupted, triggering overinvestment, overproduction and overconsumption, and stagnation in innovation, with damaging consequences.[105]

Perhaps more importantly, fossil fuel subsidies present a major impediment to a successful fight against climate change.[106] The extraction and burning of fossil fuels have deleterious impacts on the environment, climate, and public health.[107] Fossil fuel subsidies increase the use of private automobiles with the attendant increase in carbon dioxide emissions.[108] Carbon dioxide and other greenhouse gases 'trap heat in the earth's atmosphere and contribute to climate change.'[109]

It is imperative that subsidy reforms should promote, and not undermine, sustainable development. Sustainable development is commonly defined as 'development that meets the needs of the present without compromising the ability of future generations to meet their own needs.'[110] Sustainable development is a tripod consisting of economic progress, environmental progress, and social progress.[111]

Sustainable development goals (SDGs) were adopted by world leaders at the United Nations in 2015 to end poverty, protect the planet, and ensure prosperity for all.[112] Pertinent SDGs include SDG 1, which aims to end poverty of all forms at every place, and SDG 7, which focuses on ensuring access to affordable, reliable, sustainable, and modern energy for all.

There is a need to incorporate alternative measures before the elimination of subsidies.[113] A significant increase in wages and direct cash transfers to boost the income of low-wage earners should be incorporated into subsidy removal or reduction plans.[114] Providing sound public transportation, for instance, is *conditio sine qua non* for the removal of fossil fuel subsidies in countries where the average resident can barely afford the cost of transportation to work and other places, even with subsidies. On this issue is where the recent announcement on the removal of subsidies by the Nigerian government missed the point. Without a set of palliatives in place to cushion the effect of subsidy removal, the people of Nigeria were thrown into unanticipated, serious hardship.

The federal government as well as state governments in Nigeria should, as a matter of priority boost public transportation by purchasing and providing mass transit buses that ease the movement of the people at affordable costs. This gesture will serve multiple purposes. It will create jobs for the bus operators. It will increase the productivity of workers, as people will not have to struggle to get the work, as is currently the case, spending hours on the road. It will reduce transport expenses for the average person in the country. An effective public transport system will also augur well for the environment, as carbon emissions from thousands of cars will be reduced drastically.

After the provision of mass transit buses, governments should deploy the savings from subsidy removal toward the provision of solid infrastructure, notably good roads, and bridges, to facilitate both public and private transportation in the country.

It appears that the Nigerian government has started retracing its steps on the subsidy removal. The government seems to be mindful of the hardship inflicted on the people by the unexpected removal of the subsidy and may be bowing to the public outcry that attended the removal announcement. Notwithstanding the government's announcement that the petrol subsidy has been removed completely, there is strong reason to believe that the Nigerian National Petroleum Company Ltd has continued to pay subsidies. The government has also moved to negotiate with labor unions, leading to wage increases for some workers in the country.[115]

For petroleum-rich countries, the citizens have come to view the subsidies as their only guaranteed share of the national treasure. The sentiment is that politicians and public officials help themselves to the proceeds of oil and gas production, leaving the needs of the citizens unattended. In removing fossil fuel subsidies in such countries, it is imperative that an alternative guarantee for benefiting from their natural endowment be secured for the people. Policymakers have a range of options to consider, one of which is the payment of petroleum dividends to the citizens as is done by the government of Alaska.[116] Ultimately, the best guarantee that the authorities can offer the citizens is good governance. If the government is properly run and public revenue is deployed appropriately, every citizen or resident of these countries will have a sense of belonging and would hardly bother about periodic palliatives and temporary amenities.

9.6 Conclusion

Fossil fuel subsidies are politically popular initiatives that are warmly embraced by the beneficiaries. Unfortunately, they are fraught with implementation problems that seek to undermine the benefits. They orchestrate or exacerbate environmental problems that frustrate the fight against global climate change. They drain public coffers of funds that can be directed more effectively to promote economic growth. In some places, they fuel corruption ensuring that only a small but connected segment of the society corner the gains of budgeting huge sums of money for payment of subsidies. International financial institutions, including the IMF and World Bank, have invested efforts in advancing the case for fossil fuel subsidy reform. It is possible to implement reforms that protect vulnerable members of the society while ensuring that the negative impact of fossil fuel subsidies is curtailed.[117] This chapter has examined the role of subsidies in influencing individual and firm behavior, the contributions of the IMF and the World Bank to the fossil fuel subsidy discourse, and steps that can be taken to ensure optimal deployment of public resources for the overall good.

Notes

1 It is remarkable to note that opposition to renewable energy subsidies also exists. *See* Timothy L. Meyer, 'Energy Subsidies and the World Trade Organization' (2013) 17 *ASIL INSIGHTS* 1.
2 Orin S. Kerr, 'Norms of Computer Trespass' (2016) 116 *Colum. LR* 1143, 1149.
3 Eric A. Posner, 'Symbols, Signals, and Social Norms in Politics and the Law' (1998) XXIX *JLS* 1. *See further* Eric A. Posner, Law, 'Economics, and Inefficient Norms' (1996) 144 *Upenn. LR* 1697, 1699 ("The concept of a "norm" is slippery, and scholars use it in different ways."); Robert C. Ellickson, *Order Without Law: How Neighbors Settle Disputes* (Harvard University Press, 1991) 127 (defining social norms as rules that emanate from social forces while defining rules that emanate from organizations as organization rules); Paul G. Mahoney and Chris W. Sanchirico, 'Competing Norms and Social Evolution: Is the Fittest Norm Efficient?' (2001) 149

Upenn. LR 2027, 2028 (defining social norms as "informal, decentralized systems of consensus and cooperation").

4 Richard A. Posner, *Economic Analysis of Law* (8th edn, Wolters Kluver 2011) 339 (defining social norms as "rules of behavior that are not enforced by courts or other public authorities.").

5 Richard H. McAdams, 'The Origin, Development, and Regulation of Norms' (1997) 96 *Mich. LR* 338.

6 Cass R. Sunstein, 'Social Norms and Social Roles, (1996) 96 *Colum. LR* 903, 914.

7 Posner (n 4) 340–342 (discussing various ways of enforcing social norms, including emotion, expressions of disapproval, ridicule, and ostracism).

8 Juliet P. Kostritsky, The Law and Economics of Norms, (2013) 48 *Tex. ILJ.* 465, 473 ("Norms embody the belief systems that govern behavior."); Eric A. Posner, *Law and Social Norms* (Harvard University Press 2000) 3.

> In a world with no law and rudimentary government, order of some sort would exist. So much is clear from anthropological studies. The order would appear as routine compliance with social norms and the collective infliction of sanctions on those who violate them, including stigmatization of the deviant and ostracism of the incorrigible.

9 Stewart Macaulay et al. (eds) *Law & Society: Readings in The Social Study of Law* (W.W. Norton & Co 1995) 44 (discussing the highway cloverleaf).

10 Lawrence Lessig, *Code: Version 2.0* (Basic Books, 2006) 128.

11 Robert S. Pindyck and Daniel L. Rubinfeld, *Microeconomics* (5th edn, Prentice Hall 2000) 669.

12 Hee Jhee Jiow, 'Cyber Crime in Singapore: An Analysis of Regulation Based on Lessig's Four Modalities of Constraint' (2013) 7 *IJCC* 18, 20.

13 Lessig (n 10) 122.

14 Lessig (n 10) 122.

15 Lessig (n 10) 122.

16 Lessig (n 10) 122.

17 Lessig (n 10) 123.

18 Lessig (n 10) 123.

19 Lessig (n 10) 123.

20 Jiow (n 12) at 20 states that 'The constraints are interdependent, supporting or opposing one another, yet they are distinct.'.

21 Lessig (n 10) 124.

22 McAdams (n 5) 340.

> Sometimes norms govern behavior irrespective of the legal rule, making the choice of a formal rule surprisingly unimportant. Sometimes legal rules facilitate or impede the enforcement of a norm, and the selection of the formal rule matters in entirely new ways, the exact consequence depending on whether the formal rule strengthens or weakens a desirable or undesirable norm. Indeed, in some cases, new norms arise in the presence of different legal rules, making the relevant policy choice one between two or more law-norm combinations.

23 Robert Cooter, 'Normative Failure Theory of Law' (1997) 82 Cornell LR 947 (1997).

24 Eric A. Posner (ed), *Social Norms, Nonlegal Sanctions, and the Law* (Edward Elgar Publishing 2007) xiii, state that the achievement of societal order through social norms 'poses problems and opportunities for formal legal regulation.'.

25 Cooter (n 23) 949; Posner (n 4) 341–342.

26 Lessig (n 10) 128.

27 Lessig (n 10) 128.

28 Lessig (n 10) 127.

29 Lessig (n 10) 127.
30 Lessig (n 10) 127.
31 Clayton Coleman and Emma Dietz, 'Fossil Fuel Subsidies: A Closer Look at Tax Breaks and Societal Costs' (*Environmental and Energy Study Institute*, July 2019) 1; Johannes Urpelainen and Elisha George, 'Reforming Global Fossil Fuel Subsidies: How the United States Can Restart International Cooperation' (*Brookings Institution*, 14 July 2021) stating that 'key production subsidies are embedded in legislation, namely the tax code.'.
32 Simon Lester, 'The Problem of Subsidies as a Means of Protectionism: Lessons from the WTO EC – Aircraft Case' (2011) 12 Melb. JIL. 345, 348 quoting Paul A. Samuelson and William D. Nordhaus, *Economics* (13th edn, McGraw-Hill, 1989) 982.
33 Oil Change International, 'Fossil Fuel Subsidies: Overview https://priceofoil.org/fossil-fuel-subsidies/ accessed 14 October 2023.
34 Björn Ólafsson, 'What Farm Subsidies Are and Why They Matter, Explained' (*Sentient Media*, 11 August 2023) ("A subsidy is money from the government that is intended to keep the price of a commodity low."); Ken Silverstein, 'COVID-19 Is Killing Oil And Gas But The Virus Could Also Poison Renewables' *Forbes* (6 April 2020) (stating that 40% of the fossil fuel subsidies existing globally "are designed to make oil cheaper and more affordable.").
35 According to Joshua Mackinnon, 'The African Century: Renewable Energy Opportunities in Sub-Saharan Africa' (2023) 47 *Wm. & Mary ELPR* 427, 439.

> Fossil fuel subsidies take two forms. Production subsidies are tax breaks or direct payments intended to reduce the costs of turning oil or coal into usable energy. Consumption subsidies involve the act of fixing fuel prices, which keeps fuel affordable for the end user.

36 Chris Wold, Grant Wilson, and Sara Foroshani, 'Leveraging Climate Change Benefits Through the World Trade Organization: Are Fossil Fuel Subsidies Actionable?' (2012) 43 *Geo. JIL* 635, 643 states that 'Whereas consumption subsidies are intended to benefit consumers, production subsidies are designed to assist producers increase production.'.
37 Nicolas Loris, 'The Wind Production Tax Credit and the Case for Ending All Energy Subsidies' (2013) 23 *Duke ELPF* 323, 324 posits that 'The definition of a subsidy as a direct transfer of money to a group or industry is underinclusive'; *See also* Cleo Verkuijl et al., 'Tackling Fossil Fuel Subsidies Through International Trade Agreements: Taking Stock, Looking Forward' (2019) 58 *Virginia JIL* 309, 318 stating that fossil fuel subsidies include different government measures, such as cash payments or other direct transfer of funds, purchase of goods above the market rate, funding for research and development, tax revenue forgone, including deviations and exemptions from standard tax rules, other revenues forgone, such as beneficial terms of access to resources, allowing transfer of risks by providing loans, loan guarantees, insurance or indemnifications at below-market rates, and inducing the transfer of funds through price controls or purchase requirements.
38 Wold, Wilson and Foroshani (n 36) 643.
39 Savannah Bertrand, 'Proposals to Reduce Fossil Fuel Subsidies' (*Environmental and Energy Study Institute*, 23 July 2021) ('The fossil fuel industry is also subsidized through inexpensive leases and low royalty rates on fossil fuels extracted from public lands.').
40 Wold, Wilson and Foroshani (n 36) 643.
41 Oil Change International (n 33).
42 Wold, Wilson and Foroshani (n 36) 643–644.
43 International Energy Agency, *Fossil Fuel Subsidies in Clean Energy Transitions: Time for a New Approach?* (February 2023) ('The methodology is a "price gap

approach" where we establish a market reference price and then compare it with the price paid by consumers. When the end-user price is lower than the reference price, it is counted as a subsidy.') https://www.iea.org/reports/fossil-fuel-subsidies-in-clean-energy-transitions-time-for-a-new-approach accessed 14 October 2023.

44 Jakob Skovgaard, 'The Devil Lies in the Definition: Competing Approaches to Fossil Fuel Subsidies at the IMF and the OECD' (2017) 17 *International Environmental Agreements* 341, 343.

45 Jakob Skovgaard, 'The Devil Lies in the Definition: Competing Approaches to Fossil Fuel Subsidies at the IMF and the OECD' (2017) 17 *International Environmental Agreements* 343.

46 Timothy Meyer, 'Free Trade, Fair Trade, and Selective Enforcement' (2018) 118 *Colum. LR* 491, 542 n. 284.

47 Kenina Lee, 'An Inherent Conflict Between WTO Law and a Sustainable Future? Evaluating the Consistency of Canadian and Chinese Renewable Energy Policies with WTO Trade Law' (2011) 24 *Geo. IELR* 57, 88 (stating that 'the purpose of subsidies to wind and solar manufacturers are to lower their manufacturing costs and spur greater growth in an economy's energy sector… '); Urpelainen and George (n 31) ('Production subsidies increase the profitability of extracting and transporting fuels, usually by offering tax breaks, production credits, or accelerated depreciation for capital investment.').

48 Charles J. Delmotte, 'The Case Against Tax Subsidies in Innovation Policy' (2021) 48 *Florida State University Law Review* 285, 306.

49 Robert W. Adler and Carina E. Wells, 'Plastics and the Limits of U.S. Environmental Law' (2023) 47 *Harv. ELR* 1, 55–56.

50 Robert W. Adler and Carina E. Wells, 'Plastics and the Limits of U.S. Environmental Law' (2023) 47 *Harv. ELR* 1, 55–56. *See also* The Environmental Literacy Council, 'Externalities' Updated by Dawn Anderson ('Arthur Pigou, a British economist best known for his work in welfare economics… supported taxes to discourage activities that created harmful effects and subsidies for those creating benefits to further encourage those activities. These are now known as Pigovian taxes and subsidies.') http://enviroliteracy.org/environment-society/economics/externalities/.

51 Richard Valdmanis, 'Biden Budget to Target U.S. Fossil Fuel Subsidies' *Reuters* (9 March 2023).

52 Carol A. Dahl, *International Energy Markets: Understanding Pricing, Policies, and Profits* (2nd edn, PennWell, 2015) 281 (noting that pollution abatement subsidies can create a distortion because '[t]there may be the political temptation to use such subsidies as a trade policy to favor domestic industry and contravene free trade agreements.').

53 Lester (n 32) 346.

54 Lester (n 32) 348.

55 Urpelainen and George (n 31) ('Without any alternatives, scaling up domestic fossil fuel production was part of the United States' aggressive push for energy security following the OPEC oil embargo in 1973.').

56 Loris (n 37) 323–324.

57 Loris (n 37) 323–324.

58 Loris (n 37) 323–324. *See also* Virginia R. Hildreth, 'Renewable Energy Subsidies and the GATT' (2014) 14 *Chi. JIL* 702, 706–707 (stating that 'government assistance is often key to encourage investment in industries like renewable energy.').

59 Loris (n 37) 323–324.

60 Loris (n 37) 323–324.

61 Loris (n 37) 323–324.

62 Loris (n 37) 323–324.

63 Paul Kuruk, 'The Subsidies Issue in International Trade: Musings of the Economic Partnership Agreement Negotiations' (2013) 38 N.C. JILCR 327, 332.

64 International Energy Agency, *Fossil Fuels Consumption Subsidies 2022* (stating that a sharp increase in energy consumption subsidies by governments in 2022 'reduced hardship but diminished the incentive for consumers to save or to switch to alternative – and cleaner – sources of energy, thereby delaying a lasting resolution of the [energy] crisis.') https://www.iea.org/reports/fossil-fuels-consumption-subsidies-2022 accessed 14 October 2023.
65 Skovgaard (n 44) 343.
66 Skovgaard (n 44) 343.
67 Skovgaard (n 44) 343.
68 Skovgaard (n 44) 343.
69 Skovgaard (n 44) 343–344.
70 Dahl (n 52) 91 ('The opposite of an energy tax would be an energy subsidy.').
71 Loris (n 37) 324 (2013) ('The general economic rule of thumb is that if you want less of something, tax it, and if you want more of something, subsidize it.').
72 Dahl (n 52) 78.
73 Skovgaard (n 44) 346 ('Multilateral development banks and the IMF have long advocated that countries phase out 'poorly targeted' subsidies of all kinds without using the concept of fossil fuel subsidies.').
74 Ian W.H. Parry, Simon Black and Nate Vernon, *Still Not Getting Energy Prices Right: A Global and Country Update of Fossil Fuel Subsidies* (24 September 2021) 6 https://www.imf.org/en/Publications/WP/Issues/2021/09/23/Still-Not-Getting-Energy-Prices-Right-A-Global-and-Country-Update-of-Fossil-Fuel-Subsidies-466004 accessed 3 October 2023.
75 International Monetary Fund, *Climate Change: Fossil Fuel Subsidies* https://www.imf.org/en/Topics/climate-change/energy-subsidies accessed 2 October 2023.
76 *See* Skovgaard (n 44) 347–348.
77 International Monetary Fund, *Climate Change* (n 75).
78 Parry, Black and Vernon (n 71) 8 (stating that 'explicit subsidies as undercharging for supply costs and producer subsidies (i.e., pre-tax subsidies), and implicit subsidies as undercharging for environmental costs and general consumption taxes (i.e., post-tax subsidies less pre-tax subsidies').
79 International Monetary Fund, *Climate Change* (n 75).
80 International Monetary Fund, *Climate Change* (n 75).
81 International Monetary Fund, *Climate Change* (n 75).
82 International Monetary Fund, *Climate Change* (n 75).
83 International Monetary Fund, *Climate Change* (n 75).
84 Michael Shellenberger, 'Haiti Riots Triggered by IMF Advice to Cut Fuel Subsidies' *Forbes* (22 September 2022) https://www.forbes.com/sites/michaelshellenberger/2022/09/22/haiti-riots-triggered-by-imf-advice-to-cut-fuel-subsidies/ accessed 23 October 2023 ('And, it's not just Haiti. Over 40 nations since 2005 have triggered riots after cutting fuel subsidies or otherwise raising energy prices. It happened earlier this year in Kazakhstan, Ecuador in 2019, Nigeria in 2012, Bolivia in 2010, and Indonesia in 2005.').
85 International Monetary Fund, *Climate Change* (n 75).
86 Richard Damania et al., *Detox Development: Repurposing Environmentally Harmful Subsidies* (The World Bank Group, 2023).
87 Damania et al. (n8 86) The publication contains a disclaimer that the 'findings, interpretations, and conclusions expressed in this work do not necessarily reflect the views of The World Bank, its Board of Executive Directors, or the governments they represent.'.
88 Damania et al. (n 86) xxi.
89 Damania et al. (n 86).
90 Damania et al. (n 86) 242.

91 The World Bank, *Carbon Pricing Dashboard, Main Types of Carbon Pricing* https://carbonpricingdashboard.worldbank.org/what-carbon-pricing accessed 13 October 2023.

92 Damania et al. (n 86) 38.

93 Damania et al. (n 86) 38. ('For instance, lower gasoline prices would result in higher consumption, which, intuitively, would increase the level of pollution from fine particulate matter.').

94 Damania et al. (n 86) 240.

95 Damania et al. (n 86) 240.

96 Damania et al. (n 86) xxvi.

> Reforms of fossil fuel subsidies are typically pro-poor. By owning more cars and by heating and lighting bigger houses, the rich consume more energy and benefit disproportionately from energy subsidy schemes. Hence the richest income group always loses more from the removal of subsidies than the poorest—on average, 13 times more in 19 countries examined in this report. And while conventional wisdom holds that subsidies constitute a larger share of the income of the poor, who therefore lose more from subsidy reform, the data offer mixed evidence.

97 Urpelainen and George (n 31).

98 Damania et al (n 86) 249.

99 Damania et al (n 86) 249.

100 Damania et al (n 86) 249.

101 Damania et al (n 86) 249.

102 Parry, Black and Vernon (n 74) 29 ('It is rare to find near universal support among economists for a major policy action, but reforming fossil fuel prices is one such policy').

103 Pamela S. Chasek et al., *Global Environmental Politics* (7th edn, Routledge 2017) 340.

> Subsidies distort markets by sending signals to producers and consumers that fail to reflect the true costs of production, thus misallocating financial and natural resources. Subsidies on goods traded internationally also give unfair advantage to exports that are subsidized over others. Subsidies can have negative impacts on the environment, especially in the commodity sectors (e.g., agriculture, forests, fossil fuels, fisheries, and mining). They draw more investment into these sectors and exacerbate the overexploitation of land, forests, water, and fish. They also reduce the cost of particular practices, products, or technologies that harm the environment, such as flood irrigation, mining, fossil-fuel extraction and use, or excessive use of pesticides.

104 Chris Edwards, 'Ten Reasons to Cut Farm Subsidies' (*CATO Institute*, 28 June 2007) ('Farm subsidies damage the economy. In most industries, market prices balance supply and demand and encourage efficient production.') https://www.cato.org/commentary/ten-reasons-cut-farm-subsidies accessed 14 October 2023.

105 Chris Edwards, 'Cutting Federal Farm Subsidies' (*CATO Institute Briefing Paper* No. 162, 31 Aug. 2023) ('In most industries, markets steer investment, businesses balance risks and rewards, and entrepreneurs innovate to reduce costs. Federal farm programs blunt those market mechanisms, which can cause overproduction, inadequate cost control, and distorted decisions about land use and choice of crops.') https://www.cato.org/briefing-paper/cutting-federal-farm-subsidies accessed on October 14, 2023; Urpelainen and George (n 31) ('[Subsidies] create market distortions by artificially lowering the price of fossil fuels, which leads to overconsumption, particularly in energy and capital-intensive industries like power and transport. A 2014 study estimated that global fuel subsidies generated $44 billion in deadweight loss each year…').

106 Parry, Black and Vernon (n 74) 10 ('The environmental costs of coal, natural gas, and liquid fuel combustion include global climate and local outdoor ('ambient') air pollution damages.').
107 Coleman and Dietz (n 31) 7 ('Burning fossil fuels creates air pollutants such as particulate matter, carbon monoxide, sulfur dioxide, ozone, and mercury. These pollutants lead to health impacts including asthma, lung disease, bronchitis, and other chronic respiratory diseases that may lead to premature death.').
108 Dahl (n 52) 297.

> [C]urrent subsidies to fossil fuel industries cause market distortions. Removing these subsidies would raise costs in these industries and help reduce CO_2 emissions. Automobiles cause local air pollution problems as well as traffic congestion. Policies to reduce the amount of driving and amount of fuel used would help solve these problems plus contribute to CO2 reductions. Taxing parking subsidies given to employees by businesses would reduce a market distortion, increase the cost of driving to work, and cause some to switch to mass transit. Encouraging bicycling and walking to work could improve health in countries where obesity is an increasing problem.

109 Savannah Bertrand, 'Climate, Environmental, and Health Impacts of Fossil Fuels' (2021) (*Environmental and Energy Study Institute* 17 December 2021).
110 *Our Common Future*, Report of the World Commission on Environment and Development (Brundtland Commission) (1987).
111 Owen L. Anderson et al., *International Petroleum Law and Transactions* 584 (Rocky Mountain Mineral Law Foundation, 2020).
112 Ved P. Nanda, 'The Journey from the Millennium Development Goals to the Sustainable Development Goals' (2016) 44 Denv. JILP 389, 392; United Nations, 'Sustainable Development Goals: The Sustainable Development Agenda' https://www.un.org/sustainabledevelopment/development-agenda/ accessed 9 May 2024.
113 Parry, Black and Vernon (n 74) 8 ('A comprehensive strategy, for example with measures to assist lowincome households, displaced workers, trade-exposed firms/regions, and the use of revenues from price reform to boost the economy in an equitable way, can improve acceptability.').
114 Direct cash transfers contributed to the acceptance of fossil fuel subsidy reform in Indonesia. *See* Asian Development Bank, *Fossil Fuel Subsidies in Indonesia Trends, Impacts, and Reforms* (Asian Development Bank, 2015.); Oil Change International (n 33)

> However, not all subsidies are created equal – the intent of consumption subsidies in developing countries is often simply to help make access to energy and transport more affordable – even if they do not often accomplish this goal efficiently. While consumption subsidies must be phased out as part of the global transition away from an extraction-based, fossil fuel-powered economic system, a great deal of care needs to be taken in removing these subsidies so as not to harm the populations that rely on them for affordable energy.

115 Obas Esiedesa, 'Why I removed subsidy on petrol – Tinubu,' Vanguard (Nigeria) 27 February 2024 https://www.vanguardngr.com/2024/02/why-i-removed-subsidy-on-petrol-tinubu/ accessed 9 May 2024.
116 See generally Emeka Duruigbo, 'Managing Oil Revenues for Socio-Economic Development in Nigeria: The Case for Community-Based Trust Funds' (2004) 30 N.C. JILCR 121.
117 Parry, Black and Vernon (n 74) 6 ('Underpricing fossil fuels not only undermines domestic and global environmental objectives but is a highly inefficient policy for helping low income households and has a sizable fiscal cost—too little revenue is raised from fuel taxes, implying other taxes or government deficits must be higher or public spending lower.').

Bibliography

Robert W. Adler and Carina E. Wells, 'Plastics and the Limits of U.S. Environmental Law' (2023) 47 *Harv. ELR* 1.

Owen L. Anderson et al., *International Petroleum Law and Transactions* 584 (Rocky Mountain Mineral Law Foundation, 2020).

Asian Development Bank, *Fossil Fuel Subsidies in Indonesia Trends, Impacts, and Reforms* (Asian Development Bank, 2015).

Savannah Bertrand, 'Climate, Environmental, and Health Impacts of Fossil Fuels' (2021a) (*Environmental and Energy Study Institute* 17 December 2021). https://www.eesi.org/papers/view/fact-sheet-climate-environmental-and-health-impacts-of-fossil-fuels-2021

Savannah Bertrand, 'Proposals to Reduce Fossil Fuel Subsidies' (*Environmental and Energy Study Institute*, 23 July 2021b). https://www.eesi.org/papers/view/fact-sheet-proposals-to-reduce-fossil-fuel-subsidies-2021

Pamela S. Chasek et al., *Global Environmental Politics* (7th edn, Routledge, 2017).

Clayton Coleman and Emma Dietz, 'Fossil Fuel Subsidies: A Closer Look at Tax Breaks and Societal Costs' (*Environmental and Energy Study Institute*, July 2019). https://www.eesi.org/papers/view/fact-sheet-fossil-fuel-subsidies-a-closer-look-at-tax-breaks-and-societal-costs

Robert Cooter, 'Normative Failure Theory of Law' (1997) 82 *Cornell LR* 947.

Carol A. Dahl, *International Energy Markets: Understanding Pricing, Policies, and Profits* (2nd edn, PennWell, 2015).

Richard Damania et al., *Detox Development: Repurposing Environmentally Harmful Subsidies* (The World Bank Group, 2023).

Charles J. Delmotte, 'The Case Against Tax Subsidies in Innovation Policy' (2021) 48 *Florida State University Law Review* 285.

Emeka Duruigbo, 'Managing Oil Revenues for Socio-Economic Development in Nigeria: The Case for Community-Based Trust Funds' (2004) 30 *N.C. JILCR* 121.

Chris Edwards, 'Ten Reasons to Cut Farm Subsidies' (*CATO Institute*, 28 June 2007) ('Farm subsidies damage the economy. In most industries, market prices balance supply and demand and encourage efficient production.') https://www.cato.org/commentary/ten-reasons-cut-farm-subsidies accessed 14 October 2023.

Chris Edwards, 'Cutting Federal Farm Subsidies' (*CATO Institute Briefing Paper* No. 162, 31 August 2023 https://www.cato.org/briefing-paper/cutting-federal-farm-subsidies accessed 14 October 2023.

Robert C. Ellickson, *Order Without Law: How Neighbors Settle Disputes* (Harvard University Press, 1991).

Obas Esiedesa, 'Why I Removed Subsidy on Petrol – Tinubu' Vanguard (Nigeria) 27 February 2024 https://www.vanguardngr.com/2024/02/why-i-removed-subsidy-on-petrol-tinubu/ accessed 9 May 2024.

Virginia R. Hildreth, 'Renewable Energy Subsidies and the GATT' (2014) 14 *Chi. JIL* 702.

International Energy Agency, *Fossil Fuel Subsidies in Clean Energy Transitions: Time for a New Approach?* (February 2023) https://www.iea.org/reports/fossil-fuel-subsidies-in-clean-energy-transitions-time-for-a-new-approach accessed 14 October 2023.

International Monetary Fund, *Climate Change: Fossil Fuel Subsidies* https://www.imf.org/en/Topics/climate-change/energy-subsidies accessed 2 October 2023.

Hee Jhee Jiow, 'Cyber Crime in Singapore: An Analysis of Regulation Based on Lessig's Four Modalities of Constraint' (2013) 7 *IJCC* 18.

Orin S. Kerr, 'Norms of Computer Trespass' (2016) 116 *Colum. LR* 1143.

Juliet P. Kostritsky, 'The Law and Economics of Norms' (2013) 48 *Tex. ILJ* 465.

Paul Kuruk, 'The Subsidies Issue in International Trade: Musings of the Economic Partnership Agreement Negotiations' (2013) 38 *N.C. JILCR* 327.

Kenina Lee, 'An Inherent Conflict Between WTO Law and a Sustainable Future? Evaluating the Consistency of Canadian and Chinese Renewable Energy Policies with WTO Trade Law' (2011) 24 *Geo. IELR* 57.

Lawrence Lessig, *Code: Version 2.0* (Basic Books, 2006).
Simon Lester, 'The Problem of Subsidies as a Means of Protectionism: Lessons from the WTO EC – Aircraft Case' (2011) 12 *Melb. JIL* 345.
Nicolas Loris, 'The Wind Production Tax Credit and the Case for Ending All Energy Subsidies' (2013) 23 *Duke ELPF* 323.
Stewart Macaulay et al. (eds) *Law & Society: Readings in The Social Study of Law* (W.W. Norton & Co, 1995).
Joshua Mackinnon, 'The African Century: Renewable Energy Opportunities in Sub-Saharan Africa' (2023) 47 *Wm. & Mary ELPR* 427.
Paul G. Mahoney and Chris W. Sanchirico, 'Competing Norms and Social Evolution: Is the Fittest Norm Efficient?' (2001) 149 *Upenn. LR* 2027.
Richard H. McAdams, 'The Origin, Development, and Regulation of Norms' (1997) 96 *Mich. LR* 338.
Timothy Meyer, 'Free Trade, Fair Trade, and Selective Enforcement' (2018) 118 *Colum. LR* 491.
Timothy L. Meyer, 'Energy Subsidies and the World Trade Organization' (2013) 17 *ASIL INSIGHTS* 1.
Ved P. Nanda, 'The Journey from the Millennium Development Goals to the Sustainable Development Goals' (2016) 44 *Denv. JILP* 389, 392; United Nations, 'Sustainable Development Goals: The Sustainable Development Agenda' https://www.un.org/sustainabledevelopment/development-agenda/ accessed 9 May 2024.
Oil Change International, 'Fossil Fuel Subsidies: Overview' (n.d.) https://priceofoil.org/fossil-fuel-subsidies/ accessed 14 October 2023.
Björn Ólafsson, 'What Farm Subsidies Are and Why They Matter, Explained' (*Sentient Media*, 11 August 2023). https://sentientmedia.org/why-are-farmers-subsidized/
Our Common Future, *Report of the World Commission on Environment and Development (Brundtland Commission)* (1987). https://digitallibrary.un.org/record/139811?ln=en&v=pdf
Ian W.H. Parry, Simon Black and Nate Vernon, *Still Not Getting Energy Prices Right: A Global and Country Update of Fossil Fuel Subsidies* (24 September 2021) 6 https://www.imf.org/en/Publications/WP/Issues/2021/09/23/Still-Not-Getting-Energy-Prices-Right-A-Global-and-Country-Update-of-Fossil-Fuel-Subsidies-466004 accessed 3 October 2023.
Robert S. Pindyck and Daniel L. Rubinfeld, *Microeconomics* (5th edn, Prentice Hall, 2000).
Eric A. Posner, 'Law, Economics, and Inefficient Norms' (1996) 144 *Upenn. LR* 1697.
Eric A. Posner, 'Symbols, Signals, and Social Norms in Politics and the Law' (1998) XXIX *JLS* 1.
Eric A. Posner, *Law and Social Norms* (Harvard University Press, 2000).
Eric A. Posner (ed), *Social Norms, Nonlegal Sanctions, and the Law* (Edward Elgar Publishing, 2007).
Richard A. Posner, *Economic Analysis of Law* (8th edn, Wolters Kluwer, 2011).
Michael Shellenberger, 'Haiti Riots Triggered by IMF Advice to Cut Fuel Subsidies' *Forbes* (22 September 2022) https://www.forbes.com/sites/michaelshellenberger/2022/09/22/haiti-riots-triggered-by-imf-advice-to-cut-fuel-subsidies/ accessed 23 October 2023.
Ken Silverstein, 'COVID-19 Is Killing Oil and Gas But The Virus Could Also Poison Renewables' *Forbes* (6 April 2020). https://www.forbes.com/sites/kensilverstein/2020/04/06/covid-19-is-killing-oil-and-gas-but-the-virus-could-also-poison-renewables/
Jakob Skovgaard, 'The Devil Lies in the Definition: Competing Approaches to Fossil Fuel Subsidies at the IMF and the OECD' (2017) 17 *International Environmental Agreements* 341.

Cass R. Sunstein, 'Social Norms and Social Roles' (1996) 96 *Colum. LR* 903.
The World Bank, *Carbon Pricing Dashboard, Main Types of Carbon Pricing* (n.d.) https://carbonpricingdashboard.worldbank.org/what-carbon-pricing accessed 13 October 2023.
Johannes Urpelainen and Elisha George, 'Reforming Global Fossil Fuel Subsidies: How the United States Can Restart International Cooperation' (*Brookings Institution*, 14 July 2021).
Richard Valdmanis, 'Biden Budget to Target U.S. Fossil Fuel Subsidies' *Reuters* (9 March 2023).
Cleo Verkuijl et al., 'Tackling Fossil Fuel Subsidies Through International Trade Agreements: Taking Stock, Looking Forward' (2019) 58 *Virginia JIL* 309.
Chris Wold, Grant Wilson and Sara Foroshani, 'Leveraging Climate Change Benefits through the World Trade Organization: Are Fossil Fuel Subsidies Actionable?' (2012) 43 *Geo. JIL* 635.

Part C

Tax Compliance and Development

10 Digital taxation

Sustainable use of digitalization and tax justice in Africa

Olusegun Vincent and Olaniyi Evans†*

10.1 Introduction

The advent of the digital revolution in the 1980s, marked by the onset of the Third Industrial Revolution, has heralded transformative changes across various facets of society and the economy.[1] This paradigm shift has not only redefined economies but has also given rise to new challenges and opportunities in public policy domains.[2] The emergence of the digital economy presents a host of advantages over traditional economic models, offering scalability and efficiency in tax management at both micro and macro levels. Central to this digital transformation is the indispensable role of big data, which facilitates rapid cross-verification of information and augments taxpayer compliance.[3]

According to a study conducted by the African Tax Administration Forum,[4] digitalization holds immense promise in the revolution of tax collection methodologies in Africa, to bolster the efficiency of African tax organizations and augment tax revenues. Nonetheless, it is necessary to recognize that technological solutions alone are insufficient in combatting tax fraud and evasion; complementary measures such as legislative reforms, robust enforcement mechanisms, and international collaboration are indispensable.[5] African tax systems necessitate preparedness to navigate the transformations ushered in by digitalization and to evaluate international tax regulations considering their ramifications for governmental structures and the future trajectory of tax systems.

In numerous African nations, the digital economy has experienced exponential growth, presenting governments with formidable challenges in tracking taxpayer activities, ensuring income accuracy, and fortifying reporting mechanisms. This reality engenders revenue losses and fiscal deficits. While the traditional taxation framework has long been a stalwart revenue generator, its efficacy is constrained. This chapter therefore undertakes an exploration of the

* School of Management and Social Sciences, Pan-Atlantic University, Lagos, Nigeria. Email address: ovincent@pau.edu.ng.

† School of Management and Social Sciences, Pan-Atlantic University, Lagos, Nigeria. Email address: oevans@pau.edu.ng.

DOI: 10.4324/9781003432890-13

potential of digital taxation by investigating the application of technology in tax collection and administration, with a particular focus on issues such as unreported income, tax fraud, and evasion.

Importantly, despite the growing attention paid to digitalization's impact on taxation, there remains a literature gap in the systematic exploration of the challenges, opportunities, and strategies associated with the leverage of digital innovations to promote tax justice. This chapter aims to address this gap by elucidating the intersection of digital innovations and taxation, particularly tax justice in the digital era. The research thus endeavors to achieve three primary objectives:

i Explore the impact of digital innovations on taxation.
ii Investigate challenges and opportunities for tax justice in the digital economy.
iii Analyze strategies to leverage digitalization to combat tax fraud and illicit financial flows.

Based on a conceptual methodology which draws on extant theories, findings, and frameworks found in the literature, this study seeks to contribute to a deeper understanding of the dynamics of digital taxation. It informs policymakers about the transformative impact of digital innovations on taxation. It identifies challenges and opportunities for the promotion of tax justice in the digital economy, to offer guidance for the design of equitable tax policies. Ultimately, it emphasizes the importance of proactive policymaking to leverage digitalization for the reinforcement of fiscal governance in Africa.

10.2 Methodology

The methodology is a conceptual study based on the literature, which draws on extant theories, concepts, and frameworks found in the literature. Using conceptual study anchored in extant literature, we contribute to the theoretical development of the field and provide a foundation for future empirical research. By synthesizing extant literature and theories on the topic, the conceptual methodology facilitates a deep understanding of the subject matter.[6] The focus on theoretical analysis, conceptualization, and framework development allows for the integration and refinement of extant theories and models, essential for addressing the research objectives.[7]

To begin, the methodology entails a review of academic and professional literature related to digitalization and taxation in Africa. This literature review, guided by the research questions, encompasses various sources such as journal articles, books, and reports, selected based on their relevance.[8] Subsequently, a critical analysis of the literature will be conducted, which aims to identify the current dynamics of digitalization and taxation in Africa, particularly challenges, best practices, and recommendations.

10.3 Digital innovations in taxation

The digital revolution has permeated all aspects of life, particularly taxation, triggering profound shifts in economic and managerial paradigms.[9] Modern technologies have disrupted traditional tax norms, to influence market dynamics and governmental entities.[10] Moshkova[11] argues that these technologies facilitate the evolution of new tax authority frameworks, which enable conceptual changes in tax data collection and analysis, and provide convenient avenues for taxpayers to fulfill their obligations.

Digital innovations have the potential to amplify efficiency, transparency, and simplify tax-related tasks, and thereby foster trust between taxpayers and tax authorities.[12] Automation mitigates errors, eliminates subjectivity in tax collection, and fosters transparency, transforming tax authorities into more user-friendly entities.

Furthermore, the restructuring of trust dynamics in tax systems and the consumerization of tax organizations represent fundamental shifts in the taxation of industrialized nations. The infusion of digital technology into tax frameworks intensifies the metamorphosis of traditional tax models. Digital innovation targets shadow and deficit budgets, exemplified by studies showcasing the development of tax policies through automated investment design technologies, remote monitoring, and control technologies.[13]

Blockchain technology holds promise for tax authorities and regulators, which furnish reliable, shared information conducive to early transaction-related tax collection and oversight. This technology's transparency aids in the detection of fraud and errors, particularly in value-added tax (VAT) fraud scenarios. In addition, blockchain technology can incite behavioral change to curb the costs and repercussions of noncompliance, and thus narrow the tax gap.

The digital revolution has also significantly influenced tax accounting policies in businesses globally. Digitalization has positively impacted the accounting profession and thus fostered increased transparency, accuracy in tracking, permanent records, reduced processing costs, and heightened public trust in audit outcomes.[14] Substantial progress has been made in the structure of tax accounting procedures in businesses.

In Africa, digitalization has significantly influenced tax accounting policies as well. For instance, Kenya's implementation of the iTax system has streamlined tax payment and filing processes for businesses, to foster efficiency, transparency, and accountability.[15] Similarly, South Africa's introduction of the eFiling platform by the South African Revenue Service (SARS) facilitates electronic tax return submission and payments, to simplify tax compliance and improve accuracy.[16] Moreover, Nigeria's Federal Inland Revenue Service (FIRS) has launched the TaxPro Max, a digital platform aimed at fostering tax collection efficiency and reduction of administrative burdens for taxpayers.[17] The FIRS has also introduced the Electronic Tax Invoice System (ETIS) to further streamline tax compliance processes. Similarly, in Morocco, the E-taxation system introduced by the government offers electronic tax return filing and payment options, to ease administrative burdens.[18] Rwanda's Rwanda Revenue Authority (RRA) has implemented the Rwanda Online Tax System (ROTS), providing electronic tax filing, payment, and information access, which reduces administrative burdens and fostering tax collection efficiency.[19]

The digital transformation of taxation has thus facilitated businesses' compliance with tax obligations and fostered tax collection efficiency globally, particularly in Africa. These digital platforms have streamlined tax payment and filing processes, improved tax collection efficiency, and bolstered transparency and accountability. By simplification of tax compliance, reducing administrative costs, and fostering transparency, digitalization has empowered businesses to become more competitive and efficient, and thereby foster tax justice.

10.4 The challenges of tax justice in the digital economy

The emergence of the digital economy has posed novel challenges for tax authorities, necessitating the development of a comprehensive framework to encompass digital elements crucial for economic transactions and a taxonomy of tax-disruptive business models.[20] These challenges stem from factors like the intricacy of digital transactions, heavy reliance on intangible assets, lack of physical presence, and the difficulty in qualifying assets, activities, and revenue streams.

However, taxation of the digital economy could alleviate the tax burden on less volatile sources, such as labor income. New tax regulations are necessary due to the wide gap between economic realities and tax systems that have lagged behind new business models.[21] Large tech corporations purportedly bear lower tax burdens compared to their traditional economic counterparts. The globalization of the digital economy introduces fresh challenges for international taxes, characterized by an unprecedented reliance on intangible assets, significant data consumption, and the potential migration of core business processes.[22]

Developing countries face a heightened risk to the tax base from the burgeoning digital economy compared to wealthier nations. Corporate income tax (CIT) and VAT, two tax systems particularly vulnerable to the digital economy, constitute a larger share of overall tax collections in developing countries, particularly African nations, than in wealthier countries. Developing nations would encounter greater difficulty in managing any decline in CIT and VAT, given the feeble nature of personal income tax (PIT) and the already concerning overreliance on trade taxes. In addition, the objective of ensuring tax neutrality between digital and traditional businesses presents an excessively intricate task unlikely to be achieved, considering the simplistic and unclear mechanism of the approach, which merely assumes taxation of the attributed profit of foreign digital companies through low-rate turnover taxation.

Moreover, the digital economy complicates VAT collection, particularly when private customers purchase products, services, and intangibles from suppliers in other countries. The extant international taxation system fails to equitably allocate the tax base among nations in the digital environment, which contravenes the principle of taxes based on value added in the specific country.[23] In the absence of international agreement, governments have unilaterally altered their tax systems by imposing digital services taxes.[24] These indirect taxes are levied on the turnover of international digital enterprises in the market country, by nature, as the source of income country.

One of the primary challenges of taxation of the digital economy in Africa lies in the determination of the taxable presence of digital companies. The digital economy is characterized by companies' ability to provide services across borders without any physical presence in the market, which renders it problematic to ascertain where tax liabilities lie. For example, in South Africa, the SARS has grappled with this challenge in the taxation of multinational digital companies in the country. Similarly, Kenya's government has faced difficulties in the taxation of digital companies due to their overseas base and lack of physical presence in the market. Nigeria's FIRS has encountered similar challenges in the taxation of digital companies. Likewise, Ghana's tax authorities strive to improve tax collection mechanisms for digital companies. Egypt's Ministry of Finance has also fostered tax collection mechanisms to ensure fair taxation of digital companies.

10.5 Opportunities for digital taxation

From tax planning for digital companies to tax fraud and illicit financial flows (IFFs), the integration of digital technologies offers promising solutions. Tax justice emerges as a central theme, ensuring fairness and transparency in fiscal policies. Through initiatives like digital tax systems and collaboration among governments, efforts are underway to foster tax compliance and governance.

10.5.1 Tax planning for digital companies

The burgeoning global presence of the digital business model prompts nations to adopt diverse strategies to foster its growth.[25] Yet, its novelty and departure from traditional accounting practices often render digital companies targets for audits or confusion by tax authorities. Taxation, seen by governments as an indispensable tool for fostering economic development and digital leadership, highlights the significance of tax justice in this domain.[26]

Classical taxation theory advocates taxation of earnings where economic activities occur, and value is generated. However, the advent of digital enterprises, with intangible production factors and virtual establishments, complicates the delineation of economic activity and value-creation locations, to challenge profit taxation.[27] In response, the international community advocates for a digital services tax to address these complexities, with some countries enacting their versions while others pursue a global minimum tax approach. The debate on the basis, initiation point, and tax rates for digital services highlights the necessity for equitable tax governance, which emphasizes the principle of tax justice.[28]

Various governments have implemented measures to tax digital enterprises. For instance, the United Kingdom imposes a 25% Diverted Profits Levy, Mato Grosso in Brazil levies a commodities tax on internet downloads, Israel deems heavy internet dependence as a fixed base for corporations, and Colombia applies a 19% VAT on internet services.[29] With global governance responsibilities, the safeguarding of the interests of digital companies becomes paramount, which emphasizes the principle of tax justice.

In Africa, the surge of digitalization creates new vistas for tax planning among digital companies. With a mushrooming online business, innovative tax planning strategies tailored to the digital economy's unique attributes are necessary. For instance, Kenya offers tax incentives for technology-based startups, particularly a five-year corporate tax holiday and reduced tax rates for software and tech companies, to nurture the growth of the tech sector.[30]

Similarly, Nigeria's two-year tax holiday for technology companies and South Africa's tax incentives for research and development in the tech sector foster innovation and competitiveness. In Morocco and Tunisia, tax incentives such as tax holidays for technology companies spur investment and growth in the digital sector. These initiatives highlight the importance of tax justice in an equitable environment for digital businesses to thrive across the continent.

10.5.2 Digitalization against tax fraud and evasion

Tax evasion and fraud remain persistent challenges, resulting in substantial annual losses. Beyond contravention of the law and depriving governments of revenue, they engender an unfair environment for law-abiding taxpayers, which highlights the necessity of tax justice.[31] Tax revenues serve as crucial resources for finance of social programs and public investments aimed at societal well-being and economic advancement.

Tax evasion entails the deliberate use of deceptive tactics by taxpayers to evade tax obligations, which pose significant threats to revenue mobilization, particularly in developing countries.[32] Tariff evasion and cross-border trade fraud exacerbate revenue losses, especially in regions reliant on international trade.[33] The challenge for governments lies in tracking taxpayers' activities and earnings, especially in cash transactions without a paper trail.[34]

Digitization emerges as a potent tool for combating tax evasion and fraud, which empowers governments with accurate data to monitor transactions effectively.[35] The integration of digital technology into fiscal policies fosters operational efficiency and trade information accuracy, and thus bolsters tax compliance efforts.[36] While digitalization facilitates information flow to governments and thereby reduces tax fraud, it also necessitates vigilance against new forms of tax avoidance as technology advances.[37] Sophisticated digital tools enable tax authorities to identify suspicious transactions and non-compliance, which mitigates tax evasion risks.[38]

In Africa, the rise of digitalization offers significant prospects for combating tax fraud and evasion. Implementation of digital tax systems in various African nations fosters government oversight and thus reduces opportunities for fraudulent activities. Systems like Kenya's iTax and South Africa's eFiling enable real-time monitoring of tax compliance, which contributes to a decline in tax fraud incidents. Similarly, Nigeria's Integrated Tax Administration System (ITAS) improves tax collection efficiency and provides real-time information on liabilities, which curb tax evasion.

Ghana's Tax Platform and Uganda's Electronic Tax Management System (ETMS) bolster tax compliance efforts through real-time monitoring and detection of fraudulent activities. The Uganda Revenue Authority (URA) has implemented the ETMS, which has improved the efficiency of tax collection and reduced the likelihood of tax fraud and evasion. The system provides real-time information on tax liabilities and enables the government to monitor tax compliance and detect fraudulent activities. These initiatives highlight the transformative potential of digitalization to foster tax justice and curb tax evasion across the African continent.

10.5.3 Digital taxation and illicit financial flows

IFFs, the unlawful movement of money across borders, pose significant challenges, which impede governments' ability to promote and safeguard human rights.[39] These illicit flows encompass diverse illegal activities and methods aimed at the transfer of money and assets across national borders, which violate national or international laws. They comprise illegally obtained funds as well as legally sourced money used for illegal purposes like terrorist financing or illicit transfers, which highlights the multifaceted nature of the issue.

Studies highlight the persistent prevalence of IFFs, particularly in developing regions like Sub-Saharan Africa, where they erode resources crucial for public-sector development, which emphasizes the significance of tax justice. These flows stem from various factors such as mis-invoicing, trade in illegal goods, corruption, and illicit activities like human and drug trafficking, often involved in complicity from officials in key government institutions.[40]

Digital taxation emerges as an indispensable strategy to mitigate revenue losses in African nations due to tax avoidance, which highlights the role of tax justice. IFFs, intricate and transnational in nature, necessitate comprehensive measures to curb them, particularly via digital technologies and the closure of tax treaty loopholes.[41] These illicit funds often originate from jurisdictions with limited resources, which deplete foreign reserves and impede investment inflows.

The global community recognizes the threat posed by IFFs, which align with Sustainable Development Goals (SDGs) objectives to combat them, to emphasize the importance of tax justice in promoting equitable fiscal systems.[42] Consensus on the definition and accurate measurement of IFFs remains a challenge, with proposals to encompass both illegal actions like tax evasion and legal activities that impact tax revenue.

Digitalization offers favorable avenues for governments to foster tax collection and allocate resources to poverty alleviation programs, to promote social and economic progress. Inter-agency collaboration is indispensable for effective policymaking in this realm, alongside international financial and technological cooperation to bolster the rule of law, protect property rights, and uphold contractual obligations, which embody principles of tax justice.

In Africa, where limited resources hinder tax law enforcement and exacerbate IFFs, digitalization presents transformative opportunities. Initiatives like South Africa's Transfer Pricing Regulations (TPRs) and Nigeria's adoption of similar regulations aim to curb base erosion and profit shifting by multinational companies (MNCs), which foster tax transparency and justice. Kenya's Base Erosion and Profit Shifting (BEPS) initiative and Ghana's TPRs further highlight the commitment of African governments to combat IFFs through digital means.

These examples from South Africa, Nigeria, Kenya, Ghana, and Morocco illustrate the continent's concerted efforts to utilize digital tools to tackle IFFs, foster tax collection, and promote transparency. Using technology, African governments can strengthen tax enforcement, curb tax fraud and evasion, and foster equitable tax systems, to embody the principles of tax justice and fairness.

10.6 Conclusion and implications

Based on a conceptual methodology which draws on extant theories, findings, and frameworks found in the literature, this chapter has shown that the digital revolution has reshaped taxation to bring about significant changes in tax administration. These innovations offer the potential to improve efficiency, transparency, and accountability in tax systems, to foster trust between taxpayers and tax authorities. In addition, the integration of digital technology into tax frameworks has altered traditional tax models, to address shadow and deficit budgets and increase transparency and reduce tax fraud. Despite these advancements, challenges remain, particularly in tax justice in the digital economy. Tax authorities face difficulties in the determination of taxable presence, management of tax liabilities of digital companies, and achievement of equitable taxation across traditional and digital businesses. Nevertheless, digitalization presents opportunities to combat tax fraud and IFFs, foster tax compliance, and advance fairness and transparency in fiscal policies. Initiatives such as digital tax systems and intergovernmental collaboration are underway to leverage digital technologies for tax enforcement and governance, which align with principles of tax justice and fairness.

To maximize the benefits of digitalization in taxation, the following are recommended:

1 Promotion of tax justice and compliance

The integration of digital technologies into taxation systems presents a significant opportunity to foster tax justice and compliance. Governments should prioritize the development and implementation of digital tax platforms, like

Kenya's iTax and Nigeria's TaxPro Max, to streamline tax processes and provide real-time information to taxpayers.

2 Closure of tax treaty loopholes
Developing countries, particularly in Africa, should collaborate with international partners to close tax treaty loopholes that facilitate IFFs. By renegotiation of tax treaties and adoption of international tax standards, governments can prevent MNCs from exploiting loopholes to shift profits and avoid payment of their fair share of taxes.

3 Inter-agency collaboration
Effective policymaking and enforcement require seamless collaboration among government agencies, particularly tax authorities, law enforcement agencies, and regulatory bodies. Governments should invest in robust data-sharing mechanisms and cross-agency collaboration frameworks to combat tax fraud, evasion, and IFFs.

4 Tax incentives for digital innovation
To foster digital innovation and competitiveness, governments should consider tax incentives targeted at digital companies. Tax holidays, reduced corporate tax rates, and research and development tax credits can incentivize investment in digital technologies and promote economic growth.

5 Investment in digital tax enforcement tools
Governments should prioritize investment in digital tax enforcement tools, such as data analytics, artificial intelligence, and blockchain technology, to foster tax compliance and enforcement efforts. Using advanced technologies, tax authorities can identify tax fraud patterns, detect non-compliance, and enforce tax laws more effectively.

6 Capacity building and training
Reinforcement of the capacity of tax authorities and equipment of tax officials with the necessary skills and knowledge to leverage digital technologies is essential for effective tax administration. Governments should invest in training programs and capacity-building initiatives to empower tax officials to effectively use digital tools for tax administration, compliance monitoring, and enforcement.

7 International cooperation
Given the transnational nature of tax evasion and IFFs, international cooperation is essential for addressing these challenges effectively. Governments should collaborate with international organizations, such as the OECD and the UN, to develop common standards, exchange information, and coordinate efforts to combat tax evasion and IFFs.

8 Access to digital tax services
Governments should prioritize access to digital tax services for all taxpayers, particularly small- and medium-sized enterprises (SMEs) and individuals. The provision of user-friendly digital platforms, technical support,

and promotion of digital literacy initiatives can help ensure that all taxpayers can effectively fulfill their tax obligations.

9 Public awareness and engagement

Governments should invest in public awareness campaigns to educate taxpayers about their rights and responsibilities, the benefits of tax compliance, and the consequences of tax evasion. Engagement with taxpayers through digital channels, such as social media and online forums, can help build trust, transparency, and accountability in tax administration.

10 Monitoring and evaluation

Continuous monitoring and evaluation of digital taxation initiatives are essential to assess their effectiveness, identify challenges, and make necessary adjustments. Governments should establish robust monitoring and evaluation frameworks to track key performance indicators, measure outcomes, and ensure accountability in tax administration.

While this chapter has shown that the integration of digital technologies into taxation systems presents numerous opportunities, there are areas for future research. Firstly, the rapid pace of technological advancement may outpace regulatory frameworks, which can lead to challenges in maintaining tax justice and fairness. Secondly, the digital divide, which encompasses disparities in access to technology and digital literacy, may exacerbate extant inequalities in tax compliance. Future studies could explore strategies to bridge this gap and ensure equitable participation in digital tax systems. Furthermore, there is a need for thorough research on the long-term implications of digitalization on tax administration, particularly its effects on revenue distribution, taxpayer behavior, and overall economic development. Understanding these dynamics is important for policymakers to design effective tax policies that promote inclusivity and sustainability in the digital economy. Moreover, investigations into the potential risks associated with digital taxation, such as data privacy concerns and cybersecurity threats, are essential for the mitigation of adverse impacts and building trust in digital tax systems. Moreover, future studies should adopt a multidisciplinary approach, considering technological, economic, social, and legal dimensions to address the complex challenges and opportunities that may arise from the digital transformation of taxation.

Notes

1 H Strauss, 'Tax reform within a digitalised economy: tax, technology and assurance' (Doctoral dissertation, North-West University (South Africa, 2021).
2 O Adeola, O Evans, and I Ngare, 'Climate-Smart Technologies for Empowerment of Women Farmers in Africa' in Gender Equality, Climate Action, and Technological Innovation for Sustainable Development in Africa (Springer International Publishing 2023) 131.
3 O Vincent and O Evans, 'Fintech and tax revenues: Does political institution matter?' (2024) *Asia-Pacific Journal of Accounting & Economics* 1–9. https://doi.org/10.1080/16081625.2024.2356106.

4 African Tax Administration Forum, '5th High-Level Tax Policy Dialogue: A Collaboration Between the African Tax Administration Forum and the African Union Commission' (17 May 2021) https://www.ataftax.org/5th-high-level-tax-policy-dialogue-a-collaboration-between-the-african-tax-administration-forum-and-the-african-union-commission accessed 17 November 2024.
5 African Tax Administration Forum, '5th High-Level Tax Policy Dialogue: A Collaboration Between the African Tax Administration Forum and the African Union Commission' (17 May 2021) https://www.ataftax.org/5th-high-level-tax-policy-dialogue-a-collaboration-between-the-african-tax-administration-forum-and-the-african-union-commission accessed 17 November 2024.
6 JW Creswell, *A Concise Introduction to Mixed Methods Research* (SAGE Publications, 2021).
7 J Bettany-Saltikov, 'Learning how to undertake a systematic review: Part 2' (2013) 24 (51) *Nursing Standard* 47.
8 MJ Grant and A Booth, 'A typology of reviews: An analysis of 14 review types and associated methodologies' (2009) 26 *Health Information & Libraries Journal* 91.
9 Vincent and Evans (n3).
10 N Lagodiienko and I Yakushko, 'Digital innovations in taxation: Bibliometric analysis' (2021) *3 Marketing and Management of Innovations* 66–77.
11 DM Moshkova, 'Digitalisation of tax administration in the context of the development of high-tech municipalities' (2021, April). In *IOP Conference Series: Earth and Environmental Science* (Vol. 740, No. 1, p. 012024). IOP Publishing.
12 Lagodiienko and Yakushko (n 10).
13 AE Nemade, SS Kadam, RN Choudhary, SS Fegade, and K Agarwal, 'Blockchain technology used in taxation' in '2019 International Conference on Vision Towards Emerging Trends in Communication and Networking' (ViTECoN 2019) 1.
14 I Guzov, G Soboleva, and D Artemova, 'Digital technologies in accounting and taxation: some issues from Russian literature and experience' (2019) Third International Economic Symposium (IES 2018) 258.
15 Kenya Revenue Authority, 'iTax' (2021) https://www.kra.go.ke/itax/ accessed 17 November 2024.
16 South African Revenue Service, 'eFiling' (2021) https://www.sars.gov.za/Home/eFiling/ accessed 17 November 2024.
17 Federal Inland Revenue Service, 'Public notice – introduction of firs' tax administration solution (Taxpro-Max)'. (n.d.) https://www.firs.gov.ng/public-notice-introduction-of-firs-tax-administration-solution-taxpro-max/ accessed 17 November 2024.
18 Ministry of Economy, Finance and Administrative Reform, 'Tax Incentives for Technology Companies in Morocco' (2020).
19 Rwanda Revenue Authority, 'Rwanda Online Tax System (ROTS)' (n.d.) https://www.rra.gov.rw/index.php?id=2 accessed 8 February 2023.
20 Lagodiienko and Yakushko (n 10).
21 Guzov et al (n 14).
22 OECD, 'Addressing the Tax Challenges of the Digital Economy' (2014) https://www.oecd.org/ctp/addressing-the-tax-challenges-of-the-digital-economy-9789264218789-en.htm accessed 17 November 2024.
23 Moshkova (n 11).
24 OECD, 'Addressing the Tax Challenges of the Digital Economy, Action 1 – 2015 Final Report' (2015) https://www.oecd.org/tax/addressing-the-tax-challenges-of-the-digital-economy-action-1-2015-final-report-9789264241046-en.htm accessed 17 November 2024.
25 AS Alekseev, 'Opportunities for tax planning for digital companies: International experience' (2021) 14 (2) *Russian Journal of Industrial Economics*.
26 W Cui, 'The superiority of the digital services tax over significant digital presence proposals' (2019) 72(4) *National Tax Journal* 839.

27 A Aslam and A Shah, 'Taxing the Digital Economy' in Ruud A. de Mooij, Alexander D Klemm, Victoria J Perry (eds.) Corporate Income Taxes under Pressure: Why Reform Is Needed and How It Could Be Designed (International Monetary Fund 2021) 189.
28 Strauss (n 1).
29 OECD, 'Tax and digitalisation', OECD Going Digital Policy Note, (OECD, 2018) www.oecd.org/going-digital/topics/tax accessed 17 November 2024.
30 Kenya Revenue Authority, 'Kenya Revenue Authority' (2020) https://www.kra.go.ke/ accessed 17 November.
31 A Riahi-Belkaoui, 'Relationship between tax compliance internationally and selected determinants of tax morale' (2004) 13 (2) *Journal of International Accounting, Auditing and Taxation* 135.
32 J Alm, J Martinez-Vazquez, and C McClellan, 'Corruption and firm tax evasion' (2016) 124 *Journal of Economic Behavior & Organization* 146.
33 O Farny, M Franz, P Gerhartinger, G Lunzer, M Neuwirth, and M Saringer, 'Tax avoidance, tax evasion and tax havens' (2015) *Gerechtigkeit muss sein*.
34 J Alm, 'Tax evasion, technology, and inequality' (2021) 22 (4) *Economics of Governance* 321.
35 E Kitsios, J Jalles, and G Verdier, 'Reducing tax evasion from cross-border fraud: The role of digitalization' (2019).
36 RD Picur and A Riahi-Belkaoui, 'The impact of bureaucracy, corruption and tax compliance' (2006) 5 (2) *Review of Accounting and Finance* 174.
37 Alm (n34).
38 OF Atayah and MM Alshater, 'Audit and tax in the context of emerging technologies: A retrospective analysis, current trends, and future opportunities' (2021) 21 *International Journal of Digital Accounting Research* 95–128.
39 AJ Cockfield, 'Tax wars: The battle over taxing global digital commerce' (2018) 161 *Tax Notes* 1331.
40 M Forstater, 'Illicit financial flows, trade Misinvoicing, and multinational tax avoidance: the same or different' (2018) CGD Policy Paper (26 March 2018) https://www.cgdev.org/publication/illicit-financial-flows-trade-misinvoicing-and-multinational-tax-avoidance accessed 17 November 2024.
41 I Ritter, 'Illicit financial flows: An analysis and some initial policy proposals' (2015) Managerkreis der Friedrich-Ebert-Stiftung.
42 C. Goredema, 'Combating illicit financial flows and related corruption in Africa: Towards a more integrated and effective approach' (U4 Issue 2011).

Bibliography

O Adeola, O Evans and I Ngare, *'Climate-Smart Technologies for Empowerment of Women Farmers in Africa' in Gender Equality, Climate Action, and Technological Innovation for Sustainable Development in Africa* (Springer International Publishing 2023) 131.

African Tax Administration Forum, '5th High-Level Tax Policy Dialogue: A Collaboration Between the African Tax Administration Forum and the African Union Commission' (17 May 2021) https://www.ataftax.org/5th-high-level-tax-policy-dialogue-a-collaboration-between-the-african-tax-administration-forum-and-the-african-union-commission accessed 17 November 2024.

AS Alekseev, 'Opportunities for tax planning for digital companies: International experience' (2021) 14 (2) *Russian Journal of Industrial Economics*. 214.

J Alm, 'Tax evasion, technology, and inequality' (2021) 22 (4) *Economics of Governance* 321.

J Alm, J Martinez-Vazquez and C McClellan, 'Corruption and firm tax evasion' (2016) 124 *Journal of Economic Behavior & Organization* 146.

A Aslam and A Shah, 'Taxing the digital economy' in Ruud A. de Mooij, Alexander D Klemm, Victoria J Perry (eds.) *Corporate Income Taxes under Pressure: Why Reform Is Needed and How It Could Be Designed* (International Monetary Fund 2021) 189. https://www.imf.org/en/Publications/Books/Issues/2021/03/01/Corporate-Income-Taxes-under-Pressure-Why-Reform-Is-Needed-and-How-It-Could-Be-Designed-48604

OF Atayah and MM Alshater, 'Audit and tax in the context of emerging technologies: A retrospective analysis, current trends, and future opportunities' (2021) 21 *International Journal of Digital Accounting Research* 95–128.

J Bettany-Saltikov 'Learning how to undertake a systematic review: Part 2' (2013) 24 (51) *Nursing Standard* 47.

AJ Cockfield, 'Tax wars: The battle over taxing global digital commerce' (2018) 161 *Tax Notes* 1331.

JW Creswell, *A Concise Introduction to Mixed Methods Research* (SAGE Publications 2021).

W Cui, 'The superiority of the digital services tax over significant digital presence proposals' (2019) 72 (4) *National Tax Journal* 839.

O Farny, M Franz, P Gerhartinger, G Lunzer, M Neuwirth and M Saringer, 'Tax avoidance, tax evasion and tax havens' (2015) *Gerechtigkeit muss sein*. https://www.arbeiterkammer.at/infopool/wien/Studie_tax_avoidance.pdf

M Forstater, 'Illicit financial flows, trade Misinvoicing, and multinational tax avoidance: the same or different' CGD Policy Paper (26 March 2018) https://www.cgdev.org/publication/illicit-financial-flows-trade-misinvoicing-and-multinational-tax-avoidance accessed 17 November 2024.

C. Goredema, 'Combating illicit financial flows and related corruption in Africa: Towards a more integrated and effective approach' (U4 Issue 2011). https://www.u4.no/publications/combating-illicit-financial-flows-and-related-corruption-in-africa-towards-a-more-integrated-and-effective-approach

MJ Grant and A Booth, 'A typology of reviews: An analysis of 14 review types and associated methodologies' (2009) 26 *Health Information & Libraries Journal* 91.

I Guzov, G Soboleva and D Artemova, 'Digital technologies in accounting and taxation: some issues from Russian literature and experience' (2019) *Third International Economic Symposium (IES 2018)* 258.

E Kitsios, J Jalles and G Verdier, 'Reducing tax evasion from cross-border fraud: The role of digitalization' (2019) (IMF Workimg Paper). https://www.bancaditalia.it/pubblicazioni/altri-atti-convegni/2019-xxi-wpf/8_tovar_jalles.pdf

N Lagodiienko and I Yakushko, 'Digital innovations in taxation: bibliometric analysis' (2021) 3 *Marketing and Management of Innovations* 66–77.

DM Moshkova, 'Digitalisation of tax administration in the context of the development of high-tech municipalities' (2021, April). In *IOP Conference Series: Earth and Environmental Science* (Vol. 740, No. 1, p. 012024). IOP Publishing.

AE Nemade, SS Kadam, RN Choudhary, SS Fegade and K Agarwal, 'Blockchain technology used in taxation' in *2019 International Conference on Vision Towards Emerging Trends in Communication and Networking (ViTECoN)* (2019).

OECD, 'Addressing the tax challenges of the digital economy' https://www.oecd.org/ctp/addressing-the-tax-challenges-of-the-digital-economy-9789264218789-en.htm (2014) accessed 17 November 2024.

OECD, 'Addressing the tax challenges of the digital economy, action 1 – 2015 final report' (2015) https://www.oecd.org/tax/addressing-the-tax-challenges-of-the-digital-economy-action-1-2015-final-report-9789264241046-en.htm accessed 17 November 2024.

RD Picur and A Riahi-Belkaoui, 'The impact of bureaucracy, corruption and tax compliance' (2006) 5 (2) *Review of Accounting and Finance* 174.
A Riahi-Belkaoui, 'Relationship between tax compliance internationally and selected determinants of tax morale' (2004) 13 (2) *Journal of International Accounting, Auditing and Taxation* 135.
I Ritter, 'Illicit financial flows: An analysis and some initial policy proposals' (2015) *Managerkreis der Friedrich-Ebert-Stiftung*. https://library.fes.de/pdf-files/managerkreis/11487.pdf
H Strauss, 'Tax reform within a digitalised economy: tax, technology and assurance' (Doctoral dissertation, North-West University South Africa 2021).
O Vincent and O Evans, 'Fintech and tax revenues: does political institution matter?; (2024) *Asia-Pacific Journal of Accounting & Economics*, 1–19. 10.1080/16081625.2024.2356106

11 Tax Implications of Fiscal Social Contract on Sustainable Development in Nigeria

Newman U. Richards

11.1 Introduction

Sustainable development is understood as meeting the present needs of society without compromising the capacity of future generations to meet their own needs.[1] In other words, sustainable development implies the resultant effect of consistent measures to meet the needs of any given society which will invariably include the provision of essential infrastructures in critical areas such as health, education and transportation. The attainment of the developmental objectives of any nation requires huge funding and resource mobilisation constraints often inhibit progress in delivering on sustainable development imperatives.[2] While it is the responsibility of the government to drive development, there is a need for government to mobilise resources from all quarters including taxation. This, in essence, calls for a collaboration between the government and its citizens to mobilise resources towards sustainable development.[3] The social contract theory helps to understand the imperatives of collaboration between the government and its citizens in the pursuit of sustainable development in any given society. While it explains the role of the government in the development of any given society, it considers taxation as the corresponding obligation of the citizens.

The social contract theory is hinged on the notions of reciprocity, which implies that citizens will be willing 'to pay tax if they believe the state has the ability to provide effective and fair public goods from which they will benefit.'[4] This chapter argues that social conditions invariably affect the attitude of people towards the payment of taxes. Confidence in the ability and preparedness of the government to fulfil its side of the social contract motivates citizenship participation in governance through the payment of taxes. Thus, government disposition towards the welfare and security of its citizens may well be a major catalyst in instigating voluntary tax compliance. Consequently, it may be unfair for the government to expect citizens to continue to pay taxes if it fails to discharge its obligation to provide much-needed social benefits to the people. Taking the argument further, it is argued that tax evasion is likely to be high in a tax system where the government is not accountable and has not been able to utilise, manage or deploy available resources in a prudent manner to deliver

DOI: 10.4324/9781003432890-14

sustainable development.[5] At the same time, failure to pay tax may frustrate the social contract, as it is important for citizens to fulfil their concomitant obligation to contribute towards the cost of meeting their social needs and by implication sustainable development. The foregoing implies the integral role tax compliance plays in the attainment of sustainable development.

This chapter contends that good governance is a major catalyst for tax compliance and, by extension, sustainable development. It contends further that in developing countries like Nigeria, where the provision of public goods and services is often inadequate, citizens often see the social contract as an agreement they can opt out of and consequently; they are less inclined to comply with their tax obligations. This raises some concerns, considering that taxation has a critical role to play in mobilising domestic resources to meet the commitment of the state to drive social welfare imperatives and sustainable development. The essence of the social contract is to build trust between the government and the taxpayer. This is anchored on the rights of the taxpayer to enjoy public goods and services. In other words, human rights standards are critical in the debate on creating an effective tax system in Nigeria. This chapter relies on the social contract theory as a basis to understand or analyse the relationship between, good governance, tax justice and taxpayer behaviour.

The chapter is organised as follows: after the introduction, the next part discusses the concept of social contract considering its fundamentals and highlights the context it is used in this work. This is followed by an analysis of the legal foundation of a social contract and taxation in Nigeria, and the human rights implications. Thereafter the chapter examines the effect of tax compliance on sustainable development within the context of the social contract and particularly underscores the importance of tax as a fiscal contract and a tool for fiscal exchange that demands reciprocity by the state. The chapter concludes by recommending that good governance is fundamental to the attainment of sustainable development and tax compliance.

11.2 Theoretical Framework: Fiscal Social Contract and Sustainable Development

The social contract trade-off theory implies that in a society, individuals give up some rights in expectation of some benefits. In other words, the relationship between the state and its citizens can conveniently be described as an implied social contract with obligations and benefits. Hence, Castañeda *et al.* opine that 'At the heart of the social contract is an agreement that the state will provide for its citizens through public goods and that citizens will contribute what they can to help the state to function.'[6] For Gribnau and Dijkstra, the concept of social contract was a consequence of classical contractarian thinkers' rejection of the view that there is natural political authority among men on the basis of which rulers are entitled to rule by birth and the subjects are obligated to obey the rulers.[7] They argued that since man by nature is born free and equal, political authority must be a product of negotiation and consent.[8] Thus, social contract theorists hinge on the source of political power in the people and are concerned about the legitimacy of sovereigns and the legal obligations of the subject.

Also, an important feature of social contract doctrine is that people agree to move from a state of nature to a state of society and their consent is expressed either as an actual or a hypothetical contract. Therefore, the relationship between the state and the people can be said to be 'contractual, explicitly or implicitly, and which specifies or implies the respective rights and duties of the contractees.'[9] For Rawls, the fiscal social contract is horizontal between the citizens and the state and vertical between citizens.[10] In conceptualising the social contract, Rawls appears to approach it from a tripartite perspective which goes beyond the state and its citizens and includes the relationship between citizens. This implies that citizens collectively agree to share a part of their resources with others by contributing towards the provision of public services by the state.[11] Accordingly, fiscal contract theorists, opine that there is an implied distribution of obligations/responsibilities and benefits/rights between the states and its citizens in what can be termed a social contract.[12] This suggests that underlining the formative process of modern states is an implied contract in which citizens exchange some rights for the provision of social benefits. This includes a fiscal exchange where citizens are also expected to contribute via payment of taxes to the state funds for the provision of social goods.[13]

Considering the foregoing, Adekoya *et al.* opine that the 'social contract leads to the concept of fiscal exchange and legitimacy theory' which is expected to make the government more accountable and responsive in the management of resources and provision of public goods and services.[14] In other words 'tax is a form of fiscal exchange between the government and the citizens, where the government provides goods and services as return for tax payments.'[15] The political legitimacy theory drives the fact that 'tax compliance is influenced by taxpayers trust in government and its institution.'[16] Moore notes that the essence of the fiscal exchange theory and political legitimacy theory is to deliver governance dividends.[17] That is a negotiated relationship between the government and citizens that could enhance government revenue through voluntary tax compliance driven by the expectation of dividends from the government in the form of improved social conditions.

Furthermore, Moore argues that this social pact which includes taxation helps to understand the relation of the state and its citizens within the context of taxation and helps to understand the political legitimacy of states in the formation of states.[18] In that context, revenue from taxation was exchanged for policies and incentivised to ensure the prosperity and survival of the state.[19] The summation is that although the idea of a fiscal contract is rooted in European history, countries that are heavily dependent on non-tax revenues could become more effective, democratic and accountable if they adopt the dynamics of a tax state.[20] This is underscored by Alm *et al*, in their experiment on factors that drive tax compliance.[21] They found that the understanding that taxes are used to provide public goods that citizens value, drives them to pay taxes, as it guarantees their continuous enjoyment of government goods and services.[22] In other words, citizens see tax payment as a form of fiscal exchange or fiscal contract wherein they have an obligation to contribute towards the funding of public goods and services. This implies that their continuous contribution is catalysed by the government's consistency in providing those goods and services that citizens value.[23] In summary, good governance is a major catalyst for voluntary tax compliance.[24] This implies that taxation could have far-reaching implications on the political future of government, the development of public trust in the government and its critical in the economic development of an effective state.[25]

Additionally, the philosophical underpinnings for the social contract theory can be found in the work of Marshall on social citizenship and social rights where he posited that 'If citizenship is invoked in the defence of rights, the corresponding duties of citizenship cannot be ignored.'[26] He argued further that

> a contractualist conception of social rights suggests that contractualism might be defended as a requirement of economic fairness or distributive justice: more precisely, as a way of ensuring that those who willingly share in the social product satisfy a corresponding obligation to make a productive contribution back to the community.[27]

Also, the essence of the implied social contract is the sustainable development of a society; where the social and economic rights of citizens receive considerable attention and the citizens are willing to reciprocate by contributing towards the sustenance of the state. For Dahl, the ultimate purpose of development is to improve the prosperity and well-being of everyone on this planet and therefore the ethical principle for a global social contract becomes the oneness of humankind. Therefore, society needs a new economic model that is supported by a just and thriving social order that is cooperative in nature.[28] The social contract theory therefore advocates that sustainable development which entails the provision of social goods and services by the state, demands some form of cooperation and reciprocity in the form of financial contributions by citizens.

Notwithstanding the foregoing, there is no consensus about the concept of a social contract. For example, Hume does not see the role of a social contract in society, for him we need convention rather than contract as human sociability makes the idea of a social contract superfluous.[29] Similarly, Gribnau and Dijkstra note that opponents of the social contract theory opine that although man is competitive, at the same time they are dependent on others as mutual assistance is critical to self-preservation. Hence, they are naturally inclined to cooperate and despite the differences and often conflicting interests among themselves, they prefer to live together in a society.[30]

Similarly, Tengs observes that the fiscal social contract hypothesis although established theoretically was yet to be endorsed empirically due to the fact that it only considers the aspects between the state and its citizens but did not consider the vertical relationship between the citizens.[31] He seems to agree with Rawls[32] that for the social contract to be viable its protagonist must look beyond the relationship of the state and its citizens to consider the effect of the interactions among citizens on the relationship between the state and its citizens. In the same vein, Tengs noted further that the social contractarian theorists argue that, while the social contractarian theory was based on establishing a welfare state, the advocates did not consider that the interaction amongst citizens is essential to the formation of a welfare state.[33] He concludes that how the government handles the interaction among its citizens impacts their level of tax compliance.[34] In other words, opponents of the social contract theory do not seem to agree with the attempt to explain the relationship between the state and its citizens from a contractual perspective. They rather see it from the social stabilisation and solidarity perspective which implies that citizens cooperate for their self-preservation and pay tax as part of their duty to obey the sovereign and laws made by the sovereign.[35]

Although there are divergent views regarding the import or utility of the social contract theory; it is relevant to modern-day political, social and economic development discourse. For example, it is often used as a template to evaluate state and citizenship relationships in the pursuit of sustainable development.[36] In this way, social contract theory underscores the need for collaboration between the state and its citizens in the quest for sustainable development and it is in this context that the social contract theory is used in this work.

11.3 Legal Basis for Fiscal Social Contract and Taxation in Nigeria

In modern states, the fiscal social contract is not only implied but its terms are often expressed in a seemingly contractual document which is the Constitution. This is certainly true in the case of Nigeria. Chapter 2 of the Constitution of the Federal Republic of Nigeria, 1999 (CFRN 1999) shows the responsibility of the government to harness the resources of the State and pursue the security and welfare of its citizens; while the citizens have a corresponding obligation to pay taxes and contribute towards the provision of common social goods. For instance, section 14(2)(a) of the CFRN 1999 provides that 'sovereignty belongs to the people of Nigeria from whom government through this constitution derives all its powers and authority.' Therefore, the government derives its powers and legitimacy from the people and, by extension; the constitution can be understood as a contractual document that allocates rights and obligations between the people and the government. Hence it provides that 'the security and welfare of the people shall be the primary purpose of government'[37] and mandates the government to harness the resources of the nation to improve the welfare and living conditions of the people by the provision of transport, health, education and other social facilities.[38] On the other hand, sections 24(d) and 24 (f) of the CFRN 1999 puts a reciprocal obligation on every citizen to contribute towards the advancement of his immediate community by declaring his income honestly and paying tax timeously. Accordingly, it is argued that the CFRN 1999 created a fiscal social contract between the people and the government. It mandates the government to pursue issues of security and welfare of the people as its primary objective and it demands a reciprocal commitment from the citizens to pay taxes as consideration for the enjoyment of social benefits.

Although, chapter 11 of the CFRN 1999 are provisions on the specie of human rights collectively referred to as social economic rights (SERs), which regrettably are generally non-justiciable in Nigeria.[39] It is important to protect these rights, notwithstanding, the arguments that SERs are mere aspirations which may be difficult to implement especially in low-income countries due to limited resources.[40] This is because, payment of taxes is an implied contribution to economic development and nation-building, which demands the legal protection of the taxpayers' rights and interests to enjoy public goods and services. It is opined that SERs provide this legal protection, and it is imperative to remove all hurdles inhibiting the enjoyment of these rights. Commendably, liberal interpretation of these provisions by some courts and reliance on the provisions of international standards for human rights provide some succour. For instance, in *Centre for Oil Pollution Watch v Nigerian National Petroleum Corporation*,[41] the Nigerian Supreme Court held that 'the non justiciability of section 6(6) c of the constitution is neither total nor sacrosanct as the sub section provides a leeway by the use of the words except as otherwise provided by this constitution.'[42] The implication of this is that the court can rely on other provisions of the constitution to hold that a provision in chapter 2 of CFRN 1999 is justiciable. Hence, the court although obiter, recognised that the right to a safe and clean environment is justiciable.[43] This is a commendable approach as the court has a duty under section 13(1) of the CFRN 1999 to give effect to the provisions of chapter 2 of CFRN 1999 and to ensure that citizens enjoy SERs provided in the constitution.

Furthermore, this chapter contends that human rights standards should be invoked in the debate on creating effective tax regimes in Nigeria and their implications for sustainable development. Considering that the provisions of chapter 2 of CFRN 1999 are equally guaranteed and justiciable in some human rights instruments to which Nigeria is a signatory. For instance, Nigeria is a signatory to the African Charter on Human and Peoples' Rights (African Charter).[44] In *Social and Economic Rights Action Centre (SERAC) & Another v Nigeria*,[45] the African Commission on Human and Peoples' Rights held that the Nigerian Government violated the socio-economic rights of its citizens to a clean safe environment and health guaranteed by the African Charter. Arguably, this implies that SERs are enforceable in Nigeria under international standards. Also, Nigeria is a signatory to the International Covenant on Economic, Social and Cultural Rights (ICESCR). The ICESCR imposes general and specific obligations on state parties to take steps towards the realisation of SERs.[46] It recognises that states may be unable to completely ensure the enjoyment of these rights within a short time due to funding constraints.

However, it advocates for a progressive implementation, which will require a gradual but consistent protection of these rights in proportion to available resources.[47] The approach towards the realisation of SERs at the international level is a direct consequence of the efforts of Judges, academics and human rights advocates which has led to the formulation of several theories to promote some level of enforcement for SERs. One such theory is the principle of minimum core obligations which expects states to strive to meet the basic minimum demands of SERs,[48] such as the provision of health, education, housing, sanitation and transport facilities among others. It is given that SERs 'cannot be enforced in the absence of adequate fiscal resources,'[49] which may provide some reasons Nigeria has not fared too well in the realisation of SERs. However, based on international human rights standards, scarce resources are no longer an acceptable excuse for a state to equivocate on its minimum core obligation[50] to provide basic social amenities for its citizens.

The nexus between the enjoyment of SERs and tax compliance is arguably premised on the appropriate utilisation of resources to drive government programmes on SERs in Nigeria as a catalyst for voluntary tax compliance. In other words, taxation plays a facilitative role in the realisation of human rights and sustainable development.[51] While the enforcement of human rights especially SERs is an effective catalyst for voluntary tax compliance. It follows that tax policies must be designed to assist in the realisation of SERs. Hence, an effective tax system should be designed to reduce the tax burdens of low-income earners and increase funding for programs that promote SERs.[52] In other words, the imposition and collection of taxes on citizens confers some rights which can be encapsulated as legitimate expectations from the states as benefits for surrendering their proprietary rights through the payment of taxes for the development of the state. Thus, voluntary tax compliance is critical to the attainment of sustainable development which is the goal of fiscal social contract.

11.4 Tax Compliance and Sustainable Development within the Context of a Social Contract in Nigeria

It is the contention of this chapter that the social contract theory helps to understand the responsibilities of citizens on one hand and that of the government on the other hand in the pursuit of sustainable development. In other words, sustainable development may elude a state if the citizens fail to pay taxes and the government reneges on its responsibility to provide social services as envisaged under the social contract. The relationship between socio-economic development and non-compliance in the payment of taxes in Nigeria may be explainable under the social contract theory. Hence, the level of tax compliance is critical to the development of any state as tax evasion will hinder the government's ability to raise significant revenue to provide public goods and services and could impede the development of the state.[53] However, voluntary tax compliance can be induced by governments' response to issues of accountability. The level of taxpayers' confidence, that revenues from taxes will be accounted for and channelled efficiently towards the provision of the social needs of the state has a considerable impact on voluntary tax compliance.[54] In Nigeria, there seems to be a trust deficit. While the Government does not seem to trust that citizens will pay their taxes voluntarily; the citizens on the other hand do not trust the government to deploy the revenue prudently to provide necessary public goods and services.[55]

Appah and Aganaba note that trust influences the level of tax compliance in any society and where citizens trust the government, compliance will be high but, where there is mistrust, tax evasion will be high.[56] They argue that 'good governance practices, transparency, accountability of tax revenue, expenditures that improve public welfare, minimal corruption level of public officials enhances taxpayers' trust and voluntary tax compliance.'[57] However, while tax payment is necessary to mobilise resources for the provision of public goods and services, the government must recognise that tax morale and taxpayers' behaviour are largely determined by the level of satisfaction or dissatisfaction with the provision of public goods and services. Hence, with the rate of poverty, unemployment, insecurity, corruption and economic challenges in Nigeria, tax evasion will certainly be high as the perception of governance affects tax compliance behaviours.[58]

For illustration, despite the interventions of the government over the years, the infrastructural deficit in Nigeria is huge and it constrains the economic growth of the country. It is projected that about 2.3 trillion dollars is needed over the next 30 years to bridge the infrastructural deficit in Nigeria.[59] This is more so as it has been observed that Nigeria will require about 100 billion dollars to provide infrastructure between 2018 and 2024.[60] The challenges of infrastructural development in Nigeria need urgent attention as the lack of educational, transport and health facilities create a large efficiency gap in the quantity of infrastructure to an extent that could impede sustainable development[61] and the enjoyment of socio-economic rights. In addition, there are issues of corruption and accountability, for instance, the Corruption Perception Index (CPI) 2023 report by Transparency International puts Nigeria at 145 out of the 180 countries surveyed and on a scale of 100, it scored 25.[62] Furthermore, the state of insecurity is worrisome as there are increasing cases of armed robbery, kidnapping, rape, banditry and terrorism which have kept many Nigerians in fear daily.[63]

On the other hand, the foregoing may have invariably affected voluntary tax compliance in Nigeria. Voluntary tax compliance implies the willingness to pay taxes without any coercion[64] this contrasts with 'Enforced Compliance' where the taxpayer is compelled to pay tax through enforcement mechanisms including litigation, imposition of fines and penalties.[65] To stimulate voluntary tax compliance, the Nigerian Government introduced the Tax Administration (Self Assessment) Regulations, 2011. However, there has not been a significant improvement in voluntary tax compliance since the regulation was introduced.

Nigeria's tax to GDP is presently put at 9.4% by the International Monetary Fund (IMF) which is one of the lowest in the world.[66] This is below the African average of about 15.6%.[67] While Nigeria's tax-to-GDP ratio is reported to have increased from 6.7% in 2021 to about 10.6% in 2023.[68] The Nigerian Minister of Finance, admits that a tax-to-GDP ratio of about 10% clearly indicates that Nigerians do not pay significant amounts of taxes.[69] This is evident from the fact that South Africa's tax-to-GDP ratio is above 20%.[70] The low level of tax compliance in Nigeria suggests low tax morale of its citizens and affects the ability to generate significant revenue to address the developmental challenges in Nigeria. Non-payment of taxes could distort the functional utility of the fiscal social contract in developing countries[71] and frustrate their efforts towards sustainable development.

The foregoing could be the reasons sustainable development has eluded Nigeria for a long time and the social contract theory provides an explanation for the high infrastructural deficit and low tax to GDP in Nigeria. It demonstrates an inability of the government to harness resources to provide public goods and services which may have led to a lack of confidence on the part of the citizens resulting in the unwillingness to pay taxes. Although tax evasion is criminal and should be deprecated, taxpayers seem to view tax payment from the economic perspective of cost and benefits.

Taxation arguably is one of the visible ways a social contract can be consummated between citizens and the state.[72] It is a potent way for citizens to collaborate with the government in resource mobilisation in modern states towards achieving sustainable development. Hence, under the social contract while the state is expected to harness and administer the resources of the state in the interest of all; citizens pay taxes as an implied consideration for a social contract between the government and the people. Accordingly, Umar *et al.* argue that 'fiscal social contract implies that citizens should pay tax which is utilized by government to execute programs for the collective good.'[73] In other words 'citizens consent to pay taxes because they receive public goods in return.'[74] This implies that government can enhance voluntary tax compliance by providing public goods and services to its citizens more efficiently and effectively.[75] This invariably means that the more the government spends public revenue on the provision of necessary amenities, infrastructure and services efficiently in Nigeria, the higher the propensity of its citizens towards voluntary tax compliance, as public expenditures can drive tax compliance.[76] In other words, the perception of citizens to the pattern of government spending affects their attitude towards their tax obligation. If taxpayers, consider that the government is spending the national revenue judiciously and applying it towards the provision of basic infrastructure, such as public health, education, security and public transportation, it is likely that voluntary compliance of taxpayers will increase. In contrast, if taxpayers perceive that the government is misapplying public funds, unaccountable and spending too much on unnecessary projects, it is very likely that some Nigerians will continue to evade the tax system.

To reiterate, taxation is a means by which citizens can cooperate with the government to pursue sustainable development objectives and to deliver social benefits that are enjoyed collectively. Therefore, access to social benefits is one side of a social contract between citizens and the State which has, on its reverse side, the obligation of citizens to pay tax. Thus, 'taxes payment in social contract theory is people surrendering their economic independence through the taxes payment in order to realize common interests to state. In return, state uses the tax payments to create prosperity for all people.'[77] For Marshall 'the duty most obviously and immediately implied by our social rights is the duty to pay taxes and insurance contributions.'[78] Similarly, Umar *et al.* observed that 'The fiscal social contract implies that members of the society pay tax in return for sharing in the benefit of governance.'[79] Furthermore, Spinoza suggests that taxes are a means of contributing to the provision of public goods and it is comparable to military service and the effective deployment of tax revenue to provide public goods stimulates tax compliance.[80] He further argues that citizens accept payment of taxes as a moral obligation to contribute towards the financing of public goods. Thus, the Government has a duty to instigate trust to enhance cooperation and voluntary compliance in the payment of taxes.[81] For Hume, since citizens enjoy some benefits in the society they live, they are expected to make reasonable contributions to society based on the principle of reciprocity.[82]

Accordingly, it is argued that taxation has a critical role to play in every society in mobilising resources to fund and sustain the continuous provision of social welfare and sustainable development. Therefore, Mangoting *et al.* observe that 'In taxation context …taxpayer is party who offers while the government accepts the offer. Taxpayer offer is to provide economic resources to obtain welfare, whereas the government accepts the offer and use the economic resources to create wealth for society.'[83] The contention in the chapter is that there is a strong correlation between the propensity to pay taxes and the attitude of the government towards its responsibility to the people. The implication of the foregoing is that the only justification for the imposition and collection of taxes is the expectation that the government will discharge its obligation to deliver a better society and improve the quality of life of the citizen/taxpayer which will invariably lead to sustainable development. For Prabhakar: 'Costs of taxpayer in form of tax payments must be commensurate with benefits that will be received in form of public service.'[84] Hence, Mangoting *et al.* conclude that

> taxpayer resistance to pay taxes is also motivated by principle that every economic sacrifice must give economic benefit as return. When paying taxes, taxpayer will not get a direct return for the tax payment but the benefits will be provided in form of public service, good facilities and infrastructure built by government as results of tax payments.[85]

In the same vein, it has been opined that 'the massive tax noncompliance in developing countries may be better understood as "tax boycott" arising from taxpayers' frustration with the fiscal social contract of governance.'[86] Thus, in most cases default in the payment of tax is a subtle protest against maladministration and lack of accountability over the years. However, the government also has a legitimate expectation that citizens will pay their taxes to complement government efforts in domestic resource mobilisation because public goods and services come at a cost. To put it in another way, the response to the quest for citizenship participation in resource mobilisation can be understood as being underpinned by the attitude of the government to issues of development. Therefore, payment of taxes is a demonstration of citizens' cooperation and commitment towards the attainment of sustainable development and should therefore be catalysed through the provision of public goods and services.

11.5 Conclusion and Recommendations

Sustainable development is achievable in Nigeria and taxation could play a facilitative role. Stimulating voluntary tax compliance in Nigeria requires a confidence-building process. The government must begin this process by demonstrating a stronger commitment to provide infrastructure and social development. This is because from the findings above, the infrastructural deficit is high in Nigeria and the lack of basic infrastructure such as electricity, hospitals, schools, roads, bridges, etc., is a major catalyst for tax evasion. While it is necessary for the government to enforce tax compliance considering that, tax evasion is an offence; it is contended that reliance on traditional statutory enforcement measures such as penalties, fines, interest and prosecution of tax defaulters may not yield the desired result, unless deliberate efforts are made to address the developmental challenges in Nigeria. This study agrees with Mangoting *et al.* that

> governments need to understand that tax evasion by taxpayer cannot be solved by sanctions and fines as a deterrent. But in a different dimension, a taxpayer may become resistant and attack behind the government by questioning the commitments and seriousness of government to provide public services.[87]

Furthermore, it is argued that it may be difficult to achieve sustainable development, without taking steps to address the issues discouraging voluntary compliance in the payment of taxes. A situation where every Nigerian is like a local authority to itself, providing its own electricity, through generating sets and plants; portable water, through sinking of personal boreholes and security, through private local vigilante groups; will not encourage the voluntary payment of taxes. For businesses, providing these infrastructures from their capital increases the cost of doing business and affects their competitiveness globally. The foregoing may justify the perception of the payment of taxes as an exploitation; since citizens and firms do for themselves what the government is primarily set up to do. When a government fails to make its impact felt by the people, it is a pointer to the fact that it has reneged on its obligation under the fiscal social contract and therefore its citizens may be reluctant to observe their reciprocal duty to pay tax. Hence, non-compliance in the payment of tax could be a protest against the misgovernance over the years. Therefore, the government should commit to deploying available resources towards the provision of critical social goods and services. It is expected that this will be reciprocated by increased voluntary tax compliance.

Currently, the fiscal social contract theory seems to have failed and is of no value to the ordinary Nigerian. This is accentuated by the trust deficit between the government and the citizens. Thus, to gain the trust of the citizens, the government needs to align its tax policies with its human rights obligations and the state must institutionalise ways of holding the Government accountable. For the social contract to function, every party must be held accountable to their obligation under the social pact. While citizens should pay taxes, the government must be accountable and be ready to channel the resources towards the provision of the social needs of the citizens. This will promote tax justice and an inclusive fiscal social contract.

Going forward taxpayers and government should begin to see the payment of taxes and the proper utilisation of tax revenue as obligations under a social contract. It is therefore recommended that confidence building through good governance with demonstrable impact in the areas of infrastructural development, security of lives and property and provision of social goods like hospitals, schools, roads and other social infrastructure across the country should be prioritised. This is a more effective tax compliance strategy because the people will be motivated to pay taxes when they see positive developments around them. Also, accountability in resource management improves the confidence of the people in the government and helps to meet Nigerians' obligations under international human rights standards and the CFRN 1999. This is more so as the judicious distribution of resources to effectuate government policies on socio-economic rights in Nigeria will stimulate voluntary tax compliance. In addition, corruption must be addressed frontally, and anti-corruption institutions should be strengthened to check the corrupt tendencies of government officials. If this is done, it will signal the beginning of the confidence-building process and lead to increased public trust in the government, which is a vital ingredient for the sustenance of the social contract and voluntary tax compliance and the consequence over time will be sustainable development.

Notes

1 Rebecca M Kulik, 'Sustainable Development' *Britannica* https://www.britannica.com/topic/sustainable-development accessed 11 September 2024.

2 Newman U Richards, 'SDG's and Public Private Partnerships in Nigeria' in Eghosa O. Ekhator, Servel Miller and Etinosa Igbinosa (eds) *Implementing the Sustainable Development Goals in Nigeria* (Routledge, 2022) 152.

3 Newman U. Richards, 'SDG's and Public Private Partnerships in Nigeria' in Eghosa O. Ekhator, Servel Miller and Etinosa Igbinosa (eds) *Implementing the Sustainable Development Goals in Nigeria* (Routledge, 2022) 152.

4 N Castañeda, D Doyle, and C Schwartz 'Opting Out of the Social Contract: Tax Morale and Evasion' (2019) *Comparative Political Studies* 8.
5 McCulloch, Neil and Moerenhout Tom, 'What Nigerians Really Think About Tax' *ICTD Blog Post*, 25 March 2019. https://www.ictd.ac/blog/what-nigerians-really-think-about-tax accessed 19 September 2023).
6 McCulloch, Neil and Moerenhout Tom, 'What Nigerians really think about Tax' *ICTD Blog Post*, 25 March 2019. https://www.ictd.ac/blog/what-nigerians-really-think-about-tax accessed 19 September 2023) 32.
7 H Gribnau and C Dijkstra 'Social Contract and Beyond: Sociability, Reciprocity and Tax Ethics' in R Van Brederode (ed) *Ethics and Taxation* (Springer, 2019) 3.
8 H Gribnau and C Dijkstra 'Social Contract and Beyond: Sociability, Reciprocity and Tax Ethics' in R Van Brederode (ed) *Ethics and Taxation* (Springer, 2019) 3.
9 H Gribnau and C Dijkstra 'Social Contract and Beyond: Sociability, Reciprocity and Tax Ethics' in R Van Brederode (ed) *Ethics and Taxation* (Springer, 2019) 3.
10 John Rawls *A Theory of Justice* (rev edn, Harvard University Press) 1999, Culled from Gribnau and Dijkstra (n 7) 5.
11 E. Tengs, 'Taxation as a Social Contract: Public Goods and Collective Action: An empirical analysis of determinants of tax compliance in Sub-Saharan Africa' (2016) (Master's thesis, June 2016, Department of Sociology and Political Science, Faculty of Social Sciences and Technology Management, Norwegian University of Science and Technology) 2, https://ntnuopen.ntmu.no/ntnu-xmlui/handle/ accessed 19 August 2023.
12 E. Tengs, 'Taxation as a Social Contract: Public Goods and Collective Action: An empirical analysis of determinants of tax compliance in Sub-Saharan Africa' (2016) (Master's thesis, June 2016, Department of Sociology and Political Science, Faculty of Social Sciences and Technology Management, Norwegian University of Science and Technology) 2, https://ntnuopen.ntmu.no/ntnu-xmlui/handle/ accessed 19 August 20231.
13 Castañeda, et al. (n 4) 1.
14 Augustine A Adekoya, Enyi P Enyi and Rufus I Akintoye, 'Government Accountability and Voluntary Tax Compliance Behaviour in Selected States in South-West, Nigeria' *International Journal of Advanced Studies in Business Strategies and Management* (2019) 7 (1) 115.
15 Augustine A Adekoya, Ifayemi M Olayinka, and Oluwatosin G Aina, 'Good Governance and Voluntary Tax Compliance Behaviour in Lagos State, Nigeria: An Empirical Analysis' (2023) 9 (12) *International Journal of Management and Economics Invention* 3169.
16 Augustine A Adekoya, Ifayemi M Olayinka, and Oluwatosin G Aina, 'Good Governance and Voluntary Tax Compliance Behaviour in Lagos State, Nigeria: An Empirical Analysis' (2023) 9 (12) *International Journal of Management and Economics Invention* 3172.
17 Mick Moore, 'Revenues, State Formation, and the Quality of Governance in Developing Countries' (2004) 25 (3) *International Political Science Review* 310.
18 Mick Moore, 'Revenues, State Formation, and the Quality of Governance in Developing Countries' (2004) 25 (3) *International Political Science Review* 313.
19 Mick Moore, 'Revenues, State Formation, and the Quality of Governance in Developing Countries' (2004) 25 (3) *International Political Science Review* 299–300.
20 Mick Moore, 'Revenues, State Formation, and the Quality of Governance in Developing Countries' (2004) 25 (3) *International Political Science Review* 302–303.
21 James Alm, Gary H McClelland and William Schulze, 'Why Do People Pay Tax?' (1992) 48 (1) *Journal of Public Economics* 21–48.
22 James Alm, Gary H McClelland and William Schulze, 'Why Do People Pay Tax?' (1992) 48 (1) *Journal of Public Economics* 36.
23 James Alm, Gary H McClelland and William Schulze, 'Why Do People Pay Tax?' (1992) 48 (1) *Journal of Public Economics* 34.
24 Adekoya et al. (n 15) 3170.

25 Emo Idornigie Pearce and Chisa Onyejekwe, 'Taxation and the Implementation of Sustainable Development Goals in Nigeria' in Eghosa O Ekhator, Servel Miller and Etinosa Igbinosa (eds) *Implementing the Sustainable Development Goals in Nigeria* (Routledge, 2022) 139–141.
26 TH Marshall, 'Citizenship and Social Class', in Marshall, *Citizenship and Social Class* (Cambridge University Press, 1950) 1–85. Cited in Stuart White, 'Review Article: Social Rights and the Social Contract - Political Theory and the New Welfare Politics' (2000) 30 *British Journal of Political Science* 507.
27 Marshall, (n 26).
28 AL Dahl, 'Putting the Individual at the Center of Development: Indicators of Well-Being for a New Social Contract' in F Mancebo and I Sachs (eds) *Transitions to Sustainability* (Springer, 2014) 86–87.
29 D Hume, 'A Treatise of Human Nature' in LA Selby-Bigge and PH Nidditch (eds) (Clarendon Press, 1978). Also cited in Gribnau and Dijkstra (n 7) 4.
30 Gribnau and Dijkstra (n 7) 18–19.
31 Tengs, (n 11) 3.
32 Rawls, (n 10).
33 Tengs, (n 11) 3.
34 Tengs, (n 11) 3.
35 Tengs, (n 11) 3.
36 T Goodfellow and O Owen, 'Taxation, Property Rights and the Social Contract in Lagos' ICTD Working Paper 73 (Institute of Development Studies 2018) 6, 33.
37 S 14(2)(b) CFRN.
38 Ss 15(2) a; 16(1)b and (2)b; 17 (3) d and 18 of CFRN 1999.
39 S 6(6) of the CFRN 1999.
40 Daniel Olika, 'Taxation and Human Rights: Towards a Sustainable Realisation of Minimum Core Obligations in Nigeria' (2024) 24 (1) *African Human Rights Law Journal* 35.
41 [2018] LPELR 50830 (SC).
42 [2018] LPELR 50830 (SC) 59–60, per Chima Centus Nweze, JSC.
43 [2018] LPELR 50830 (SC) 62. Also see, Eghosa Ekhator, Sustainable development and the AU legal order' in Olufemi Amao *et al The Emergent African Union Law: Conceptualization, Delimitation, and Application* (Oxford University Press, 2021) 335–58.
44 See articles 2, 14–18, 20–22 and 24.
45 (2001) AHRLR 60 (ACHPR 2001).
46 International Commission of Jurists 'Adjudicating economic, social and cultural rights at national level: A practitioners guide' 2014, https://www.icj.org/wpcontent/uploads/2015/07/Universal-ESCR-PG-no-8-Publications-Practitionersguide-2014-eng.pdf accessed 28 September 2024.
47 See Art 2 of ICESCR; Olika, (n 41) 34–35.
48 Olika, (n 40) 31.
49 Olika, (n 40) 31.
50 Olika, (n 40), 35.
51 International Bar Association's Human Rights Institute 'The obligation to mobilise resources: Bridging human rights, sustainable Development Goals, and economic and fiscal policies' (December 2017) https://www.right-to-education.org/resource/obligation-mobilise-resources-bridging-human-rights-sustainable-development-goals-and accessed 28 September 2024.
52 Olika, (n 40) 43.
53 Adekoya et al. (n 14) 114–115. Generally, see Eghosa Ekhator, Chisa Onyejekwe and Newman Richards, 'Human Rights and Taxation in Developing Countries: A Case for Tax Justice and Accountability in Africa' in Damilola Olawuyi and Oyeniyi Abe (eds) *Business and Human Rights Law and Practice in Africa* (Edward Elgar, 2022) 127–150.

54 Adekoya, (n 14) 115.
55 Adekoya (n 14) 116.
56 Ebimobowei Appah and Doubara Aganaba, 'Tax Knowledge and Voluntary Tax Compliance: The Role of Public Trust in Nigeria' (2022) 12 (2) *British Journal of Psychology Research* 55.
57 Ebimobowei Appah and Doubara Aganaba, 'Tax Knowledge and Voluntary Tax Compliance: The Role of Public Trust in Nigeria' (2022) 12 (2) *British Journal of Psychology Research* 55–56.
58 Adekoya et al. 'Good Governance and Voluntary Tax Compliance Behaviour in Lagos State, Nigeria: An Empirical Analysis' (n 15) 3169.
59 Dennis Amata, 'All Eyes on Tinubu to Close Nigeria's $2.3 Trillion Infrastructural Gap' (Dataphyte 26 April 2023) https://dataphyte.com/latest-reports/all-eyes-on-tinubu-to-close-nigerias-2-3-trillion-infrastructure-gap/ accessed 10 June 2024.
60 Infrastructure Concession Regulatory Commission, 'Filling Nigeria's Infrastructure Gap' http://www.icrc.gov.ng/filling-nigerias-infrastructure-gap/ accessed 12 December 2023.
61 Dhruv Gandhi, Africa in Focus: Figure of the Week: Gaps in Nigeria's Public Infrastructure', https://www.brookings.edu/blog/africa-in-focus/2018/03/14/figure-of-the-week-gaps-in-nigerias-public-infrastructure/amp/ accessed 19 September 2023.
62 Transparency International 'Nigeria Corruption Perception Index 2019' https://www.transparency.org/en/cpi/2019 accessed 4 February 2023.
63 TS Akinyetun, VC Ebonine and IO Ambrose, 'Unknown Gunmen and Insecurity in Nigeria: Dancing on the Brink of State Fragility' (2023) *Security and Defence Quarterly*, 42(2), 16–34. https://doi.org/10.35467/sdq/163462.
64 Say Youde and Seunghoo Lim, 'Tax Compliance' (2019) Global Encyclopedia of Public Administration, Public Policy, and Governance. https://link.springer.com/referenceworkentry/10.1007/978-3-319-31816-5_3828-1 accessed 3 December 2023.
65 Larissa Batrancea, 'What's in a Name?: Insights on Tax Compliance Behavior and Ethnic Diversity' in Emilia Alaverdov and Muhammed Waseem Bari (eds) *Handbook of Research on Ethnic, Racial, and Religious Conflicts and Their Impact on State and Social Security* (IGI Global Publishing, 2021) https://www.igi-global.com/dictionary/whats-in-a-name/102924#:~:text=Chapter%2014,non%2Dcompliant%20citizens%2C%20etc accessed 3 December 2023.
66 Desmond Okon, 'The International Monetary Fund (IMF) says Nigeria recorded a tax revenue to gross domestic product (GDP) ratio of 9.4 percent in 2023' (The Cable, 10 May 2024) https://www.thecable.ng/imf-at-9-4-in-2023-nigerias-tax-revenue-to-gdp-ratio-among-lowest-in-the-world/ accessed 10 June 2023.
67 OECD, 'Revenue Statistics in Africa 2023 – Africa' 1/2023 https://www.oecd.org/tax/tax-policy/revenue-statistics-africa-nigeria.pdf accessed 30 November 2023.
68 Chisom Michael, 'Nigeria's climb to 10.6%: Tax-GDP ratio rollercoaster across African countries as SA's dip to 21%' BusinessDay Available at https://businessday.ng/business-economy/article/nigerias-climb-to-10-6-tax-gdp-ratio-rollercoaster-across-african-countries-as-sas-dip-to-21/ accessed 10 June 2024.
69 Desmond Okon, 'Wale Edun: 10% Tax-to-GDP Ratio Shows Nigerians Don't Pay Taxes' The Cable available at https://www.thecable.ng/wale-edun-10-tax-to-gdp-ratio-shows-nigerians-dont-pay-taxes/ accessed 10 June 2023.
70 Desmond Okon, 'Wale Edun: 10% Tax-to-GDP Ratio Shows Nigerians Don't Pay Taxes' The Cable available at https://www.thecable.ng/wale-edun-10-tax-to-gdp-ratio-shows-nigerians-dont-pay-taxes/ accessed 10 June 2023.
71 Akan David Chucks, and Odita Ogomrgbunam Anthony, 'Tax morale and its effect on taxpayers' compliance to tax policies of the Nigerian Government' (2022) (12) (6) *Journal of Business and Management* 35; B Torgler 'Speaking to the Theorists and Searching for Facts: Tax Morale and Tax Compliance in Experiments' (2022) (16) *Journal of Economic Surveys* 657.

72 N Makovicky and R Smith, 'Tax Beyond the Social Contract: An Anthropology of Tax' (2020) 64 (2) *Social Analysis* 5.
73 Mohammed Abdullahi Umar, Chek Derashid, and Idawati Ibrahim, 'What Is Wrong with the Fiscal Social Contract of Taxation in Developing Countries? A Dialogue with Self-Employed Business Owners in Nigeria' (2017) 7 (4) Sage Open 2158244017745114.
74 Tengs, (n 11) 1.
75 Alm et al. (n 21) 27, 32, 24.
76 Alm et al. (n 21) 27; Moore, (n 17) 308–310.
77 Yenni Mangoting, Eko G Sukoharsono and Rosidic Nurkholis, 'Developing a Model of Tax Compliance from Social Contract Perspective: Mitigating the Tax Evasion' (2015) 211 *Procedia-Social and Behavioral Sciences* 966–971.
78 Marshall, (n 14) 511.
79 Umar, et al. (n 74) 1.
80 Gribnau and Dijkstra, (n 4) 17.
81 Gribnau and Dijkstra, (n 4) at 20 and 25.
82 Hume, (n 29) 4.
83 Mangoting, et al. (n 78) 968.
84 R. Prabhakar, 'What Do the Public Think of Taxation? Evidence from a Focus Group Study in England' (2012) 22 (1) *Journal of European Social Policy* 77–89.
85 Mangoting, et al. (n 78) 967.
86 Umar, et al. (n 74) 1.
87 Mangoting, et al. (n 78) 970.

Bibliography

Augustine A Adekoya, Enyi P Enyi, and Rufus I Akintoye, 'Government Accountability and Voluntary Tax Compliance Behaviour in Selected States in South-West, Nigeria' (2019) 7 (1) *International Journal of Advanced Studies in Business Strategies and Management* 115.

Augustine A Adekoya, Ifayemi M Olayinka, and Oluwatosin G. Aina, 'Good Governance and Voluntary Tax Compliance Behaviour in Lagos State, Nigeria: An Empirical Analysis' (2023) 9 (12) *International Journal of Management and Economics Invention* 3169.

TS Akinyetun, VC Ebonine, and IO Ambrose, 'Unknown Gunmen and Insecurity in Nigeria: Dancing on the Brink of State Fragility' (2023) 42 (2) *Security and Defence Quarterly* 16–34.

James Alm, Gary H McClelland and William Schulze, 'Why Do People Pay Tax?' (1992) 48 (1) *Journal of Public Economics* 21–48.

Dennis Amata, 'All Eyes on Tinubu to Close Nigeria's $2.3 Trillion Infrastructural Gap' *Dataphyte* 26 April 2023. https://dataphyte.com/latest-reports/all-eyes-on-tinubu-to-close-nigerias-2-3-trillion-infrastructure-gap/ accessed 10 June 2024.

Ebimobowei Appah and Doubara Aganaba, 'Tax Knowledge and Voluntary Tax Compliance: The Role of Public Trust in Nigeria' (2024) 12 (2) *British Journal of Psychology Research* 55.

Larissa Batrancea, 'What's in a Name?: Insights on Tax Compliance Behavior and Ethnic Diversity' in Emilia Alaverdov and Muhammed Waseem Bari (eds) *Handbook of Research on Ethnic, Racial, and Religious Conflicts and Their Impact on State and Social Security* (IGI Global Publishing, 2021) https://www.igi-global.com/dictionary/whats-in-a-name/102924#:~:text=Chapter%2014,non%2Dcompliant%20citizens%2C%20etc accessed 3 December 2023.

N Castañeda, D Doyle, and C Schwartz, 'Opting Out of the Social Contract: Tax Morale and Evasion' (2019) 53 (7) *Comparative Political Studies* 8.

Akan David Chucks, and Odita Ogomrgbunam Anthony, 'Tax Morale and Its Effect on Taxpayers' Compliance to Tax Policies of the Nigerian Government' (2022) (12) (6) *Journal of Business and Management* 35.

AL Dahl, 'Putting the Individual at the Center of Development: Indicators of Well-Being for a New Social Contract' in F Mancebo and I Sachs (eds) *Transitions to Sustainability* (Springer, 2014) 86–87.

Dhruv Gandhi, 'Africa in Focus: Figure of the Week: Gaps in Nigeria's Public Infrastructure' (14 March 2018) https://www.brookings.edu/blog/africa-in-focus/2018/03/14/figure-of-the-week-gaps-in-nigerias-public-infrastructure/amp/ accessed 19 September 2023.

T Goodfellow and O Owen. 'Taxation, Property Rights and the Social Contract in Lagos' ICTD Working Paper 73 (Institute of Development Studies 2018). https://www.ictd.ac/publication/taxation-property-rights-and-the-social-contract-in-lagos-summary-of-working-paper-73/

H Gribnau and C Dijkstra, 'Social Contract and Beyond: Sociability, Reciprocity and Tax Ethics' in R Van Brederode (ed) *Ethics and Taxation* (Springer, 2019).

Hume D, 'A Treatise of Human Nature' reprinted from the Original Edition in three volumes and edited, with an analytical index, by Selby-Bigge LA and Nidditch PH (eds) (Clarendon Press, 1978)

Infrastructure Concession Regulatory Commission, 'Filling Nigeria's Infrastructure Gap' (2017) Available at http://www.icrc.gov.ng/filling-nigerias-infrastructure-gap/ (accessed 12 December 2023).

International Bar Association's Human Rights Institute, 'The Obligation to Mobilise Resources: Bridging Human Rights, Sustainable Development Goals, and Economic and Fiscal Policies' December 2017, https://www.right-to-education.org/sites/right-to-education.org/files/resource-attachments/IBA_Obligation_toMobilise_Resources_SDG_2017_En.pdf (accessed 28 September 2024.

International Commission of Jurists, 'Adjudicating Economic, Social and Cultural Rights at National Level: A Practitioners Guide' 2014, https://www.icj.org/wpcontent/uploads/2015/07/Universal-ESCR-PG-no-8-Publications-Practitionersguide-2014-eng.pdf accessed 28 September 2024.

Rebecca M Kulik, 'Sustainable Development' *Britannica* (last updated 7 March 2025). https://www.britannica.com/topic/sustainable-development accessed 11 September 2023.

N Makovicky and R Smith, 'Tax Beyond the Social Contract: An Anthropology of Tax' (2020) 64 (2) *Social Analysis* 5.

Yenni Mangoting, Eko G Sukoharsono, and Rosidic Nurkholis, 'Developing a Model of Tax Compliance from Social Contract Perspective: Mitigating the Tax Evasion' (2015) 211 *Procedia-Social and Behavioral Sciences* 966–971.

TH Marshall, 'Citizenship and Social Class', in TH Marshall (ed), *Citizenship and Social Class* (Cambridge University Press, 1950), 1–85.

Neil McCulloch and Tom Moerenhout 'What Nigerians Really Think About Tax' *ICTD Blog Post*, 25 March 2019. https://www.ictd.ac/blog/what-nigerians-really-think-about-tax accessed 19 September 2023.

Chisom Michael, 'Nigeria's climb to 10.6%: Tax-GDP ratio rollercoaster across African countries as SA's dip to 21%' *BusinessDay* (8 January 2024). Available at https://businessday.ng/business-economy/article/nigerias-climb-to-10-6-tax-gdp-ratio-rollercoaster-across-african-countries-as-sas-dip-to-21/ accessed 10 June 2024.

Mick Moore, 'Revenues, State Formation, and the Quality of Governance in Developing Countries' (2004) 25 (3) *International Political Science Review* 310.

OECD, 'Revenue Statistics in Africa 2023 – Africa' 1/2023 https://www.oecd.org/tax/tax-policy/revenue-statistics-africa-nigeria.pdf accessed 30 November 2023.

Desmond Okon, 'The International Monetary Fund (IMF) says Nigeria recorded a tax revenue to gross domestic product (GDP) ratio of 9.4 percent in 2023' *The Cable*

(10 May 2024) Available at https://www.thecable.ng/imf-at-9-4-in-2023-nigerias-tax-revenue-to-gdp-ratio-among-lowest-in-the-world/ accessed 10 June 2023.

Desmond Okon, 'Wale Edun: 10% tax-to-GDP ratio shows Nigerians Don't pay taxes' *The Cable* (19 April 2024) Available at https://www.thecable.ng/wale-edun-10-tax-to-gdp-ratio-shows-nigerians-dont-pay-taxes/ accessed 10 June 2023.

Daniel Olika, 'Taxation and Human Rights: Towards a Sustainable Realisation of Minimum Core Obligations in Nigeria' (2024) 24 (1) *African Human Rights Law Journal* 35.

Emo Idornigie Pearce and Chisa Onyejekwe, 'Taxation and the Implementation of Sustainable Development Goals in Nigeria' in Eghosa O Ekhator, Servel Miller and Etinosa Igbinosa (eds) *Implementing the Sustainable Development Goals in Nigeria* (Routledge, 2022) 139–141.

R Prabhakar, 'What Do the Public Think of Taxation? Evidence from a Focus Group Study in England' (2012) 22 (1) *Journal of European Social Policy* 77–89.

John Rawls, *A Theory of Justice* (rev edn, Harvard University Press, 1999).

Newman U. Richards, 'SDGs and Public Private Partnerships in Nigeria' in Eghosa O Ekhator, Servel Miller, and Etinosa Igbinosa (eds) *Implementing the Sustainable Development Goals in Nigeria* (Routledge, 2022).

E Tengs, 'Taxation as a Social Contract: Public Goods and Collective Action: An empirical analysis of determinants of tax compliance in Sub-Saharan Africa' (2016) (Master's thesis, June 2016, Department of Sociology and Political Science, Faculty of Social Sciences and Technology Management, Norwegian University of Science and Technology) at 2. Available at https://ntnuopen.ntmu.no/ntnu-xmlui/handle/ accessed 19 August 2023.

B Torgler 'Speaking to the Theorists and Searching for Facts: Tax Morale and Tax Compliance in Experiments' (2022) (16) *Journal of Economic Surveys* 657.

Transparency International, 'Nigeria Corruption Perception Index 2019'(2020) https://www.transparency.org/en/cpi/2019 accessed 4 February 2023.

Mohammed Abdullahi Umar, Chek Derashid, and Idawati Ibrahim, 'What Is Wrong with the Fiscal Social Contract of Taxation in Developing Countries? A Dialogue with Self-Employed Business Owners in Nigeria' (2017) 7 (4) *Sage Open* 2158244017745114.

Stuart White, 'Review Article: Social Rights and the Social Contract – Political Theory and the New Welfare Politics' (2000) 30 *British Journal of Political Science* 507.

Say Youde and Seunghoo Lim, 'Tax Compliance' (2019) Global Encyclopedia of Public Administration, Public Policy, and Governance. https://link.springer.com/referenceworkentry/10.1007/978-3-319-31816-5_3828-1 accessed 3 December 2023.

Index

Note: Pages in *italics* refer to figures and pages in **bold** refer to tables.

Kolibri 360 GmbH
Ferdinand-Jühlke-Straße 7
99095 Erfurt, Deutschland
produktsicherheit@kolibri360.de